SMOKEY BEAR

The Cub Who Left His Pawprints on History

A Novel

Karen Signell

Copyright © 2014 Karen Signell

All rights reserved.

All photographs unless otherwise noted are courtesy of the USDA Forest Service. Several other photographs are identified by their photographers. Still others, identified by a number, were obtained through Shutterstock, Inc.

The name and character of Smokey Bear* are property of the United States, as provided by 16 U.S.C. 580p-1 and 18 U.S.C. 711, and are used with permission of the Forest Service, US Department of Agriculture.

This book is licensed by the USDA Forest Service/Cooperative Forest Fire Prevention Program. A portion of the proceeds from this book are paid to the Forest Service to further wildfire prevention education.

*'Smokey Bear' is the official name for the live bear and the icon. The name 'Smokey *the* Bear' is well-known because of the 1952 song with that title.

About This Novel

For the historical facts about the live bear and the fire, this novel relied upon the nonfiction book *Smokey Bear 20252: A Biography* by William Clifford Lawter, Jr., for which he interviewed hundreds of eyewitnesses and researched over a thousand contemporary documents. See "What's Fact and What's Fiction in the Novel" toward the end of this book.

The Smokey Bear story would not have become well-known without three important contributions: first, the highly successful campaign—from the early 1940s through the present—by the US Forest Service, the National Association of State Foresters, and the Advertising Council to bring the message of the icon Smokey Bear to the public; then, the rescue of a burned cub by the insightful game warden Ray L. Bell; and last but not least, the personal sacrifice and fortitude of the real-life Smokey Bear.

Photographs of the bear cub were given to the author decades ago by the US Forest Service Headquarters in Washington, D. C. Many additional photographs and posters in recent years came from the National Agricultural Library. Others were given to the author by Don Bell.

Cover design by Ann MacLeod

Published by Karen Signell, Boca Raton, Florida

Publisher Cataloging-in-Publication Data has been applied for.

Library of Congress Control Number: 2014914012

ISBN-10 0-990-61850-1
ISBN-13 978-0-9906185-0-8

Dedication

Dedicated to the wild animals and the wilderness we love, and those who protect them.

From time far older than memory, the bear has been a special being. Like us, the bear stands upright . . . sits on his tail end . . . worries with moans and sighs . . . We cannot shake off the impression that behind the long muzzle and beneath the furry coat so unlike our naked skin there is a self not so different from us . . . wily, smart, strong, fast, agile, independent in ways that we humans have left behind when we took up residence in the city.
–Paul Shepard and Barry Sanders

Preview

The little bear cub whimpered. His legs felt too heavy to keep up the fast pace. Mother Bear glanced back, but she didn't slow down. It wasn't until he lagged far behind that Gersa rushed back. "You can do it, my boy!" Her massive paw pushed his rump and swept him forward.

Smokey stumbled, and in that moment turned, and for the first time saw fire. It was big and red and hot. The fire sizzled his fur, and prickled his nose like sharp pine needles. He plunged ahead. A bush burst into flame as he ran by. The monster was catching up. The cub collapsed and screeched. Gersa let out a wail, and came rushing back to his body splayed on the ground.

She fixed her eyes on his frightened ones and her urgent voice penetrated his being. "See this stump?" She thumped the rotten old tree trunk with her paw. "It's hollow inside. Now do as I say: Reach up to the opening on top and climb in." She boosted him up the stump to the open hole on top. "Quick, drop down inside!"

As soon as his footpads hit the damp floor inside, Smokey stretched up and frantically looked for her. She was still there, amid the flames. The acrid smell of her singed fur assaulted the cub's nostrils. "I must leave you, and run down the mountain to the beaver pond where the fire can't hurt me.

"Smokey, listen! Be my brave little bear, and stay in the tree trunk—no matter what." She nuzzled his face, and pulled away. "Dearest Smokey! Good-bye.

"Good-bye," Smokey cried, his throat tight with anguish as he watched her familiar furry rump until it was out of sight. 'My brave little bear' she had called him. He didn't feel brave at all. His throat rasped out a small sob and he slumped onto the earthen floor of the tree stump.

The forest fire roared closer.

Contents

Chapters 1 - 58 1-461
Epilogue 477
Author's Backstory 480
Afterword 483
What's Fact and What's Fiction in the Novel 485
Smokey Bear's Message 489
Websites and Places to Visit 490
Wild Animals in Confinement 493
Questions for Discussion 494
Acknowledgments 495
Selected Readings 497
To My Readers 502

Photographs

Strut	2
Smokey ventures out	6
Young Duke and Strut	41
Smokey sees fire	64
Ray rescues Smokey	104
Doc Smith bandages Smokey	110
Lightning	118
Smokey safe	132
Ray and Dean among the embers	136
Smokey poses with posters	138
Smokey licks Judy's chin	141
Little Smokey and Ray	143
Smokey and Ray at airport	144
Smokey's had enough!	144
Don	145
Baby Beaver	148
Ray	153
Smokey and Jet scuffle	164
Smokey in the back yard	168
Smokey up a tree again	171
Smokey plays indoors	174
Smokey and Jet share kibble	175
Scared Smokey and playful Ruby	178
Smokey and Ruby: a truce	179
Smokey plays with a doll	180
Smokey at ABC radio	185
Smokey and kids	189
Smokey's last bath at home	196
Smokey uneasy in Homer's lap	199
Smokey and his plane	201
Smokey and a Cub Scout	206
Smokey and TWA hostesses	207

Photographs (cont'd)

Smokey with Doc Mann and Homer 208
Mr. Dazzle 212
Smokey dons Chief Watts' hat 216
Smokey and AAA kids 221
Trish and Trash 226
Freddie 234
Smokey in Rock Creek Park 256
Sophia 304
Smokey forlorn 320
Smokey hopeless 320
A swim helps Smokey 321
Smokey's bored again 321
Strut and Robbie 371
Strut spies Smokey 414
Smokey and the crowd 421
Smokey disappointed 426
Smokey enjoys a good scratch 430
Judy and Ike 440
Judy poses with Smokey 443
Smokey "signs" Judy's poster 443
Ray and Smokey reconciled 447
Goldie 448
Goldie and Smokey 453
Smokey awaits Tilly 454
Smokey's mail 460
Smokey still caged, age 24 462
Goldie and Smokey, old together 468
Smokey's gravesite 490
Our family 502

Chapter 1

Draw your chair up to the edge of the precipice, and I'll tell you a story.
–F. Scott Fitzgerald

Without wilderness no fish could leap and flash, no deer could bound soft as eternal waters over the field; no bird could open its wings and become buoyant, adventurous, valorous beyond even the plan of nature. Nor could we.
–Mary Oliver

The young bear cub nuzzled deep into his mother's fur until his belly felt the gentle rise and fall of her breathing. As Smokey awoke further, he missed the familiar press of the other cubs against his body. Where were they? His eyes were still closed and sticky at the corners, so he had to wrinkle his forehead to raise his eyelids. No matter how hard he strained to see in the dim light of early morning, he couldn't detect the familiar shapes of the two cubs anywhere in the mountain cave. An uneasy feeling gripped the back of his neck. Then he remembered: They were gone.

A bright shaft of sunlight pierced the entrance of the den, and a monstrous shadow flickered across the far wall. Smokey's body stiffened in alarm. He gasped for air, assaulted for an instant by a flashback of stifled shrieks from his brother and sister. Then his body collapsed and he shrank against his mother.

After a while, when the cub dared to scan the cave again, he breathed out a huff of relief. The shadow came from a small animal flitting about a ledge on the cave wall. The cub crept over to the low ledge and rose on his hind legs to investigate. Wings flailed his face and he was tilted backward to the sound of a loud "Caw!"

Smokey caught his balance. "Hey! Who are you?"

"Caaaw. Hello yourself, little bear." The bird stood on tall legs and looked over at Smokey. Puffing out his chest, he took slow deliberate strides along the rocky ledge, abruptly stopped and combed his long tail feathers with quick darts of his black beak. Then, cocking his head to catch the cub's eyes, he stretched his neck and held his head high. "See how big I am, and all this purple sparkling among my black feathers? That makes me a *crow*. Caw!"

His eyes riveted on the fascinating creature, Smokey asked, "Do you live here too?"

Strut   © GLORI BERRY

"Caaaw. I only hide my treasures here. Want to see them?" The crow stepped aside on the shelf to reveal an array of glittering trinkets. The bird lifted a silver gum wrapper with his beak and set it down, then slowly picked his way through his hoard, gloating over a piece of tin, a silver button, and a shoe lace. He ended the tour by sweeping his head over the entire array and fanned out his tail in satisfaction.

Smokey stepped closer, eagerly grasped the ledge with his curved claws, and reached out an arm. Lickety-split, the bird hopped in front of his treasures, and thrust his beak in the cub's face. "Caw! Don't you dare touch my stuff!" The bear jumped back, folded his paws on his stomach, and looked up in dismay.

The crow's eyes softened. "Caaah. Sorry to insult you, little fellow. My brothers and sisters try to steal my things all the time. They think it's funny. Caw-ah! So they've made me awfully suspicious of everyone. My mistake, in this particular case.

"You're welcome to look and sniff." He leaned toward Smokey with a friendly tilt of his head. "I can tell you're a good-natured bear. Caaah. In fact, little guy, why don't you call me by name? It's Strut!"

"Hello, Strut. I have a name too: It's Smokey. And sleeping back there in the cave is my mother. She's a Medicine Bear. I had a brother and sister, too. Just now I heard their cries again—like in a dream. Something must have happened to them because they're not here anymore."

"I know . . . I saw what happened to them." The crow looked at Smokey, opened his beak as if to continue, and then clamped it shut. He shuffled his feet back and forth, bent down to peck at a trinket and looked into the distance.

The cub scrunched his eyebrows and stared at Strut, demanding that he speak. But the next moment, confusion crossed his face. Did he really want to face the scary scene that took place during the shrill cries? The cub hung his head.

Finally Strut broke the silence with an enticing toss of his glossy head. He motioned Smokey closer to his shelf. "Don't you want to hear where my treasures come from? Well, it's really The Story of My Life."

The cub brightened and sat down on the cave floor with his legs in front of him. Expectantly, he craned his head up toward Strut.

The crow began, "I was very young, like you are now, when I spied a two-legged creature tromping through the forest. He suddenly veered straight toward our tree. I was leaning over the side of the nest to get a better look at him when I fell. Or, I suspect, I was pushed by one of my nestlings—caw!

"I landed with a hard thud. The wind was knocked out of me. My head was buzzing. Caah. I flailed my legs to hide under the bushes. There was no hope of flying since my flight feathers hadn't even grown out. It was terrible! Being helpless is the worst thing of all.

"I was afraid a predator would find me. Then something amazing happened. I felt hands cup my body and lift me off the ground. The hands were smooth, like the soft moss lining our nest. I was supported so gently, with my feet tucked nicely underneath, that I relaxed. I had a fleeting qualm that I was being taken to a nearby lair to be eaten, but before long I realized that, instead, I was being carried a long way down the mountain.

"The next thing I knew, I was inside the two-legged ones' nest with its gigantic square walls. Caaah, the people were so good to me! They nursed me back to health in a few days. But I was clever enough to pretend I was still weak so I could stay longer in the house. Maybe I'll tell you more about it sometime — what it's like to be in a house with humans."

Smokey leaned forward and blurted out, "I sure do want to hear. Tell me everything!"

The cub caught a flash of excitement in Strut's eyes. With long-legged strides, the crow walked along the shelf and grabbed something up with his bill.

"See this red ribbon?" He dangled it down toward the bear's face. "It's my favorite treasure. The two-legged one tied it to a bush near my nesting tree so he could return me home later on. Caaaw. But there isn't a happy ending to The Story of the Red Ribbon. At least not so far. I'd been saved . . . only to be hurled down to The Great Hurt of Rejection by my own kind."

Smokey raised sympathetic eyes to his new friend. "Why did that happen?"

"The reason? It's these bands on my legs. See?" Smokey watched the crow teeter on one leg to show him the other scaly black leg. "The human put these shiny bands on my legs before he returned me to the nest. It made me into an outcast among the other crows — like it was a *jinx*."

The crow hung his head. In the hush that followed, Strut and Smokey heard the rumbling snore of the sleeping Mother Bear suddenly erupt into a rasping snort. The two swiveled their eyes to the back of the cave. Gersa lifted her massive head, widened her eyes at the bird and roared, "What are you doing here?"

Strut whispered, "Oops. Gotta go, Smokey. Tell you more about the jinx later." He whooshed out the cave entrance.

A moment later, Smokey found himself walloped from behind so hard that his face was slammed on the cave floor. His mouth was gritty with dirt and he angrily spat it out. He waited to catch his breath before he faced his mother. Gersa towered over him. She narrowed her beady eyes down at him. "Don't I ever catch you with that crow again."

Smokey was stunned. What had he done wrong? He stood defiantly and stared at her with blazing eyes. "He's my new friend."

"Don't you dare defy me!" She lurched forward, opened her big mouth to grab him by the scruff of his neck, and shook him. Then tossed him down again.

Shaken, but still mad, Smokey grumbled to himself, "Can't I even have a friend? She won't let me do anything!"

Gersa turned and sat with her back to him. A few moments passed until the little cub became stricken with sadness. He slowly picked himself up and tottered over in her direction. Mother Bear reached out and drew Smokey to her. He whimpered in her arms and she murmured, "I can't lose you, too, my little runt."

Then she switched to her voice of calm authority, "You must beware crows. That crow, in particular. Too smart for his own good. Fraternizes with two-legged ones. They're dangerous."

The bear cub mulled over his mother's warning, but had no idea what she meant.

Chapter 2

Smokey ventures out

Courage stands halfway between cowardice and rashness, one of which is a lack, the other an excess, of courage.
–Plutarch

During the following week, heeding the stern warning from Mother Bear, Smokey saw his new friend Strut only fleetingly. Then one morning the cub woke early and meandered to the entrance of his cave to see what might be happening outside. He smelled Chittery before he saw him. Once he'd spied one chipmunk moving about, the bear knew, he'd see many more. And sure enough, there were Chittery's brothers and sisters and cousins dashing back and forth, stopping every so often to freeze in place.

The early morning chorus of insects began to hum as the sky lightened. As soon as the golden ball in the sky finally peeked over the mountaintop, first one bird, then another, began singing. Everyone was busy except Smokey. The cub slumped down and leaned against the side of the cave entrance, wishing something would happen.

"Bored, bored, bored," he thought. He chafed at being restricted to the cave. Until his mother woke, he was forbidden to pursue the intriguing smells from the forest. And whenever she did take him foraging, he was required to stay within sight, or within the sound of her tongue-clicking. If he ran off, she'd swat his behind, and, if he dared snap at her, she'd make him stay up in a tree until he cooled off.

The cub's legs and arms felt restless. How he yearned to run into the dense forest. He felt itchy and twitchy just waiting.

For lack of anything better to do, he sat and bent his knees to scratch the bottoms of his feet, as if to soothe their restless desire to be on their way and crunch twigs underfoot.

What was that smell in the wind? Smokey stood on his hind legs at the cave entrance, and pointed his nose across the mountain. Something musky was wafting his way: a scent stronger than his mother's fur, more like the tufts of fur left on trees where other bears rubbed their backs. His insides roiled. Smokey went into body-alert. His muscles tensed and his breath came fast.

A large animal was within smelling range, intruding on his territory! The cub dropped onto all four feet and stiff-walked out the cave. His throat vibrated with a low moaning sound, "Wa-wa wha-wha-wa," but he was careful to stifle the noise enough so he wouldn't wake his mother and face her wrath.

Then, as if the tension in the cub's chest had drawn the crow down from the sky, Strut appeared and alighted on a nearby branch. The bird looked alarmed. "I've never seen you like this—like a tiny but mighty bear with your ears flattened and fur bristling. What's up?"

"Strut, I've got the strangest feeling. I don't know what it is, but I'm raring to go. It's a musky smell that scares me and makes me mad at the same time. I have to see who it is!"

"You sure can smell things. But, then, I can *see* things you can't. And I sure saw something big out there. That's why I came. I think it might be your father!"

"Let's go then!" Smokey said.

Before Strut could raise his wings to take off, the young cub stretched up on his hind feet and widened his nose to zero in on the smell. He quickly dropped onto all fours and bolted, scattering the chipmunks. He dashed along the well-worn animal path that led to the other side of the mountain. Now and then, wherever the bushes and tree cover thinned, a flickering shadow crossed his path. It was the crow above him, cawing, but he paid no heed. Finally, Smokey paused when the path brought him to a rocky overlook.

"Caw! Caw! Wait a minute. I have to tell you something. Before it's too late!"

Smokey had halted to catch his breath, but stayed on all fours ready to be off again. Ignoring the crow, he leaned over the ledge to sniff the breeze intently. As he jerked his body back to the path, Strut suddenly appeared on the ground blocking his way.

The crow began urgently. "You don't know what you're getting into! Listen to me! Back in the nest I saw my mother — and my father. They both fed me and stayed around. That's how it is with crows — unlike bears. So I've always thought you'd like to see what a father-bear looks like. That's why I came to fetch you . . . but there's something you gotta know first."

The cub stared at Strut impatiently. What was this long-winded crow talking about? Smokey told him, "I gotta go. Come with me, or not." He plunged past Strut and sped along the path again.

But Strut didn't give up. He flew alongside Smokey's head and cawed loudly. "No, wait a minute. I meant to say something more. It's important. You have to be careful. A male bear can *eat* you!"

That was ridiculous, Smokey thought. He tossed his head in a dismissive way and didn't stop until he reached a large clearing, a high alpine meadow. His eyes swept down the gentle slope to a wide river meandering down the middle. On his side of the river smooth boulders were strewn here and there, the biggest ones with patches of snow on their shaded sides.

It came to mind that his mother had warned him never to enter a large clearing like this without trees to climb or thick bushes to hide in . . . What had Strut been trying to tell him? About some kind of danger?

The strong odor certainly came from somewhere in this meadow. Smokey stood tall and flared his nostrils to inhale the heavy musky smell, so potent it made him shake. He trusted his nose much more than his eyes, but nevertheless squinted hard in the direction of the odor.

Then he saw him—a bear ambling along the river bank. At that moment, the bear rose to his full height, arms bent at the elbows with his forepaws dangling in front of his stomach. The bear thrust his muzzle in the air, then sharply jerked his head to stare directly at the cub.

Smokey's eyes were riveted on the creature, but out of the corner of his eyes he could see Strut on a slender bush nearby. The cub stole a quick glance his way, then continued looking in the distance, only half-listening to the crow blathering away.

"Smokey, that's what I've been trying to tell you. It's a bear. An enormous male bear! I didn't realize how big he was from my aerial view. And he's on this side of the river—your mother's territory. He could be your father. Then again, maybe not. In any case, you can see how big you'll be when you grow up."

The cub was too entranced with the male bear to react to the crow until Strut alighted on Smokey's shoulder and poked his beak sharply into the bear's neck. He gave the cub a hard stare as if trying to hypnotize him into listening. "Cubs are eaten by big male bears—if they're hungry enough. Like now, when there's been a drought! And they can kill you just because they find you in their territory. Especially if you're another male. This one already senses you're a male—just like you sense he's a male. So let's get out of here! Before it's too late."

But Smokey paid hardly any attention. "I have to see him up close! I want to see how big he is!"

"That's crazy! I wouldn't do that—Smokey! Caw! Caw!"

Smokey was off, racing down the slope toward the river, and shouting across the meadow, "Are you my father?"

The bear looked gigantic. He came closer, huffing low menacing roars that made the cub's hair stand on end. Smokey stopped short in terror, wheeled around and started to run back up the slope, faster than he'd ever run before. The guttural roar and chomping teeth came closer, loud enough to block out thought. Musky male bear-scent overwhelmed the cub.

Smokey chanced a quick look behind him and shrieked. The massive head was almost upon him, the huge mouth open with its enormous teeth ready to chomp down. The creature's large shadow fell over Smokey's body, and the horrific smell of the bear's breath engulfed him.

A loud caw split the air. "Kr-aak." It was Strut! The bear's low rumbling huff turned into snarls of irritation. Smokey stole another look behind him as he ran. He saw Strut's spread wings whopping the bear's head, slowing his headlong rush.

Not looking where he was going, the cub tripped, was thrown on his back, and whacked his head on a rock. Everything went blank for a moment. Then, from his prone position, he raised his eyes. The standing bear towered over him.

The big animal swayed from one foot to the other, swatting at the crow as if he were a bothersome horsefly. Suddenly Strut squawked. A few dislodged feathers drifted away from his body, and he flapped out of range.

"Run, Smokey, *run*." The cub scratched the earth in haste and scrambled onto his feet. The next instant the little bear was thumped from behind by a powerful paw, thrown onto the ground, his haunch slashed by tremendous claws. The cub screeched.

Lying on his back, Smokey looked up and saw the huge bear rear up on his hind legs above him, ready to wallop him again. For an instant, the big bear's intense eyes held him paralyzed in their grip. With a mighty effort, Smokey twisted his body aside and swiveled his head to search with frantic eyes for Strut.

"Kr-aack!" The brave crow came zooming toward the bear's huge head and beat his wings on his snout so he couldn't see. The bear halted to snarl and swat at the bird. Then he jerked his head away and lunged with his mouth open toward Smokey's neck.

But teeth didn't close on Smokey's neck. The cub raised his

head. The great bear had halted and stood with his attention fixed on a spot far up the slope. Moaning, Smokey hastily gathered his feet under him and streaked away. Barely out of danger, he shot a glance up the hill.

It was his mother! In an explosive burst of energy, she was charging down the slope, head lowered, snorting loudly. As she came closer, the cub heard Gersa clacking her jaws, and saw slobber spurting right and left out of her mouth. With ears laid back and her upper lip curled, she headed straight toward the male bear. Smokey could hardly believe what he saw. Although Mother Bear looked much smaller than the massive male, she appeared so fierce and determined that the cub knew nothing would stop her. Her momentum would ram the bigger bear.

Just in time, the male bear abruptly turned and fled back toward the river. Gersa pursued him, loudly huffing with each fast breath, and she didn't stop until he'd splashed through the water and reached the far bank. Smokey stood, in stunned amazement at his mother's victorious deed. Then huffs of relief escaped him. The cub blew out his nostrils as if to free himself from the atrocious smell of the male bear, still heavy in the air. It was an odor he knew that he'd never forget, one that still made his fur bristle with anger and his insides quail.

At last Smokey's panting ceased and his heart stopped beating so fast. Then the cub took in a deep breath and inflated his chest. How thrilling it had been to see such an enormous bear! He could imagine how big he, himself, would be some day. It made him feel bolder than he'd ever been in his life. He gave a proud nod to beckon Strut. With the crow on his shoulder, the cub headed toward Mother Bear who stood tall at the river bank, the fur on her neck and back still erect.

They arrived in time to hear Gersa roar at the retreating back of the male bear across the river, "*Don't you dare hurt my cub!* And remember: This side of the river is my territory. Berry-picking later on, okay. Fishing from your side, okay. But no more assaults. I know your temper, and I'll match you any time."

The panting and the heaving of her chest gradually subsided. She paused, and, with a lilting sound in her voice, called after him, "Take care, Clem. Perhaps I'll see you sometime later—in a year or so."

Mother Bear then turned to glare at the crow who remained on Smokey's shoulder. Strut hastily flew just out of reach, landed on a nearby bush and desperately clung to the flimsy twig on top. Gersa pursued him and raised her huge arm as if to strike. She said, "If this was your idea, crow—"

Smokey cut in. "Don't hurt him. It was my idea. This is my friend, Strut. Before you came, he dared to fly right into that big bear's muzzle." The cub screwed up his face into a half-hearted smile, and told her in his most earnest voice, "He saved my life!"

The little bear quickly continued. "I smelled the bear and just had to see it. I thought it might be my father." He groaned. "Aaaaah. I know it was a mistake . . . But since it turned out okay, I'm glad I did it! It really was my father, wasn't it? Now I know how big I'll be some day. And where I got my temper from." He flashed his mother a triumphant grin.

For the first time in his short life, the cub saw her at a loss for words. After a pause in which she studied his hopeful face, she sighed.

He continued. "I'm going to grow up to be just as big and fierce as he is. Oh, mom, I've always felt so little . . . but now-- I've never felt so big in my whole life!"

Mother Bear gave Smokey 'the eye' for a long time, then turned to Strut. Her mouth, usually soft with its loose lips, was clamped down to a firm slit, and she narrowed her small eyes at him. The crow held his breath and tried to keep his balance on the twig. For once, he knew enough not to say anything. Instead, he hung his head contritely.

She thought a moment. Finally her demeanor softened and she said, "Thank you, Crow. You are a brave friend. A true friend of the family."

The crow was taken by surprise, and nervously stood on

one foot then the other, making his unsteady perch on the bush wobble even more. He looked up, and, not quite meeting her eye, he said, "Caaah. Me and my big mouth! I have to admit that I told Smokey that I might have seen his father. I didn't mean to tempt him to go look. When he took off, I really tried to warn him. Believe me, I just couldn't stop him."

"I know what you mean. Smokey can be very determined!"

At a lull in their conversation, Smokey spoke up. "Mom, there's something you should know. Don't get upset, but I think you ought to see this." Smokey turned his slashed leg toward her. "It hurts, but maybe it's not so bad after all."

"Stay on all fours . . . Now stand still!" Mother Bear commanded, and bent her head low to examine his wound. Then she made him lie on his good side. Bending down to his outer thigh, she licked the dirt off his blood-matted fur to reveal three parallel gashes in his flesh. The claw marks were deep and several inches long. The cub's eyes widened to see so much blood flowing onto the ground.

"It's going to be all right," she said, assuming her familiar Medicine Bear tone. "Cold water is best. See how this river water is clear and icy with fresh snow-melt? Lie over here at the edge, up to your hip in water. It'll stanch the bleeding."

Smokey did as he was told. Cold stabbed his leg a moment before the leg went numb. After a while, the red rivulets of blood in the water turned light pink and disappeared. Mother Bear ordered, "Now, onto the shore." She slurped gobs of saliva onto the wound with her big tongue. "That'll help heal it. Now, you do it. You have to learn these things. I won't always be around."

The cub licked his wound as he rested on the river bank. Eventually Mother Bear got up and said, "Now let's get you more powerful medicine. The best grove of herbs is back up the slope and a short way into the forest. Can you walk okay?"

"Sure. It doesn't hurt much." He shined a bright face at her. "What's a little pain, when I could've been killed?"

"Yes, you could have been killed!" Gersa snorted, and fixed

harsh eyes on him until his spunky look shifted to a crestfallen one. She announced, "Let's go ahead — walk in front of me — so I can see whether your wound starts bleeding again."

"Mom?'

"Yes?"

"You sure were fierce! And, uh, I'm sorry to give you such a scare."

"Well, thank the stars I came in time." She gave him a meaningful look. "You are an impetuous bear. It's in your blood, so you must be careful until you're much bigger — like Clem. Then you can put yourself in danger — and get by with it."

Mother Bear sighed, and rested her eyes on him, then turned her head away to emit a heavy-hearted moan before she said, so softly he could barely hear, "I can't imagine losing you, too, my precious Smokey."

"I know," replied the cub in a small voice. "I'll try to be more careful."

Chapter 3

The Navaho and Blackfeet Indians of North America watched wild bears dig up and use the roots of Ligusticum *plants so frequently, and with such obvious benefit, that they named the plant "bear medicine."*
–Cindy Engel

Smokey crossed the meadow, blood trickling down his leg, and labored up the hill with Mother Bear behind and Strut overhead. As they entered the forest, mosquitoes swarmed around the bears, and a large horsefly bit the cub on the raw flesh of his wound. He yelped, and Mother Bear swiftly motioned him to an evergreen tree. In her serious Medicine Bear voice, she rumbled instructions to wiggle against the bark to rub strong-scented sap into his fur. "The resin keeps pests away," she said.

After the cub had rubbed enough sap on his fur, she continued. "You should remember that you can also smear honey on a wound, or smack globs of mud or clay on it. And if it's a bad wound, eat the clay, especially if it's red or yellow." She paused a moment and bored her eyes into his. "Remember, Smokey: Someday it'll be your mission to pass on this ancient wisdom to others."

Gersa swung her body away and urged, "Come along now, or you'll miss what's in this meadow. There are flowers to eat." Smokey gamboled after her to mouth clover, which was wonderfully sweet, and pounced on the bright yellow tops of dandelions. "These are the best, Mom. Too bad the others can't be here. They would've loved these!"

Mother Bear acted as if she hadn't heard him, and quickly diverted his attention, as she always did when he mentioned his brother and sister. "Here, Smokey, a real delicacy!" She bent down a young aspen so he could reach the upper branches. Smokey feasted on buds, catkins, and tiny green leaf sprouts, then yanked the slender aspen from her, let it go, and laughed to see it whip back upright.

As the two moseyed along the meadow the cub chattered about each discovery, and his mother nodded absentmindedly and said, "Yes, my dear." She stopped at a large area of crushed grass. "That means deer have been sleeping here." She snuffled among the smashed weeds. "Ah," she said, "See these pebbles of scat? When you're older and eating a lot of grass, you won't be able to digest it, like Hoofed Animals can. So deer droppings can help out. Taste this. It's still fresh." As soon as Smokey mouthed a moist brown pebble, his mouth watered for more. He nosed among the grasses and scooped up another with his flexible lips, rolled it around with his tongue to savor the flavor, and swallowed it.

Strut swooped down from a tree and ambled over to Smokey, then hopped back a short way. "You know what? I can't smell things as well as you can, but you smell yucky and your fur looks quite odd."

Smokey chortled. "That's probably the sap to keep insects away."

"Ugh," said Strut. "I'd never use sap! It'd make my feathers sticky. Birds have a better way to handle insects! If an insect pesters me, I snap my beak at it. Clack! Clack! Or eat it." The garrulous crow continued, "What I can't stand are mites and lice that crawl all over my soft skin under my feathers. Have you ever hear of 'anting'?"

Smokey shook his head, and Strut launched forth. "If creepy-crawlies are really driving me nuts, I find an ant hill and spread my wings till all the ants crawl under my feathers and go to work, eating up all the mites. You can't imagine how ticklish it is, but hey, it works pretty well."

Strut shook his feathers and continued. "And you won't believe this, Smokey. If I'm really overrun with mites, there's heavy-duty anting. I pick up ants on an anthill and crunch them with my beak, and while they're still squirming I poke them through my feathers as fast as I can. They're so scared they let out stinky stuff that kills all the little nasties. And what's more, smelling the stuff gives you quite a thrill. Some other crows—Duke and his gang—go out of their minds sniffing it, just for the fun of it."

"That sounds like fun! Why don't you ask to join them?"

"Well, I don't ask to join other crows much now-a-days. It's partly the jinx on me. And I'm certainly not friends of those guys, in particular." Strut shook his head and quickly added, "Anyway, I got scads of things to do. I want to go off and see the world, and bring back stories that'll amaze everybody. Then I can really be accepted!"

Smokey exulted, "Let's go together!"

"Yes, indeedy. That'd be great." Strut waggled his long tail from side to side.

"We'd be a great team. You could scout things from the air, and I'd search the wind for interesting things to go see." And, he boasted, "I'd be so big that no one would dare to bother us."

"Well, first you'll have to stay out of danger till you're grown up and can leave home, okay?"

"What do you mean?"

The crow motioned Smokey out of earshot of Gersa. He spoke in a quiet voice. "Smokey, you have to be careful. Everyone knows that a bear cub has only one chance in three to survive the first year."

The cub just said "Uh" but he felt stricken at the news. His chest raced as he was reminded of the cries of his brother and sister and his close call with Father Bear. To banish these thoughts, Smokey twisted to his thigh and frantically slurped saliva on his wound.

Strut hastily added in an authoritative voice. "But, my friend, *you* can beat the odds. As Elder Crow says, 'Once warned, twice careful.' And this mountain's great. Lots of food for us, and they don't shoot bears here. You could live to twenty."

Smokey's breathing had slowed, but he had to swallow past the tight lump in his throat and ask, in a small voice, "But how long will *you* be around?"

"Crows also live to about twenty. So we can be friends for life. I promise."

"Thank Ursa's tail! Someday we'll explore the whole mountain," the cub exclaimed.

Just then Mother Bear appeared. "Come along, Smokey. Enough of that crow's prattling. We need herbs." Smokey rose awkwardly on his stiff hip, and they soon entered a small field of grasses and bushes. Gersa instructed Smokey, "Follow your nose. What's the smelliest plant around here?"

"This one."

"That's it. Dig up the root. Chew it well, and spit it on your leg." After he'd done so, Mother Bear rubbed the paste into the wound.

The bear cub let out a slow "Aaah," and slumped onto the ground. "That really helps."

"Smokey, did you know that bears have been using *osha* root so long that we call it The Bear Medicine? Birds use it too; they must have learned about it from bears a long time ago. Isn't that so, Crow?"

Strut stopped walking on the ground near Smokey, and fixed a beady black eye on her. "Well, now, wait just a minute!" He sashayed over to the plant and pronounced, "That's a relative of the wild carrot. We crows call it The Birds' Nest Root. So *bears* must've learned about it from watching *us*!"

Gersa loomed over the crow. "How dare you contradict me — in front of my son? What arrogance. I'll have you know I come from a long line of Medicine Bears. You black birds think you know everything, making a racket all the time."

She glared at him. "And you in particular. You lured him away from the safety of his home. You could have had him killed."

Strut opened his beak, but nothing came out.

Smokey looked from one to the other. Their eyes were locked, Strut's wing feathers were spread wide, and the fur on Gersa' back stood up stiff.

Smokey's little body shook, and he bravely wedged himself between them. His loud voice cut the air. "STOP IT! What does it matter, anyway, who's *first*? Who cares?"

At first they frowned at him. Finally, his mother's fur softened and Strut's wings settled. The crow addressed the cub. "Yeah. So what—who's first? Maybe *each* of us found it, so that makes it *doubly* right. So there!"

Gersa wheezed out a breath, and at the same time Strut flashed a slight smile to the cub. Then, in a sober tone, the crow addressed Gersa, "Uh, Mother Medicine Bear, I didn't mean to get my feathers up just now. I'm truly sorry."

Slowly, as if she were very tired, Gersa heaved her bulk down on the ground close to Strut. She furrowed her brow and her small eyes studied him a long time. He held his breath so he wouldn't give her the satisfaction of seeing him flinch.

At last her tight lips relaxed and she emitted a soft grunt of satisfaction. She carefully conceded, "You know, I never thought I'd say this to a *crow*, but after today I think you can call me by my name—Gersa. Would you do that?"

Strut swallowed hard, and his voice was solemn as he answered, "I'd be very honored to do so." After a pause he said, "And, you probably know I'm called Strut the Storyteller." Suddenly, so pleased to be accepted into the family, he jittered from one foot to the other. Mother Bear gave him a benign look. As if in slow motion, Smokey feasted his eyes on one and the other, then beamed a wide-lipped happy smile at them.

After a few moments, though, the bright sun of Smokey's wholehearted happiness unexpectedly brought its opposite—a dark cloud. He let out a plaintive sigh of foreboding. It came over him again in flashes like a bad dream—glimpses of the mountain lion, his brother, his sister . . .

Smokey hesitated. If he asked about the other cubs, would his mother get so mad that she would hit him, or even worse, look away from him in heavy sorrow? 'Now or never,' he thought.

Chapter 4

Silence propagates itself, and the longer talk has been suspended, the more difficult it is to find anything to say.
 –Samuel Johnson

A little loss borrows its powers from the greater loss [that] comes like a creditor clawing its demands upon memory.
 –Halldór Laxness

Smokey felt his head grow hot as he plunged ahead to ask Gersa, "What about the others?"

"What do you mean?"

"Mother, you never want to talk about it . . . but I keep remembering bits and pieces of what happened to the other cubs. It got worse right after Father Bear attacked me and I was soaking my leg in the creek."

The cub's words jolted Gersa, but after a while she recovered her serious Medicine Bear demeanor. "Yes, it's about time . . .

"First, tell me what you saw before I came home that day." She sat down close by and gazed at him with soft eyes for a long moment and lowered her muzzle to gently lick his lips. Then her big arms gathered Smokey into a close embrace against her big round belly. His tight throat relaxed and he heaved out a great sigh.

She gently prompted him, "Do you remember me leaving that day?"

"I remember it was early morning when you said goodbye to us and left to find food. We waited a long time but you didn't come back. We were getting hungry! The other two cubs started play-wrestling — rolling around and mouthing each other's necks. I was watching them from inside the cave. Even though you'd told us to stay in the cave, they somehow ended up half-inside and half-outside.

"Suddenly a dreadful smell from outside made my body tremble. I backed against the wall and peered out. It was a big mountain lion. But I can't quite remember what came next . . . It only comes in bits and pieces like a bad dream."

Smokey whimpered. Mother Bear squeezed him and said, "Never mind. Maybe your crow friend saw what happened next." She looked over at Strut.

The crow alighted on the ground a discreet distance away. She nodded for him to move closer. "Strut, you probably know the whole story. Would you be so kind as to relate it to us?"

The crow walked closer and stood before the two seated bears. "I was on a tree branch just outside the den. I can see it now. The mountain lion slowly slipped her long body out of the bushes, one soft padded foot after the other, and crouched outside the cave entrance, perfectly silent. So close to me that I could clearly see the small rounded ears on her head. So still that only the thick tuft of fur at the end of her long tail twitched. Actually, I saw her pink nose twitch, too, as she gazed at the two cubs.

"I should have known what would happen. I could have warned the two. But I must have been too scared. And . . . I guess I didn't want to let her see *me*. All I did was hold my breath and just watch for what seemed like the longest time."

Smokey squirmed his rump against the ground and muttered, "I remember now . . . I saw her too, but I didn't do anything either. Then everything went blank, like I wasn't there anymore."

"Yeah. At that point I'd glanced around to see where you were — safe in the cave — and saw you squeeze your eyes tight and melt into the shadow against the wall."

Mother Bear became agitated and huffed at Strut, but before she could interrupt him, the cub leaned forward with determination and asked, "What happened next? Tell us. I can take it!"

"Right after Smokey faded into the shadows, I saw the mountain lion tighten her haunches and launch her body through the air. Killed the girl cub with a quick slash. The boy cub had nimbly jumped aside, but the lion snarled and grabbed his neck with her big teeth. He squealed, and for a moment put up a brave fight, jerking his body to fling himself out of her grip. But the mountain lion quickly silenced him. Then she swiftly seized both of them with her jaws and carried them away."

"Strut!" Gersa protested.

"I'm so sorry! I guess I got too carried away, as a storyteller, with something so dramatic! It's an awful failing of mine — to momentarily forget who is listening. I'll try to be more careful." He hung his head contritely.

A few moments later, the crow raised his eyes and saw Mother Bear look expectantly at him. Strut pondered a moment and began again. "It was very quick," he said. That's what I really wanted to convey. They hardly suffered at all."

Mother and son relaxed more in each other's arms and gave small sighs of relief.

Soon Gersa told the crow, "Proceed, if you will, Strut. Tell Smokey what happened next."

"Well, I'm not sure how long you kept your eyes shut there in the back of the cave, Smokey. Anyway, it wasn't long before your mother came running up to the cave, panting hard. She paused at the entrance. Looked around this way and that, as if confused. Then rose up on her hind legs and sucked in long, loud sniffs.

"Then Gersa let out a mighty roar. Loud enough to wake frogs-in-the-mud. Bent over and frantically scratched the earth at the entrance. Flared her nose at the bloodied ground. Heaved her body to the ground and sat next to the scuffed-up dirt. As if in a daze. Swayed back and forth, moaning and wailing.

"Then . . . oh my . . . I shall never forget how she reached out her arm to nudge some tufts of fur on the ground. Carefully laid the soft pads of her paws on them, and drew the bits of fur toward her body. So sad it was, that it shattered my heart."

The crow paused and gazed at the two bears listening to his story. They tightened their arms around each other and exchanged sorrowful looks.

He addressed the cub, "You might not recall what happened next, Smokey, so I'll tell it. You mewed out loud from the back of the cave — where you must have crept by then. Your mother sat straight up and turned her head in your direction, but then, as if she couldn't believe that she'd really heard anything, she slumped again. At that moment, little bear, you must have felt so forlorn!"

Facing the storyteller, Smokey froze his shoulders and stifled a small sound, but he quickly made a brave face at Strut to continue.

"Then, little bear, you let out a high-pitched screech that cut the air. Your mother was so glad to hear you that she called out, 'Oh, thank the Spirits you're alive, my dear little runt! Where are you?'

"In the blink of an eye, I saw her great hulk lurch toward the back of the cave."

Smokey interrupted. "Wait, I know the rest. Mom, you lay down next to me on the cave floor, scooped me up with your arms, and gathered me to you. I thought I'd never stop shaking and whimpering . . . At last I found myself sink into your fur and just listen to your soft rumblings.

"Soon after, though, I heard your Mother Medicine Bear voice say, 'Let me see you by the light of day.' You carried me out into the sunlight and set my four feet on the ground. I was examined all over, and I even let you turn me over onto my back. 'You seem perfectly fine,' you told me. 'Unscathed.' You patted my fur and asked where the gray dust came from. I explained that I'd crept to the back of the cave to hide, and burrowed into the old ash-heap.

"Of course, you had to clean me up right away. You patted my fur all over and sent clouds of powdery ash into the air. It made us both sneeze. Then you licked me all over with your big tongue until I couldn't stop giggling."

Silence descended on the three animals. At length, Gersa broke the silence and addressed the crow, "Well, then, Strut, at last we're done for a while—first our close call with Clem's attack today, then hearing about the mountain lion attack.

"It has indeed been an exhausting day. It's a long way home, especially since Smokey will be limping along. So if you don't mind, Strut, I'd like to spend some time alone with my son. So feel free to go on ahead, if you'd like. We'll look forward to seeing you—our new family friend—in the next few days."

Strut nodded to Gersa, hovered overhead a moment to say goodbye to Smokey, and winged away.

Mother Bear motioned for Smokey to proceed on the path toward home, but he balked and stared into her eyes. "You must tell me," he said. "I have to know!" His voice turned plaintive. "Is it *my* fault—what happened to my brother and sister?"

"Oh, no, dear Smokey. If it's anyone's fault, it's *mine* . . . in a way."

She switched to her Mother Medicine Bear's forthright voice. "You're right: We have to address this question. It's a long story that we must sort out. We'll talk about it when we get home. I promise."

Later that night, after they had rested for a while in the cave, Mother Bear examined the cub's thigh, and said it was healing well. Gersa also told him she was sorry that when he'd been so wounded and tired, she had forced him to march at great length and dig up a root by himself. "I wanted to teach you how to take care of yourself, but I wish I'd taken more time to comfort you." She gave him a small squeeze. "I have to keep you safe!"

"Now that we're home, you promised to tell me if it's my fault—that *they* were killed—and not *me*." He held his breath.

Gersa looked away. A mournful sound escaped from deep inside. "Dear little one, don't worry. Actually, no one's to blame. If there was any negligence, it was *mine*."

"But I have this terrible feeling—that I should have warned the other cubs!"

Mother Bear waited, as if thinking about what to say. She finally broke the silence to tell Smokey that it was not his fault that the other two had died. She carefully explained: Even if he had called out to warn them, it wouldn't have stopped the mountain lion. It would only have jeopardized him, too.

In fact, he had been in the automatic grip of a bear cub's instinct to shut down and save his own life. And, afterward, it was brave of him to maintain his quiet throughout.

Gersa told Smokey that it was actually *her* fault to leave the cubs for so long. Yet, it had seemed to her at the time that she had little choice. He must know, though, that she meant well. She had to take a risk for all her dear ones, especially him.

She pondered a moment, and then asked Smokey if he'd like to hear the whole story about the three cubs so he could understand. He nodded assent.

"As you must have realized, you were the runt compared to your robust litter-mates. From the time you were only a few inches long, Smokey, suckling here in our winter cave high in the mountains, the two bigger ones pushed you aside so you couldn't get as much milk.

"But from the beginning, Smokey, you were a plucky bear—the first to scramble onto me and clamp onto the nearest teat and fiercely grasp my fur with your claws. More often than not, however, the other cubs knocked you out of the way, so they grew bigger and stronger while you grew thinner. You probably remember being hungry during that time, don't you?" Smokey nodded in reply.

"You should know that I tried my best to include you at my breasts, but the drought had left me with only a thin layer of fat, and my milk began to run dry. At first I could graze just outside the cave on the tender chartreuse grass you've seen that poked through the late-melting snow, but it wasn't enough. So I sought food farther from the cave, despite my worries about leaving you cubs alone.

"At first I made short excursions nearby. I tore bark off fallen trees so I could gather up fat grubs with my tongue, and stomp on scurrying termites to lick them off my feet.

"But one day when I rushed back and heaved myself onto the earthen floor so you three could nurse, you — the little runt — seemed too weak and slow to even reach a breast before the other cubs shouldered you aside. I tried to make room for you, but wondered whether I should relinquish hope and admit that you'd soon die anyway.

"However, Smokey dear, whenever I searched your face, expecting a dull look of defeat, I was always surprised by the sparkle of determination in your eyes. I'd think, 'You are a struggler. If you can't be fat, maybe you can be lean and lucky.' Perhaps, after all, you could survive on the small amount of remaining milk after the others had finished."

Mother Bear paused a moment to smile at Smokey, and he smiled back.

"Even though you were weak from hunger, I noticed what curiosity you could muster at times, and how restless you were for adventure. And you seemed so smart, with such an inquisitive spirit, that I harbored the great expectation that you were 'the one' who might eventually pass on my knowledge of medicinal herbs!

"At the time, though, I also wondered with foreboding, whether you'd be too bold for your own good and venture past the dangerous lands beyond our boundaries.

"Then, one day when you tried to suckle after the others, there was no milk left. You were still inquisitive, and sniffed the edges of the cave with what energy you had, but from then on, you slept more and more. I considered The Way of the Ancient Mothers of the Forest: 'Let nature take its course for those who have no chance to survive.'

"Smokey, I want you to know: You were always very special to me. In fact, my favorite. I argued against my love for you. Wouldn't it be merciful to let you go? It would give the other two a better chance of survival. Somehow, though, I couldn't go against my heart and stop feeding you!

"So, in my desperation to find enough nourishment for all three of you. I reached a dangerous decision. I risked leaving you cubs alone for the long time it would take to climb above the timberline for an abundant source of great nourishment. There, in the rock-falls beneath the peak of the mountain, I devoured the newly-hatched moths in the air, and overturned boulders to gobble up the fat larvae underneath.

"Afterward, I hurried home as fast as I could. Well . . . we already heard Strut tell us what happened next. I had taken a terrible risk, and it made us all suffer. I'm sorry. Do you understand, my little runt?"

In response, Smokey leaned over and licked her muzzle.

A big cloud passed by. The moon shed light on the mountain and bright stars studded the sky. The forest seemed empty, and pregnant with waiting. Murmuring softly Mother Bear told her cub how glad she was that he'd stayed hidden so her precious one could live. Then, with their arms holding each other close, they both cried about the two cubs. And it seemed as if the flow of tears began to melt away the terror, the guilt, the sorrow. A long silence carried their relief.

The last thing Smokey heard, before he sank into sleep, was his mother whispering to him, "I promise: I'll always protect you, my little Smokey, so no harm can ever come to you."

Chapter 5

One of the most difficult of all things to endure for a crow, a raven, a wolf, or a human is to feel alone and separated from one's own kind. A sense of belonging is one of the most universal of all feelings.
–Lawrence Kilham

The next morning Strut paced on his shelf in the den. Mother and cub were sleeping late. Finally he became impatient and dared to utter a caw. Gersa stirred, suddenly alert, and raised her head to swiftly survey the den. "Oh, it's you, Strut!" Careful not to wake her cub, she slipped from his side and rose onto her four feet. "It's already late. I must be leaving to forage, but Smokey should remain here to recuperate from his wound. So, my noble friend, would you be so kind as to make sure he rests here inside the cave—and not get into any trouble?"

"Yes, indeed! I'll keep him here with my stories. And if any predator happens to come by, I'll attack it myself." With a grateful nod at the crow, and a lingering look at her sleeping cub, Mother Bear left.

As soon as Strut saw Smokey stretch awake, wince at his stiff leg, and start to vigorously lick his wound, the crow launched his plan for a storytelling day. The crow was surprised to find the cub remembered to ask about the 'jinx' that had made the crow an outcast among his flock.

Strut eagerly took his former position on the edge of the low shelf, and Smokey sat on the ground with his legs in front of him, eyes raised expectantly. The crow waited in silence for a moment, then dramatically thrust out one leg with the band on it.

"Now: about this mysterious jinx! When I returned to the

flock bursting to tell them about Ray's house in town, did everybody welcome me? No! To my consternation, my own family and the rest of the flock gave me the cold shoulder. At first it was subtle, just a turn of the head or a few hops away from me on a branch. Then, as time went on, the bolder ones would land next to me and suddenly peck at a band, not minding whether they might cut my leg with their sharp bills. Not to give them any satisfaction, I didn't flinch, and the harassment seemed to die down."

Strut paused and cocked his head toward the bear. "Remember this, Smokey: Just ignoring bullying like that seemed to work, but it really didn't—in the long run. One day, one of the flock flew over and plunked himself next to me on a branch. It was the pipsqueak who dragged his ragged tail feathers behind him. How pathetic, I thought, that this bedraggled nobody might be my only friend. But misery loves company, so I turned to greet the damaged little crow.

"The next thing I knew—that scumbag darted me a nasty look and pecked me on the head, then he skedaddled before I could slash him back with my beak. A bunch of young crows laughed, 'Caaaw, caaw, caaw.' I felt my stomach plummet. Caah. I dropped from my branch and hid in the bushes from everyone.

"But let this be a lesson for you: Before long, though, I shook off the shame and fumed. How dare they drive *me* away! Anger filled my throat with a sour taste, and I screwed up my courage. You may not know this, Smokey, but once one of the flock pecks you badly on the head, others follow suit. Pretty soon you have a raw bleeding wound. They'll end up killing you!

"So, I used my noggin. I'd prove myself to them—on their own terms. I flew over and taunted them. I boasted outrageously so they'd dare me to do something. And wouldn't you know, Smokey, the dare that they gave me was a whopper: to fly over to the Great Horned Owl perched nearby on a tall skag.

"I was so mad that I zoomed straightaway to the owl. As I drew near he loomed so large I could hardly believe it. Big wicked-looking talons clasped the wood and his cold eyes glared at me. I pumped my wings right in his face and squawked 'KR-AACK.' Then I blasted away.

"After I landed back on a branch in front of the other crows, I nonchalantly combed my feathers, and sneaked a glance. They were looking at me with wide-open beaks. Actually, I had even astonished myself. So, little bear, do you think that fierce deed of bravery got me some respect? It sure did! But a feeling of belonging? Not really.

"So I tried something else. You probably don't know that each family of crows has a Long Song. It's like a secret password to find your own flock, even among a gathering of hundreds of crows. So I sneaked off each morning and practiced our Long Song—to show I was really one of them.

"One sunset, I stood tall before the crows roosting in our tree and sang it loudly and flawlessly, with every caw, coo, click, chirp, rasp, rattle, and screech. Guess what, Smokey? They made noises of approval. They were impressed!

"Encouraged, I improvised a variation with a nifty rhythm and poignant pauses, hoping they'd join in the jazz, but no one chimed in. Determined to win them over, I stretched my neck to sing lusty barks, trills and chortles in the longest sequence imaginable. Certainly they couldn't resist such an exciting song! I finally stopped. Those stupid idiots had resumed cawing among themselves as if they couldn't appreciate real artistry.

"I knew I'd sounded great! But not one crow had the gumption to go against the flock and join in, or even come up afterward and befriend me! I felt so mad that I flew to the pine tree above them and hammered on the trunk as hard as I could. Then I launched a barrage of pine cones at them and got some direct hits. Were they surprised! You should have seen me, Smokey. Caw-ah!"

Smokey chortled, his chest filling with exuberance at

having found such an exciting friend.

Strut nodded at him and continued, "As time went on, after I'd grumbled to myself a lot, I finally figured out why they didn't consider me one of them. When I'd returned from the humans' house, I must have smelled strange. Crows can't smell as well as you can, Smokey, but they must have sensed that I smelled like people, and they don't like people. Even mountain crows have heard how two-legged ones down in the grasslands think all the land is theirs. They shoot us, even though *we* were here first! Caw! Caw! And they frighten crows from cornfields with a scarecrow — made of straw to look like a human.

"Anyway, Smokey, to get back to my story, after the human smell finally wore off, my fellow crows treated me better, although to this day they still regard me as a bit different. After a while, I figured out why. Crows see very well and really notice small things. It's these shiny bands on my legs. They must catch their eyes all the time. It makes them look down on me, and there's nothing I can do about it. Caaah.

"They don't pick on me anymore, but I'm left on the end of a branch all by myself. Crows belong to a flock. Not loners like ravens. We always have sentinels on duty, so the rest of us feel safe to eat and talk. We do love to talk. Tell each other everything when we return to the roost. Argue and squabble over whose branch it is. Then, as the sky darkens, we huddle together and murmur among ourselves. Preen each other. So, to be left out of the group is really hard on me, in particular, because I happen to be a very talkative crow!"

The cub smiled broadly and said, "I can see that!"

"And the worst part, Smokey, is that I'm from a long line of storytellers. How can I tell stories without an audience? In my earliest days, everyone liked my stories and asked for more. Even the Old Crows cah-cahhed their approval.

"So I was bursting to tell everything I'd seen in town. You know how smart and inquisitive crows are, but they avoided my eyes. Can you imagine that, Smokey?" The cub shook his head.

"They acted like something was wrong with me." He paused. "Is there something wrong with me?"

Smokey replied emphatically, "Of course not!" He thought a moment before he spoke again. "I know! The other crows couldn't imagine being taken captive and put into a strange house with two-legged ones. It's too scary."

"Well, that's very insightful of you, little bear! I think you're right." The crow looked sharply at Smokey. "Would you be upset to hear all about it?"

Smokey took a deep breath and heaved it out. Then he gave Strut a strong, steady look. "No, I'm not afraid. I want to hear everything."

Strut met the cub's eyes with his own penetrating ones. It was as if the crow was recognizing Smokey for the first time as quite an intelligent friend, not just a little cub.

The crow softened his gaze, and, with a twinkle in his eyes, said, "Anyway, you look like a mighty curious bear to me. So you really want to hear about the world down there? I've been dying to tell someone. It might even be useful for you some day."

"Oh, yes!" Smokey leaned forward to hear about people and their intriguing world below the mountain.

Chapter 6

Men have forgotten this truth, but you must never forget it. You remain responsible forever for what you have tamed.
–Antoine de Saint-Exupery

The real voyage of discovery lies not in new landscapes but in seeing with fresh eyes.
–Marcel Proust

Days of storytelling went by while the cub was recovering his strength. At last, when Gersa came home one day and Smokey was full from nursing, he couldn't contain his news any longer. He eyed his mother lying on her back on the cave floor. Would she be surprised! He pounced on her belly with all four feet and blurted out what the crow had told him about the two-legged humans. Did she know that humans didn't have any tails? Instead of fur, babies have delicate soft skin, and just lie on their backs or crawl. Adults walk upright, but mostly sit on wooden sticks."

Mother Bear warned, "Don't get entranced by those stories. Humans can get you in terrible trouble."

The cub's exuberance was hardly deterred. He moved out of reach. "But, Mom, wait till you hear what happened to Strut. When he fell out of the nest, a man rescued him and he stayed in his house—like a marvelous cave."

Mother Bear swatted him. "Listen to me! Don't ever let any men see you, or you might never see our forest again."

"But they were kind to Strut. And returned him to the forest."

Mother Bear rose to her full height and towered over Smokey. "Then he's an exception. You shouldn't listen to him.

He's a bad influence. He'll fill your head with dangerous notions."

She stomped over to the crow's shelf and abruptly raised her forearm to sweep everything off of it.

"No, don't! He's my friend. Those are his treasures!" As she hesitated, he quickly admitted, "You're right. Humans keep animals *captive* in the house. They call them pets. They can't see the sky or even smell what's happening outside. I couldn't stand that!"

She lowered her arm. "That's what I mean! People can lock you up. Or shoot you. So don't let that crow tempt you to go anywhere near them."

Smokey nodded to her, but decided to be more careful in reporting what Strut told him.

Not long afterward, when Smokey saw the crow swoop into the den saying, "Caw! Today . . ." the cub frantically waved his paw to hush him. "Don't let her catch you talking to me about people!"

The cub scrambled out the cave on all fours and lowered his head toward Strut who was on the ground by then. The crow began, in the low voice of a conspirator, "Actually this is about some bold moves I'm about to make. Today is the last day of class this spring. I've just completed the course, How to Pest-Proof a Nest. I've been cutting class to spy on the savvy old crows. Guess how they line their nests to repel blood-sucking mites? They pick only the upper green tips of the herbs. That's what I'll do someday. So a female will choose me as her mate. Not anytime soon, though. First, I gotta see the world!

"Tomorrow's my last exam: Defending the Nest and Mobbing. It's how we attack red-tailed hawks. Caw! Caw! After that, I'm free.

"What do you suppose I'm going to do? I'm going to cut summer school. Skip all that heavy-duty stuff, like The Mechanics of Nest Construction. Caw, that's fifteen hundred twigs! I'll miss Robbing Nests—that's other birds' eggs. That'd be fun, but some other time.

"This summer I'm bailing out of classes to do my own independent field work. Since the crows still think I'm different, I'm going to *be* different! I'm not ashamed of who I am. I'm Strut the Storyteller! I'll fly down to the village . . . and see what I can see."

"Glad to hear!" Smokey danced around on his hind legs. "That's the way, Strut! And come back and tell me all about it."

During the next days every time the crow sneaked into the den Smokey feasted his curiosity on tidbits of news and the trinkets Strut had found for his collection — a copper coin, a key, a clothes pin.

Then, early one morning the cub was startled to see Strut come back soon after he'd left. The crow rushed in flapping his wings frantically. "Quick. Gotta get my red ribbon. To take it down to town. They're leaving! Oh, here it is!"

In mid-air, dangling the red ribbon from one foot, his wings thrashing, Strut craned his neck back toward the astonished cub. "Smokey, I may be gone for a while. A few days, a long time, maybe *forever*. I don't know. Take care."

Smokey stood up, his heart thumping. "Wait! What's come over you?" He cried, "Don't leave me!" but his friend had already flown off without a backward glance. The cub's throat tightened so hard it hurt. He scrunched down and laid his chin on the ground.

Not long afterward, Smokey heard a noise from the crow's shelf. Careful not to wake his mother, who was still sleeping, the cub crept over and stretched up to the ledge to see a slumped form. The crow greeted him in a weary voice, "Caaa, caaa," but the cub turned his head away, his throat still tight at having been left. He plunked his four feet onto the cave floor and paced.

Mother Bear snorted in her sleep, then was quiet again. Smokey narrowed his eyes at the crow and whispered. "You looked crazy when you left. You said you might be gone *forever*!"

"Caah. I'm sorry, Smokey."

The cub frowned and sputtered, "It's okay this time, but don't ever fly off like that again." Strut nodded, and looked so remorseful that Smokey couldn't contain himself longer. "So tell me. What happened? Let's go to the end of the shelf away from my mom — and not so loud."

"The people wouldn't take me with them. I guess it was asking too much." Slowly the bird stirred his crumpled body and locked his long legs to stand. He looked around the den. "Anyhow, it sure feels good to be back."

He abruptly exclaimed, "Great Crow in Heaven! What was I thinking? I must've been crazy. Those humans could've taken me anywhere. Then who knows whether I'd ever see you again? Or our forest!" Strut's bill drooped. "But I'm sure going to miss them."

"Strut, my old pal. Tell me what happened!" Smokey sat on the cave floor, expectantly lifting his face toward the crow.

"Don't worry. I'll speak quietly and tell you the whole story. I flew down to the house where I stayed with that family. Did you know humans have names like we do? I figured out that the guy who rescued me was called Ray, his mate was Ruth, their son, Don, and little daughter, Judy. And a rambunctious black puppy called Jet. Until now, whenever I've gone to town I've always gone to their house. That's where most of the trinkets come from.

"I'd swoop down on the house with loud caws, and Ray'd come out. He'd sit on the back stoop and throw out corn for me. I'd even take it on-the-wing from his open hand. If he's not home, he's walking around town. I can spot him from high in the air — from the way he walks and that silver cowboy hat. I'd dive-bomb him and whizz by with my beak open as if I'm going to yank his hat away. But I always let him take it off in the nick of time and he shoos me away with it. He acts mad, especially if someone's watching. I squawk and flail at his hat with my feet and wings until he laughs and yells, 'You crazy crow!' He's a real friend — like you, Smokey.

"He's sure proud of that cowboy hat. I think he's afraid I'll land on it and soil it, but I'd never do that, Smokey. Anyhow, he doesn't dare put it back on when I'm around or I'll attack it. So I flutter in front of him to pull the dangling leather strings of his western tie, or I stand on his shoulder and nibble at his ear — till he stops laughing and says, 'Ouch! Cut it out!' Then I fly down near his feet so he'll toss kernels of corn on the ground. They're so delicious!"

Smokey moved his legs restlessly. "But what happened this morning?"

"This morning was different. No teasing. No corn. The whole family was loading all their stuff into a huge van. At first I couldn't figure out what was happening. Could they be leaving their house? Our nests would never be so infested with mites this early in spring that we'd have to abandon them. If I'd realized their house had already become infested, I could have brought herbs. Or, did they have to leave because a predator had moved nearby? If so, I could've tried to drive it away." The crow tipped his head from side to side. "I'll never know.

"So I stood on each cardboard box they moved to the curb and cawed for them to take me with them. But they only brushed me aside. One after another, neighbors stopped by and said goodbye. Ray and his son, Don, shook hands or clapped a hand on the shoulders of the men. Ruth and little Judy hugged their friends and cried at leaving the neighbor's little baby — the one who used to visit them.

"Well, I'm a good friend too, so I beat my way back here as fast as I could — to fetch the red ribbon — and remind them that I'm a member of the family. After all, Ray and I've known each other practically my whole life. Ever since he rescued me.

"I returned with the ribbon just in time. I saw Ruth and the children driving away in the family car, and Ray was getting into the driver's seat of the big van. He was going to leave without me! I flew to the front of the van, clung to the windshield wiper and stared into Ray's eyes. I beat my wings frantically against the glass. He finally cranked down the side window.

"I sped into the van, stood on the passenger seat next to his cowboy hat, and leaned my head forward like a person going for a ride. I tilted my head to see his reaction. Ray opened his mouth in surprise and his eyes twinkled. Then he closed his mouth and looked intently at me. At last I had his attention!

"I remembered the red ribbon I'd been carrying. I shook my beak to make it wave in the air and looked meaningfully at Ray. He didn't laugh or shoo me off. Humans are so smart! Almost as savvy as crows. So I hoped that he'd recognized the ribbon as the one he'd put near my nesting tree so he could return me to the right place in the forest.

"A moment passed between us. Male people don't cry, certainly not cowboys like Ray or ranchers, but his eyes brimmed. He pointed to his metal badge—the one he always wears—and, as he said words to me, I knew from his tone that he couldn't take me with him. He looked at me intently, then kindly slipped the ribbon from my bill. Then he seemed at a loss about what to do with it.

"As a crow-of-action, I took charge of the situation. I alighted on his wrist and tugged the ribbon out of his fingers. Then I flew over to his cowboy hat on the front seat, and tucked it into the hat band. He reached over and softly stroked my bill with his finger. Then he put on his hat for a moment, and tipped it to me. That's what people do, Smokey, to honor each other. Caah.

"Then—imagine this, Smokey—he caught my eye. He slowly reached up, and undid his stringy cowboy necktie with its silver tips, and held it out to me. I closed my bill over it and bowed. Then, thinking I'd never see him again, I took my leave out the van's window. I was very tired and slowly flew back here. It seemed a long way home to the mountain and you."

Smokey looked at the western bolo that Strut showed him. "Yeah, that's nice, I guess. But I'm sure glad you didn't leave!" When Strut still looked morose, Smokey added, "What about your own flock? Wouldn't they have missed you?"

"I doubt it," Strut said gloomily. "They don't really like

me."

Smokey frowned. "Really? *All* of them?" he prompted.

"Well, actually, five of them are the worst." Strut perked up. "You've given me an idea. See you tomorrow," and he flew off.

The next morning after Gersa had gone foraging, Strut flew into the cave. "Remember what you said yesterday? Well, here's my idea. The biggest bully is Duke who is always backed up by his four nest mates. They're all bullies. Somehow, I gotta get Duke on my side. Lately, every time he flies by, he swerves over toward me and takes a jab at the metal ring on one of my legs, making his gang laugh. If I don't stop him now, his whole gang will think me fair game and start doing it too. I couldn't ever relax. So I must do something."

"Yeah, Strut! But what?"

"Well, I can't peck Duke back—he's too big, and I don't have any other crows on my side, like he does."

"So why don't you befriend him?" Smokey said. "Tell him some of your exciting stories. He'd love those!"

"Nice of you to say, Smokey, but I'm afraid that's kinda naïve. He wouldn't deign to listen. He doesn't even like me. But maybe you're on the right track. I'll have to use my noggin to think up something . . ."

"Isn't there anything that *you* have that he might want?"

"I won't be blackmailed out of my treasures, if that's what you mean! Anyway, that'd just make him despise me, like I'm some kinda pushover."

The crow looked at the sky, mumbling "Something he might want . . . Show him something new, something irresistible, dazzling . . . I got it!"

Without a word to Smokey, the crow flashed out of the cave, hopped onto a branch, stretched his neck out and screeched in the direction of the nesting tree, "Duke, where are you?" Other crows clamored for Duke and buzzed with questions, but Strut shushed them, saying, "It's for his ears only. A secret expedition. If Duke dares."

Strut cawed to Smokey, "Here he comes."

A big crow banked in mid-air at the sight of the bear cub, then reached down his big black feet to grasp the branch above Strut.

"What's up? You interrupted my grooming, you little twerp. This had better be good."

Young Duke and Strut   © GLORI BERRY

"Wait till you hear what it is." Strut lowered his voice. "There's something you gotta see. Humans have caught the sun in globes. It's absolutely dazzling. All the streets are aglow at night. Something called Rural Electrification's suddenly come to all the small towns down there. Like nothing you've ever seen."

Seeing Duke's bulky body jittering with excitement, Strut added, "We'll have to go at night. The owls will be out. But I'm game for night-flying. Aren't you? So, how about tonight as soon as the moon breaks over the ridge?"

"Well . . . yeah. Why not?" Then Duke narrowed his eyes. "CAWK! This better not be some kinda wild goose chase, buster, or you'll be sorry."

Strut met the big crow's eyes with a steady stare. Then, in a cagey tone, he said, "Not afraid to take a chance, are ya, big boy? Meet you here at moon-break."

Smokey had fallen asleep that night before the two left, but he heard their loud return by the time the moon was high in the sky. They were cawing and laughing together, Duke's voice exclaiming with awe: "Wasn't that mind-boggling? I'll never forget the moment—all those towns getting bright all at once. Wow! Humans are far out! So you go to town all the time? Hey, pal, you gotta show me more of this kinda stuff."

"Well, I suppose so . . . Why not? See you later, big guy."

Smokey smiled to himself, rolled over and went back to sleep. The cub only learned much later about the crows' trip to town—the first of their ventures that would be portentous for his own future life.

Chapter 7

Bunham bunaham: To be about to speak, and about not to speak.
–Boro language

The next evening Strut swooped over to the nesting tree where the crows were already flying hither and yon to find their places for the night. It was a frenzied scene with dozens of crows squabbling over roosting places and cawing about the news of the day. As a junior storyteller, Strut took his place on a lower perch. It was beneath other crows, where he had to endure occasional splats on his head or back. Thank goodness, he thought, spring foliage was budding forth above him and would soon become thick enough to shield him.

He awoke the next morning free of splats but his feathers covered with dew. Half-asleep in the misty gray mountain fog, he shivered. How he wished he could be higher in the tall tree to bask in the warm sunlight, like the senior crows and the more aggressive ones. It wasn't fair that Duke and his pals were higher than he was! Why was their fighting prowess more esteemed than his storytelling skill? He glared toward the Older Crows who could change things if they wanted to.

Strut had no sooner had these thoughts when Duke alighted on a branch nearby. The big crow looked warm and dry. He fluffed out his wings in a self-important way and announced, "A summons from Elder Crow. For both of us. Follow me."

Strut was so impressed with Duke that, despite his reservations about the big crow, he was pleased to be seen with him. "Do you suppose we're in trouble about last night?"

Duke shrugged. "I dunno. That old fogey is always chewing me out for goofing-off. Just wait and see: I'll be the one who'll be blamed, not you — you-goody-two-wings.'"

"Don't worry. I can talk us out of anything."

"Good enough, pal. I can't afford any more warnings or I'll be demoted. Elder crow is always down on me. No sense of humor — the old sour-beak." As if embarrassed at admitting so much, he cawed 'follow me' and abruptly took off. Strut stood a moment, whirred his wings to send the dew droplets flying, and bolted in pursuit.

Moments later, Strut and Duke stood side by side before Elder Crow. The branch he had indicated for them was a spindly one. They bounced for a while, getting more and more off balance, realizing that Elder Crow had no doubt planned it that way. Even knowing this, they found to their consternation that the more they flapped their wings, the more the branch teetered.

With an amused glint in his eyes, Elder Crow opened his beak so wide that his pointed tongue showed. Strut nudged Duke. "Go slow. More subtle," and they soon barely raised their wings — not in unison but in alternation — until the branch stopped and they could fold their wings. Duke shot Strut a grateful sideways look. By now, his usual cockiness had faltered, and he seemed merely relieved to be standing still.

"Since you two scalawags have seen fit to finally settle down on that branch," the old crow began, "let me say that I'm not particularly pleased with your foolish escapade to the towns down in the valley and your noisy return in the middle of the night. I'm getting fed up with your tomfoolery. But that's not why I summoned you.

"Duke, I want you to show Strut where the Apache meeting ground is. Close your beak, Duke. Don't pretend you don't know where it is. You frequently go there to mock the Mescalero Indians. I know — that you know — where it is. That's why I have need of you."

Elder Crow turned to address Strut. The old one had an impressive stance. His broad back, that usually looked solid black, sparkled resplendent purple and green in the sun's early rays.

"You're a good storyteller, Strut, but you are not a *great* storyteller." Strut was crest-fallen. "You do have real promise, though. At least you know how to talk. However, you don't know how to listen: Not to nature, nor to the past and future. Not to the waters of inspiration that spring forth from deep inside or what streams from the farthest stars — where true stories are created. Caw! Close your beak and listen to me.

"You don't know what you don't know. You know only these new arrivals — the white men, who don't know much about the forest nor its inhabitants. On the other wing, the red men have always lived in nature amongst us. And we have lived in harmony with them back to the beginning of Crowkind. Go. Be with them this afternoon, experience their dance, and see what happens. Show what you're made of. *Remember: Don't let anything distract you.*"

Strut bowed his head low in acquiescence as well as to hide his bewilderment.

Elder Crow motioned with a slight upward nod of his head for Duke to hop over to his branch. Elder Crow spoke softly to Duke in a crafty, closed-beak sort of way. "Keep up your banter and antics at the Apache meeting ground — no more or less than usual. If you do that, you can keep your place in the nesting tree — for the time being. In fact, I'll take off one of your demerits."

"Glad to oblige."

With a parting "Crowspeed to the both of you," Elder Crow flew off.

Strut cawed at Duke, "So what was all that mumbo jumbo about?"

"Well, I'm not sure I should tell you." He cocked his head in a sly tease. Strut glared until Duke relented. "Old Sour Beak must be planning some kind of test for you. Here's how I figure it: Just act the opposite of me and my pals. That'd be the shrewd move here. You know how the old geezer is always keen on initiations and gobbledygook like that. This is one of those things."

Duke abruptly said, "Stay here," and took off. Strut waited impatiently. In a few minutes the big crow came into sight, accompanied by his loud nest-mates and a few others. As he sped by, he cawed down at Strut to catch up.

After they'd crossed the mountain and entered the territory of the Mescalero Apaches they floated down and perched in a tall tree overlooking a clearing in the Apache reservation. The cleared area had a flagpole in its center.

At first Strut took a limb below the other crows as they jockeyed for position and yakked away. On a whim, he changed his mind and flew to the top of the tree. Oddly enough, Duke touched down on a branch nearby as if to endorse Strut's position. Then Duke returned to the noisy fray below, cawing like the others.

Before long, a car drove up and the door opened. Ray Bell, in his game warden jacket and sharply-pressed jeans, sprang out the door. "Mendez! Sorry I'm late. Just flew the Piper Cub into Capitan."

Strut felt his heart leap at the sight of Ray. How his throat yearned to be with him, as if a strong force was pulling him down to alight on his friend's shoulder. "*No distractions,*" Strut thought, and gripped the branch tightly with his feet.

The crow watched as Ray and Mendez handed out a kortick—a sharp metal hoe with a wooden rake on the other end—to each of the two dozen men in jeans and white cotton shirts lined up below the tree. Aloysius Mendez, a full-blooded Apache, beamed a quick smile at Ray. "You know, ever since they were youngsters, they've fought fires on the reservation, but after all the practice, wait till you see how fast they are now!

"Let's begin." Drummers took up a fast beat, the men worked in synchrony at a fast clip. The first man bent to chop and rake a wide swath of ground, then stood to take four steps forward, and the next man bent to do likewise, thus saving their backs with the one-chop method and rapidly cutting a fire-line three-feet wide.

Two crows who were below Strut mimicked the dancing. In time with the drumbeat, they swaggered sideways on a branch, and suddenly tottered before lurching upright again. The other crows laughed so raucously that Strut could hardly resist and had to clamp his beak shut with a foot.

After a while Strut grew drowsy from the monotonous beat, and found himself bobbing in time with the drumbeats. With his eyelids half-closed, his body became lighter until he imagined himself a speck hovering in the sky.

Scenes from stories he'd never heard flashed before him, as if they were floating up from a mysterious origin: great flocks of crows migrating above herds of great hoofed beasts on the plains below; then a crow blown off course finding safety along a river; a medicine man sending off a young crow to search for something important . . . The jumble of images piqued intense curiosity, and he tried to concentrate on the fragments, hoping they might weave themselves into stories before new images appeared.

Both drums abruptly stopped on the same beat, and the firefighters stopped the same instant. Strut had no idea how long his trance had lasted. Opening his eyes, he felt like a different crow—his body heavier yet somehow lighter too.

The Apaches were standing at ease, chatting among themselves. Far below Strut, he saw Ray and Mendez smiling broadly at the men. Ray said, "You are true Hot-Shots. I've never seen any firefighters cut such a fast fire-line." He walked briskly to the car and returned with a large wooden box.

Mendez announced, "Congratulations, men. Here are your well-deserved firefighter hats—to protect you from falling rocks and embers." As the men filed by, Mendez and Ray shook their hands and gave each a red helmet. Afterward, their bodies still wet with perspiration, the men stood milling around, laughing boisterously.

Over the ensuing years, more Native Americans swelled the ranks of the Red Hats, and they became so famous for their extraordinary speed and stamina that they were called upon to fight fires throughout the land. They earned the Department of Interior's highest honor — the Meritorious Service Award — for protecting the country's natural resources.

Strut watched Ray return to his car. The crow felt a pang in his throat, and raised his wings to fly down to his friend. But he was halted by Elder Crow's low voice: "If your human friend can come back this time, he can come back another time. Let it be."

Strut looked around. Elder Crow wasn't there. How confusing. Did the voice come from himself? He shook his whole body and took a deep breath. It was strange: He felt bolder than before, but somehow more humble. He shook his head, perplexed whether he wanted this change from his familiar self.

The storyteller saw the other crows flying about, having fun. Why couldn't he be light-hearted like they were? He lowered his head and sighed. "Caaa." Then he pumped his wings vigorously and folded them close to his body. "Do I dare hope," he thought, "that I've found my true flight-plan in life — as a storyteller?"

Duke jarred the branch as he landed. "Let's go back. Gotta report to Old Sour Beak. Sure was a lot of fun, wasn't it?" Strut nodded, but felt dismayed that he couldn't quite recapture his newfound feeling of camaraderie with Duke.

Back home, Elder Crow thanked Duke, who shot a smug look at Strut. The big crow flew back to the Crow Tree for more rowdying with his pals. "Come join us," he motioned to Strut, but the crow looked away. It was what he'd always wanted but he didn't feel like it at the moment. His eyes were still turned inward to some new kind of intriguing place.

Strut remained standing before Elder Crow, who looked him in the eye and scrutinized him a long time. He declared, "I see you have been truly initiated. You've passed across a boundary in the skies. There's no going back. Let me counsel you: Learn how to be still and nurture the spring that wells up within you. It means that at times you will be among others, but not truly with them. Henceforth you will be their friendly Storyteller. And, in time, you might become their esteemed Storymaker, the one who creates stories from inspiration, from our history and from your imagination—plucked out of the skies. You can aspire to an honored place among all crows, my son. Embrace your fate willingly, for it is your special destiny."

Softening his voice, Elder Crow continued, "A word of advice. You know, I'm often too serious an elder. You don't have to be as . . . well, as solemn as I am. You're different. Your nature is, well, irrepressible. With you, wisdom and laughter can go together. However, beware the temptation to be too daring. Take only well-calculated risks. Don't jeopardize your life: I foresee an important mission for you to undertake in the years ahead."

The two crows bobbed their heads twice to each other. Then Elder Crow led Strut to his new place, high up the tree, not yet among the elders, but about equal to the level of Duke and his friends. "A wise choice," thought Strut, "so Duke won't be envious. Anyway, at this height, I won't have to dodge splats anymore." Although the afternoon had been quite sobering, all-in-all, excitement stirred him, and a short note of bittersweet triumph escaped Strut's beak. "Cah-ah!"

Chapter 8

"Well," said Pooh, "what I like best" . . . and then he had to stop and think. Because although Eating Honey was a very good thing to do, there was a moment just before you began to eat it which was better than when you were, but he didn't know what it was called.
–A. A. Milne

In German, there is a beautiful little word for it: Vorfreude . . . A single word captures the relationship of time, the pleasure of waiting for the moment to arrive . . . Spend your life in the eternal bliss of always having something to hope for, something to wait for, plans not realized, dreams not yet come true.
–Kai Krause

One morning when Smokey awakened early and started to patter out of the cave, Mother Bear suddenly towered over him. "Stop. Today I must show you an important boundary of our territory. You must never go again to the place where I'm taking you, except in an emergency."

She barged ahead of him and Smokey chattered at her back as he padded behind her to the other side of the mountain. At last she halted and hushed him with a stern look. She commanded, "See that drop-off ahead of us? Whatever you do, don't go any closer to it than right here."

From below the cliff came a shattering din. "I have to see what it is," Smokey blurted out and bounded ahead. From the creepy feeling on the nape of his neck he knew that his mother was glaring at him. Careful not to snap twigs, he crept toward the noise below. As he neared the drop-off, Gersa tongue-clicked and lip-smacked, then kept up a low chomping sound.

The loud sound below muffled her warnings. "Clang,

clang," reverberated from below as if one rock was hitting another repeatedly. What Smokey heard didn't seem real, so he lifted his snout. The strange stench of machinery assaulted his nose and made his fur bristle. As if compelled, he slowly crawled ahead on his belly and peered over the rim of the cliff. Far below a gigantic beetle was making the rasping noise, and pouring out its back end were black clouds.

From what Strut had told him, he recognized a truck chugging along a dirt road. Upright creatures scurried around like ants, but they walked on two legs with limbs dangling from their shoulders. They must be men!

He rose on his hind legs to feast on the scene below. A man held a machine with growly noises against a tree trunk. Then he stepped aside, and the tree crashed to the ground, snapping branches off other trees as it fell. Another man did the same to another tree. Then they ran to the fallen trees and buzzed off the branches until only long trunks remained.

The cub's jaw hung open and his eyes widened at the tremendous power men had. He'd seen Mother Bear rip the bark off a fallen tree with one swipe of her mighty paw to expose grubs and ants. He'd seen deep claw marks—long gouges—that male bears had left high on the trunks of trees. But these men left their mark in the forest like no other animal.

Dropping onto all fours, Smokey gawked for a long time. A wave of excitement shook his body. He remembered Strut telling him that people lived in huge square nests made of wood. Would these logs make homes for people? He took a deep breath and a great yearning swept over him to know more about men.

The cub slowly headed back to Gersa, not daring to look at her. But he heard her "huh-huh" of displeasure and sensed her stiff-walking toward him. She thwacked him with a cuff that knocked him down and rolled him over. "You're too strong-minded, just like your father, Clem!"

Still sprawled on the ground, the cub hardly listened. He was trying to remember what Strut had told him about humans and houses and cars. His mother glowered and gave him a penetrating look. "It's that crow's fault! Men can be dangerous! They don't know the Rules of the Wild. And don't you ever let them turn you into a Garbage Bear!"

The cub gave her a puzzled look. "What's a Garbage Bear?"

"That's a bear who gorges on garbage heaps at campgrounds and begs for sweets along the road. Smokey, listen to me! If you hang around humans, they'll trap you in a cage and take you away."

Mother Bear bored harsh eyes into his. "Listen to me! People are coming farther into our forest every year. That means trouble. Humans are powerful but ignorant.

"They don't know the simplest body language! They stride right into your territory past all your markers — as if they can't see or smell. And if they blunder into you on a path, they have the atrocious manners to stare you in the face! So, any self-respecting bear is forced to huff-and-rush them to scare them off. Then they can become so frightened that they shoot you."

In a warmer voice she said, "Remember, Smokey, you'll always have a good life within our territory. High in the mountains here, there's plentiful food. I'll show you each season where to find good things to eat: grubs and fish, acorns and pine nuts, and berries of all kinds."

Smokey nodded dutifully, but he already felt gripped by a force that lured him to explore the enchanting world beyond the mountains.

Late that evening Mother Bear, having sensed his curiosity, said, "I'm sorry I hit you so hard, but you must always avoid men."

The next day Strut appeared in the cave and shushed Smokey so he could concentrate on rearranging the collection on his shelf. Nevertheless, he himself talked non-stop. "Caw-caw. What a mess! Keys, tin foil, clothes pins every-which-way. I must put this jumble in proper order — to suit the new me! Elder Crow would endorse this as some form of 'meditation' — whatever that is."

Smokey stood up to watch, but the black bird firmly insisted that the cub not look until the masterpiece was completed. The bear went back onto all fours. But he could still follow Strut's shadow on the cave wall as he bustled about, moving things around with his beak as he muttered to himself. At last the shadow-bird stopped. "Cah, that's almost perfect. But there's a blank space in the center where the red ribbon—the one I gave Ray—used to be. Caah-Caah. It's like an empty space in my heart."

The crow suddenly flew out of the cave and soon blasted back, carrying a magpie's tail feather. "Don't look yet," he commanded. But Smokey watched his shadow place the feather in the center and fiddle with it a long time to make it stand upright. "Cah! That does it!

"Now you can look. You know, little bear, life is wonderful and terrible, so I needed something black and white." He surveyed his shelf, with a dip of his head and a satisfied wag of his tail feathers.

Smokey stretched up on his hind legs and exclaimed, "I don't understand all that mumbo-jumbo about what you did, but the new arrangement does have a nice feel to it.

"So, Strut, now that you're finished, I've been wanting to tell you what happened to me yesterday . . ."

"Caw-caw. First let me tell you—"

As the crow opened his beak and expanded his breast feathers to launch into his own story, Smokey stood and bristled his fur. "Huff-huff! There you go again, you . . . you birdbrain! Always running at the beak! When I finally have a story to tell you, you can't shut up!"

Strut stood stock-still. Then he bent forward. "Cah. I really want to hear. But I'm a crow and just can't stop myself. I'm glad to shut my beak—"

"So be quiet!" In response, the crow quickly reached up with one black foot to clutch his beak shut, and wobbled on the remaining foot until Smokey got a fit of giggling. The cub rolled onto his back with his feet in the air, and they both laughed until their stomachs hurt.

The crow recovered first. "I really do love to hear a story, so cut to the chase!"

Smokey proceeded to tell how he disobeyed Gersa's warning and looked below the cliff, and how thrilling it was to see men — buzzing down trees and loading them onto a truck. Strut listened in open-beaked surprise, which greatly pleased Smokey. At one point the crow interjected, "Those are logs. Men use them to build their houses, like birds use twigs to build nests."

"I was wondering about that myself!" the cub said.

Except for this small interruption, Strut restrained himself from talking until the cub was finished. "Yes, indeed. A great story." He beat his wings. "I must go see! Toodle-oo."

For a while Mother Bear had been telling Smokey that sometime in the spring they would be leaving their den to venture forth to find spring and summer food, and not return until hibernation in the fall. As soon as Smokey heard, he had meant to inform Strut — so the crow would know where they'd be going — but somehow he kept forgetting to tell him.

So one morning Smokey was startled to hear Mother Bear abruptly announce that they were going to leave the den right away.

"But what about Strut?" he asked.

"He'll find you."

Smokey's throat tightened at the thought of losing his good friend. "Are you sure he can find us?"

"Yes. Crows are good at finding anything they set their minds to. We're just going part way down the mountain. That's far enough for you to go — with your little legs, but not very far for him, flying in the sky."

Smokey concentrated on putting each of his four paws down solidly on the ground, imitating his mother as she lumbered ahead of him. For each of her big steps, he had to take many small ones, so when he looked up after a while she was already at the bottom of a small slope. "Wait for me!" He leaped ahead, stumbled, and suddenly was rolling downhill. He bumped against her at the bottom and he laughed, and she joined in.

"Now, come along, Smokey. There's a treat waiting for you in a tree. I'll show you where it is—near a meadow at the edge the woods."

It was a sunny day in the beginning of May, one of the brightest and hottest Smokey had known since he'd first emerged from the dark cave weeks before. As he went along, the cub saw shimmering spots of sunlight on the ground and sprang from one to the next. When he looked up, Mother Bear was out of sight.

A tinkling sound ahead lured him forward just in time to see Mother Bear slosh across a narrow creek splashing glints of silver in her wake. The cub halted at the water's edge, so abruptly that his seat slammed hard onto the ground, arching him backwards so he almost fell onto his back. His eyes fastened forward on the water with its moving flashes of light and dark. What was this writhing creature? He tentatively reached out his front paw and poked it.

Just then Gersa's impatient huff reached him. She half-turned as if to proceed down the path on the other side of the river. He raised his head and beamed a wide-lipped smile at her and slapped the water. With a shrill whoop he flopped his whole body in and lolled around in the shallows. Drawn to a strange rounded rock at water's edge, he stood and pushed it with all his strength and rocked it until it gave way with a sucking sound. Nothing was underneath. But the muddy bottom that swirled up into the clear water made him dizzy. He staggered, seeing again his wounded leg spreading blood into the big river.

Smokey heard himself let out a wail like a tiny cub. The next thing he knew, Gersa straightened to her full height and galloped across the water toward him. Ha! She was such an easy target that he whisked water at her and she drenched him back. The cub fought so ferociously—and they laughed so joyously — that they couldn't stop until they were breathing so hard that they collapsed together on the creek bank, soaked to their inner fur.

Mother Bear licked his muzzle with hearty slurps of her big wet tongue. "Oh, Smokey, it's so good to see you having fun!" Then, in her usual instructive voice she said, "You should remember that this creek goes to a beaver pond down the mountain. It's not far. I'll show it to you some day so you can play in it. Or in winter we might even crash the beaver house to eat one of them." She abruptly turned her back and he followed her rump across the creek. Before proceeding down the path, though, both bears felt an urge at the same time to shake their bodies vigorously to send water sparkling every which way.

When they finally came to a clearing. Mother Bear stood and raised her head. She sucked a noisy breath into her nose, and opened her mouth wide to taste the air. With saliva sloshing out right and left, she swung her head as she picked up her pace. "Come along!" Smokey bumbled after her as fast as he could, tripping so hard, time and again, that he smacked his nose on the ground.

He caught up with her in front of an old tree with patches of bark falling off. It had a gaping hole up on the trunk where bees were buzzing in and out. "Watch me," Gersa said. She stood to scoop out a paw full of pale yellow honeycomb and gobbled it down.

"I want some too!" the cub yowled, but Gersa was absorbed in stuffing her mouth. So he shinnied up the trunk, dug his back feet into the rough crumbling bark, and reached a forearm into the hole up to his armpit. To his amazement, his paw came out dripping with a gob of honeycomb to crunch and lick. Bees swarmed around him and stung his face, but he found his muzzle mainly immune to the stings. Anyway, the honey was the best food he'd ever tasted. Mother Bear paused a moment to say, "Don't let those bees get away, Smokey. Sweep your tongue all around your face and eat them. They're good food."

After they had slurped up plenty of honey, they roamed the forest again where Gersa showed Smokey places for foraging in the coming seasons. She had him sniff certain healing herbs, so that one day he could pass on her knowledge as a Medicine Bear. This made him feel very important.

Around sunset, Smokey looked up at his mother and said, "This has been one of the best days of my life. A day I will always remember . . . Can't we sleep around here? Some place where we can look up at the stars? We never had much chance to see them from the old cave." Mother Bear swept her neck forward, indicating 'up ahead.'

Walking leisurely side by side, they soon came upon a huge tree with a thick cushion of pine needles underneath. They shared a glance: This was it. Mother Bear lowered herself onto the ground and sat with her legs stretched out front. Suddenly, with a playful impulse, Smokey laughed and leaped onto her shoulder, then slid down over her head, face-first. She laughed and captured him with her encircling paws, and they both rolled onto the pine-cushioned ground. Smokey panted, caught his breath, and lay happily beside his mother's big furry body.

They listened to the evening forest. Crickets chirped a background blend of high sounds, rising and falling. A little tree frog piped up, "Peep." Another joined with a "Peep." Then came successive waves of song, "Peep. Peep. Peeeep." All was silent a moment, and there came the faint cry of a far-off owl, "Hoo, hoo. Hoo, hoo-hoo."

Smokey felt his mother draw him even closer. In response he took a deep breath and slowly let it out. His whole body soft and heavy with tiredness, belly full, he let himself drift into sleep, a very contented bear. Perfectly safe. A wonderful world ahead of him in his forest home.

Chapter 9

Remember...Only <u>you</u> can prevent wildfires.
–Smokey Bear

Ashes are the work of a moment, a forest the work of centuries.
–Seneca the Younger

Earlier in the evening, on the other side of the mountain, a camper had warmed his hands before a red and yellow fire. It was the last day of his vacation. As the crackling fire ebbed to a few dancing flames and gradually turned to embers, he realized how much he loved the wilderness: a cushioned path underfoot, glimpses of small animals scurrying away, an alluring whiff of balsam in the breeze, the sound of an owl at night. What a surprise it had been that afternoon to watch a mother bear and her cub robbing honey from a beehive.

A glance at the low sun in the sky and the fading light warned him it was past the time to leave. Reluctantly he arose, hoisted his backpack, poured some water over the charred remnants of the fire, kicked some loose soil over it all, and left. He usually at least stirred ashes with a stick but it didn't seem necessary. As he took a moment to pause on the trail and look back at his campsite, he did not realize that, under the dirt, live embers still burned pinkish-red. And little did he realize what tragedy would come to the forest he loved and to its creatures.

What would come would not be a controlled burn – a fire set by a ranger and fire teams in the cool morning of a calm, moist day, to clear away underbrush and dry timber, the kind of fire to prevent future conflagrations.

Nor would it be a fire ignited by lightning. Long before humans appeared on the scene, those fires, large and small, had been erupting periodically to renew the forest.

Instead of an unavoidable fire caused by lightning or a controlled burn, this would be a man-made wildfire, a fire caused by carelessness.

Conditions were ripe: a drought and a very hot and windy day. The fire would rage out of control and sweep across the vast mountain, so intensely hot that it would leave a tremendous destruction of forests and animals in its wake. And what happened at Lincoln National Forest, New Mexico, near the little town of Capitan, would become a legend for people across the country to recall with sadness.

As the sun set, all was calm at the deserted campsite. A breeze stirred. A puff of wind blew over the embers making them glow. A leaf from a scrub oak fell and flared into brightness, then curled up black, but not before its little flame darted over and licked at the bed of pine needles nearby. The pine needles smoldered. Sticks and branches on the ground flared up. Bushes burst into fire.

Flames leaped up a grand old tree and gulped the dry, worm-eaten wood of the trunk. The crisp bark peeled and fire licked up the dried sap inside and hurried on. Fire quickly spread to the branches, and the tree became a blazing tower. The great old tree did not crash to the ground. It withstood the damage. But it sprayed showers of sparks onto other trees and onto the ground, and the wind whipped the fire along. Underbrush ignited. The fire got hot, crackled and snapped. Where tree branches touched, flames leaped from the crown of one tree to another. The air became choked with black smoke, which rose into the sky and glowed sooty-red above the raging flames. Wind blew the fire onward. Panic-stricken animals fled.

Unaware of the danger still far away, Smokey awoke the next day to a whiff of something strange in the breeze, yawned deeply and lazily, and wandered away from his mother—still sleeping under the pine tree—to a bright spot of sunlight. He lay on his back and stretched his four paws toward the sky as far as he could. He spread out his claws, and thought, "How nice it'd be to lie here all day, just soaking up warm sunshine."

Then, with a pang, he missed Strut. Where was he? Smokey remembered the times from the very beginning, back in the cave, when the crow dangled dazzling things before him just out of reach, shiny and sparkling. He was such fun to be around. That crow could imitate anything. The cub remembered times when he would hear sounds up in the tree above him that sounded exactly like Mother Bear's snoring and grunting. He'd turn around, look up, and there would be Strut, his head tilted to one side, with a look of amusement in those crafty eyes.

Smokey scanned the sky. Where was his good friend? Was Strut searching for him right now? "Here I am!" woofed the little bear. The sky was empty except for a lone hawk moving slowly, tilting its wings now and then. Smokey sighed. He realized how much he counted on Strut—not just as a friend to tell him stories, but someone to give him the latest news of the forest. That clever crow knew everything that was going on all over the mountain. He and the other crows flew high in the sky, scouted the far reaches of the forest and rushed back to tell everyone the news.

Smokey's mother had told him, "If you want to know what's happening, watch the crows." Smokey knew he had been luckier than that. He was the first animal to hear news direct from his own personal informant, his feathered friend. But where was Strut now?

"Caw, caw, caw." The raucous, rasping sound interrupted the cub's reverie. "Here I am!"

"You found me!" Smokey jumped up, delighted.

On a branch within easy reach, the crow was doing his strut-walk as if on parade, halting to be sure his audience was watching. He placed one foot right in front of the other, in his usual pigeon-toed way, his long tail shifting from side to side. With each deliberate step forward, he halted, as if each step were very important. Strut cocked his shiny purplish-black head to the side and looked down to beam a beady eye on Smokey to see whether he had his full attention.

A playful, contrary spirit caught Smokey and he pretended to look away. But out of the corner of his eye he saw Strut suddenly clutch the wood and flip-flop upside-down, squawking, "Help!" Smokey had to look. As soon as he did so, Strut quickly righted himself and gave Smokey a smug tilt of his head, because once again Smokey couldn't resist his acrobatics.

Without warning, the cub sprang up—it was a game they played—and flicked his paw at the crow's black scaly feet on the branch above him and almost whooshed the crow off. What fun it would be to knock that saucy crow off balance. Then Smokey flung his paw with all his might. Oops! He'd been warned to beware his strength or Strut would call him a bully. But luckily, in the nick of time, the crow deftly pulled in his wing and hopped aside. The bird looked down at him with a glint in his eye. "Caw! Hello, yourself, you slow-poke."

Smokey was momentarily miffed at being called slow compared to Strut. The crow had often teased the cub by suddenly dive-bombing him to snatch food or intercept whatever intriguing bug Smokey was turning over with his paw. Yet the little bear sighed in relief and felt a warm flush of gratitude that his friend had found him.

Smokey was distracted by another whiff of the strange smell he'd been noticing in the air. It seemed much stronger than before, so he asked, "Hey Strut, any news of the forest today? Like, what's that odd smell?"

Strut didn't answer. He stood silent on the branch, his entire body turned to listen to some crows not far away. "Nothing yet. I don't know about the smell. You're the one with the big sniffer. Look: My bill only has these two small nostrils— Hey! What's going on? Those crows over there look upset about something. But then, crows are always agitated, so it's hard to tell."

Strut bowed his head and admitted, "To tell the truth, I don't have any idea of what's been happening around here. I've been away from the flock from early morning, checking out the houses in the valley. Caw! But here come our feathered friends. We'll hear soon enough."

Half the flock—other young crows like Strut—bombarded the area, shrieking hysterically, "Keek, keek, keek, keek!" They flapped their wings, hopped from branch to branch, landed on the ground and walked with fast jerky steps, all the time calling back and forth to each other, "Keek, keek, keek, keek." Crows often looked excited about things, but this time they were working themselves into a frenzy.

"Strut, what's wrong?"

"I'd tell you if I could, Smokey. Usually alarm calls say what kind of danger it is and where it's coming from—whether a sky predator or a ground one. But these crows are too wacky to make any sense."

Smokey felt as if the birds' wings were aflutter in his own chest. His body felt shaky and his heart pounded. His feeling of foreboding increased when the older crows descended from the sky—without alighting as usual. They hovered in the air right above him, tilting awkwardly, this way and that, to stay aloft. They flapped their big black wings as if they were visitors from a dark and dangerous world.

Elder Crow shrieked above the din, "Stop that noise. Red Alert! Take off. KOO! KOO! Beat those wings. Everybody get airborne! Hurry up. Terrible. Terrible." The frantic melee suddenly dissolved as the birds winged away in all directions.

Except Strut. The crow had tarried a moment on the branch, a tense but stationary figure among the chaos of panicky wings. Smokey shouted at him, "What's wrong? What's a Red Alert?"

Strut gave Smokey a meaningful look and nodded behind him toward the other side of the mountain. "Red Alert means 'Fly away as fast as you can.' *You* better get going too. Right away!"

Strut readied to take off toward town, the opposite direction from the one the other crows had taken. "I have to go down to the valley to warn the town birds that something is wrong. So they can alert the town folks—if they'll listen."

As he was about to thrust off, the crow turned his head back toward Smokey. "KO! KO! Wake your mother!" Then he flew off.

Smokey hesitated, stomping his feet and frowning his eyebrows in irritation. He thought, "Isn't it just like crows: cawing themselves into a frenzy, but so excited that they can't stop to say what it's all about!" Then he thought, "Maybe it's such a tremendous danger there's no way to describe it." Scared as he was, he pictured Strut again, the lone crow on his perch, resolute in the center of the storm. It was a small comfort that his friend had delayed leaving with the flock, to try his best to tell Smokey what he could.

As Smokey watched the black specks of the crows disappear far into the distance, he felt dazed. Suddenly he shook his head. He tore his eyes away from the sky and looked around him in full alert. He must wake his mother!

At the touch of the cub's paw on her shoulder, Gersa rolled sleepily toward him, then awoke startled, and jolted him aside. She stood up to her full height, looking bigger than ever, her nose held high to sniff the air. Her whole body stiffened as she boomed forth, "FIRE!" He'd never seen her fur stand on end like this with her eyes wide open in fright.

Smokey piped up, "What's 'fire'? Why can't anybody tell me?" He stood on his hind legs to look where she was staring. He saw a reddish-gray haze above the trees in the distance. The two stood side by side, very still, barely breathing, for what seemed like a long time.

The spell was abruptly broken. In the small clearing coyotes, rabbits and marmots scrambled away to their burrows. Then, after a short time, a long-eared mule deer crashed through the bushes, leaped through the air and sprang past the bears. A hunched-over raccoon scurried past a skunk that stood frozen with fear. Dread seized Smokey's body and he thought, "Fire must be a terrible thing if everyone is afraid, even my mother!"

"Smokey, listen!" Mother Bear intoned with her most

authoritative and solemn Medicine Bear voice. "The fire's coming toward us from beyond the meadow. Follow right behind me. Run as fast as you can." She whirled her great bulk to the path. Smokey hurried after her. Animals ran alongside the cub. Others bounded ahead. The two bears ran on and on. They followed an animal path for a while, picked their way across a small rock slide, and went through the forest again, jumping over logs and brushing past bushes.

The cub whimpered. His little legs felt too heavy to keep up the fast pace. Mother Bear glanced back, but didn't slow down. It wasn't until Smokey fell far behind that Gersa rushed back, placed her paw on his rump and swept him forward. "You can do it, Smokey, my boy!" With her pushing him, he tried as hard as he could to keep moving his legs.

Smokey sees fire

At last Smokey stumbled, and in that moment turned, and for the first time saw fire. It was big and red and hot. The fire sizzled his fur, and prickled his nose like sharp pine needles. It came roaring closer. He plunged ahead. A bush burst into flame as he ran by. The monster was catching up. Gasping for breath, Smokey collapsed and screeched. Gersa let out a wail, and ran to his body, splayed on the ground.

She fixed her eyes on his frightened ones and her urgent voice penetrated his being. "See this short tree trunk?" She thumped a rotten old tree stump with her massive paw. "It's hollow inside. Now, do as I say: Reach up to the opening on top and climb in." She gave him a boost up the side of the stump to the open hole on top. "Quick, get in!"

As soon as the pads of his feet hit the damp floor inside the tree trunk, Smokey stretched up and frantically looked out of the hole. She was still there, amid flames singeing her fur with an awful smell. "I have to leave you, and run down the mountain to the beaver pond, where the fire can't hurt me.

"Smokey, listen! Be my brave little bear, and stay in the tree trunk—no matter what." She nuzzled his face, and pulled away. "Dearest Smokey! Good-bye."

"Good-bye," Smokey cried, his throat tight with anguish as he watched her furry rump until it was out of sight. 'My brave little bear,' she had said. He let out a small sob, and with his heart thumping in his chest, slumped onto the earthen floor of the tree stump, as flames roared closer.

Fire raged around the hollow stump. A flaming branch toppled from a tree overhead and a chunk of it thudded on Smokey's back. Sparks ignited the fur on his back and the stub of his short tail. He frantically slapped where he felt pinpricks of fire. Red-hot embers landed near his feet and he angrily stamped them out. Soon his hind paws became sore, his front paw pads raw. His feet found a rhythm—hop, hop, shuffle, hop. He became determined to come down on the beat and stamp on embers as they flared, then shuffle them to the edges.

When he stopped for a brief respite, he lost control of his bladder in starts and stops of dribble. His urine made the live embers sizzle and steam. "Uh-uh," he grunted. Here was something he could do! He sprayed urine onto embers in the center of the stump floor where he'd been hot-footing it.

Then another enemy enveloped him: thick smoke. Smokey choked and coughed. His eyes got scratchy. Hot air seared his throat so raw that it hurt to swallow saliva.

He had to do something! Smokey roared in angry frustration, clawed and bit the soft wood inside the stump. That gave him an idea. His claws dug away the chunks of old wood in the bottom of the stump. He came upon earth underneath. Instinctively, he thrust his nose down to breathe. Wonderful cool air came up through the rocks and loose soil. The cub breathed out every now and then, flaring his nostrils and huffing to get rid of the fine soil. What a relief to breathe.

But there was worse to come. The full fury of the fire burst upon him like a monster. It rumbled and growled, shrieked and shrilled. Louder and louder. Booming explosions made him cover his ears with his paws. When Smokey removed his paws, his ears were still ringing. Terror seized him in its tight grip. He couldn't move. He dared to take a whisper of breath, and started to shake. It seemed as if he would be shaken loose into pieces. How could he shut out the noise? The cub mustered one mighty roar.

Where was his mother? He went blank for a moment, then as if suddenly awake, he knew he must be brave and summon all his strength to endure! It was up to him alone.

Then, in that dire moment, something unexpected happened. As if he were in a trance, an imaginary golden acorn began to glow inside him and then all around him. He slid into memories of good times — eating honey and playing with Strut. Finally, something lightened within his chest.

The brief reprieve from terror allowed the cub to take care of himself. It was too much effort to reach his burnt stomach, rump and tail, so he licked and licked the sore pads of his feet. As if in a trance, it soothed him to lick himself, even though it hurt in the places where the thick leather of his paw pads had become raw pink flesh. Eventually he had numbed himself into a daze. He stopped licking. Exhausted, he rolled into the smallest ball he could, leaned against the damp rotten wood inside the stump, and hummed a sad song to himself until he fell asleep. Too exhausted to think of what might happen next.

Chapter 10

My knowledge is pessimistic, but my willing and hoping are optimistic.
–Albert Schweitzer

Meanwhile, as Strut floated in the air above Capitan, he spotted Ray's airplane in a meadow. The crow zoomed down and peered through the plane's small windshield. The pilot seat was empty. Where could the man be? He flew aloft and quickly surveyed the entire mountain town of Capitan—seven blocks long and four blocks wide—dotted with small houses, its main road lined with seven bars, a grocery store, and a gas station. But it was no longer the sleepy town he'd known. Ranchers and cowpunchers were throwing tools into their pickups and heading for the mountain.

The bakery truck was careening down the main street. The crow swooped to the front window, surprised to see it was being driven by the baker's young boy. Drawn by the strong aroma of yeasty bread, Strut followed the truck to the high school, where boys rushed over and threw open the back doors. They grabbed loaves of bread and tossed them onto long tables in the school yard, where women and other boys snatched them up for sandwiches.

Town crows caught scraps on-the-fly as bread crusts were tossed toward the garbage cans. One crow, spotting Strut, stopped gobbling food to call out, "Cah, if it isn't Strut the Storyteller! What're *you* doing here?"

"I gotta find Ray—my friend who wears that silvery cowboy hat. You know, the one who moved away."

"Oh, yeah. Flew in early this morning. You shoulda seen him fly that plane over the fire. Wow! Close to the tree tops just like a crazy *bird*. He'd head into that black smoke and just disappear, then appear again out the other end. Finally landed back in the field here and took off in a truck."

"So where's he now? I gotta reach him."

"He went that-a-way — the far side of the mountain — with a bunch of Apache firefighters. But forget about *him*. Come join *us*. The bread is *great*."

Strut seized a piece and gave it a few polite pecks. "Thanks, pal, but I gotta split. There's something I have to do."

Meanwhile, the game warden Ray Bell and his Apache partner Aloysius Mendez were angling a fire line across the mountain. Close behind them, two dozen Mescalero Apache firefighters wielded korticks, clearing away thick brush. Ray, his shirt soaked with sweat, raised his hand to signal a halt. He took a swallow from his canteen and turned to Mendez. "How can your men cut a three foot swath, no food, no water — and still dog my heels — while all I'm doing is just running ahead to find the best fire line?"

"What's the matter? Out of shape behind that desk in Santa Fe?" Mendez sent Ray a quick smile. "Let me tell you: We've been training since we were ten — to fight fires on our own lands. You know, our Apache ancestors could run across seventy miles of high country in one day. Imagine *that*."

Mendez' brow tensed as he suddenly pointed at Capitan Gap — the two peaks of Capitan Mountain, each ten thousand feet high. "Oh, no! Look at all that smoke over there! The fire's starting to jump across the canyons in the Gap."

"That means real trouble for the crews at the base, and those higher up."

Several miles away high on the ridge — silhouetted against the smoke and sky — was the lone figure of a rancher astride his horse. It was Fred Pfingsten, an experienced forest firefighter, a congenial man whose cattle roamed the vast mountain. This day he was glad to be mounted on Schick. The light brown sorrel was his favorite horse for firefighting, and the man leaned forward and patted his neck.

Fred was keeping watch over the firefighters on the mountainside below. The leaders of the fire crews down there were on their own — without radios. So, if something happened, he'd have to move quickly on horseback to pass messages to them.

From his perch as lookout, he squinted in the bright sun to monitor the fire. The slow-moving fire on the lower slope suddenly grew larger and moved up the mountain. A fresh gust of wind tilted his Stetson — a bad sign. The wind gathered more force. What had been a stiff breeze now approached seventy miles per hour. He knew that the strong winds could sweep this fire up the mountain — if the firefighters near the base didn't stop it.

The horse caught Fred's tension and danced in place as the man held his reins firmly. The rancher let out a tight breath, relaxed into the saddle, and Schick quieted down. After many years, the two of them sensed each other's moods and were good partners. They had gone through fires and lightning storms, handled break-away cattle and made steep descents down rocky terrain. Today, Fred thought, this wildfire could become a big one, and whatever it dealt out, the two of them would have to handle it.

It was a very hot day, already one hundred degrees at this elevation of eight thousand feet. Fred loosened the reins to give Schick some slack. With hooves clattering on stones, the horse skittered back and forth, rocking Fred in the saddle from side to side. The man kept his body calm while his mind raced to the dangers ahead. He quickly surveyed the fire crews far below. First, he focused intently on the little figures spread across the broad lower slopes. The fire was still two miles below them. Could those men in that front line stop it from coming up farther?

If not, if the fire managed to pass those men and continue up the mountain, it could engulf the large group of men at midway, where it was too steep for men to outrun a fire. He must warn those midway men somehow.

The rancher squinted to scan the scrub and forest below for a glimpse of Speed Simmons, the firefighter in charge of the midway fire crews. Fred couldn't see him. His legs stiffened in the stirrups. Should he plunge down the slope to find Speed, or give warning himself? He decided to wait a bit longer. Speed must show up soon.

Fred reviewed what he knew about this cowboy turned game warden and firefighter, Lee William Simmons, dubbed 'Speed' because he was fast in foot races and extraordinarily quick with a pistol. The six-foot-two man was in his prime as an outdoorsman. He had a reputation for sniffing out danger in the wilderness and reacting swiftly in emergencies. Stern, but quiet-spoken, he was known for driving men hard and himself harder—something he'd need for corralling these volunteer firefighters, mostly raw recruits.

Fred knew Speed was a good, tough-minded leader in fighting forest fires. He weighed all possibilities in advance—some said to a fault—to be ready for any eventuality. Fred thought, "What we need now is the sharpshooter, quick-action side of Speed. No time for dilly-dallying today."

At that moment, Speed Simmons was midway down the mountain in a wooded area of dense scrub oaks and junipers. He knew he was hidden from Fred's view above, but was well aware that the big rancher was somewhere above him, keeping watch. Speed strode out of the woods and looked up the gulch. There was Fred, his hat askew, his jacket waving, astride the sorrel whose tail was blowing in the wind. That meant the wind was really gusting up on the ridge, a fierce wind that could suck the fire up the mountain. Speed had to think fast. Brush was dry. A very hot day. A very dangerous day to fight a fire.

In seconds, Speed rapidly scanned the entire scene, his senses alert: smelling the air as it changed, gauging the heat on his face, feeling the wind stirring leaves nearby and riffling his hair, hearing the changing sounds of the fire as it shifted below. And there were subtle things he couldn't name but just knew with the sixth sense of experience.

The back of his head hurt and he felt a little dizzy. It was a premonition of dreadful danger, first to the men spread over the mountain far below — too far for Fred on horseback to warn them — then to the many men up here at midway. The fire at the lower part of the mountain would probably leap the fire breaks — the swaths that firefighters had cut — and be windswept upward to his own men.

For as long as Speed could remember, he had always felt safe in the mountains. In the past, he and other firefighters had been successful in stopping the small fires that cropped up. Lately, however, he'd become acutely aware that blowups might occur in these New Mexico mountains that he loved. And blowups, once started, could not be stopped.

Speed had been shocked last August to hear about the tragedy of the Mann Gulch fire in Montana. Sixteen smokejumpers had been caught by a wind-whipped blowup in a canyon like this, and thirteen of them had died. Since then, the Forest Service had studied what made some wildfires explode into cataclysmic ones. Speed himself suspected it was very hot days, very windy conditions, and a long drought.

He had wondered: What made wildfires especially fierce in these steep high-altitude mountains in the West, and what did firefighters here need for survival? Since Mann Gulch, Speed had rehearsed what he must do to save his men in a similar situation.

Now, at midway in the wooded mountain canyon, with a terrible foreboding that a big fire would come, he quickly sought an escape route for the crews far below and the two groups nearby in the woods.

With quick flashes of thoughts and images, Speed appraised the possibilities. If the fire heated up, the firefighters on the bottom slopes were too far away to warn. They'd have to be on their own. Speed hoped they'd see the fire in time to rush for the sides of the broad slopes before the fire swept by.

What about his men in this canyon here at midway? Where could they go? The narrowing of the gorge meant there was no escape to the sides. Charging to the top would be impossible: The ridges rose over thousands of feet straight up. The fire would whip up the steep gorge faster than they could run. Moreover, from the ten-thousand-foot peaks above them, red-hot boulders, some as large as cars, could tumble down on the men.

To make a small back fire was a rash choice. With this wind and heat, it would undoubtedly ignite a large fire right at one's feet.

Nor could men run to the patches of ash that most fires left in their wake, where firefighters could step into "the good black"—areas already burned—so they could hop-scotch across blackened patches to safety.

The thought of a 'fire storm' shot a shiver of liquid helplessness through his body. Such an intense fire might whip up the mountain faster than fit men with heavy packs could scramble up the sheer slopes. The fire could be combustible-hot, instantly exploding brush and trees in its path. Hot like an oven. At one hundred and forty degrees, a person couldn't breathe and still live. Hot enough to kill someone with one intake of breath. Hot enough to melt clothes. Hot enough to blacken flesh to a crisp.

Speed faced a grim possibility. A blowup could come up as fast as a wind—seventy miles per hour or more—and unbelievably hot, as much as two thousand degrees. Like an incinerator, it could reduce everything in its path to ash and melted goo. A tree could torch in seconds; a man could suffocate in moments.

The man thought quickly. The worst fires didn't usually blast up canyons until the heat of the day, around two or three o'clock. So far, it was only eleven in the morning. However, the air temperature was already over a hundred! And the timber up here was dry from the winter drought, which meant a buildup of lots of fuel.

Those strong gusting winds could make an updraft. And that updraft would suck up the cool air from the lower elevation at the bottom of the mountain — right up these vertical slopes here to create the fire's own climate at the high elevations. Fire whirls and spot fires might join together into a giant fire storm, like a tornado destroying everything in its wide path up to the ten-thousand-foot peaks.

Speed searched with frantic emotion, but a calm mind, for a safe place for his men at midway — a group of five experienced forest firefighters and another group of twenty-four firefighting novices — scattered in the wooded area near him. He found two possibilities. The safest would be the big rock slide, but it was a hard climb up the mountain. A closer possibility was a small rockslide nearby, only two hundred feet in diameter. It was in a gully about four feet deep — too small and too shallow to offer much protection. But it would have to do.

A few minutes later Speed emerged from among the trees and hastily crested the middle ridge. He looked down the mountain and saw dark smoke billowing up toward the men on the broad slope far below. The line they'd already cut wouldn't hold. And they couldn't realize how dangerous their position was until the fast-moving fire licked their heels as they tried to plunge out of its way — to the sides. Speed could clearly see it coming, but with a sinking feeling he knew there was no way to warn them. He must pull his eyes from the men far below, and try to save his men here at midway.

The firefighter took a deep breath and steeled his body into a taut fighting stance. What Speed had been preparing for — the worst — was coming. He sensed it with his whole being. Sudden explosive heat would roar straight up the mountain. His men at midway were only minutes from being incinerated.

Chapter 11

Desperation is sometimes as powerful an inspirer as genius.
–Benjamin Disraeli

The hardest profession to leave is firefighting. You miss the camaraderie, the challenge, the adrenaline rush. I'm going to have some regrets. It's going to be rough to see a big timber fire and not help.
–John E. Kennedy

The two firefighters high on the mountainside signaled each other at the same time: Speed Simmons below on foot, Fred Pfingsten above on horseback. They rushed to get within shouting distance. It took only seconds to communicate. Speed shouted up to Fred: "Five men, and another twenty-four—in the timber here. Get them to me—quick! Or they'll be fried." Fred was already wheeling his horse around, and plunged down the steep slope as fast as he could toward the woods.

Speed waited at the danger spot in the mid-mountain gorge. Within moments, Fred had flushed the five experienced firefighters from the woods and herded them to Speed. Before they could catch their breath, Speed pointed up the mountain. "Race to that big slide up there. You have only a few minutes. Your life depends on it. When you get there, hunker down. Breathe air coming up through the rocks. Get going!"

Long minutes later, Fred and his horse herded the group of twenty-four men to Speed. In a glance he sized them up. A few were in old fatigues and battle helmets. They were veterans battle-hardened five years ago in World War II. Those he could count on. Others were in new fatigues and hard hats—green young soldiers from Fort Bliss in Texas. The rest wore only regular shoes and clothes. They were earnest-looking but ill-prepared. He recognized most as local men and boys who must have rushed to the fire—to save their forest, their ranches, their town of Capitan. All twenty-four looked ready to follow orders, but too weary from hours of firefighting in one-hundred-degree heat to go much further.

The full force of the fire was sweeping up the canyon toward them. It was too late to reach the big slide near the top where the first five had already disappeared. The only chance for this group of two dozen was the small rock slide nearby. "Follow me as fast as you can!" At a rapid pace, Speed led the weary men into the clearing where they clambered over boulders to a shallow depression lined with rocks. He barked, "Form a circle. Lie down, close together. Now!

"Onto your stomachs. Burrow into the rocks, face down. Breathe the air coming up through the rocks. Remember: Breathing's the important thing!"

As the smoke and heat increased, he shouted above the approaching roar of the fire, "Put your arm on the shoulder of the man to your right: That's your buddy. Crush any sparks that land on his clothes. Keep your canteen handy and douse him with water if he catches fire."

The blaze was soon upon them. Speed Simmons could sense fear rising among the prone men. Knowing that if one man panicked and ran, they all might panic, Speed shouted, "If anyone tries to get up and run, I'll hit him over the head with my shovel." He commanded, "If your buddy gets up, you better stop him before I do."

Speed steeled himself for the awful reality: The chances of getting out of this alive were slim. He told the men, "You have two minutes. I suggest you use those two minutes in prayer—for your survival."

Then the fire engulfed them. It leaped from the tree tops on one side of the narrow canyon to explode trees on the other side. The roar was deafening. The heat, intense.

The few veterans from World War II re-lived the

horrendous sounds of Anzio and other battles. They knew how to survive against the odds. From grim experience, every one of them knew how to obey orders and hold a position and keep his head down.

As the fire came booming at him, a local boy, Joe Phillips, asked himself why he'd volunteered to fight the fire. He didn't want to die so young. He hadn't even graduated from high school yet. His legs tensed to run for his life, but he had to stay, to take care of the man next to him.

The smoke was so thick that Speed couldn't see his wristwatch—a few inches away. Men coughed and gasped for breath. They wedged themselves deeper into the rocks to inhale pockets of air from below. Sheets of flame swept past them so hot it seemed that they might be roasted alive.

If any man stood up, the fire would have burned him instantly, but the men rooted themselves like hardy bushes into the rocky ground. No one moved, except to burrow himself deeper into the rocks, and slap at flaming clothes with blistered hands.

Shortly before, having hastily mounted the ridge again a quarter mile away, Fred Pfingsten had sat astride his horse. Schick was heaving and sweating from the exertion of climbing back from the hasty descent. The man leaned over and placed his palm on the horse's wet neck, grateful that he could count on the cow pony to stand his ground. Schick flared his nostrils to snort, and pawed the gravel with a front hoof.

The rancher—a man of action—knew there was nothing more he could do at this point for the firefighters except keep vigil. He wiped his sleeve across his forehead to catch the sweat dripping into his eyes, and squinted down the mountain, trying to locate the two groups of men trapped below at midway. He could make out the five experienced firefighters just below him, heaving boulders aside to burrow their heads deep into the big rock slide before the fire engulfed them.

Below the big slide, he tried to locate the larger group of twenty-four men. Surely they should have reached the small slide by now. And there they were! He could barely make out their prone bodies in a circle, their arms clawing small rocks aside so they could press their faces further below. His heart ached for them. The coming fire would be ferocious.

From his vantage point on the ridge, Fred could see five miles of territory below. At the base of the mountain tiny figures of firefighters were still trying to stop the blaze from spreading to nearby ranches and meadows. Above them, firefighters who had been cutting a line on the lower slopes were dashing sideways to safety.

Raising his eyes farther up, Fred once again spotted the men midway up the canyon. What would happen to these two groups hunkered in the slides just below? The sun was hot. Winds were whipping around. Timber and brush — dense and dry. He braced himself. It could happen fast.

With a horrific roar like an express train, the fire intensified. Sheets of flame swept up the mountain. Awful as it was, it was also spellbinding. Fred's eyes widened as the fire reached the rock slides. Spruce trees exploded like charges of dynamite and launched branches over the trapped men from one side of the canyon to the other.

Massive flames streamed two hundred feet in the air, and the fire sucked up oxygen to make its own whirlwind. The monstrous blaze soon reached the two-mile high mountaintop and continued high into the sky. Fred could no longer see any firefighters below. They'd been swallowed up in sheets of red and black smoke. The sun had turned blood-red.

Fred walked his horse slowly along the ridge, his eyes drawn to the wildfire. He fell under a timeless spell, every minute long and heavy. Then he snapped out of it. It occurred to him that any sane man would get out of there. And take care of his horse. Was he "fire-struck" — riveted in hypnotic fascination at the explosive force and sheer size of the fire? Was he like new firefighters he'd seen: paralyzed, staring with fixed eyes at the power of awesome destruction — instead of feeling their own helplessness? Maybe so.

He shook his head to yank himself back to the awful reality. There were no radios on the mountain. No airplane support. The game warden, Ray, had the only plane and he was now on the ground, cutting a fire line on the other side of the mountain. So Fred knew he was the only one—up here at the top—who could survey the whole scene and who also had some mobility. That meant he must stay on the ridge above the rock slides, alert to move quickly if he was needed.

The tough cowboy code—by which he'd lived his entire life—now gripped his weathered body and held him mounted there like a stone statue. It was the code they all followed for the perilous business of handling cattle and horses: Bide your time, throw yourself into an emergency, handle it yourself, and don't complain if you're hurt. Even though the muscles of Fred's arms and legs were ready to spring into action, and his chest burst to do something—anything—he must wait, no matter how long.

After a full hour of the inferno, Fred knew that the fire had reached the zenith of its fierce siege and would begin its slow burnout as it ran out of fuel. He and Schick waited three hours more until the blasting heat subsided, and the smoke cleared a bit. Soon there was more oxygen to breath.

Coughing and wheezing himself, the rancher let Schick pick his way down the canyon through small ground fires, seeking out cooler areas among the embers. The trip down seemed infinitely slower than the earlier one when they had rushed down to herd the firefighters to Speed.

It was Fred's job now to see whether any of these same men at the rock slides midway had survived, and if so, lead them down to the fire camp miles below. If there were no survivors, he would attend to the bodies. Had they all suffocated from the heat or from oxygen starvation? If they were alive, had they scorched their lungs? Been badly burned? Could they possibly be alive and able to walk?

The horseman's teeth remained clenched and his throat tight with anxiety about what he might find below. He heaved air out of his chest, loosened up, and concentrated on the steep descent, which couldn't be rushed. It was hot sitting in the saddle, but he knew it was even harder for Schick. Any other horse would have spooked, but Schick trusted his rider, and Fred could trust his horse, even in wildfires. Fred loose-reined the sorrel to let him make his own way. The horse's head swayed back and forth, sometimes jerking to recover from a clattering stumble over loose rock. It seemed a long way down. Time moved slowly.

The horse jittered across patches of black ashes with still-glowing embers and startled when hard charcoal crackled under his hooves. Fred soon caught the faint scent of burning hooves, and felt bad for his horse. He let Schick skitter sideways as small grass fires flared to sear the horse's legs and singe the end of his long, sweeping tail. "Schick, poor fellow, your tail's getting shorter and shorter," Fred muttered.

The rancher knew Schick liked to be soothed with murmurs, and strengthened now and then with commands. Hot rocks split above them and tumbled down the canyon to crash nearby, startling Schick into jumping aside. When the horse grew wild-eyed, Fred rubbed his neck and kept a firm hand on the reins to remind Schick he was still there, in charge, taking care of him.

As Fred see-sawed in the saddle, legs outstretched with boots pressed into the stirrups, the horse kept a constant pace despite the awkward terrain, and placed his hooves carefully among rocks. Once, coming upon a scree of loose gravel, Schick hesitated only a moment, then slid down on stiff legs. The descent seemed interminable.

At the same time that Fred, from the ridge, had been seeing the inferno begin its burnout, Speed down below him had been experiencing the same thing. Still beside the huddle of the two dozen trapped men at the small rock slide, Speed finally sensed that the heat and smoke had receded. His breath came easier. The young men next to him stirred. He couldn't see all of them yet, just gray lumps through the dark haze, but he called out loudly that the worst was over. At first he could see a few feet away, then a few yards.

Dreading and hoping, Speed raised his head enough to cast his eyes over the circle of men. The lumps were coming to life. Not much talking among them, but every man was stretching or moving a little—badly shaken, clothing charred, soles of their shoes curled. Unbelievable though it was, they had all evidently escaped with their lungs, their limbs and their lives.

Speed Simmons kept the men pinned down at the rock slide as long as the fire remained a hazard. Still prone, the firefighters managed to check each other's clothing to find any spots that were still smoldering. A World War II veteran named Harry Collins said, "Sometimes it sounded like a five-hundred pound bomb exploding beneath us." But most men were silent. The surrounding forest was still burning, blowing a few embers onto the small rock slide. The heat and smoke remained dense and Speed knew smoke inhalation was still a danger.

After a while, a breeze came up, and some of the smoke shifted away. Speed moved his cramped body into a crouch, then arose on stiff legs. He signaled to the men that they could finally move too. Stretching, checking their bodies to make sure they were all right, they called out to each other, relieved and cocky.

The two dozen men didn't realize how black their faces were until Fred Pfingsten arrived on his horse, herding the five firefighters down from the big rock slide above. They had all survived, too. Each group kept pointing and laughing at the other group's blackened faces and burnt hair, vying for who had the most greasy, sooty, burnt clothes and shoes. Fred's grimy face couldn't stop grinning as he greeted Speed, the two men gripping each other's shoulders for joy.

Before night fell on the long day of May 8, 1950, the exhausted men, led by Speed and Fred, slowly walked down to the fire camp at seven thousand feet. At first everyone stared at the blackened men as if they were ghosts returned from the dead. Then people rushed up to greet them with cries of relief.

The returning firefighters were told the news. At the time of the blowup that day, there had been two hundred and fifty men on the mountain. Throughout the day, all had returned except these men: the two groups numbering five and twenty-four. A local newspaper and radio reporter—Dorothy Gray Guck—had been broadcasting news of other returning firefighters from her vigil at the fire camp, but, hour after hour, she had to repeat the words "no news yet" about these men. Many people had almost given up hope. Now that the men had finally appeared, she could at last broadcast to her waiting listeners that every husband, parent, son, friend, and soldier had survived.

Two days later, the two dozen firefighters from midway gathered to leave camp and return to their military bases and homes in the village. Speed thanked them for their discipline and a job well done. They spontaneously gave Speed the honor due a hero. The rookies lined up, and as they filed past, each man saluted the senior firefighter who had saved their lives. As the high school student Joe Phillips later recalled, it was at this moment, with tears in his eyes, he knew why he had volunteered, and if the call came, why he might volunteer again.

For his ordeal in the Capitan Gap Fire, Speed Simmons paid the price that many seasoned firefighters have to pay for their devotion to saving the forest, its creatures, and people's homes. He had acquired acute and chronic lung damage from accumulated smoke inhalation. Within days Speed developed pneumonia. He would never recover the lung capacity to fight fires again. He would continue at a desk job to work for the wildlife and wilderness he had loved since he was a boy.

The fire camp remained a base for the many days and weeks it took firefighters to fully contain the fire, and check out the damage done to Lincoln National Forest: seventeen thousand acres of forest destroyed, the entire side of the mountain burned — with little grass, brush or trees left from the former array of wild grasses, sumac and scrub oak, pinyon and juniper, Ponderosa pine, blue spruce and

Douglas fir, and beautiful aspen groves. Gone was the favorable habitat for elk, bighorn sheep, bear and smaller wildlife.

Tired almost beyond endurance, the two hundred and fifty volunteer firefighters on the mountain at the time of the blowup climbed back up the mountain the next day and the coming days to mop up the smoldering fire. As news spread, their ranks swelled to five hundred men: ranchers, cowpunchers, pipeline crews from the Southern Pacific Railroad, and ordinary citizens; soldiers from Ft. Bliss, Texas; Native American firefighter crews; New Mexico game wardens; and US Forest Service officials.

Women and boys who eked out their living among the mountains worked long hours to bring sandwiches and other supplies from the village, and became overwhelmed by the increased number of firefighters—until their efforts were augmented by supply trucks from afar. The state police, operators of bulldozers, and numerous support groups from hundreds of miles around came and stayed for many weeks.

Chapter 12

It is only in the state of complete abandonment and loneliness that we experience the helpful powers of our own natures.
–Carl Jung

The bear, as the Ainu say, is the God of the Mountain. His energy, vigor, and alertness are pure expressions of the power of the wild forest. To meet him is not just an occasion of fear, but of delight and awe. We learn to accept bears in the mountains as part of the risky beauty of life.
–Paul Shepard and Barry Sanders

Throughout the fire on the day of May 8, 1950, Smokey had stayed inside the hollow tree stump—not far from the gulch where the firefighters were hunkered down. In the aftermath of the fire, his burnt paws hurt. So did his belly and rear end. His throat scratched when he breathed. Finally, exhausted from dread, pain and coughing, he fell into a fitful sleep through the long afternoon and night.

The cub awoke the next day to silence. He peeked out the opening at the top of his tree stump. It was a bewildering scene. As far as he could see, trees were blackened. A dead branch fell with a thud and ashes bounced into the air. On the gray floor of the forest, an occasional wisp of smoke arose from embers beneath the ashes. Then there was silence again. Nothing moved. Relieved that he was safe from the fire, yet heartsick about the strange new world outside and his body throbbing with pain, he sank back to the earthen floor inside his stump, curled up and slipped again into oblivion.

In the deep sleep that followed, Smokey dreamed of his mother. The dream was so vivid that he could smell her presence beside him. She was bigger than he remembered. A bright light silhouetted her face and gave a reddish-brown glow to her fur. "Oh, Smokey," she said, "I'm so glad you survived! I'm very proud of you."

In the dream she looked into his eyes with her sorrowful ones. "But I have something to tell you." She paused. "It will be difficult for you to hear . . . Are you ready?"

Smokey murmured, "I guess so. Yes."

She took a deep breath and said, "I want you to know that I died on the way to the beaver pond. So I can never return to you in my fur-body. I have gone to Rainbow Bridge, a safe place far away. I will wait for you there until the day—a long time from now—when you finally join me . . . at the end of your life." Her eyes softened, as she said in a whisper, "I'm sorry to leave you so young."

After a long silence, she continued in her strong and familiar 'listen carefully' voice. "Please forgive me, Smokey, for the times when I cuffed you to teach you a lesson." She paused and swallowed. "Remember our good times together. Whenever you need me during your life, imagine me beside you, like I am now.

"And remember the Ancient Bear's saying, 'It's the wounded tree that yields the sweetest honey.' You might be like that wounded tree. I have always thought you had a special destiny in life, Smokey. You are spunky like your crow friend Strut. This tragedy launches you on a new path of great hardship. Meet it like a hero and perhaps you'll bring something sweet to the world."

Mother Bear hugged him good-bye. "Take care, my dearest cub." Smokey said farewell, his chest sore with sadness. The dream drifted away.

Smokey awoke but kept his eyes shut, holding onto the good feeling of closeness with his mother to shield him from the dark cloud of anguish that threatened to descend upon him full force. He basked in Mother Bear's presence and her warm embrace until they were stored deep inside.

However, as soon as he opened his eyes to the dim light inside the stump, the reality of her death stabbed him like a lightning bolt. His throat ached at the thought of never seeing her again. He went limp, his limbs heavy. He never wanted to move again. He would stay in his safe place now, the hollowed-out tree stump. It would be easier to die than face living without his mother. Exhaustion overcame him. Smokey sensed his life energy leaving him. His eyes closed.

Then something happened. It was as if a flash of early sunlight broke through the darkness of his closed eyelids. The image of a golden acorn appeared with enough power to reassure him. His chest slowly began to expand and gave him some new strength. Inner resolve came to him as if out of the blue: He would do what he must to meet the new world!

Hadn't his mother always called him a scrappy, adventurous fellow? And Smokey thought of his plucky friend Strut. What would Strut do? As he pictured the cocky crow, the cub's own fighting spirit returned. Strut dared to leave the flock and go exploring. He, too, could dare to face life alone.

Smokey's curiosity quickened. What would he find if he dared look outside again? He stretched his body to its full height, grasped the top of the stump with his sore paws, and poked his head out the big opening. The forest was still eerily quiet. No chorus of morning insects, no birdsong, no rustle of animals, no stirring of leaves. The air was hazy, but the red flames were gone as far as he could see. Through the charred trees he saw, far away in the distance, the tall pine tree under which he and his mother had slept the day they had found the honey. It was black and ugly now, a spear piercing the sky. Was that just yesterday? The day before yesterday? It seemed a long time ago.

"Caaaaw." It was not the usual loud, hoarse sound of Strut, but a weak and humble one. Smokey peered down at the ground next to the stump. It was Strut! His back was no longer a sleek black color glistening with purple, but frosted dull with ashes, his feathers tattered at the edges, one wing slightly askew.

The tired cub perked up at the sight of his friend. Despite his burnt paws, he clung to the top edge of the stump and called down, "Am I glad to see you!" His round ears spread wide in happiness. But the crow wouldn't meet his eyes, just hung his head until his bill almost touched the ground, and mumbled, "There's something terrible I have to tell you."

Smokey's eyes misted, and he murmured, "You don't have to tell me, Strut. I know about my mother."

Strut fluttered up, landed on the rim of the stump and leaned against Smokey's shoulder. The weakened cub staggered. Strut quickly said, "Sorry, I didn't know you were so fragile. Shall I move?"

"No, but . . . It hurts all over. My head feels strange, and I can hardly stay up by myself."

Strut rested his bill very gently on the cub's shoulder for a brief moment, then wiped his beak softly back and forth on the fur. "Caaaaaaah. I'm sorry buddy-bear. You look awful, but at least you're alive."

Smokey looked questioningly at his friend. "How . . ."

"Do you want to know how I found you? Caaaaah. The forest looks very different. Even the brush is all gone. The fire uncovered boulders I didn't know were there. But I found some landmarks like the tall pine."

"Cah!" he continued with some of his old spirit. "The truth is, buddy-bear, with your little nose poking out of the stump, you weren't that hard to spot. Not much is moving. The whole forest on this side of the mountain is gone."

Strut lowered his head. "I saw things you can't imagine. Some of the animals — never mind." He muttered awhile, then stopped talking and his body drooped.

"What happened to them?"

"Caaw, caw. Good news first. As far as I know, my flock of crows escaped. Our sentinels saw the fire first so we could all fly away. That warned other animals to flee, too. So, thanks to us, lots of them escaped. The Hoofed Ones, like deer, elk and moose, could go fast even where it was steep. Furry Ones like some of the fox and coyote also ran fast enough. And others hid in burrows or in the mud."

The crow looked away a moment. "There's some bad news. Caaah."

Smokey found himself fading in and out as Strut continued. "Some animals didn't know what to do, and ran every which way. The fire ate them up—a quick death. Then there were other Furry Ones who headed down the gulch to the beaver pond, but the fire blasted up the gulch before they could reach the water."

Smokey and the crow were silent together for a long time. Then the little bear looked over with a pang, as the crow stretched out his neck and began to flutter his wings. "I have to be off," Strut said. "You need help—like I did, when I fell out of my nest. I'll try to find my friend Ray and I'll be back. You can count on Strut. I won't desert you. After all, you're my best friend." He lifted off and was gone.

The cub felt a void upon being left, but his sad mood was interrupted by stomach pangs. Reluctant as he was to leave his safe place, he recalled his mother saying that, no matter what, bears must eat. He scanned the ground with alarm. How could he find ants under a dried-out rotten log when there weren't any logs? Where could he find berries and acorns, when everything was shriveled up and blackened? His heart pounded. What was he going to do?

The cub made a half-hearted attempt to climb out of the stump, but his limbs felt too weak, and his paws throbbed anew with pain. He slumped back inside and whimpered himself to sleep.

Strut slowly flapped his tired wings above the hundreds of men at the fire camp until he spotted someone with a familiar stance. It was Ray! Strut dive-bombed, but the tired man just shooed him away with an impatient hand. Couldn't humans distinguish one crow from another? He himself always recognized Ray no matter what clothes he wore. And he recognized the Apache with him, whom Strut had seen with Ray training firefighters on the reservation.

Mendez appraised the crow with a keen look, and turned to Ray. "Isn't this a friend of yours?" Ray frowned, but the Apache continued, "He looks bedraggled, but see those leg bands?"

Ray laughed and declared, "Well, well, well. Danged if it isn't my old friend!" He extended his arm and Strut flew up and grasped it through the sleeve. The crow leaned forward hopefully and flashed black eyes at him. Noticing the intent expression, Ray asked, "What brings you here? Sorry I don't have any corn. Not today. Not here."

Strut wondered how he could let this dumb cluck know about the urgency of Smokey's plight. In frustration, he lifted into the air and fluttered his wings in Ray's face. The man flailed his arms to ward him off.

Then Ray stopped slapping at the crow for a moment, and, shielding his head with one arm, rubbed his sooty face with the other hand. By now, Strut was settled back on his arm, and Ray stared hard at the crow in exasperation. "You ornery birdbrain. What's got into you?" Now that he had the man's full attention, Strut looked at him meaningfully. Ray looked back, puzzled.

"Mendez! You're so good with animals. What's going on? He's never done anything like this before."

The Apache suddenly jerked his chin at the crow in recognition. "Come to think of it, this looks like the scrawny crow I've seen hanging around a bear cub up on the mountain lately. Maybe those two are buddies. The cub's awfully small. Not even two months old."

Ray said, "That reminds me. One of the firefighters thought he saw a bear cub yesterday, somewhere at midway, not far from the rockslide. Now I wonder. It's farfetched, but maybe the crow's trying to tell us about that cub."

The game warden's face broke into a big smile, and turning to Mendez, he exclaimed, "If there's a bear cub up there, I want him!"

Mendez raised his eyebrows, and Ray said, "I know. The rule is to leave wildlife to fend for themselves after a fire. But if there's a cub who has made it, his mother hasn't survived—or she would be with him. That firefighter just mentioned a lone cub. A little orphan like that can't find things to eat on his own in a burned-out forest."

Ray found himself excited, like a horse so full of raw energy that it must have its head and gallop. It was disconcerting to feel so wild, but he couldn't stop himself. He told Mendez, "The other fire bosses won't like it, but dang it all, I'm the game warden here. I have jurisdiction."

With Strut hovering high above to watch, Ray strode over to various men. "I know it's against regulations . . ." he began with each. The tired fire bosses argued with him, opposed the idea of wasting energy to rescue a bear cub who might not even exist. Ray admitted it sounded crazy, but he was adamant. He debated with some, cajoled others, joked, called in favors, and prevailed. He gave the order, "Pass word to your fire crews going up the mountain: If they see a little cub, bring him down. I want him!"

Chapter 13

Chiku – 'eat bitter' – meaning 'endure hardship.'
–Chinese language

It was a momentous day in Smokey's life. By May 9th, the smoke had lifted enough for him to breathe more easily. "Huh!" He sneezed out some ashes, and his sense of smell returned. Weak and hungry, he searched with his nose for a whiff of food. Sensing an unusual animal scent, he stretched his neck out of the stump, and lifted his nose into the air. The odd smell grew stronger, coming closer. It was the greasy smell of a strange animal's sweat — anxious sweat. Perhaps dangerous.

Through the gray haze came some big upright animals. They were searching the ground foraging for food. They were angling his way. Perhaps they'd pass him by. He backed down into the stump, leaving only his eyes and ears showing. As they came closer, he saw that they didn't have fur, and walked on hind legs. They were men!

The humans were big, as tall as his parents standing on their hind feet. Smokey felt his chest tighten as he flashed on the image of his mother upright sniffing the air, and his father standing across the meadow. Now, out of the world of ashes and smoldering embers, the men loomed large in their blackened clothes and forest ranger hats. With axes in hand, they were concentrating on the ground and occasionally looking at trees — as if they were seeking grass or nuts to eat. Then they came rapidly in his direction, headed straight toward his stump.

Suddenly, they no longer appeared to be foragers, but predators hunting him down to eat. Smokey leaped out of the hollow stump, squeaked shrilly as his sore paws hit the ground, and ran to the nearest tree. Weak as he was, he managed to climb far above the tall humans. Then he slowly turned his head to look down.

A plaintive cry escaped his lips. One of the men had spotted him, and was pointing and shouting to the others. All of them gathered at the base of the tree. Smokey boosted himself even higher. He had to grip tightly because the rough bark had been stripped away to uncover the smooth surface beneath. How long must he hold on?

The trunk still retained heat from the fire, and felt hot and hard against his burnt belly. His legs soon became weary clinging to the tree, and his paw pads hurt. Smokey dug his sharp claws farther into the wood. Then his body could go limp and just hang there without much effort. He closed his eyes. He could wait as long as it took until the humans left to seek easier prey.

A hand in a leather glove suddenly grabbed Smokey's back. Someone below shouted, "Hey kid, watch out for those claws and teeth!" In an instant, the cub's fighting spirit burst forth and he twisted, trying to rake the boy with his claws . . . but he couldn't. His neck was gripped firmly by a hand, and he was being held at arm's length. The young man dangled him in the air while shinnying down the tree trunk. Smokey screamed all the way. Then he was jolted as the young man jumped onto the ground.

Smokey was so dazed that he soon gave up struggling and went limp. The boy called out something, stood still, and pressed the cub against his chest to take off each glove. Smokey became aware that the hands that now held him were gentle, like his mother's paw pads when she gathered him to her furry body. He sensed that he was not going to be hurt and must trust his captor. With relief, he let out a long moan and sucked his paw. The fellow tucked him inside his shirt, and, hidden in the dark against the soft skin, Smokey felt safe. He whimpered softly. One big hand braced his back through the shirt, careful not to rub his sore paws, belly, or burnt rump. Smokey settled against the chest of the young man who now held him close.

The boy lurched as he moved across the ground, and momentary panic seized the cub. He twisted to face forward and poked his head out the shirt below the man's chin so he could see. They stopped a short distance from other men. Smokey looked at the men, and they looked at him. Then, one by one, they approached very slowly, making soothing sounds in their throats. Whenever they reached out their hands to touch his head, though, Smokey recoiled and snapped his teeth in warning.

A canteen was tipped above Smokey's head, and something wet splattered his face. Water! He stretched his neck out, his parched throat desperate. Although he coughed at first as he swallowed water, he was soon swallowing easily, feeling energy flow down his throat into his body.

Then he was being carried again in a jostling, swaying movement. Peeking out the top of the shirt, he could see that the boy was taking him down the mountain. Smokey gave in to his woozy weakness. He dozed now and then from the rocking motion as they descended farther and farther.

The cub had been feeling secure and sleepy, when he was startled by sudden noise nearby. He looked out. Like a swarm of giant ants, young soldiers with dingy faces came up close to beam at him.

Curious to see everything, Smokey clambered to the top of the boy's shirt, and the boy undid another button so the cub could stick his shoulders and paws out. The cub hastily surveyed the wide level ground of the busy fire camp. Just then, a mammal walked slowly toward him. It seemed like a large gray wolf but it wore a studded collar. The cub recoiled against the boy's neck and tried to crawl back inside the shirt but it was too late. The boy had already crouched and was leaning toward the animal. It loomed over Smokey's head to sniff him. The bear roared, thrust out his paw and swatted it hard, his claws raking the big nose. The German shepherd backed off, and the boy quickly stood and made comforting sounds to the whimpering cub.

Hearing the commotion, a man in white bustled over. "That little fellow is dehydrated." Making enticing sounds, the camp cook held out a can of condensed milk for Smokey to smell, and tipped it for him to grab with both paws. The cub gulped the liquid down and licked the dribbles from his chin. Soon his stomach clutched in pain, and he let out a loud wail.

Then a man, smelling of wood-smoke and sweat, strode over to stand in front of the boy. Erect, with hands on hips, his bearing exuded authority, like Mother Bear, like the man Strut had told him about. Smokey couldn't understand the words addressed to the boy, but he tried to gather what he could from the man's body language and tone of voice.

"Son, I'd like to talk to you. I'm Ray Bell, the chief wildlife officer for this area. You're the firefighter — the young soldier — who climbed the tree and brought this cub back, right?"

"Yes, sir."

"He's awfully small, isn't he? Thanks for bringing him back to the camp. I'm here to take him off your hands now."

The boy recoiled, stepped back, then protested. "You don't have to. I mean, begging your pardon, sir, I'm taking him home to my folks. They've never seen a little bear."

"And just how do you plan to take him home?"

"Well, I don't rightly know. But he's mine. I climbed up that tree and brought him clear down the mountain."

Ray took a deep breath that expanded his chest, and he pulled himself to his full height. Smokey sensed sparks of anger. "Now you listen to me! That cub is probably going to die. I know wild animals. And from the looks of him, even if he lives through the night, he'll die for sure tomorrow — if I don't fly him to a vet at daybreak."

Ray reached toward the cub. Smokey flinched, and the boy stepped back, pressing the bear closer to his chest. Smokey burrowed down deeper inside the boy's shirt with only his nose and eyes above the collar, watching.

The boy said, "See! He's afraid of you. He feels safe with

me, and I like him. I don't have to give him up if I don't want to. He's mine. How do I know what you say is true? Anyway, you're not Army. You can't make me do it."

"No, I'm not Army. I can't order you, not that way."

Ray's solid body seemed to expand with anger. He stepped nearer and put his face up to the boy, the beak of his cap almost knocking the boy's forehead. "See this badge? New Mexico Game and Fish. I'm in charge of the whole area here as far as *animals* are concerned. I'm above the Army here, even the Forest Service fire bosses and anyone else helping put out this fire."

Smokey felt the young man's breath quicken and his arms clench in defiance for a moment, then his body slump in defeat. There was a long silence. Smokey felt agitated. What was going to happen? The boy suddenly seemed different, holding him in a distant way.

Ray's tone of voice altered as he put his hand lightly on the boy's upper arm. "I know it's hard, son. I've had to give up wild animals too. There's something special about rescuing an animal. Being so close to a wild thing. That's why I like my work. I know it's why you like this little bear." He paused, and his eyes softened to look into the boy's. He gave a little cough and said, "It's always sad to let them go."

Then the game warden continued. "Some die, but most I can take back to the forest, and that feels good." He smiled at the boy. "I can't fly the cub to the vet until there's enough light for the plane, so why don't you keep him with you tonight. I'll pick him up as soon as day breaks in the morning."

The boy hugged Smokey to him, hung his head and mumbled, "Yes, sir."

The bear spent the evening in a blur of fatigue and discomfort from the dull ache of his burnt underside. When the boy finally laid him on the ground beside him, Smokey was too weak to stir and took comfort from the familiar smell of the boy against his body. He tensed at the small noises that humans made as they settled down for the night. Smokey desperately wished for the blackness of sleep, but became more and more aware of stomach pains, and how much his burned body hurt. Finally, he began to shriek as loud as he could.

The cub suddenly saw Ray standing above, silhouetted against the early moon in the night sky. The game warden leaned down and shook the boy's shoulder. "We have to get this little bear out of here so the firefighters can sleep. I'll have to take him. *Now.*"

The boy sleepily nodded acquiescence, and his hand reached out to pat the cub good-bye. Ray gently lifted Smokey and held his exhausted, slack body. "Why, this cub doesn't weigh much more than a squirrel!" He carried the cub to the cook tent and rubbed cowboy salve—bacon grease—on Smokey's paws, tummy, rump and tail. The little bear felt some relief, and his throat eased at sensing that this man was helping him.

The next thing Smokey knew, he lay on the front seat of a truck pressed against Ray's leg, being flopped up and down as they bumped along a rocky road. As they rounded a curve, the cub became queasy. His claws catching hold of a pant leg, he crawled into Ray's lap. Feeling better, he hunched down and held on tight until the truck suddenly stopped and rocked a moment. Ray winced as he pulled the cub's claws loose, set him aside, and got out. He patted Smokey through the open door. "Just stay put a minute. I have to see whether or not they'll take you."

The truck door slammed. Smokey clutched his ears at the harsh noise, and scrunched down. As his protector's sweaty odor grew faint, Smokey worried that he was being left behind. When he had been snuggling next to Ray, he hadn't noticed his pain as much, but, as he waited alone, he became increasingly aware of his throbbing head and aching body.

He heard a knock on a door outside, and a low, gruff voice. The next thing he knew, Smokey had been placed in a small cardboard box with a loosely closed lid. He was being carried down one jarring step after another into a dusky underground place—something like the cooler air and dust in the back of his cave. His box was set on a table. Pale light filtered through its loose top. Then light burst into his eyes as the lid was opened. He slid to one end of the box, and dug his claws into the cardboard base. "You can leave the top open. He's too weak to go anywhere."

The cub looked around. It was a large place, larger than the front part of the cave, and unlike anything he'd ever seen in the forest. It was like Strut's description of a house! He wanted to be left alone to sleep. Someone approached. A hand picked him up and laid him back down again in his box, this time on something like soft moss for his burnt belly.

"There now, little tyke." Through his misty hearing came Ray's voice. "Hope this old towel will make him more comfortable, and it can be disposed of in case he dirties himself. Though he doesn't have much in him. Looks dehydrated, and famished. Look at that raw skin. Probably smoke inhalation, too. It'll be a miracle if he lasts the night."

"Here's some water," the gruff voice said, and Ray let the liquid dribble into the cub's eager mouth. "That's enough for now, little guy." Ray turned to the other man and said, "Let's leave the box open in case it gets smelly. It's hard enough for a wild animal to be left in its own dirt. I'll be back in the morning—at first light." Footsteps receded, a door closed, and Smokey was alone.

No more surprises to brace against. The pounding in Smokey's head and his taut alertness subsided. Only weariness was left. He collapsed with a sigh and curled up at one end of the box. It was very quiet.

He must have dozed, for the next thing he heard was the door click open at the top of the stairs. He braced against the heavy-footed crunch and creak of wooden steps as someone came downstairs. The steps halted a moment.

There was nowhere to hide, trapped in the open box, unlike the forest, where he could almost always flee to a bush or tree. He could feel his heart thumping in his chest, and pulsing sounds—like a field of crickets—in his head. The stomp of hard boots on the basement floor came closer. Gulping sounds escaped his throat.

Smokey could smell the man and expected the intruder to lean over and sniff him. The cub squeezed against the far end of the box. Was this human tensing to pounce? "BaaWoo, BaaWoo!" Smokey screamed, but his own voice was so loud that it seemed to burst his head with unbearable sound, and he had to stop.

As the man bent closer, Smokey scrunched his eyes closed, and out came his wavering moan. A gruff voice whispered, "It's okay, little fellow," and the bear smelled the man who'd come down the stairs with Ray.

The steps receded toward the wall nearby. Remembering his mother's admonition to always keep an eye on a predator, he rested his chin on the upper edge of his box and watched. In the moonlight coming through a small window, the man could be seen standing upright like a bear, his bare forearms handling a glass object. He tilted it with one paw, snapped something small and shiny to light a flame, and replaced the glass object—now bright with light—on the table.

The human figure suddenly loomed large, but what was even more terrifying was his monstrous shadow moving on the far wall. The man and his shadow lunged toward Smokey before he could duck his head back into the box.

"Here's a lantern so you'll know where you are. My kids always liked a nightlight when young. We don't want you to be scared, left alone in the dark, do we?" Smokey was tempted to peek at him, but didn't want to enrage the man by staring, and just turned his head sideways to watch him climb the stairs and click the cellar door shut. Relieved, Smokey slumped down again. It took a while for his fast-beating heart to slow.

Then curiosity seized Smokey as his eyes were drawn to the flickering light on the table. Bright light at night! He blinked, looked away, and then couldn't keep his eyes from returning. A small sun right in his room! What other surprises did humans have? For a few moments he forgot his pain and fear. What kind of world had he entered? Part of the room was brighter than moonlight in the forest, but other parts were black like sun-shadows at noonday. He looked around. The room was a big square box of straight lines, just as Strut had described human houses. Footsteps sounded above his head. He must be in an underground part of a human cave.

His breath came fast and short with excitement as he looked at strange things cluttered on the floor and hanging on the wall. As he whirled his head around to look at everything, he suddenly felt faint and nauseated. He ducked into the end of his cardboard hideout and whimpered. How he wished he could call his mother to him, back in his own home, in the forest, where it was dark at night and light by day. Pain assailed him. He howled and howled for his lost world.

Smokey hated being confined to the box. No night sounds, just a dull roar in his head as if he were near the river. His stomach felt like claws were tearing his insides. His burned belly, rump and paws throbbed. Where was that crow? Strut had promised to return.

Alone and deserted, Smokey had fallen into confusion, when he was startled alert by the terrifying sound of a screech owl right next to him. He started to raise himself to look, then crouched down to hide. The screeching kept on and on. At last, it dawned on him that it was his own voice screeching. The cub couldn't stop even though the sound hurt his ears and his throat got tight and sore, as he cried into the long night.

A strange feeling like a buzzing sound filled his head, as if he was sliding into a hazy memory of his cave in early morning. He was falling into a trance where nothing could hurt him. Despite his dream-like sense of something terrible having happened, he was once again feeling his mother licking him, her long tongue sweeping down the length of his body.

Smokey jolted awake, his flesh raw. Shrieking so hard that it echoed in his head, he plunged into terror, like his terror in the cave hearing his brother and sister cry out. Then it seemed as if he was lost in the forest and couldn't find his way home.

Just before dawn, his spirit sputtered out. He cried out in a hoarse whisper, "Mother, mother." His body splayed itself on the bottom of the box, his neck extended with his chin flattened on the cardboard. Relieved that he would never have to raise his head again, the cub entered into Nothingness.

Chapter 14

Life shrinks or expands in proportion to one's courage.
–Anais Nin

Whatever you dream you can do, begin it. Boldness has genius, power and magic in it.
–Johann Wolfgang von Goethe

After Strut had alerted Ray at the fire camp that afternoon, the crow wearily flapped his wings up the mountain to wait with Smokey for his rescue. Before he had gone very far, though, he flopped on a branch, exhausted from his strenuous trips. His eyes closed and he fell into a deep sleep. When Strut awoke, it was dark. With the thought that Ray might have already rescued Smokey, he headed back down to the fire camp as fast as he could.

Upon arrival, the crow descended to a tree limb overlooking the fire camp. There was no cub in sight. Everyone seemed asleep except a German shepherd who sat on his haunches as if on guard. They regarded each other, and something about the dog caught the crow's attention. The black bird flew to a nearby branch and noticed that the dog's long tongue was licking a fresh scratch on his nose.

"Hey, dog-o. Did that scratch come from a little bear? If so, where is he?" When the shepherd turned his head aside, as if he didn't deign to answer a mere bird, the crow hovered so close that the wing-wind fanned the dog's face. "If you know something, tell me. Or beware my beak. Caw!" The shepherd flattened his big body onto the ground and rolled his eyes up, his tail held low, thumping the ground.

In response, Strut alighted on the ground, folded his wings

firmly to his body and positioned himself a short distance away. The shepherd turned intelligent eyes on the crow. He nodded first toward a truck and then toward the dirt road leading down the valley. Strut bowed and fluffed out his feathers. "Thanks, pal!"

A wave of warmth flushed his body before he felt a shudder of grief at the thought that he might not find his friend Smokey alive. "If only I can be at his side, Smokey will take heart and not die," he thought. Hope filling his chest, the crow leaned forward, raised his wings, and flew down the road.

As soon as Strut approached the far end of the valley, he beamed onto the sound of screaming and swooped down to the basement window of the ranch house where the sound was loudest. In the flickering light of a small lamp inside, he spied a dark shape in a box.

The crow tried to perch on the wood frame at the base of the window, and had to frantically clutch the wood in a tight grip. Strut pecked the glass so hard it hurt his beak, "Tat! Tat!"

But apparently Smokey was screeching too loud to hear him. He called out as loud as he could, "Caw! It's Strut. Here I am! You're not alone anymore." Strut spread his wings wide in the window to get Smokey's attention, but the little bear had stretched his neck toward the ceiling to screech. The crow felt desperate. And mad at the cub. How could he rescue Smokey from this prison, or at least give him some comfort in his distress, if the cub kept screaming so loudly?

He hastily scouted around the building. No open windows. No other way inside. He returned and tried to get a grip on the slim window sill, flapping his wings slowly to remain visible in the window. His wings grew tired.

One last sound escaped from Smokey's hoarse throat and the crow saw his friend's body sag and become still. Strut called in a cracked voice, "No, don't die! Here I am. I came like I said I would. Don't give up. Please." But the cub's figure remained unmoving.

A surge of angry frustration aroused the crow once more.

"Well, I won't give up, not Strut!" He struck the glass hard with his beak, "Tat-tat-tat." And he emitted a guttural, rasping shriek, "Aaarr-cak! Cak! Cak!"

At that moment, Smokey felt the heavy stone of his being rise without any will of his own, as if someone had picked him up. His ears tilted forward and his eyelids lifted to the window. His heart leaped as he saw — silhouetted in the moonlight — the black wingspread of his friend Strut. The crow fixed him with eager eyes. "Don't slip away! Hold on till daybreak!" Smokey nodded in accord, sighed, breathed more easily, crumpled, and fell asleep.

His mission accomplished so far, Strut paused and felt his exhaustion. How weary his muscles felt from the exertion of traveling up and down the mountain, then his desperate efforts to rouse Smokey. He had hardly slept or eaten for a long time. He thudded to the ground below the window, teetered on his feet a few steps, repeating to himself, "I'll keep watch through the night. I won't leave you." His body drooped and settled on the ground, and his eyes fluttered closed.

The next thing he knew it was early daylight. Strut darted to the window pane and looked inside. Smokey's body remained inert. Strut squinted his eyes to see whether the cub was still breathing, but he couldn't tell.

Gravel crunched as a pickup truck came to a stop beside the ranch house. Strut thrust himself through the air toward the driveway. Ray was already springing up the steps to the back door. "Caw!" the crow cried, and dug his claws into his human friend's shoulder. "Hurry, before it's too late!"

"Crow, how did you get here?"

Strut, impatient to save Smokey, bit the man's ear.

"Hey, that hurt!" Swiping with his hand, Ray whisked the beak from his ear and flipped the crow into the air. Strut flopped onto Ray's shoulder again and the man sighed and rubbed the bird's neck. Ray opened the door and went down the stairs two at a time. Strut got there first, and swooped down into the box and nudged Smokey's limp form with his bill. "Get up! We're here." With one hand, Ray cradled the fuzzy body, lifted Smokey and pressed him to his chest. The cub's head lolled to the side, and the man's other big hand quickly supported his neck.

The little body squirmed and suddenly the cub sank his sharp teeth into the top of Ray's hand. "Hey, you little demon!" But Ray was laughing in relief to see the cub alive. The game warden replaced the cub in his cardboard box. "Let's get this little fellow to the vet." And they were up the stairs and into the truck. Ray placed the box with the cub on the passenger seat and Strut quickly wedged himself next to the box.

Ray rescues Smokey

Down at the village, they finally came to a lurching stop in a grassy field. Ray scooped up the dazed cub and strode to his red-and-white airplane. As he opened the cockpit door, Strut tried to fly in. Ray held up his hands. "Sorry, my friend, you belong here with your flock—and what's left of the forest. Don't worry—I'll take good care of your bear friend." The door slammed shut and the propellers whirred their furious wind. The Piper 115, specially fitted for short runways, bumped along the uneven ground, gathering speed.

Strut followed the plane as it climbed steeply into the sky. He strained his wings to keep up with the noisy machine, but soon fell behind. He finally gave up, waving his wings slowly as he watched the plane shrink to a dot in the sky. He stumbled awkwardly onto the ground and looked in the direction of the departed plane.

"Good-bye, Smokey," he said aloud, "I know you'll make it. I'll try to find you again, some day. I promise." With a heavy heart at the loss of his friend, but some hope, too, that he'd live, the crow turned to face the mountain. Once more, he beat his wings up the mountain to find his flock—his family, Duke, Elder Crow and his fellow crows.

Once the plane became airborne and leveled off, Ray heard a small "huff-huff" of fear from the box on the seat beside him. He moistened his forefinger to reach over and gently rub the cub's lips, and felt the end of his finger being grasped and sucked. After emitting a few whimpers, Smokey fell silent in sleep. Unexpected tenderness welled up in Ray's chest, and he thought, "I can't go soft on this bear. Chances are, he won't make it."

But a fierce desire seized him: This bear must survive! As the engine throbbed, his thoughts swirled, as they usually did while flying. He was gripped by a sense of mission. His imagination leapt: If the cub survived, maybe his sad eyes could somehow tell the story of how wildfires hurt animals in the forest.

Ray cast a far-away gaze toward the horizon—and beyond. Memories came to him unbidden of a darker mission five years earlier. It was 1945, during World War II, when he had been stationed with the Allies in India. Why had they picked him? He remembered the moment he was called to US Army Air

Corps headquarters. He stood at attention, expecting a reprimand.

Loving to fly, he had hoped to pilot military planes in the war, but had been assigned to repair them instead. His job was to fix the turrets on Allied planes in China. For some time he had been flown back and forth from the base in India over the Himalayas, the perilous route called, "Over the Hump."

During the endlessly boring down-time at the air base in India, he'd whiled away the days showing the other guys some rodeo stunts. The soldiers had whooped as Ray set out to bulldog a Brahman bull standing below the wing of a B-29. The stunt had started out fine. Ray climbed onto the airplane's wing and flung himself through the air to grab the bull's horns. Startled, the beast ran toward the jungle, entangling Ray in a clothesline and causing the cowboy to break his ankle.

Ray thought that stunt was responsible for his being summoned to headquarters. So he was puzzled, when he showed up, that the brass treated him with a curious kind of respect. Instead of reprimanding him, they were entrusting him with a top secret mission. He must tell no one, and report directly to a remote Pacific island. They told him nothing else, but he soon discovered that the tiny island was between Hawaii and the Philippines. It was one of the Mariana Islands, close to Saipan. Its name was Tinian.

As soon as Ray arrived on the island, he knew something was up. He sensed it all around him: everyone close-lipped, the air crackling with electricity, the intense concentration of the officers in charge, the adrenalin rush of the soldiers working as fast as they could on the B-29—any mistake or delay deemed unthinkable.

Ray was ordered to work on the turrets while others altered the structure of the plane. The purpose: to lighten the plane enough so it could carry the weight of a five-ton bomb on a long non-stop flight over the Pacific—and still have enough gas to return.

They had just accomplished the renovation of the plane

when President Truman's "go" order came for the important mission. On the island of Tinian the local date was August 6, 1945. Painted on the side of the bomber was its name: *Enola Gay*. Ray and others in the ground crew awoke early and watched the B-29 take off at 2:45 a.m. and disappear into the night sky. They didn't know that it carried an atomic bomb and that its target was Hiroshima. And upon the plane's return, when no surrender came from Japan, another plane carrying an atomic bomb would strike Nagasaki.

Those dark missions brought the surrender of Japan and, finally, the end of World War II. It had been a horrendous war in which the Axis powers — Nazi Germany, Fascist Italy, and Imperial Japan — had invaded and occupied Europe, the Middle East, North Africa, Asia and the Pacific. Although the war had ended in Europe, the fierce warfare in the Pacific and Asia had continued with heavy casualties on both sides, so the final defeat of Japan brought enormous relief.

After years of anxiety about the outcome of the war — with its worldwide devastation and loss of life — the end brought not so much an attitude of triumph as a feeling of solemnity at the gravity of what the world had suffered. Hundreds of thousands of soldiers — and millions of civilians displaced by the war — could start their return home. But the image of the atomic blasts in their horror and tragedy and their unforeseen consequences must have haunted some of those who worked at Tinian.

Memories crowded Ray's mind—the return of the *Enola Gay* crew holding their thumbs up and beaming like heroes for the cameras, but, afterwards on the base, keeping to themselves, some looking grim-faced. Later on, the reason became known:

Before turning the plane back from Hiroshima the crew had looked below at the utter devastation of buildings and life. Eventually Life Magazine *showed photographs of Hiroshima and Nagasaki — incinerated to cinders and the surviving people burned, and, later, it turned out, many to suffer and die from radiation.*

Ray turned attention to his Piper Cub for a moment before he gazed again at the horizon. This time, a fresh image haunted him: the burned mountainside he had just left. In his mind's eye, he saw again the forest at Capitan with its blackened trees and eerie silence. Then, from the devastation of the forest floor of thick ashes, he imagined the little cub holding onto a tree, the sun breaking through and bathing his fur with its golden rays.

The game warden stole a glance at the cardboard box where the little fellow snuffled in his sleep. Here was one survivor from the animals lost in the wildfire. And right now, he himself was this cub's only guardian. At least, this was something he could do, if all went well. He sighed with relief. It felt like he'd just watched the end of a war movie, but there was a double-feature, and he was hoping a more upbeat film might begin.

Ray's thoughts returned to the war. He'd worked on those turrets of the *Enola Gay*—and other turrets throughout the war—because the Army Air Corps had ordered him to do so. But his dream of flying had been strong. Before the war, any time he'd saved a few dollars from household money, he'd taken a lesson. He loved flying: the exhilaration of lifting off the ground, the ease of banking in any dimension, the awe he felt among the clouds, the magic of seeing the world in miniature below.

Before the war, he had loved the thrill of flying low over tree tops and swooping under telephone wires. He wouldn't do such daredevil stunts now, just for the thrill of it, but was glad he'd had the experience when he was young and reckless. Flying near the ground was now invaluable in his work—surveying game, finding lost people, seeding lakes with fish, and, as he'd done yesterday, doing low-flying, wind-whipped reconnaissance over forest fires.

He'd always liked challenges. As a ranch hand, he'd handled big animals, and had dared to woo the rancher's daughter—a strawberry-blonde who could ride a horse and handle cattle as well as any man on the ranch. Ruth had been his wife through all the hard times. Ray remembered when he had had to shoot game for their dinner table—with only one bullet, because bullets were expensive. And she had been his champion, with resilience and humor, those years when he threw his body into the rodeo circuit.

After the war he'd returned in one piece and was fortunate enough to land the job of New Mexico's "flying game warden." And he was especially grateful to return home to his wife and two children. He felt like a lucky man.

Santa Fe appeared on the horizon. Ray rehearsed how quickly he could ground the plane, then sprint to his car holding the cub without jostling him too much. He must drive to the veterinarian before it was too late. How many times had he been through this kind of emergency with crippled deer, wounded elk, sick geese and smaller animals? He looked forward to the day when there might be special facilities for wild animal rescue and rehabilitation, but for now, he had to depend on a willing vet for emergencies and hospitalization, then house the recovering animals at his own home.

Ray knew he was fortunate: His old neighbor and hunting buddy, Edwin J. Smith, was the best vet in New Mexico. Ed would see any wild animal Ray brought—without a fee. But a bear this young would be a first for both of them.

Chapter 15

So ended an era and so began another.
–Allen Drury

In captivity, especially if separation from its mother was frightening, the cub's demands for comfort and contact are excruciating. It becomes a clinging, clawing, climbing, screaming brat terrified by any sign of rejection.
–Irving Petite

Doc Smith bandages Smokey

Ray carried the cub into the veterinarian's office. Jolted awake by the hasty pace, Smokey still managed to snuggle his nose as close as he could to the familiar sweaty smell of the man's armpit.

"So this is the little bear burned in the fire," said the woman at the desk. "Isn't he a cute little fuzz-ball? Why, curled up like that, he's not much bigger than a man's fist! But he doesn't look very well, does he? I'll tell Dr. Smith, and he'll be right out."

A moment later she returned with Ed Smith, a middle-aged man in a white coat, with a high forehead and an earnest—but calm—manner. The vet said, "The airport called. Well, well, well. What do we have here?" He inclined his head toward the cub. "So this is the bear I've been hearing about! Much younger than I'd have thought. Come on in. I'll see what I can do."

As soon as the door to the small examination room closed, the acrid scent of Smokey's singed fur filled the air. Ray gently placed the cub on the table but Smokey's four feet slipped on the smooth shiny surface and he fell onto his shoulder. His claws frantically scraped at the table, and the scratchy noise seemed to frighten him.

Ray scooped up Smokey in his arms but the bear desperately dug his claws through Ray's clothes to his skin. The man's shirt was torn trying to pull him off. "Now look what you've done! Let go, you little—" The cub's gulping sounds of fear made Ray stop struggling with him.

"Ed, you'd better do it. He's already bitten me too many times."

When the doctor reached for him, Smokey closed his eyes, arched his back, and let out a shrill howl as the vet freed his claws from the shirt. It was soon obvious that Ed was used to babies, for he treated Smokey like his own, holding him in his arms and intoning soft baby-talk until he quieted. He gradually eased the cub upright onto the table and let him brace against his own body.

Smokey whimpered pitiably as calm hands stroked his fur down the length of his back. It felt like being licked by his mother's long tongue. Then the hands pressed softly but firmly against the sides of his body, as if Smokey were braced against his brother and sister inside the cave. Smokey took a deep breath and let out a sigh. His heart was no longer beating so fast. Maybe some humans were like bears after all, some kind of relative that stood on two hind legs.

Ray said, "You sure have a way with animals. Guess I'm a bit rough. From all those years of handling ornery cattle."

The vet's voice made soothing sounds to Smokey as his hands moved slow-motion to hold him lightly and firmly by the shoulders. "This is a very young bear, something like ten weeks old. Couldn't have weighed more than half a pound or so at birth around the end of February. Let's weigh him . . . Just four pounds — underweight for his age. See those bright blue eyes? They'll turn brown later. Now for a closer look."

Smokey heard a click as a bright light suddenly blazed. He was momentarily blinded, and squinted to ward off the glare — brighter than a patch of spring snow in the noonday sun. He closed his eyes tightly again and held his breath. He heard the vet's voice, which seemed to come from afar. "There, there, little fellow. It'll be okay." Smokey mewed and dropped into a quiet, trance-like state.

The cub felt the vet's hands touch all over his body: his paws, his ears, and his burnt underside. The hands even lifted up Smokey's stub of a tail, which he'd never let anyone touch — except his mother when she groomed him. His limbs were squeezed, flexed and slowly stretched. "No broken bones, just a torn tendon in his right foreleg. See the pad here under the right front paw — worse than the other one. Raw flesh where the skin peeled off."

It was strange for Smokey to experience his body so limp that he was turned onto his side without willing it. The slight breeze from the vet's breath came close to his stomach and continued toward his behind. "This poor little fellow. Burnt all over his softest parts! Burned bare — no fur left. He must have sat down on some live embers!" Smokey felt in good hands, and let the man do whatever he wanted.

Smooth fingers pushed against both outer sides of his mouth and pressed it open wide. Smokey tightened his eyes shut as a shiny round light on the vet's forehead came close.

"The gums have a pretty good color — a good sign. But a badly scorched throat, probably seared clear inside. Lungs undoubtedly damaged by smoke inhalation. Like firefighters' lungs."

Smokey felt the skin on his neck being pinched and rolled between fingers. "No fat under the skin at all, and badly dehydrated to boot. This one's probably the runt of the litter. Already thin to begin with, then starved since the fire began."

Ray spoke. "I forgot to tell you. All he's had is some water from the boy who found him, and the little I gave him last night. The fire camp cook also fed him condensed milk from a can, and some of the fire crew gave him candy."

"That water might have saved his life." Gentle fingers pushed deep into Smokey's stomach and the cub winced. "Hard painful spots here. That condensed milk — or whatever — might have given him stomach cramps."

"Maybe that's one reason he was howling most of the night."

"We'll have to find something he can keep down. He desperately needs liquid and food. But let's see what else might be wrong."

The vet held his finger in front of the cub's face and moved it from side to side. With the bright light shining in Smokey's eyes, he watched the finger waggle in front of the vet's nose in a fascinating way, like a leaf quivering on a twig. "Good sign. He's tracking. Alert. The pupils are okay so he's not in shock.

"Now for the lungs and heart. I'm afraid of what we'll find." The vet held up something in his hand for Smokey to see. It was shiny, silver and round. Then, moving slowly, so Smokey could see what he was doing, the vet pressed the metallic thing against the cub's body and listened intently to the silver vines in his ears. Smokey felt the metal rest a long time on his chest, then touch his back here and there.

Dr. Smith held the cub's nose shut to make him take deep breaths through his mouth. "Well, his lungs are scratchy. His heartbeat's slow. The pulse a little low. It's remarkable he's alive, having gone through the fire—all that terror and pain. Enough to knock the life out of anybody. He must have a will to live like nobody's business.

"Ray, would you hold him still a minute?"

The vet felt Smokey's armpits. "The lymph glands are okay, so he's not infected. That's good news. Because infection's the real danger with burns." He slowly pressed fingers into Smokey's stomach and kidneys to see if there was any internal damage, then felt his ribs and the rest of his body, and beamed a small light into each ear. "The rest of him is okay. It's good someone carried him down from that tree, rather than let him fall. Now, let's see how badly burned his body is."

Smokey felt himself being turned on his side. He could tolerate that. But when they forced him spread-eagle onto his back he became alarmed to find his feet in the air and his armpits pinned down. The cub squirmed mightily to twist back onto his feet, and tried to rake the men with his hind claws. But his hind legs wouldn't obey him and flailed weakly in the air. He hated that he couldn't resist. It reminded him of when he was very small and his mother would turn him with her paw to lick his behind or anywhere else she wanted.

At least, the cub thought, I can huff, but it came out like a ragged cough. Something broke in him. He gave up and became inert. The vet made cooing sounds reminding him of those his mother had made when she was grooming him. Maybe the humans meant well and would lick his wounds like Mother Bear.

Smokey jerked his head at the popping sounds as bottles of peroxide and antiseptic were opened. Awful smells assailed him. With a wet cloth the vet scrubbed the black charcoal off his fur, and dabbed smelly liquid on his burned places, making them sting. But immediately afterward comforting salve was smeared on the tender wounds—his belly, his behind, his singed tail and blistered paws. He was feeling soothed until the vet started to wrap his wounds in white gauze and adhesive tape. He snarled and struggled to resist, but Ray resolutely held him down, pressing him onto the hard table.

They finally let Smokey sit, and he immediately went to work licking himself. But when he tried to lick his underside, his bound paws slipped, He lost his balance and would have skidded off the table if the vet hadn't blocked the edge of the table with his body. Smokey yowled, and, bracing against the man's body, scrambled into a sitting position to work on his stomach, but it was covered in bandages. And he couldn't twist his body enough to yank off the patch on his rear end. It was always a comfort to lick his paws, so he tried in vain to bite the tape off his ankles. "Looks like those bandages will hold, you little demon," the vet said. He looked into the cub's small eyes. Smokey glanced up, then succumbed. He slumped onto the table, his head resting between his bandaged paws.

When Ed Smith set his scissors on the metal table, the metallic clink made Smokey flinch. The vet said, "Did you see that, Ray? Let me try an experiment." He clanked a metal bowl onto the counter and Smokey cried out and covered his ears with his paws. Then Ed gently set a glass bottle on the counter, making a barely audible clash. Smokey winced. The vet said, "It's just a hunch, but you know how soldiers come back with shell shock? For some of them I think it's more than psychological. It can also be physiological — the soldiers' hearing is damaged by loud explosions in the front lines. It can make a kind of tinnitus — that's an irritating and continuous buzzing in your ears. This variation, though, is called hyperacusis — that's extreme sensitivity to loud sounds, especially sharp high-pitched ones. Watch the cub when I drop this metal spoon. See him flinch and grimace? That hurt his ears, as if I'd crashed cymbals together.

"So this bear apparently was subjected to explosive sounds in that firestorm like some soldiers subjected to explosive devices in war. It looks like this cub has 'noise sensitivity' on top of everything else. So let's shield him for a while from loud sounds — above ninety or a hundred decibels — so his hearing has a chance to recover."

Ray leaned over the cub, "Poor little soldier, as if you haven't already suffered enough in the front lines."

"One last thing. I'll hydrate him." Smokey felt a sudden pinch of fingers and a quick prick into the skin on his side, then a cool flow of energy into his body. "Even though his burns may hurt a lot, he's too far gone to risk painkillers. He's probably light-headed anyway. That'll help. Mercifully, if pain gets too bad, wounded animals often slip into a coma or trance. Nature has its ways of limiting suffering. When a predator sinks its teeth into an animal's throat, it takes only about eight seconds for endorphins to kick in so the prey feels nothing more and dies without too much suffering."

The vet let out a sigh, shuffled his feet, and turned off the bright light. He said to Ray, "We've done all we can for now. It's mainly up to him. We'll keep the cub here and see how it goes. He's actually not in as bad shape as I'd feared—no broken bones or infection."

"So he'll be okay?"

"Well, I wouldn't get my hopes up too high. Burns present a serious trauma for the whole system. There's a big danger of infection afterward. And there's another big problem: This cub is badly undernourished. To survive he'll need fluids, food and rest. And a quiet atmosphere. And we've never had a bear cub this young, so we don't really know what he can eat or keep down. Hospital life will be very different from what he's known in the wild. Let me warn you: He's likely to refuse to eat and just give up. He'll have to be a very strong little bear to make it. But I'll do my best."

Ray stood there a moment, his eyes cast down, then he looked over at Smokey, and finally at Ed Smith. "Well, you're the best there is. I've seen you save animals before, when it seemed impossible—almost all the animals I've brought in so far. But this little fellow—" Ray caught Smokey looking up at him with the whites of his eyes showing. He stroked the cub's fur with his finger. "You've gotta make it, little guy."

Ray faced the vet, then turned his head aside. "I know he's

just a bear. But— I don't know what to say. I've had a gut feeling about this bear from the very beginning. You know, whoever started that fire . . . would I like to see him look this bear in the eye! He has a lot to answer for."

Ed said, "Yeah. Well, it's too late to save the other animals and their habitat—all that forest land. But at least we might be able to save this little runt."

"I know he's in good hands. I'll be visiting to see how he's doing. This bear cub knows me, so maybe he'd like that. You know, we live close by now, here in Santa Fe. We moved last month from Capitan—me and the family. So call us any time and let us know how he's doing, for better or worse." Ed placed his hand on Ray's shoulder a moment, and then the game warden turned to leave.

As Ray disappeared through the door, Smokey had a moment of panic at being abandoned by the only man he knew. The cub screeched, and before he knew what was happening, the vet had cradled him in his arms, taken him down a corridor to a spacious room, placed him in a roomy wire animal cage, and was gone. Left alone at last, he moaned, then let out a slow sigh, and sank into sleep.

Chapter 16

Lightning #196878872

Cats seem to go on the principle that it never does any harm to ask for what you want.
–Joseph Wood Krutch

Animals not only have a sense of justice, but also a sense of empathy, forgiveness, trust, reciprocity, and much more as well ... Animals have rich inner worlds – they have a nuanced repertoire of emotions, a high degree of intelligence (they're really smart and adaptable), and demonstrate behavioral flexibility as they negotiate complex and changing social relationships.
–Marc Bekoff

Smokey awoke to bandaged paws and his underside throbbing with pain. High windows showed the sun fading and night falling.

"So, little one, you're finally awake," came a high voice. "You were whimpering so pathetically in your sleep. If I were not confined in this cage, I'd have come over and let you sleep next to my soft fur. My lovely purr would have rumbled right into your ribs, my darling."

Smokey turned toward the annoyingly intimate voice, then roused himself on awkward bandaged feet and lifted his head toward a cage across the way.

An animal was leisurely stretching out one pink-padded paw after the other. It licked the paws, rubbed its cheeks with them, and then scrunched its eyes shut to clean its forehead and ears. Gray and black stripes covered its body like streaks of light in tall sun-struck grasses. The cub made a small huffing sound and looked inquiringly at the strange animal.

"Let me introduce myself. I'm a cat—a domestic short-hair. The most *elegant* of my kind: a tiger-stripe. I have these *distinctive* markings. See?" She slowly pranced about the cage.

Smokey couldn't help being impressed. The animal moved as gracefully in the cage as a bird in the sky. Although it hurt to speak, he agreed, "You are very beautiful."

"Thank you. I'm named 'Lightning' because I run so fast. What's your name?"

"Smokey. I'm a bear. I was hurt in a big fire."

"The only fire I've known is a small one, in a fireplace. I once presided over a suburban household, you know—from my position in the master's armchair. But it was a dull life. That house didn't have any holes for mice to enter, nor any window sills to watch birds outside.

"Which reminds me, Smokey, it's quite boring here in this *health-prison*, don't you think? Perhaps I'll tell you my life story to pass the time."

In her talkativeness, the cat reminded Smokey of Strut. A wave of sadness came over him, but he also felt curious. "Okay, yes."

"I *love* to talk about myself. Let's see . . . One day the family with the armchair and fireplace started packing boxes. Being *intuitive* I knew immediately they were going to move to another house. So I lay down in one cardboard carton after another, but they yanked me out each time and sealed the boxes. So I hid on the lawn and watched them load the car. They were calling 'Lightning! Come, kitty-kitty' and I was going to relent and pad my way over to them when they suddenly closed the car doors and drove off. I had become *homeless*."

At the word 'homeless,' Smokey felt drawn to the cat. He was homeless now too. The bear fixed his eyes on her.

She went on in her melodic voice, "Not one to cry over spilt milk, I set out to see the world. I walked past all the neighbors I knew, until I came to the Fields Beyond. I soon found myself living in the Wilds among feral cats: Scrawny mothers with kittens hanging onto half-empty tits. Big males circling a squalling female in heat—the rivals hiss-fighting and leap-screaming at each other. We shivered in the cold, became soaking wet when it rained.

"You had to be constantly on your guard there, let me tell you! I snapped a twig once, and a one-eyed cat sprang into the air, came down with its back arched high and spit in my direction. It stiff-walked closer and its remaining yellow eye-slit bored into me. Scared to death, I turned and ran.

After a while I reached the city. I had to slink along alleys eluding scrawny and scruffy dogs—those I consider Trash Dogs. I had to be very crafty to avoid those dogs and the big rats and find a safe place to sleep. Those animals would snarl and fight over restaurant leftovers. It was disgusting stuff—all the colors of that goopy food running together into a sloppy mess. Yuk! I knew I had to leave."

Smokey perked up. "Mother warned me never to become a Garbage Bear—hanging around campgrounds. But tell me, how did you get away from all that?"

"It was a pack of big dogs. I ran for my life and dashed under a parked car. You should have seen how frustrated they were—big splayed feet scratching the pavement, blazing eyes and slathering mouths. They snarled, trying to scare me into running out. Of course, no *self-respecting* cat would budge from a safe place, so I waited until they all slunk away.

"There's a moral to this tale for you, Smokey: If you're ever in big trouble, but have found a safe enough place, just *stay put* until things change. It's a cat custom called 'biding your time.'

"When I crawled out onto the sidewalk, I found horrible grease on my back, nasty oil on my feet and stomach and a cut on my side—one of the dog's claws must have slashed me. Have you ever tried to lick grease off your back or crud off your feet? Yow!

"I decided the city was not for me. I needed a home. So I made my way to the suburbs. I found the house of an older couple. I positioned myself on the front steps so they'd see me when they opened the door to get their newspaper every morning. Before long, they set out a saucer of milk. I was famished, but I slowly sauntered over, lapped it up, and daintily rubbed my whiskers dry. How could they resist the eyes I raised to them, so eloquent in gratitude? I meowed softly and leaned against their legs. I charmed them!

"Unfortunately, as soon as they discovered my wound, instead of letting me heal it with my saliva they brought me straightaway to this vet. Fastidious as I usually am, I turned out to be infested with fleas and worms. I do hope those humans weren't too repulsed to come back and adopt me. They haven't even come back for a visit. I've been abandoned to await an unknown fate." Her voice lost its vitality and her green eyes looked pained. "Well, that's my story," she finished.

Smokey would have liked to cheer her up. Strut would have known how, he thought. He missed his mother and his bird friend and, as the silence lengthened, he escaped the pain of his wounds by remembering his times with Strut and that last day with his mother at the honey tree. "Sleep tight, little fur-ball," he heard the cat say and he was just able to murmur a thank you to this new friend before his breathing slowed and he fell asleep.

After he left the veterinarian and stopped briefly by his office, Ray headed home. As he drove, he debated whether to tell Ruth and their children about the bear cub. By the time he had pulled into the driveway alongside the small adobe house, he had resolved to wait—until he knew whether the cub would live. Ray sprang up the back steps and poked his head into the kitchen, where he saw his red-headed wife at the counter. "Honey! I'm home." Her broad face broke into a beaming smile, and he folded her in his arms for a long time.

"Thank goodness! We've been glued to the radio, but haven't heard a thing about you." Ruth called out, "Dad's home, safe and sound."

Everyone came running. Judy, the four-year-old, reached up her arms to Ray, her eyes glistening, as he gathered her up. She pressed her face against his shirt. Jet, the cocker spaniel puppy, bounced up and down against Ray's legs.

Fifteen-year-old Don appeared, his face lit up, and Ray punched his shoulder. "Hey, Dad! Did you see any of my friends? I heard kids from my old high school were helping out. If only we were still in Capitan, I could've been there too."

"You bet your boots—you would've been on the fire line. I didn't see any of them, 'cuz I was working like the dickens or out cold at camp catching a little sleep."

Don asked, "So what's the latest about the fire? Getting under control?"

"Not completely. Not for a while. There're still men on certain fire lines, but the main crew is cleaning up. You know how long a mop-up takes. It was an awfully big fire. Very steep, and a lot of ground to cover. I'll be flying back down tomorrow."

Ray looked at Don and Judy a moment, then burst into a big smile. He forgot his resolution and blurted, "Guess what I brought back? A bear cub! Just four pounds. Really young—maybe ten weeks old. About the size of my cupped hands—like this—when he's curled up asleep. A cute little fellow, but burned so bad that it hurts to look."

Judy cried, "Oh, Daddy, can I see him?"

"He's still at Doc Smith's."

She tugged his sleeve. "So let's go visit him!"

Ray found it hard to say no to his little girl. "Later. He's very, very tired and needs to rest. For a couple of days or so. Maybe then." He set her down. "Let's go sit and I'll tell you everything. You two kids go ahead. Your mother and I'll be right along."

Ray assumed a subdued tone with his wife. "Darn! I didn't mean to blurt that out—about the cub."

"Oh, you can never keep anything from us."

"The thing is, Ed doesn't know whether the cub will pull through. I have such hope for the little fellow! But the chances are . . . even though he might hang on a while, he might very well die."

"In that case," Ruth darted him a serious look, her brow grim. "I really don't think we should get attached to him. It's hard enough with these wild animals you bring home, only to give them up, one way or another. You know how Judy *loves* her teddy bear. It'd tear her heart out if she got to know this cub and then he didn't make it."

The two went to join Judy and Don in the living room. Judy bounced on the couch and exclaimed, "A real bear cub! Can't I see him?"

Ruth answered, "Not for a while, anyway. He's a very sick little bear. You do want him to get well, don't you?" She turned to Ray, "Now tell us all about the fire, and how in the world you ended up with a young cub."

Chapter 17

It is a miserable thing to live in suspense; it is the life of a spider.
–Jonathan Swift

Believe, you were not born in vain . . . Stop trembling. Prepare to live.
–Gustav Mahler

Smokey awoke the next day with the feeling he'd fallen into a dark hole. How long had it been? Was this the next day? He stirred, trying to find a comfortable position, and whimpered, "Uh-ruh."

Lightning greeted him. "I'm so glad you're okay! I've been wondering: Aren't you awfully young to be away from your mother?"

"She's dead," he replied in a small, sad voice. "She died in that big fire."

"I'm sorry, little bear . . . So who's your *other* family? I mean to say, are you someone's pet?"

"What's a 'pet'?"

"Oh, my. You *are* from the *country*! Except for that terrible time in the Wilds and the city, I've always been a pet. It means I live with humans."

Smokey remembered how Strut had lived with humans for a while, and yet his mother had warned him that humans shot and killed bears. "How do you tell which humans are good?"

"Good question." Lightning paced around her cage. "I better be adopted soon. I belong in the suburbs: a house, decent food and a litter box. Ahh, to be contented, as befits by nature, a beloved pet in a respectable home." Then she cried, "Yooow. I hate waiting in this cage!"

Smokey joined in yowling, "I want to go home to the mountains!" His throat hurt but crying out felt good.

The cat stopped yowling and looked at him. "Oh, Smokey dear, you're too little. You can't survive in the Wilds without your mother."

Smokey frowned at her and then lowered his head toward the floor of the cage. He remembered how his mother planned to show him where in the forest he could find food in the different seasons. Now, if he went back to the forest alone, how could he find berries and acorns by himself? Or learn how to catch fish?

Lightning said, "I'm sorry I've been so tactless. But Smokey, perhaps you could be a pet like me."

He lifted sad eyes to Lightning. "But how could I get food in a house? The food here makes me queasy just to smell it."

"You certainly don't look well-fed. A young animal like you should have a rounded belly, like puppies do."

"What if I'm cooped up in a house and get terribly hungry?"

"Don't worry, my darling. Humans will give you scrumptious food — eventually. Refuse food that doesn't smell good till they proffer something more pleasing.

"I'm sure, given you're so young and cuddly, you'll become a pet, Smokey. So let me give you some advice: No matter how tempted, don't harm another household pet. And never hurt a human child — not even a scratch. They're precious to adults. If one grabs or hugs you in a displeasing way, maintain your dignity and just leave the scene."

Smokey imagined living with humans, felt afraid and asked in a small tight voice, "Lightning, may I ask you something?"

"Anything."

"If we do both become pets, can we still be friends? I like to hear your stories, like I used to do with my friend the crow. And I'll need your advice about how to live with humans — if that's to be my fate."

The cat perked up, sat on her haunches facing him again, and sighed with satisfaction. "Dear little bear, I'd like nothing better than to stay friends with you. Let's hope it can happen."

She turned and pleaded to the wall behind her, "I don't want to be put to sleep! Someone has to adopt me—and the little fellow, too."

"What are you saying? Tell me it's going to be okay!"

"Yes, little he-bear. I know you're sick and hungry. That's why I've tried to fill your belly with stories. It's the best I can do."

Smokey remained with his head resting between his front paws. After a long silence, Lightning's wistful voice turned fervent. "Someone must adopt us!"

Three days went by, and Smokey became much weaker. He didn't eat any food the vet brought. After a while, hungry and hurting, he didn't care what happened to him, and meekly submitted to the vet changing his bandages. Lightning, too, dozed a lot and became increasingly despondent. Whenever someone opened the door, the cat roused herself to pose in a statuesque way, hoping to be adopted, but was disappointed each time.

Then, late one afternoon after closing hours, the two animals heard someone turn the door knob and creep in. It was the vet's ten-year-old son, Tom. Lightning arched her back and spat at him, but Tom's voice quickly soothed her. He turned to face the cub's cage and slipped something under the door. It was a slice of honey-laden bread.

Smokey was intrigued with the sweet smell he remembered from the honey-tree. He slurped up the thick golden liquid and pushed the bread back to Tom. "I knew you'd like this! Much better than that stuff my dad foists on you, isn't it?" The famished cub shook with eagerness, and cried out, "Uh, uh!" so the boy slipped a second honey-laden piece of bread to the little bear.

Lightning let out a yowl. Tom poked his finger through her cage to rub her cheek and the cat purred loudly. After that, each day after the clinic closed, Smokey and Lightning listened to the empty corridor outside, alert to the approach of Tom's stealthy steps and the arrival of honey for the bear, and comfort for the cat.

During the daytime the cub rarely raised his head. A week passed before he heard a welcome voice outside the door. In strode his friend Ray in his cowboy hat, sporting a wide grin and holding the hand of a little girl. She ran up to his cage. "You poor teddy bear!" Smokey sniffed her. He liked the soft female smell of this little human, and responded with small chirps, "Eh-eh." He had been lying flat on the floor of his cage, but rose on wobbly legs to press his nose against the wire mesh of the door, his small eyes searching her face.

Ray said, "See, Judy, he's a cinnamon-colored bear. Isn't he cute with those long eyelashes and tan eyebrows?"

"And look, Daddy. He has round ears that stick up just like Mickey Mouse." She fiddled with the door latch.

"CAREFUL!" Ray's voice cut the air. "Sweetheart, he may look small and weak, but he's still a *wild* animal." Before he could stop her, Judy had unlatched the door and opened it wide. The little bear lifted his nose to her and snuffled noisily. His big ears spread outward with a pleased look on his face. The little four-year-old leaned forward, and though he was very weak, he leaned forward to slow-lick her closed eyes. "Well," Ray said, "It looks like love at first sight!"

The vet, who had been standing in the doorway, interrupted. He told them that the cub was getting progressively weaker. "I'm keeping him hydrated, but he won't eat. I've tried formulas that usually work with young animals, but he doesn't like any of them. He hasn't gained an ounce, and he's still only half the weight he should be. It's a mystery to me how he's managed to live this long."

The curly-haired girl pleaded with her father, "We have to save him! Let's take him home to Mom. She knows how to feed wild animals. Please!"

Ray looked over at the vet. After a long moment, Ed said,

"Well, it's worth a try. Otherwise, he'll die. Let's take him to the next room. I'll show you how to change his bandages so you can pick him up in the morning." Ed gathered the lax body of the cub in his arms, and the two men left, motioning Judy to stay in the room.

A commanding "Yeoow" brought Judy's attention to the upper cage. Lightning rumbled a loud purr. The girl beamed and clapped her hands about finding a striped cat—exactly what her best friend Barbara had been wanting. The girl's reaction portended good news for Lightning and her eyes glistened. But when Ray returned to the room, they both departed without her.

The next day, May 16th, the animals were waiting expectantly when Ray and Judy returned. This time another girl as small as Judy came with them. At first, Ray tried to pull Smokey from his cage, but the cub clung to the wire-mesh floor with the claws of his hind feet. Ray let go, allowed the cub to smell his fist, then slowly spread his palms under the cub's body and gathered him to his chest.

Meanwhile, Judy had pointed out the tiger-striped cat to the other four-year-old. Judy rose on tiptoes, unlatched the cage, and signaled her friend Barbara to reach up. Lightning leaped, and almost knocked the girl off balance before the youngster could draw her close. Lightning purred loudly, enchanted with Barbara, hoping she had found a home at last.

But a few moments later, to the cat's disappointment, she was returned to her cage. Barbara stroked her one more time before swinging the door closed. Lightning examined her face, and wished she knew what the girl was saying to her. The tone was promising. "I'll have to ask my parents," Barbara was saying. "They'll *have* to let me adopt you."

Before Smokey knew what was happening, he was being carried out the door by Ray, with the two girls waving back at Lightning. The two animals realized they were being separated—perhaps forever. Smokey craned his neck to take one last look at his cat friend. His throat ached at one more good-bye in his life, and Lightning gave him a wide-eyed look of dismay.

Fortunately, as Ray drove home, the cub lay quietly in his lap. Pulling up in the driveway, Ray scooped Smokey into his arms and motioned Judy to open the front door of the house. They fast-walked past Ruth—her hands on her hips, her eyes cool, red hair blazing. Without exchanging a word with her, the two proceeded past the living room to the small laundry room at the back of the house. While Judy fetched towels and newspapers, Ray cleared a space along the wall. He peeled the cub's claws from his shirt and lowered him onto the floor. The cub nudged Ray's hand with his furry muzzle, making him chuckle softly. The man lifted the cub momentarily so Judy could lay down towels, and Smokey fell promptly asleep in his new bed.

The family's black cocker spaniel came barking and bounding from the back yard to crash against the outside door. Ray yelled, "Jet, sit!" The four-month-old puppy kept barking, throwing his weight against the door and clawing it. The man called through the screened top-half of the wooden door, "Jet, you nut, sit! STAY!" Ray motioned the dog with his hand, then let his arm drop to his side. "Okay, we might as well let you in, and see how you two get along."

Judy undid the latch and the puppy leaped in, then skidded to a stop just inside the threshold. Baffled, he sniffed noisily. He cocked his head to the side and his big brown eyes questioned Ray. He then sprawled on his back with his legs sticking up, showing his pink speckled belly. Ray stroked his smooth stomach. "It's okay, Jet. Just another wild animal, too tuckered out to do you any harm."

Fortified by the reassuring voice and soothing touch, the cocker succumbed to his curiosity. He rolled his flexible body onto his stomach, then plastered himself on the floor like a frog. With his back legs splayed flat behind him, he wiggled slowly toward the newcomer in the corner. He sniffed the fur, shook his head vigorously, and sneezed. Then he gathered his legs under him, scooted back and thrust himself between Ray's boots. Giggling, Judy knelt down and petted the silky black body and whispered, "Just you wait. You two can be friends, I know you can!"

That night Smokey met the human mother of the household as he awoke from a beautiful daze, being rocked and cradled against Ruth's bosom. She was humming softly. He snuggled closer to the sweet smell and sounds of a mothering animal. He spied Judy seated on the sofa at her side holding a small cup. The thick paste of goat milk, Pablum and honey smelled good. Then he felt fingers press against the sides of his jaw, his mouth opened, and Ruth's finger rubbed the paste against his gums and dabbed it at the back of his mouth and throat until he swallowed. He eagerly smacked his lips for more.

Judy clapped her hands. "Oh, Mom! I knew you could do it. He likes it! But why can't he have any more?"

"One teaspoon is enough for now. We don't want to make him sick."

Ruth fed the tiny cub twelve times a day for the next two days. Ray protested at the alarm clock ringing every two hours during the night, but Ruth prevailed, telling him, "I'll feed the cub *my* way or you can take him back to the vet!"

Before long, Smokey was lying on his back like an infant against Ruth's body while Judy handed her mother a warm baby bottle. Ruth dribbled a few drops of the formula onto her little finger, and brushed it against Smokey's mouth, then gently parted his lips for him to taste. When he eagerly warbled for more, Ruth tilted the bottle to his mouth, and his lips searched desperately to latch onto the rubber nipple. At first he sucked with loud gasping sounds, and pushed his bandaged paws so eagerly against the bottle that Ruth had to hold it firmly. Then he settled into a very loud, but contented cooing-chuckling hum, with a staccato pulsating rhythm to it.

Twice a day, Smokey had to undergo being assaulted by the men in the family. Ray and Don would grab him. He'd bawl at them, his eyes spitting fury. When Don then gripped the loose skin on the back of Smokey's neck, he'd squirm to bite and claw him. Despite the cub's best efforts, the teenager always managed to wrestle him to the floor and hold him down. Then Ray crouched and hovered over him.

Smokey screeched loudly and his eyes widened in panic, knowing that the painful process of ripping off the bandages would come next. At the end, the application of salve was a welcome relief, and afterward he didn't mind so much being bound with new bandages.

The procedure was traumatic not only for the cub but also for Ray and Don. Eventually, when the wounds became less raw and hardly bled any more, the bandaging was turned over to Ruth. By then, though, Smokey had developed a grudge against the cowboy as his torturer, and, to a lesser extent, against Don. From then on, he often lay in wait to pounce on Ray and bite him on the leg.

It was different for Ruth. And later on, under close supervision, she even let Judy feed Smokey — unless the cub was in an irritable mood. Mother and daughter would sit together on the concrete stoop out back, Smokey in the girl's little arms. He'd squall and open his mouth wide, showing the pink inside, then wrap his front paws around the girl's slender arm holding the bottle, his pads pressing into her arm. As soon as he finished one bottle, the cub shrieked desperately for the next, so Ruth handed it over quickly to avoid the possibility of Judy being nipped.

The girl loved feeling the cub's taut warm body against hers, and hearing the burbled purring as he fed. She'd accompany him with her own cooing and tuneless songs until his body relaxed into deep sleep.

Once a few days had passed with Smokey sharing the back room with Jet, he took comfort in smelling the puppy's distinctive scent nearby. At first the cub had mostly slept, although the irrepressible puppy tried to coax him from his bed. Finally, one morning Jet splayed himself on the floor, belly-down, so close that the cub could stretch forth his neck to go nose-to-nose with the black cocker spaniel. They sniffed each other with great interest. Although the sick cub quickly retreated to sleep some more, that afternoon the cub succumbed to the puppy's playful invitation to scamper about a little—and thus began their friendship.

Smokey safe

Chapter 18

You must skate to where the puck is going, not to where it is.
–Wayne Gretzky

The important point is that a continuity is a historical trajectory in which, if you know what happened yesterday, you have a pretty good idea what's going to happen tomorrow. A contingency is an event that was completely unpredictable and utterly changes everything.
–Walter Alvarez.

A week before, back on the afternoon of May 10th, Ray Bell, after leaving the cub at the vet hospital, had been itching to go home and wash off the grime from the fire. Instead, he heaved out a breath, and headed to his office. On the way there, he rehearsed how to approach his superior, the Chief Game Warden of New Mexico, Elliott S. Barker. Ray could feel his chest bursting with the notion that there was something special about the cub. How could he possibly explain the odd hunch that had driven him to rescue the little guy? How could he justify his strong conviction that they should do everything possible to keep him alive? He didn't even know himself why the bear seemed so important to him.

It was crucial that he get Elliott Barker's strong backing about the rescue and the cub's future—assuming the bear might live. Ray knew that from the get-go he'd do well to toe the line and observe the government chain of command, starting with Barker—a powerhouse of a man. Barker was already a legend, fiercely protecting the state's millions of acres of forest and wildlife. He could be a powerful adversary, and had successfully prosecuted lawbreakers, whether a lieutenant governor, state troopers, or poachers.

Ray knew that Elliott Barker was also a bold champion of new ideas. The two men had a special affinity, both being westerners from their beginnings. Elliott had come West in a covered wagon as a child, as Ray had, the older man having come much earlier—in 1896. Both had started out as cowboys, and they had also known each other as neighbors back in Tesuque, where they had hunted and fished together.

It dawned on Ray how strange his request might appear to the chief. He must somehow make some sense of what had happened: the devastation of the fire and the condition of the bear with its uncertain fate. He needed to be diplomatic—and wily as a fox—while still telling the truth to Barker.

By the time Ray approached Barker's office, he still hadn't figured out what to say. As a man of action, he strode in the open door anyway, and blurted out a quick report: his aerial reconnaissance of the fire, his observations on the ground while firefighting, and the current status of the fire. Before he knew it, Barker had stood up and come around the desk to shake his hand. His eyes shined a hearty welcome to Ray, bespeaking his relief to see him alive. They both knew the calculated risks Ray had to take. As the first and only New Mexico State wildlife pilot, Ray had crashed many a plane on the job and so far had always walked away from wrecks. It was a hazardous job—to fly very low over fires, forests and lakes despite poor visibility or gusts of wind.

A sensible rule popped into Ray's mind: Always make a direct request to an administrator for a specific action. So he informed the older man that the fire crews needed six Handy-Talky radios, and he wanted permission to fly them to Capitan the next morning. Elliott nodded, and paused. Ray heeded the silent prompting. He knew that Barker had an uncanny ability to read his men. The discerning face conveyed to Ray that his boss was patiently expecting to hear more.

Ray liked Barker. After all, Barker had taken a gamble in hiring Ray despite the cowboy's lack of educational qualifications for the job. In turn, Ray had the highest respect for Elliott. So he'd better say what he really wanted — and hope for the best.

The cowboy continued: And while he was in Capitan, he could fly the fire to map remaining hot spots . . . and he'd also like to take some photographs of the still-burning forest. He was sure he could find a photographer to get some good shots. Ray hesitated. Barker waited. Ray blurted out that he had rescued a cub from the fire, and, in case the cub lived, why not take some photos of the sick bear sometime soon? Pictures might come in handy someday.

Waiting for Barker's answer, Ray stood in his usual casual stance and held his Stetson in front of him. He turned the brim slowly, trying not to show his concern. Barker had clout. The man could catch the twig of an idea, or snap the branch off.

"Okay, go ahead," Barker said, with that wise smile of his. "Why not?"

The cowboy nodded and broke into a wide grin.

Ray stopped by his own desk and phoned his close friend, Harold Walter. Could he drop everything and fly down to Capitan the next morning? Harold said he'd be delighted. Ray wasn't surprised at the response. The photographer had a keen interest in taking pictures of the wilderness and wildlife, and although he did professional quality work, he never accepted a fee, always giving away his photographs. And he jumped at the idea of a rescued cub. Perhaps, Harold suggested, photographs would be a great way to link the live bear to the Forest Service's old Smokey, the poster bear.

It was as if the phone receiver in Ray's ear crackled with electricity. Ray said, "You mean make him a 'live Smokey Bear'? That's great!" Up to then, his ideas had been half-baked, but now Ray saw where he had been headed all along: A live Smokey!

They agreed that the first step would be to take photographs of the burned forest where Smokey had been found, and so the next morning before dawn the men excitedly pushed the little Super Cruiser out of the hanger onto the runway. Harold Walter — a calm-looking man with a tall, rangy frame — reached up and carefully placed his big new reflex camera, a 4 by 5 Pacemaker Speed Graphic, into the plane, jumped the prop, and hopped in.

There were no instruments except a compass to navigate through the heavy ground fog, so Ray flew south to Capitan over rangeland hardly discernible below. Daybreak finally revealed the road approaching the village. Ray's immediate tasks were to deliver the Handy-Talky radios and, after dropping off Harold near the mop-up crews, survey the progress of the fire crews across the mountain. Once he'd flown low over the smoking and blackened areas and assured himself that the fire had not flared up again, he joined Harold on the ground. While mist still hung on the mountain, the photographer took a picture of Ray and Ranger Dean Earl among the smoldering embers.

Ray and Dean among the embers

Dean told them he'd found burned deer carcasses on the mountain, and that someone had seen wild turkeys fly into the fire.

Ray and Harold were tempted to locate and shoot the small rock slide where Speed Simmons' crew had survived the fire, and also the nearby area where the cub had been found, but it turned out to be impossible. The sites were too far up the steep mountainside to climb up and back—and still allow time for a return flight to Santa Fe before dark.

As they flew back, Ray swore Harold to secrecy about their ideas for the cub and the photographs. It still wasn't clear whether the bear would live. Plus, if he was to push for a 'live Smokey Bear,' Ray needed to carefully pave the way with the higher-ups in the Forest Service. As soon as Ray's groundwork was laid, he told Harold, they could have a photo session with Smokey.

But the next morning, Ray was thunderstruck by the headlined story in the *Santa Fe New Mexican* newspaper. It told about the rescue of a tiny bear from the fire at the Lincoln National Forest. Moreover, it had a prominent photograph of the cub with Doc Smith! Somehow, it had been taken back at the vet's office by a newspaper photographer.

How had the story leaked? Ray was startled to see that the caption called the cub "Teddy with a Hotfoot." It was a catchy name, but it didn't sound right to Ray. Instead of the bear cub he knew, it brought to his mind some kind of stuffed toy.

No one anticipated then that the name Hot Foot Teddy would catch the fancy of a group that would endure into the next century, its numerous members enthusiastically collecting posters and memorabilia of the original Smokey Bear and honoring the live bear with a newsletter and conventions across the country.

Despite Ray's misgivings about the bear cub being publicized before he'd laid careful plans in the bureaucracy, he felt compelled—more than ever—to capture his own pictures of the wounded cub. The next week Harold came to the Bells' home, laden with photographic equipment. He also had large Forest Service posters of the traditional Smokey Bear.

In the living room the photographer popped flashbulbs for his first photos. The cub flinched at the bright light and sounds, and Ray worried about harming his sensitive ears, but it soon turned out that the bear didn't seem to mind. He'd just been

Smokey poses with posters

startled at first. Harold took photos for hours, hoping for a lucky shot until the weak little bear became sluggish and crawled away to hide. They let him rest.

While they were waiting, it occurred to the two men that people might like to see the baby bear with a small child. The photographer asked Ruth whether Judy might be enlisted for a picture. She agreed and the four-year-old put on her usual western outfit—dungarees, suspenders and cowboy boots. Harold asked the little cowgirl to sit on the floor. On the wall behind the curly-haired child he taped a poster of the famous

Smokey Bear in his ranger hat, holding a shovel.

Ray had been helping the photographer set up the scenes, and he tried to shove the little bear toward Judy while she sat patiently on the floor. However, by this time Smokey had become irritable. The cub was fed up with being chased, grabbed from under furniture, and pushed this way and that. He wanted only to be left alone to sleep. He suddenly lowered his head and flattened his ears in warning, and before Ray could back off, nipped him with tiny razor-sharp teeth. Ray stood, shaking his punctured hand and swearing under his breath. They took another short break.

Ruth watched warily, knowing that once Ray wanted something, he persisted until he got his way. Her husband took a break to shower Judy with praise for sitting in a pose for such a long time. And Judy didn't resist. The bright-eyed youngster was a trooper, enchanted with her Daddy. He was now laughing with her, and catching the girl's eye, wearing the same Robert Ryan smile the ranch hand had used to charm the red-headed Ruth on her father's ranch.

Frustrated that the cub refused to approach Judy on his own, Ray asked his teenage son, Don, to fetch honey from the kitchen. Holding open the jar under the cub's nose, Ray moved it toward Judy and the bear followed his nose. Then, crouching, Ray smeared a big gob on Judy's polished cowboy boot. Smokey sniffed, licked the honey, and mouthed the boot. Harold moved in for a close up. The camera popped in Smokey's face. The cub winced and cried, "Eh-eh-eh."

"Wait a minute! Before you take any more pictures—" Ruth's voice interrupted the men. She held the photographer's arm to take him aside. "That flashgun's too close. It scares him, and I've a hunch the noise hurts his ears. I'll take down this painting off the wall and you can move the poster over here. It's a sunny wall—so you won't need the flash." Harold readily agreed. The room was rearranged, and the bright mid-morning sunlight flooded the wall, highlighting Judy and the poster.

The setting was ready, and Judy was still obliging.

However, as Ruth watched Ray smear honey on Judy's knee, then her chin, she scowled. She sensed her daughter's uneasiness as the cub had become more aggravated. Having had many rescued animals in her home, she was well aware of how unpredictable wild animals were, especially one that could be aggressive, like a bear. And this little fellow had been getting more and more irritated throughout the morning.

But she chose not to say anything. Growing up a rancher's daughter, Ruth was used to risks, and Ray took many risks, mostly well-calculated ones. She knew the kind of man he was, and she loved him because of it—and despite it. There was no stopping him anyway.

Ruth had become accustomed to the ease with which Ray threw himself into danger, and she had learned to close off her worry. During the years on the rodeo circuit early in their marriage, she had become good at appearing unruffled, and, as it turned out, Ray hadn't ever gotten badly hurt in rodeo, just banged up now and then—nothing worse than broken ribs.

Nevertheless, she couldn't help feeling occasional qualms when her husband flew the small plane in reconnaissance over fires or in remote wilderness through dust and snow storms. She knew he must skim close to tree tops and canyons—his plane had been especially retrofitted to fly low, and he'd obtained a special state license to pilot it. He was good at what he did, loved his work, and had always walked away from the inevitable crashes.

She didn't mind that he packed guns and used them. After all, she herself took her six-shooter when she went camping. Ray's dozens of trophies as a crack shot made him more than a match for anyone he came up against in his job as chief law enforcement officer in the wilderness. And Ruth had gotten used to his leaving her for days at a time without any communication while he went off into the vast wilderness—helping sheriffs track criminals and find lost people, flying low to seed high altitude lakes with fish, surveying mountains and rescuing animals. Like other men raised as cowboys, Ray was blasé about physical danger. From her long experience with the man, she had to concur with a remark their son Don once made, "Dad has no fear."

Now, as her daughter sat waiting for Smokey to pose with her, Ruth knew that her husband was absolutely determined to get his photographs. The woman stayed out of camera range, but she hovered close to Judy, ready to grab her daughter from danger. Ruth lifted her chin and caught her son's eye, so Don moved into position on the other side of Judy. He was quick-moving like his father and ready to pounce on Smokey if the bear made any move to harm the girl. Ruth knew she could absolutely count on Don. Ever since, at eleven, he had carried Judy as a baby in his arms, he had shown a profound love for his little sister and was always very protective of her.

Smokey licks Judy's chin

Inch by inch, Smokey licked his way up the honey trail on Judy's dungarees. He crawled up her pants leg and put his front paws on her shirt. As he licked her chin, Judy giggled but held steady. Ray beamed.

And so, on May 21st Harold had scored his photograph of the little bear and the young girl — a photograph that was soon to become famous across the country.

Ruth glowered at Ray, and he tilted his head and rolled his eyes at her in apology. He knew he was in trouble for endangering Judy's throat and face, but not in as much trouble as if Judy had been bitten.

After she lifted Smokey up from her daughter's lap, Ruth aimed piercing eyes at Ray. Then she showed him the cub's feet. "Look what you've done! It's hardly two weeks since the fire!" The man had removed Smokey's bandages for the photography session, not realizing that the tender pads of the wounded paws would crack and bleed. Ray looked a little sheepish, but held up his own hands, bitten and bleeding, and shrugged, as if to say, "That's the way of the West: Men and animals endure all sorts of hardship." Meanwhile Don had brought salve, and Ruth gently spread it on the cub's pads, then handed him over to Ray to re-apply the bandages. Let him wrestle with the irate bear!

Harold developed the photographs in his home that afternoon, and showed them to Ray. They were so elated with the results that the two men determined to get more photographs. However, the next day Smokey was in a particularly bad mood. He was quick to escape clutching hands, running every which way, and hardly stayed still a moment to be photographed. He bit them every chance he had.

The men often took time out, and tried to persuade the cub gently with honey. Their hard-won results were a picture of Smokey Bear outdoors with Ray holding a coke bottle, another of the cub on top of the airplane, and one in front of the poster bear, as if the older Smokey were looking down sympathetically at the forlorn, sick little cub.

When the photography session was ended, Ray sat on the floor at home near Smokey. "I know you're mad at me, little bear, and I'm sorry to put you through all that." Upon hearing the softened voice, Smokey looked up, the whites of his eyes showing.

"You have to live! And you're going to live!" Ray said, scratching the cub's chest. "From now on, I'm going to call you 'Little Smokey.' Perhaps a time will come when you'll actually have some kind of career.

Little Smokey and Ray Courtesy of Don Bell

Smokey and Ray at airport

Smokey's had enough!

Chapter 19

One does not meet oneself until one catches the reflection from an eye other than human. –Loren Eisley

Don — Courtesy of Don Bell

As time went on, instead of twice a day, Smokey needed a bandage change only at night. It had been Don's job to hold the cub while his father changed bandages. After several days, the boy saw that the cub's once-bloody paws were almost healed, although his underbelly and tail still showed pink raw skin. Lately, trying to hold the bear down, Don could tell how much stronger Smokey had become. The cub fought much more vigorously, and could occasionally even twist out of the boy's grasp to nip him. His father told him that the cub undoubtedly thought they were deliberately torturing him, but it was the men's job to be the 'bad guys.' Smokey couldn't realize that because of him and his Dad, the cub's paws had almost healed.

It seemed unfair to Don. The cub never bit Ruth or Judy. He was sweet as could be with them! When he came home from school, sometimes Don saw his little sister carrying Smokey in her arms, showing him different rooms in the house. And if her mother wasn't around, Judy would sometimes set the cub on the carpet. He would totter on his bandaged feet, following the girl's retreating ankles as she circled the living room couch. Jet twirled around them, play-bowing to the cub, his short tail up in the air tick-tocking back and forth, trying to entice Smokey to chase him. To the dog's delight, the cub pursued him with a few bursts of speed before he flopped down, exhausted.

Don knew Smokey was eating more because he was leaving more dung. It was the teenager's job to clean it up, like it or not. He hated the foul smell of bear dung, but at least Smokey was careful to use the newspaper in the corner of the back room.

One day, after school, Don was coming home along the Old Santa Fe Trail. He kicked a loose stone on the sidewalk, moving it along like a soccer ball. He turned onto his street, Coronado, where the slight incline meant the stone moved more readily.

At one point, upon straightening up—after loosening the stone from a groove along the sidewalk—Don took a gander down the street. He liked the way it looked. The homes were small like the ones in Capitan, but here in Santa Fe they had a softened Spanish look. Almost all were one-storied, flat-roofed adobe houses, arrayed in pleasing colors that changed from bright to pale pastel depending on how the sunlight hit them. Some were creamy or bright yellow, others reddish like brick, or pinkish-tan like clay. One was glaring white in the afternoon sun, but very dark on its shadow-side. Almost every house had a small front yard enclosed by a thick rounded adobe wall no higher than his waist. As he went by the walls, he saw lizards scurry away. A garter snake sunning on a flagstone walkway stayed put.

It was a warm spring day in May. He couldn't wait for school to be over. Before they'd moved to Santa Fe earlier in spring, he had wondered how he'd fit in at the city school. Although they'd lived within the six square blocks of houses back in the village of Capitan, he'd always gravitated to the ranch kids who lived a ways out of town. He'd often hung out at their ranches after school and helped with their chores, cleaning saddles and mucking out stables, so afterward they could round up some horses and go riding.

Since his parents had both grown up on ranches, most of their family friends in Capitan had been ranchers, some, like his dad, having joined the state Game and Fish Department, the US Forest Service, or law enforcement. He'd often come home to find his father at the kitchen table with a sheriff — putting their heads together to hunt for someone in the wilderness, or just telling each other tall tales over coffee.

Before they had moved, Don had been concerned that the city kids in Santa Fe might dress up for school, so he might stick out like a sore thumb in his Levis. But he had found many ranch kids here, too. And lots of sports — with great teams.

He'd expected classes to be harder. Like everyone back in his village, he had thought the big city of Santa Fe would be far ahead in everything. But it had turned out that his small classes at the Capitan high school had been more advanced than the big city's classes, so he had found himself bored. Finals wouldn't be that difficult. Then he'd be free to be outdoors for the summer.

Just two more weeks now, he thought. As he neared home, he raised his eyes from kicking his soccer-stone and saw his father's pickup whiz by, swerve into the driveway and brake, gravel rattling. Something was up. By the time Don sprinted over, Ray had already opened the back door.

"Here, take this," his father said, and thrust a brown ball of fur into Don's hands. It was a baby beaver. He added, "And come back for another. I've got the whole family. Have your mother run some water in the bathtub. No way can they chew their way out of a tub! Though we'll have to remember to keep the bathroom door closed just in case the big ones climb out. Don't forget: Have your mother start that water right away."

"But won't he drown? Can a beaver kit swim?" The little

furry animal pressed against his shirt and looked up at him with shiny eyes and a nose like a dark button.

"Don't worry. He's only a month old. He'll float like a cork. Can't even dive underwater yet."

Baby Beaver   GORDON ILLG

Don cradled the kit in his cupped palms while Ruth ran the water. The baby beaver didn't weigh much more than Smokey — only a few pounds. When Don bent his head, the kit looked at him with inquiring eyes, and the boy's heart leapt. At that moment he felt especially lucky that his father was a tender-hearted game warden and animal-lover, even though it usually meant Don had to clean up animal poop — whether porcupine, bobcat or hawk. And get clawed, bitten, or, in the case of a young deer once, kicked in the stomach.

Wait till his friends heard about the beavers! They'd be dying to see them up close. He popped the little guy into the tub where it bobbed on top of the water. Then the boy spun around and went back to the pickup for another.

After Don had plunked the second kit in the water, he returned to the pickup again. Ray motioned for him to take a full-grown beaver with thick fur in a warm shade of brown. It looked big — nearly forty pounds — and Don hesitated. "What about his teeth? They could be a couple of inches long!"

His father said, "Yeah, I know. He could cut you to the bone if he wanted. But beavers are almost always nice around people. I've never been bitten or even scratched. Real sweethearts, especially the males. Here, take the father." Don gingerly took the round bundle of fur from his dad.

"Hold on, son! He's so roly-poly—he'll roll right out of your arms. Get a hold of the far hind leg . . . that's it. Now cross your other arm underneath and hold onto the closest front leg. That-a-way. Good."

The moment Don felt the big fat beaver settle firmly in his arms, the youngster stood still in wonder, surprised at how trusting the wild animal was. He exclaimed, "Why can't Smokey be like this?" The beaver leaned into the teen's chest and wrapped its webbed hind feet around his arm. With one front hand, the animal held onto Don's thumb. The boy swallowed and let out a short laugh of recognition. The feel of its trusting grip around his thumb felt just like Judy's small hand when she'd held his thumb as a baby.

Ray said, "Stick your face in his fur. Doesn't he smell clean and fresh? Beavers smell the best of any animal I know."

"Amazing! He smells just like willows."

"No wonder. That's their favorite food."

Don had seen beavers only from a distance, and their flat oval tails had looked hard and scaly. Curious, he ran his fingers over the surface of the tail. To his surprise, it was thick leathery skin with a raised pattern, like fine tool-work on a saddle. The beaver looked up at him with small intelligent eyes, and sniffed.

Ray said, "He's full of mud from the trapping. And we got the whole family. Go ahead and take him to the tub. He'll be glad to wash it off. I'll follow with the mother."

As soon as the men reached the bathtub, Judy came running, took one look at the beaver kits and said, "I'll go get Jet and Smokey. So they can see the beavers, too!" and dashed toward the back room.

Ray yelled, "Judy, stop!" but she paid no attention. Jet came lolloping in from the back room, barking excitedly, with Smokey galumphing behind him. The two men quickly dumped the adult beavers in the tub and took positions to block the bathroom doorway. Ray pounced on Smokey while Don grabbed Jet and held tight so the puppy couldn't wiggle out of his arms.

After they had both returned from releasing the two scamps into the back room and closed the door, Judy scrunched up her face in an angry scowl and stomped her foot. "That was mean! Why can't they have any fun?" Her father squatted to her eye level and explained he didn't want Jet to bark his head off and scare the beavers. And the beavers would be able to smell that Smokey was a bear and it would frighten them terribly.

"But Smokey's just a *little* bear—smaller than a cat. He can't hurt them."

"Listen! Bears are the big enemy of beavers. They chase beavers if they find them on land. They wade into beaver ponds and tear apart their lodges to *eat* beavers. Smokey would seem like a monster to them. You wouldn't want the bear to scare these cute little beavers to death, would you? Come on, let's watch them ourselves."

The Bells knelt on the bathroom floor and watched the members of the beaver family reunite in the tub. The beaver parents and youngsters touched each other with their hands, made joyous humming-buzzing sounds, and clicked their teeth. Ray said, "That's what I hear when I go by a beaver lodge—like a concert. All the different generations—sounding happy in their home. You know, they mate for life. That's why I wanted to keep this little family together."

Ray and Don returned to the pickup for armfuls of willow branches. When the food arrived, the adult beavers were cleaning themselves, sitting in the partly-filled tub with their hands busy scrubbing and combing their cheeks, chests and bellies to make their fur glisten. At the men's arrival, they interrupted their cleaning. Eyes glowing and making small barks of pleasure, they reached for the branches. With their little five-fingered hands they stripped off the leaves and buds to eat. They broke off twigs and clutched each small stick upright with both hands to eat it from the top—like rabbits eating carrots. Then they took the larger branches, holding pieces of the wood on each end to chew the bark across in one direction, then they rotated the wood to chew in the other direction—like people eating corn-on-the-cob.

After a while, the mother beaver gathered the kits to nurse at teats that were hardly visible through her thick fur. Just then, the father beaver stood and stretched. His fists were doubled in front of his stomach and he opened his mouth in a big yawn. Judy pointed, "Look how orange his teeth are!"

Ray replied, "Yeah, they're always bright orange like that. Judy, don't you just *love* beavers? We'll have to find a rancher who'll really appreciate them. Not plan to kill them—like that so-and-so I rescued them from. I couldn't convince the guy how good the beavers would be for his ranch land. At least he let me live-trap them, instead of shooting them or drowning them in a deathtrap. I'll give him credit for that . . . In fact, I know someone who'd probably like to have these little engineers. To keep the land from flooding, and some day make a nice meadow with a good water table. I'll call right now."

Ray bolted to the phone, talked briefly, and came back. "So, Don, how about helping me drop off the beavers at Miller Ranch? Come to think of it, there's a rodeo near there, starting tomorrow. Ever since I got back from the war, I've been wanting to take you to one. We missed doing so many things together while I was away at war all those years . . . I suppose you don't even remember how we went to rodeos before I left—you were such a little squirt."

"No, I haven't forgotten. But Dad, tomorrow's Friday—a school day."

"Don't worry. I'll call the principal. It's another 'wildlife emergency,' don't you think?" They caught each other's eyes and grinned. This was not the first time.

Don loved nothing better than to skip school and escape with his father in the pickup, or even better, sit in the plane beside him, flying low to the ground and helping look for poachers, illegal trappers, or whatever. Not long ago, Don had been the one in the plane to spot a troop of lost Boy Scouts in the wilderness. But driving to the rodeo in the pickup with his Dad would be just fine.

Chapter 20

Life is like a rodeo – you can fight the bull's every buck and be worn to a frazzle (if you aren't gored first), or you can match your movements to your mount and see where it takes you.
–Janine Benyus

Ray   Courtesy of Don Bell

The next morning Ray and Don worked swiftly together to rig up the back of the pickup: tarp to shield the beavers from sun and wind, and ice bags to drip cold water onto the cages to keep them cool enough. They loaded the beavers and set off.

As usual, the western men were quiet for a while. Suddenly Don gave a short cough and blurted out that Smokey deserved to be treated like a member of the family. When he came home from school, Don said, he often found the cub whimpering pitiably. The little tyke must be terribly bored cooped up in that little back room. Why not let him stay in the yard with Jet during the day, and play in the house in the evenings? Couldn't he even go for walks in the neighborhood? After all, he'd grown up wild and was used to being free. Another thing: It bothered Don to see the bear hobble so awkwardly on bandaged feet. Wasn't it about time to let him go without bandages?

Ray was quiet a moment. He liked the way his son thought, and told him that he'd consider it. Then, after a pause, he spoke again. During all those years he'd been away at war, had Don done any cowboying back in Capitan?

A storyteller like his father, the boy told how he'd liked going out to a friend's ranch after school. The guys would muck the horse stalls, then have a chance to do some steer wrestling. One time, Don said, he was pitched off. He landed so hard on his back that it had knocked the wind out of him. For a few awful minutes, he felt like he'd never be able to catch his breath again. But, as he lay there on the ground, flat on his back, he'd heard Ray's voice in his head saying, "It'll be okay, son."

Ray glanced over at him in the truck with a grin and interrupted. "Actually, if I'd been there, I'd have said, 'Quick, get your butt off the ground and get out of there!' A bull will stomp you or gore you if you show any sign of weakness or fear. I swear, those critters can smell it."

Don said he'd actually gotten up pretty quick, but not before he'd embarrassed himself something awful. Lying there, he could tell that the insides of his jeans were completely wet. It must have been from blacking out a moment when his head hit the ground — and he knew it would soon show through his Levis. So, even though he was still dazed, he had snatched his jacket off and wrapped it around his waist so his friend couldn't see, or else there would've been no end to ribbing at school.

Ray laughed and told Don he wasn't the only one to have had that kind of thing happen, and launched into a story about himself when he was seventeen. He'd left his parents' horse ranch and found his first job away from home as a cowhand. One morning before daybreak, he'd been shaken awake by the foreman. It was Big John — all of five feet two inches tall but stout as a tree stump. The man was called Big John to distinguish him from his grown son Little John — five feet eleven and skinny. The foreman told Ray, as the newest cowhand, to go get a cow up the draw. She was the cow with a torn ear. She'd left the herd and probably wandered to Lone Tree — where she had dropped calves before.

It was February — when cows had their calves — and the dead of winter in the high country. It was still dark that morning. Ray had downed a tin cup of coffee left overnight on the bunkhouse stove and pulled Levis over his long johns. He'd donned a wool sweater and heavy sheepskin jacket, jammed on his boots, and grabbed his cowboy hat — the ten gallon kind they had in those days. It was an expensive one for how dirt-poor he was, but it was his pride-and-joy.

He'd headed for the barn. The snow was half-way to the top of his boots and getting deeper. It must have been at least ten degrees below — by the way hairs in his nose froze, how the air cut his lungs, and the way powdery snow crackled and screeched underfoot.

In the barn, he'd buckled on heavy leather chaps over his jeans, hoisted the saddle onto Rowdy, worked the bit into the buckskin's mouth without too much slobber onto his jacket, stuck a yellow oilskin poncho behind the saddle and tightened the leather straps. Holding the reins, Ray had pulled sheepskin gloves over hands already numb, led Rowdy out of the barn and mounted. The cowboy neck-reined the horse and headed into the wind. He had to pull his hat down to shield his face from the wind-whipped pinpricks of snow crystals, and scrunched down into his upright sheepskin collar.

Rowdy flared his nostrils and snorted, his breath frosting the air. The horse threw his head back and danced about for a while, stood stock still and peed, then took his time walking while plopping down a load of steaming manure, before he finally perked up and settled into his jerky trot, alternating with his smoother fast-walk.

It was a whiteout, but the horse knew where he was going — up valley straight into the wind. Rowdy was a good cow pony, and Ray could relax enough in the saddle to give him his head. A white mantle of snow soon covered the buckskin's black mane. Despite the thickness of Ray's chaps, his legs were the first to become chilled, and the rest of his body followed. He couldn't see whether his nose was turning white, but he shielded it with his hand now and then to protect it from frostbite.

At one point, the pelting snow caused his eyes to tear and the tears started to ice up, gluing his eyelids together, so he had to take off his gloves and swipe at his eyes, turning his fingers wooden with cold. Now would be the time, he told himself, to put on his slicker, but somehow he couldn't bring himself to twist in the saddle and fumble with the straps that held it.

It seemed a long way to Lone Tree, but as time passed, there was something spellbinding about being alone in nowhere, with only the rhythm of the horse and muffled hoof beats going on and on. After a while, the sun rose over the ridge, pale as a full moon in the silvery-gray sky. It crossed his mind that he might get lost, swallowed up in the whiteness, not to be found till spring thaw. And yet, quiet elation filled his chest at being free, with only his partner Rowdy, in the timelessness.

He almost missed the draw when Rowdy turned abruptly so the wind hit them on the right. There, in the midst of the white world, stood the charcoal skeleton of Lone Tree. Ray neck-reined the horse up the draw. A low bellow soon beckoned them toward the torn-eared cow, who abruptly appeared out of whiteness only a stone's throw away. She had just dropped a wet calf into the snow, and had bent her head to slurp the transparent, gooey membrane from its face.

Ray dropped the reins and slid onto the ground. He made soothing noises to the old cow as he walked over to her on stiff legs. She lowered her head to nudge the calf with her muzzle to raise him off the ground. Time and again the calf tried to rise on its spindly legs, only to nose-dive into deep snow. Ray waited, arms folded across his chest, gloved hands under his armpits. Range cattle were tough, and calves had a lot of determination, so his hopes rose every time the calf got his legs under him and teetered a moment, then listed to one side, and fell. Finally the critter stopped trying to get up. Ray had to admit that this bull calf was too scrawny and wet, the snow too deep, the wind too cold: The animal would freeze to death if he didn't intervene.

The cowboy gathered the slippery calf into his arms and hefted it across the saddle. With his left hand, he steadied Rowdy, got his numb foot into the stirrup, and after a few tries—Rowdy was always contrary and chose such moments to step forward—Ray hoisted himself into the saddle behind the calf. The little fellow bleated, and Torn Ear came over. Ray turned the horse around the way they'd come, and kneed him forward. No argument this time. Going home, Rowdy always stepped up his pace.

As soon as Ray saw that Torn Ear was following, he adjusted the calf to be more secure with its legs dangling evenly down each side of the horse. He rubbed the calf vigorously to help circulation. When he leaned sideways to look into its face, the pink-faced Hereford looked back at him with big eyes beneath long black lashes. Something about the pale, grayish cast to the calf's lips bothered the cowboy. Worried that the wet little fellow was too cold for the trip back, Ray halted the horse, took off his gloves, turned in the saddle to retrieve the oilskin poncho, and pulled it over his head to make a tent for the newborn calf and himself. He was sure the shelter would make the calf more comfortable, and it made him feel a lot better too.

With the wind behind them, and Rowdy's faster pace, they soon got home, and Ray put Torn Ear and her calf in a stall with a bedding of straw. The calf managed to steady himself on wobbly legs. Ray toweled him well and left the cow to lick the newborn with her rough tongue and nudge him toward her squirting bag to nurse.

Before he left the barn, Ray checked his face in the rusted mirror—no frostbitten nose, and he painfully thawed his fingers and toes in some cold water before he went to the ranch house for breakfast.

At this point in his narrative Ray abruptly turned toward

Don next to him in the front seat of the pickup and grinned. The cowboy said he'd almost forgotten the crucial part of the story—what had reminded him of the incident in the first place: how he'd had an embarrassing accident like Don.

At Lone Tree, right after he'd spotted Torn Ear and was dismounting, he'd felt an urgent need to go to the bathroom. Coffee always did that to him. Ray figured there was no way he could wait until he got back to the ranch.

So, as soon as his boots had hit the ground, he snatched off both gloves. But his numb fingers fumbled too slowly with the metal buttons and a flood burst forth, which at first felt like a welcome relief and a wonderful rush of warmth inside his Levis. And, of course, the outside of his jeans and even the leather chaps got soaked in the process. Right afterward, though, he became more chilled than ever. He shook all over and stamped his feet. It felt much better as soon as the heavy denim froze stiff and hard.

On top of that, no sooner had he secured the calf in front of him in the saddle, than it, too, urinated on his lap and smeared its bloody umbilical cord all across his jeans and chaps. Then the whole mess froze. Ray told his son, "When I got back to the ranch, I kept wearing the oilcloth slicker until I could change, and, in case the other ranch hands noticed anything, I told them the bull calf had peed on me, which was partly true anyway. Otherwise, they would've made life unbearable. You know how cowboys are with nicknames. They'd have called me something like 'Baby Ray' or something worse, which would've followed me wherever I went for the rest of my life."

Ray's eyes twinkled as he glanced over at his son in the passenger seat and said, "Like-father-like-son, huh?" Don grinned back.

After Ray and Don dropped off the beavers at Miller Ranch, they drove to the rodeo nearby. At first, by habit from his rodeo days, Ray steered the truck back toward the chutes. Then, grumbling in exasperation, he reversed, pulled into the public parking place near the ticket booth, and bought two tickets.

Ray led the way, drawn like a magnet to the stalls in back of the arena. Then he remembered himself. He hadn't been a contestant since before the war. Who'd remember him — a has-been? Fortunately, the old cowboy assigned to the gate did, and let them in. As soon as Ray stepped onto the sawdust, the familiar smells and sounds from his former life came to him: the pungency of leather and manure, the snorts of horses, and the whack of bulls against their wooden stalls.

Young cowboys bustled about. Adrenaline surged through his body and Ray felt young again, as if he could reach his hand onto a nearby sawhorse and leap over it. His eyes misted and his throat ached for the old world he had once known. He put his arm around his son's shoulders. "By golly, those were the days!" They followed the sounds of snorts, curses, and heavy breathing to a chute at the end. Wranglers were readying a cowboy to mount a mean-eyed bull. Ray explained to his son how this moment in the chute was the most dangerous one in rodeo. In the seconds before leaving the chute, the cowboy-contestant could be crushed against the plank walls, or thrown underfoot in the narrow space.

Suddenly the cowboy's leg was slammed against the wall, and he was thrown off-balance, in danger of slipping below the bull. The wranglers were yelling, and Ray found himself rapidly climbing up the planks of the stall. He grabbed the bull's tail with both hands while the wranglers righted the cowboy. The sliding door opened, and the bull and cowboy plunged into the arena.

Climbing back down, Ray was puffing from the exertion, and he could feel his face was flushed. A little dizzy, he lowered his head toward his knees. How out of shape he had become, compared to earlier times! But when he raised his head, with a sheepish grin on his face, he found his son looking at him like he was the hero of the day. It was a good moment and they laughed together.

While they were still standing there, a handsome older man strode over. He looked dashing in a custom-tailored western suit, a mossy-green Stetson, a gray shirt crackling with starch, and kangaroo-skin boots. With a big smile, he reached out his hand to Ray and intoned in a rich baritone, "Well, if it isn't Ray Bell! Good to see you, pardner. And this must be your boy!" Ray smiled at Don and introduced him to the rodeo announcer Cy Taillon. The man said, "I sure recognize your Dad's Silver Grey Stetson—with that same Deming crease of his."

Don replied, "Yeah. Dad bought it as soon as he got back from war."

"I'll bet your Dad returned looking to you like a 'silver knight'!" Cy turned back to Ray and pointed at his big belt buckle. "I see you're wearing one of those championship trophies. Which one?"

Ray's voice came back cowboy-modest as he partly covered his mouth. "An early one—for bronc riding." Then he proudly grinned and added. "What better place to show it off? Anyhow, it's my ticket to these chutes. To show Don where the real action is."

The two men reminisced about the old days and people they'd known. Cy showed his knack for remembering everybody and everything he'd ever seen or heard about in rodeo. He recalled—correctly—that Ray had come West in a covered wagon when he was one year old and that his parents had settled a homestead in North Dakota. And Cy guffawed in recalling how Ray had made bulldogging history in 1937—as the first cowboy at a rodeo to wrestle a buffalo. "Yeah," Ray said, "I won a $25 bet on it. That dern animal dragged me around so much it wore my boots out, and it finally slammed me against the fence and cracked three of my ribs."

After they'd talked about the old days, Cy told Ray that rodeo had almost died out during the 1940s when all the boys like Ray had gone to war. Sixteen million Americans in uniform. But when the war ended and they all came home, rodeo came roaring back.

After the man moved on, Ray explained to his son that through the decades before the war, Cy had become a legend in the West. Before he had come along, rodeo announcing had been like hearing barkers at a fairground, but Cy had raised it to a grand level. He had charisma, and always told audiences what was actually involved in performing — something that contestants really appreciated.

Father and son lingered behind the chutes for a while, then climbed onto the fence to watch the rodeo. From their perch they heard Cy's deep voice announce coming events. He explained that the contestants were not only ordinary cowboys doing usual chores on the ranch. They had become highly trained professional athletes performing feats that risked cracked ribs and broken bones. If they were slammed on the ground and couldn't spring up to get out of the way quickly enough, they had to count on the mounted hands — and the brave cowboy on foot in that clown outfit over there — to distract the broncs and steers from stomping and gouging them.

"Now," said Cy, "I'd like to introduce one of the most famous cowboy-contestants in the country. He's here today — the up-and-coming Casey Tibbs! He's the one over there dressed in those flashy duds — before he dons his contestant's jeans and white shirt later on. Started rodeo at age 14. Already a World Champion in Saddle Bronc Riding.

"And now, over there on the fence, another cowboy — Ray Bell, and his son, Don. Wave that Silver Grey hat! You too, Don." Smiling over at his dad, then blushing for himself, Don waved. Cy continued, "Some of you have probably seen another 'Ray Bell' — the one out of Wyoming — who won at Pendleton and Madison Square Garden in New York City. Our Ray Bell here is also an 'all round' contestant. He hails originally from a homestead back in North Dakota and then a horse ranch right here in New Mexico. Good at saddle broncs, steer wrestling and roping. Back from serving in the war, he's now flying around as a game warden saving wild animals, catching poachers, and finding lost hikers. A round of applause for Ray!"

Ray smiled at the crowd, but as the clapping died down, he turned to his son and confided, "My whole time in rodeo, it was awkward — being mistaken for *the* Ray Bell — World Champion in the Cowboy Hall of Fame. I did okay in rodeo, but nothing like that! I never hit the really big time — the big money. In fact, sometimes in the fall, to make ends meet, your mom and I had to hire out as field hands to pick potatoes. That's backbreaking work — bending down all day bagging potatoes."

They were interrupted by Cy's booming voice over the loudspeaker again. "Next up in Chute Number One: a spine-rattling bronc with real showmanship — Thunderstorm out of Double X Ranch in Hayward, California. Ridden by Mister Ken "Kid" Turner from Billings, Montana. Expect a great performance by both horse and rider . . ."

After a few moments, Cy announced, "There seems to be a delay, so let me tell you something. Contrary to what some folks imagine, these aren't wild horses and they aren't abused — the rodeo associations work closely with the Humane Society who can attest to that. They're horses found on ranches, and, surprisingly enough, they can be led on halters. But they'll buck off any cowboy who tries to ride them.

"I want you to know something else: This is the only national sport where contestants not only pay their own entry fees — but these cowboys also place themselves in great danger, without helmets or padding like football players.

"*And here they come!*" The horse exploded out of the chute in a big arc, struck the ground hard with his forefeet stiff and flung his back legs out. Then he corkscrewed up again — his body almost vertical — front hoofs scraping at the sky. He leaped so high that for an instant all four legs were in the air, as if he were flying. The bronc bucked some more, came crashing down once in a straight-legged, jarring thud, and kicked hoof-plugs of hardened dirt behind him across the arena.

The rider managed to hold his free hand high, and stayed on until the whistle sounded, when he was finally thrown into a somersault over the horse's head. The baggy-pants clown waved his arms at the bronc while the mounted pick-up man bent down and quickly loosened the strap from around the horse's flank. The horse headed out; he knew the way. The cowboy got up slowly from the ground, limped a bit on one foot, then stood tall in the swirling dust, smiling and hitting his hat against his leg.

Ray and Don, yelling themselves hoarse, stayed until midafternoon when they wearily headed home for a late supper.

In the truck on the way back, Ray — charged by the energy let loose by the animals he'd seen — began to think about Smokey and his wild spirit. He had a good feeling of camaraderie with his son. So he told him that he'd been considering what Don had suggested about letting Smokey into the house. Why not start that evening by removing his bandages? If the cub's paws looked tough enough, they'd let Smokey walk on the carpet awhile before they all turned in for the night.

Chapter 21

Unfortunately, many people do not consider fun an important item on their daily agenda. For me, that was always high priority in whatever I was doing.
–Chuck Yeager

The more things you love, the more you are interested in, the more you enjoy, the more you are indignant about – the more you have left when anything happens.
–Ethel Barrymore

Smokey and Jet scuffle

That evening, when Smokey was set down on the carpet, he could hardly believe he was free of bandages at last. First, though, he had to sit down and sniff the healed pads of his paws. There was only a thin layer of goo remaining, hardly visible, but he felt compelled to lick off every bit of the foul-smelling stuff. Feeling like himself at last, he romped from Ray to Don, and from Ruth to Judy, as they crouched around him, laughing.

Smokey startled for an instant when Jet dashed into the living room and came to an abrupt halt nearby. But the puppy had caught the happy mood in the room and signaled a playful invitation with a deep bow. Smokey's countenance lit up. The cub signaled back his own bear-brand of playful intention: He put a goofy look on his face and swung his head from side to side, while his body flopped around loosely.

Jet got the message. He leaped at Smokey, who lunged back with a head butt, which made the dog skid to a stop and give him a puzzled, woebegone look. Smokey gave him an impish smile with his upper lips and proceeded to pretend-swipe Jet with his paw, then lunged at his neck with open jaws. Jet immediately retaliated with his own pretend-bite, and they soon broke to chase each other around the room. They were both very fast.

Although Jet was a month older, the wild cub was nimble and seemed more than a match for the speedy puppy. And when Jet did gain on him at one point, Smokey clambered atop the sofa and sprang down to wrestle the dog in a tumbling play-fight, their open jaws on each other's necks in pretend-bites. The Bells' laughter changed to uh-oh's when the two rammed the legs of the end table and knocked it over along with its lamp. A moment's pause at the crash, and the animals' chase-and-be-chased bout was on again as they bounced through the living room. Smokey had never had so much fun in his life.

On an impulse, the cub headed for the open door of Ray and Ruth's bedroom. Ray leaped out of his chair and lunged to catch him. Smokey lowered his head, flattened his ears and scooted by. He scrambled onto the bed, clawed the blankets, spun around inside the sheets, got tangled in them and shrieked in alarm, found his way out, and collapsed on the bed, wheezing to catch his breath. Then he peered over the edge of the bed.

Below him, stubby tail drumming the air, was Jet in a play-bow, his head so cocked to one side that a droopy ear brushed the floor. Smokey huffed, and the dog stretched his sturdy body up the side of the bed so his black nose almost touched Smokey's. The cub batted him on the snout. Jet yipped, then barked in the cub's face. Smokey was ready to jump when he heard Ray shout, and turned to see him, hands on hips, towering over them.

Human arms reached out to grab him on the bed. Smokey bounded down, rolled on the floor—and found himself seized by a hind leg. He turned and bit Ray hard. The man let go, and the cub raced out the bedroom door.

With the quick-moving cowboy close behind him, Smokey turned into the kitchen, skidded on the smooth tile floor and slammed into Ruth's legs in front of the kitchen sink. When Ray dived at him, he wedged himself between Ruth's legs and the kitchen cabinet, and snapped at Ray's boots. Then he scrunched down upon hearing the two humans arguing loudly above him. Ruth said, "Leave him alone. He's just exploring." She and Ray stepped back from the sink.

Smokey darted into the freed-up space in front of the cabinet and was drawn to the tantalizing aroma of food inside. He clawed the cabinet door open, pulled over the garbage container, and thrust his muzzle in. He had happily begun strewing garbage onto the kitchen floor when Ray pushed him aside. While the man grumbled and gathered up garbage, Smokey's nose led him across the linoleum to another cabinet door where he smelled The Something Wonderful he'd often noticed on Jet's breath.

The little bear pried the door open and started to crawl past pots and pans, but just as he reached the bag of dog food, a stack of pans crashed onto his head with a dreadful clatter. He squealed in panic, backed his rump out fast, and frantically looked for something to climb. Ray stood nearby, wiping his hands. The man's tall, tough jeans looked something like a tree trunk so Smokey shinnied up one of Ray's legs and clutched his shirt.

The game warden put his big hand under Smokey's rump and brought him onto his chest. He made soothing sounds until the cub stopped whimpering and nuzzled his neck. The cub then sucked on Ray's ear and made small chirps and coos.

Ray couldn't help but soften his eyes and smile. "Well, I'll be—I thought that little devil hated me. Ever since I've been bandaging him, he's been glaring at me all the time with those small angry eyes. Bites me as hard as he can every chance he gets—even when I feed him something sweet. And lately he's taken to sinking his teeth into my leg and just hanging there. But when he's really scared, I'm his savior, his Big Daddy!" Despite the mess Smokey had made with the garbage, Ray was glad to see the cub have some fun on his bare paws.

Little Judy had been watching from the kitchen door, giggles pouring out of her so hard that she got the hiccups. Still cradling Smokey in one arm, Ray gathered his daughter under his other arm to settle her down. He dropped off Judy in her bedroom for Ruth to attend, then took Smokey to the back room. He laid the little fellow's body, limp with exhaustion, in his box. Tired as Smokey was, he managed to crawl over to Jet's old quilt on the floor. Jet was already there, tuckered out. The cub curled his body around the puppy, and within seconds Smokey had fallen asleep with his new playmate.

The next morning something unexpected happened to Smokey. Ray opened the back door and plunked the cub in the big back yard for the first time. The cub squinted in the bright sun, just as he had the first time he'd emerged from the cave months before. A scent-laden breeze ruffled his fur. He could hardly believe his nose: grasses, leaves, and sweet blossoms—

the familiar smells of home!

After having been cooped up for so many days, he loved being outside again. The feeling brought memories of his own home on the mountainside. How he yearned for those days: the cave, the trees, his mother, Strut, the honey-tree. Hadn't Strut told him that after the crow had been rescued and stayed awhile at Ray's house, the man had returned him to the forest? So maybe Ray would do the same thing with him.

Smokey in the back yard

Smokey stood tall on his hind legs and swiveled his head to check for anything threatening. Something strange near the big doors to the car garage made him jerk his head and stare. It didn't move. He cautiously crept over to the big round can and sniffed some rotten food inside. He tried to push the garbage can over, but it didn't move.

Smokey wished he could hear Strut's raucous caw, and searched the trees and sky, but his friend wasn't there. He did hear familiar cries coming from the ground over near the far trees. It was a robin. It cheered him to see it do its routine: hop three times, tilt its head to listen for a worm beneath the grass, and hop again.

How good it felt to place his own feet on the grassy earth again! A pink clover blossom beckoned him, and he mouthed it tentatively. It smelled good and tasted sweet—the same as those in the meadow back home—so he ate it and moseyed along for more, until a purple dragonfly flitted by his head and zigzagged away.

The cub pursued the flittering dragonfly along the adobe-and-stone wall until he reached the driveway to the garage. The insect flew right through the chain link fence into the driveway, and in his pursuit, the cub banged his head on the barrier. He tentatively touched the hard wire with a paw, then banged the barrier.

How maddening that he could see out, but couldn't get out. The fence was like the cage at the vet's, with much stronger wire and larger holes. Smokey ran back along the adobe wall that bordered the rest of the large yard until he found himself back at the chain links where he had started. He stood up to look this way and that, scrunching his brow.

There was no way out. And when he tried to climb the fence, his forepaws slipped through the openings and he was trapped, hanging painfully by his bent paws. He huffed in alarm, let his paws slip loose and plunked back to the ground.

Jet, who had been watching him, sprang over and nudged him with his nose. Smokey sat up a moment, and noticed a big shady elm at the back corner. Splashing through a pile of old leaves to the tree, he boosted himself with his hind legs up the trunk. It felt so good, like being back home! And it would afford a quick escape to safety if needed. He came down backwards, happily pattered after Jet and challenged him to tussle.

At one point, Jet paused to lift his leg and relieve himself on a lilac bush, and the cub was puzzled at the puppy's mistake. He himself wasn't going to follow suit! After all, when they'd been confined to the back room of the house, they had both done their business on the newspaper in the corner, where they were supposed to.

Meanwhile, Ray had been smiling at Smokey and Jet freely playing together in their outdoor world. So when Ruth called him to breakfast and he left them in the yard, he was mulling over an idea. It would be fun for the two to play in the yard as much as they wanted. It would also make his son's job easier: Don was the one who had to change the smelly newspapers in the back room. After breakfast, Ray went to that room, where he rummaged through his tools. He found what he was looking for—his saw, a drill, some metal bolts, and a rectangular piece of tough leather.

Judy came and Ray asked his little daughter, "Wouldn't it be nice to build something so Smokey and Jet could let themselves in and out?" He said that he had never heard of such a thing, but he thought a large hole could be made in the lower wooden half of the outside door. It took longer than he'd expected, like most projects did, but Judy loved her job of handing him tools and screws as he needed them. As soon as she saw the opening her father made, she clapped her hands and dubbed it a "doggie door." The job was soon completed with rawhide straps to hook the door closed at night.

Meanwhile, the cub and puppy had come to the outside stoop, jostling each other and pawing the piece of leather. The two animals became even more curious when Judy slipped through the door to join them outside. At first, Ray raised the flap and poked his hand out the little door to waggle a dog biscuit under Jet's nose. Soon Jet was blasting back and forth through the leather flap.

Smokey sat and chuffed until curiosity made him nudge the flap with his head. He put one paw through, looked up at Ray inside, and moaned to be let in. Judy ran for honey, and lured by the sweet taste, the cub finally plopped through the little door onto the floor inside, and soon followed the puppy, bopping in and out.

Before long the honey was gone and the cub returned outdoors to explore every corner of the large yard—many times the size of the small house. It wasn't endless like the forest, but it was a welcome delight. Suddenly he thought of his friend Lightning whom he'd last seen at the vet's. She might know what else the humans had in store for him. Where was that cat?

Smokey up a tree again

Chapter 22

Cats are absolute individuals, with their own ideas about everything, including the people they own.
–John Digman

If I try to be like him, who will be like me?
–Yiddish proverb

A few days later, Smokey had just come in the doggie door to escape the hot New Mexico sun and lounge in the back room, when he heard someone scratch at the back door. "Yeooow." His heart thumped. He poked his head out the leather flap. There was Lightning, his tiger-striped friend from the vet's, this time in a pink collar, looking sleek and saucy. He jumped outside, and the cat rubbed against his haunch, her tail held high and happy.

She told him that little Barbara and her parents treated her like a princess, except for one thing. They hadn't let her out of the house until now to do her walkabout—to sniff what pathways other cats had marked so she could claim her own safe path through the back yards. Smokey's scent in the air had drawn her across back yards to this one, just around the corner from Barbara's house. Wasn't it wonderful that they could be together again?

Lightning admired the leather flap and yowled in protest: Why couldn't she have a door like this? It was unfair! She told Smokey he was lucky to have such good humans. This puzzled Smokey, because most of the time he hated Ray, but he didn't say anything.

At that moment, she spied Jet. She arched her back and hissed in warning, and when the puppy bounded up to her, she clawed his nose. Shocked, the puppy leaped aside and sat down, whimpering. Lightning streaked to the elm. From a high tree branch, she narrowed her eyes and flattened her ears disdainfully at the cocker far below. Smokey climbed up and settled himself in a crotch of the tree just below her. She sighed, spread her body onto the broad branch, and licked her paws.

"Smokey, my little bear, that dog could *kill* you. You must act *fierce* to make him afraid of you."

"But Jet's my friend. Don't worry. When we play together I can hold my own. My problem is the strangers who come to the house. I can't tell who will bother me, so I hide."

"Generally speaking, there are two kinds of humans. There are quiet ones, like a shy dog or cautious child. They let you come to them and usually prove to be quite likeable. Others stand tall and walk around with the confidence of a big dog like a German shepherd."

"That reminds me of Ray and some of his male friends. They make me bristle!"

"That kind usually doesn't like cats, so I don't rub against their legs, or they'll boot me aside."

Lightning continued, "You must learn how to read your keepers' *moods*. First, don't believe chirpy intonations or boisterous voices. It's their *bodies* that reveal how they *really* feel. One more thing you'd never guess: If someone stares at you, it doesn't necessarily mean they're mad at you or trying to dominate you."

"So when Ray looks right at me, he's not challenging me?"

"Not necessarily. He's just a confident man. And if he gives you a long steady look right into your eyes, it means he really *likes* you."

Smokey stared at her with his rounded ears splayed outward. "Oh . . . That's hard to believe! I'll have to think about *that*."

The next moment, the two animals heard someone calling and looked down through the leaves to see Judy standing on the ground far below. Smokey started to back down the tree, then stopped to look up at the cat, expecting her to follow. Instead, the cat was standing stiffly on the limb.

Lightning cried out to Smokey, "I can't remember whether I should climb down head first like a squirrel or bottom first like you. In fact, I've never been this high off the ground. I'd better not move at all!" Smokey stopped his descent, not knowing what to do.

The cat yowled down to Judy. The girl called up comforting sounds to no avail, then went back inside and returned with Ray. The two animals watched below to see Ray place a tall ladder against the tree trunk and climb toward them. Smokey was reached first and Ray's thickly gloved hand scooped the cub onto his shoulder. Lightning backed down the trunk a short way, then leaped onto Ray's head. He tried to grab her, but she wouldn't be budged, so he steadied her atop his head. Down the ladder they all moved, Ray yelping in pain each time the cat stabbed her claws into his scalp, then shouting expletives as the cub bit his arm and urinated all over his shirt . . . while Judy doubled over with giggles.

Smokey plays indoors

Mid-June arrived. It had been almost six weeks since the cub had come to the house. In addition to his mash of Pablum, goats' milk and honey, he was now eating moistened kibble. The family was amazed that the wild cub wasn't territorial about food. Nor was Jet, who, as a cocker spaniel, loved food above all else. Ruth had at first given them plentiful kibble in separate rooms, then fed them nearby, and soon they were amiably standing side by side eating from the same bowl.

Smokey and Jet share kibble

It didn't take Smokey long to notice that Ruth replenished the kibble whenever the bowl was emptied. The bear cub could hardly believe that whenever he was hungry he could easily snack until his belly was full. And he didn't have to search for water. He liked immersing his muzzle in Jet's water bowl and noisily sucking up the liquid. It seemed strange to him that Jet lapped up water awkwardly with his tongue.

After the humans had their supper, the family often took a walk, and cars slowed down to see the procession: Ray and Ruth side by side, then Don holding a slack leash on little Smokey in his red halter, shuffling along with his bear-gait, Jet dancing around the cub, and finally Judy and her little friend Barbara giggling at the animals. Far behind was Lightning, who walked only to the end of the first block where the Bells' street, West Coronado, met her street, Don Gasper. There the cat posed like a statue at the corner, waiting for them to return.

One afternoon Ray brought home a surprise: a female black bear about Smokey's age. This newcomer had been chained to a gas pump in the hot sun by the owner of a Standard Oil station. The man had wanted to draw in customers, who were urged to feed the cub candy and bubble gum. But one of the customers reported to the New Mexico Game and Fish Department that the cub looked sickly and starved.

Without delay, Ray drove across the state to confront the owner. The man was known as a tough character once convicted of felony murder. When Ray appeared in his uniform, the man stepped back inside his station door and armed himself with brass knuckles. In his doorway, facing Ray, he stood with legs apart and arms akimbo, and refused to yield the cub. Ray took a short step toward him, his body relaxed with a sense of quiet authority. After a short impasse, without a word being exchanged, Ray walked over, undid the chain, seized the sick animal, and drove off.

A few miles down the road, Ray stopped the car. Worried that the female cub was dehydrated, he splashed water into her mouth from his canteen and watched her with tenderness as she swallowed eagerly and na-na-na'd. Then he sped home to his wife.

Ray went to the front door, since Smokey and Jet were at the back. "Honey, come help!" Ruth was busy in the kitchen, alert for his return. Her arms reached out to the miserable-looking orphan. With a twinkle in his eye, Ray remarked how the little reddish-brown bear was another 'redhead' like Ruth, but didn't smell nearly as good.

Ruth said, "So let's name her Ruby. This little redhead needs a bath! She reeks of gasoline and motor oil." Ruth carried her to the bathroom, followed by Ray. After soaking the cub in the bathtub, Ruth pulled clods of gunk from the bear's fur as gently as she could, and cut off fur caught in sticky wads of pink bubble gum. Despite the mistreatment Ruby had endured at the gas station, she didn't protest, and leaned against the woman's supporting arm. Ruth briskly toweled and fluffed Ruby's fur. The cub reached up her forearms to be picked up, and Ruth gathered the cub to her bosom and murmured softly to her.

Ray had been squatting on his heels near the tub, and the little cub looked over at him with amiable eyes. The cowboy tentatively stroked the white spot on her chest, and found to his surprise that she loved being petted. The Bells exchanged a look: What a sweetheart compared to Smokey!

During her recuperation, Ray hoped the female cub would be a companion for Smokey. Seeing how good-natured she was, he hoped Smokey would follow her example and become sweeter too. That evening, as soon as Smokey saw Ruby enter the living room, he backed into a corner, stood stiffly, and sniffed suspiciously across the room. Curious, but mostly leery of the intruder, Smokey twitched his eyes indecisively in his taut readiness to attack. She didn't heed his warning, and took a tentative step forward. Eyes fixed on hers, Smokey dropped to all fours, his ears plastered back, and slowly stiff-walked toward her. His throat rumbled a warning.

The Bells watched him closely. What was wrong with Smokey? He had first seemed agitated, as if afraid, but also seemed to be threatening her. Was it the strange smell of gasoline and oil still clinging to Ruby's fur, so he didn't recognize her as another bear, much less a potential playmate? Or was it natural for orphan bear cubs to be wary at first, challenge each other, and then settle into an accommodation?

Ruby took a few slow steps in Smokey's direction. He clicked his teeth in warning not to come closer. Then he burst across the room so fiercely, popping his jaws and snapping his teeth, that she shrieked and Ray leaped to her rescue. The way she clung to his neck, Ray could tell she was badly frightened. But he didn't know whether Smokey's assault was only a black bear's usual bluster in a bluff-charge, or more dangerous than that. After all, Smokey might have stopped his charge in the next moment. And he hadn't actually bitten her. For the time being, Ray decided that he didn't want to risk any harm to the sweet little girl bear. Ruby had already been traumatized enough in her life.

Nevertheless, during the next days the Bells ventured a few more attempts to get the two bear cubs together, trying to gauge whether there might be serious fighting over territory or food. Although Smokey clacked his jaws and raised the fur on his neck and back, he never actually injured Ruby. Ray worried that a young male bear might play more roughly than a female, but their encounters didn't develop into play-wrestling either.

Ray made one last attempt on neutral ground. One evening, after hours, he lifted Smokey onto the wooden crossbar at the entrance to the Santa Fe National Park. Then he

Scared Smokey and playful Ruby

Smokey and Ruby: a truce

hoisted up Ruby to play with the cub. Smokey just backed away.

The Bells finally gave up. They confined Ruby to the kitchen where she'd be safe. Three days later, they reluctantly entrusted her to the Albuquerque Zoo.

The family treated Smokey like a member of the family, and he soon had the run of the house. By now the Bells had resigned themselves to Smokey's ways and temperament. It wasn't his nature to be compliant and sociable toward everyone like Ruby had been. The little bear was never aggressive toward Ruth, Judy or her friend Barbara, but lately when they tried to pet him, he'd politely slip away.

Visitors were a problem. He had definite likes and dislikes. The cub looked cuddly, but if a man started to pet him he'd usually bite. When excited chirpy-sounding people arrived, he hid under a chair to avoid them, yet he lingered around calm people. Smokey was not persuadable. He'd chase Jet as fast as he could one moment, then suddenly crash to the floor asleep the next, and nothing Jet could do would make him stir.

Smokey plays with a doll

Ray admired the cub for being a real character. Smokey knew what he wanted and wouldn't succumb to being a docile pet. He remained a wild animal. And although Ray considered him a mean little bear who regularly and deliberately ambushed him to bite or rake his body with sharp claws, he knew he'd miss the rambunctious cub when he finally had to leave. They'd all miss their evenings watching Smokey's antics.

They had learned what to expect of him. During evenings in the living room, as soon as Smokey wanted something, he would give the family meaningful looks. If they didn't notice, he'd whine and prance on his two back legs until they laughed and one of them brought him something sweet. If it was Judy who returned from the kitchen, he'd make nah-nah noises and nudge her arm with his nose until she opened her hand. Then he'd lick honey off her small palm and play with her fingers. If it was Ray, he'd grumble, slurp up a treat with his loose lips, and then sink his teeth into the proffered hand.

And, to the family's consternation, the scalawag never learned to do his business in the yard, like the dog did, even though he now had a doggie door. Instead, he'd whimper urgently in the house to be let into the back room so he could dash to his newspapers in the corner. His scat was so smelly that the nearest family member had to rush the soiled paper to the garbage can outdoors to keep the back room fresh. Yet Ray respected the cub for sticking to what he thought right, instead of copying Jet. The bear always maintained his dignity.

Ray found himself thinking fondly of the cub as an individual—and as a real westerner following the cowboy code. He was gentle toward women and children, but held his own with any man who tried to force him to do something he didn't want to do.

The man liked to play with the little scamp, chasing him in the yard and letting Smokey chase him. They had a lot of fun, but sooner or later in the game, Smokey would lock his teeth into Ray's leg—above his tough leather boots. The cowboy couldn't help but suspect that Smokey deliberately bit him there for the satisfaction of hearing Ray let out a cry of pain. Although most of the time Ray harbored the thought that Smokey was just plain mean, he also considered the likelihood that the cub assumed Ray had skin as tough as a bear's so felt free to play rough with him.

One day Ray tried an experiment in the back yard. Knowing that mother bears discipline their young by giving them a cuff, the next time Ray was bitten he tried a gentle backhanded cuff to the cub's head. He was appalled at the reaction. Smokey rolled over with his paws on his head and yowled, then proceeded to screech so loudly for three full minutes that it alarmed the neighbors. First to come running was next door neighbor Juan Heurera. Then, from across the back yards came Elida Ragle and her little daughter Barbara. They peered over the adobe wall and asked whether Smokey was all right.

Ray tried to explain what had happened, and looked very sheepish, but he needn't have worried. Instead of admonishing him, the neighbors assured him they knew he'd always been as careful as anyone could be with Smokey.

The incident, however, made Ray realize how terribly frightened the cub was of anything unexpected, especially if it smacked of harsh treatment. It revealed to him why the little bear was so determined to fight anyone dominant—anyone who might be a threat. After all, Smokey probably had lingering trauma from the fire, then had suffered pain during the three weeks of having his wounds dressed. And Ray knew that everyone—especially wild animals—hated being helpless and pinned down on their backs, as the cub had been while being bandaged. That had been obvious from how desperately the bear fought at that time against what must have felt like abuse.

So Ray had to reconcile himself to the prospect that no matter how hard he'd tried to take care of Smokey subsequently, this smart cub would probably always remember being manhandled, and never understand Ray's good intentions. Yet the man still had a wistful hope that he was wrong. Perhaps, with time, the cub would somehow think of him as fatherly.

Chapter 23

Every truth passes through three stages before it is recognized. In the first it is ridiculed; in the second it is opposed; in the third it is regarded as self-evident.
–Arthur Schopenhauer

All the forces in the world are not so powerful as an idea whose time has come.
–Victor Hugo

By the time Smokey had been in the household for seven weeks, he had doubled his weight to eight pounds and had become much stronger. When Ray carried him to bed, the bear resisted with powerful limbs, and he tussled fiercely with Jet, even though the puppy had grown to twice the cub's size. The Bells had to sternly warn guests to be careful around him. At moments when a family member saw the bear's strength, a lump of sadness would catch in their throat. Although no one mentioned it, the evidence indicated that soon the bear would become unmanageable at home. Before long, they would have to give him up.

Difficult as Smokey was, the Bells had come to love him like a member of the family. They were used to coming upon him around any corner of the house, and accustomed to finding him underfoot in the kitchen. Yet they knew he needed a new home. He was too small to return to the forest; he could not survive alone. There wasn't any place that rehabilitated bear cubs for eventual return to the wilderness. And it was unthinkable for the family to have Smokey put to sleep.

At the office, Ray continued working with his boss, Elliott Barker, to find a suitable place for Smokey. Elliott—the top game warden in the state — was a powerful ally. Nevertheless, they kept slamming up against obstacles. Ray and Elliott had forged a clear idea of what they wanted: The 'live' Smokey could remind people about the dangers of careless wildfires and the need to preserve wildlife and the wilderness. They first checked New Mexico zoos. When they learned no space was available, they were relieved, for they both wanted the entire country to hear his message. However, they themselves belonged only to the Game Department of their own state. What informal networks did they have to the federal government?

At first Ray felt stymied, but in talking with Elliott one day, he recalled that he did know someone in the United States Forest Service. It was his old friend, Kester "Kay" Flock, supervisor of the nearby Santa Fe National Forest. The slender, serious-minded man had served in the Forest Service for twenty-eight years. The outdoorsman loved animals and cared deeply about preserving the environment. So when Ray received a request from an elementary school to bring Smokey to classes and talk about the cub's rescue and fire prevention, Ray enlisted Kay to accompany him and meet the cub.

Things got off to a bad start. En route to the school, Kay got his shirt slashed as well as his hands badly bitten. Nevertheless, he gamely offered to walk Smokey around the classrooms on a leash. As Ray had hoped, the man became intrigued with the wild cub, and was impressed with children's reactions to him. Fortunately, Smokey was in a good mood and stood on hind legs to look inquiringly into children's eyes. The youngsters became quite sad upon hearing how the cub had been burned in a fire caused by a careless camper.

Kay Flock then volunteered to help Ray take Smokey to a radio interview. When they arrived at the radio station, Kay saw how well Ray, with his engaging way of telling tales, related the dramatic story of Smokey's ordeal-by-fire and answered the interviewer's questions. Kay watched the cub mouth the microphone, which had been smeared with honey.

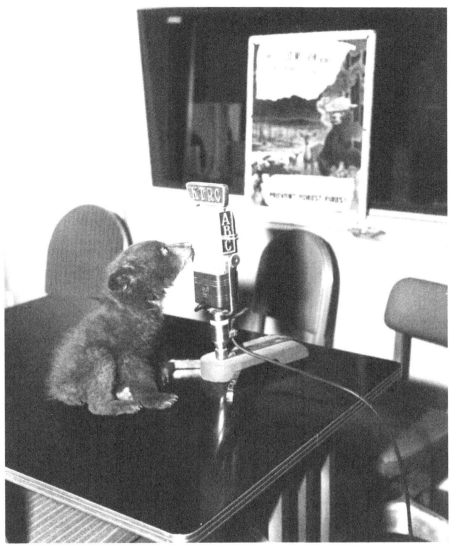

Smokey at ABC radio

Then, when Ray deliberately moved the mike away, Smokey squalled mightily — to send the cub's penetrating voice over the air. Ray and the radio announcer laughed so hard there were tears in their eyes. Smokey looked like he could become a national hit.

By then, Kay Flock had become so enthusiastic that he

called his boss, the federal director for his region, and suggested that he broach the idea of the cub as a 'living symbol of fire prevention' to federal officials at national headquarters in Washington, D. C. Unfortunately, Kay's boss called it a "crazy idea." He didn't want to make a fool of himself. Moreover, he forbade Kay to go over his head to do so.

Ray simmered at the news. Bringing Kay Flock into the quest had boomeranged. Kay—as well as Ray and his boss Elliott—now faced the likelihood that they would be reprimanded or even lose their jobs if they dared contact any Forest Service official in Washington. But Smokey was becoming stronger and more dangerous by the day, so something had to be done to make him a national treasure—soon.

Ray Bell, Elliott Barker and Kay Flock were all strong-minded outdoorsmen, and, like the three musketeers, they didn't give up without a fight. Their mission now would require subtle backdoor diplomacy. They had to think of someone in their network of old friends and colleagues at the national Forest Service headquarters—someone who could *initiate* a call to them in New Mexico and request the bear.

It was a long shot, but Elliott recalled someone from Washington headquarters he'd taken elk hunting twenty years before, back in the early 1930s: Clint Davis. Elliott knew that Clint would remember the special bond the two men had forged in the New Mexico wilderness. Wet and miserable, they'd hunted and gutted elk, and had long talks in the evenings over campfires.

Elliott was a good judge of character. He knew Clint Davis was bold, and a man who'd be receptive to new ideas. And he was the kind of man who could be very persuasive with the powers-that-be in Washington. Elliott, Ray and Kay got excited: Clint could be the key to unlock the door at headquarters.

With discreet phone calls to friends of friends, the three men prompted Clint in Washington to initiate a call to Elliott Barker in New Mexico. Fortunately, by this time Clint had become director of Forest Fire Prevention and was enthusiastic about the idea of a live Smokey Bear. He'd drum up support in his department, he said, and then approach the Chief of the Forest Service, Lyle Watts.

Just then, a monkey wrench threatened to quash the team's plans. The Advertising Council, the highly effective group that had made the Smokey poster bear such a spectacular success throughout the years, heard about plans afoot in Clint's department for a 'live Smokey Bear' and objected. They had a legitimate concern: People might confuse the live bear with the poster bear. If so, when the live bear eventually died, people might think that their poster Smokey Bear had died, and it would jeopardize the long-standing Smokey Bear campaign.

The Council was powerful. It could swing Chief Watts' decision against the New Mexicans. Clint Davis went into high-gear in Washington. He showed Council members photographs of the cub and described the great appeal of the little bear to children and adults.

When the Council members eventually registered accord, the men in Santa Fe got their hopes up. Perhaps Clint could now stir up enough interest within the Forest Service to bring Chief Watts on board.

While the three in New Mexico awaited a decision from Chief Watts, they faced another big question: If they got a green light, where could Smokey actually go? Ray and Elliott weren't familiar enough with Washington, D. C. to have any idea where Smokey Bear could actually stay. Then Kay Flock recalled visiting the Smithsonian's National Zoological Park when he'd been stationed at the capital during the war. He had been so impressed with how well the zoo took care of its animals that he'd become acquainted with the zoo director—"Doc" William Mann.

Kay dared not phone Doc from his office under the nose of his boss—he might get fired. So Kay took vacation time, meticulously documented that his telephone calls were made from home at his own expense, and managed to get the persuasive Clint Davis and Doc Mann together.

The most important piece of the New Mexicans' plot fell into place when Doc Mann agreed to take the cub. He promised to give Smokey a home at the national zoo for as long as the bear lived.

Upon hearing that Smokey would have a good home, Ray heaved a sigh of relief. But then his spirits sank—imagining his wild and rowdy friend confined to a wire enclosure for the rest of his life. He shrugged off the painful thought. This was the best solution for the cub under the circumstances. Smokey could not make it on his own. This way he would be well-fed and taken care of, and the loss of his freedom would be for an important cause: fire prevention. At the same time, Ray knew that the cub would probably never understand why he must accept one terrible loss after another.

By this point Santa Fe reporters were mobbing Ray with requests for interviews. Speed Simmons—his lungs still wheezing from the fire—brought his young daughter to visit, and Ray enjoyed seeing these old friends. Santa Fe neighbors also dropped by, and since the Bells were new in town, they liked meeting new people. But soon so many people drove by the house hoping to see the cub that there were traffic jams on West Coronado, especially whenever the cub with his teddy-bear ears stood at the screen door looking out. And so many strangers came to the door with their children that it seemed to the Bells that their small rented bungalow had become Grand Central Station. Every dinner was interrupted by the doorbell.

Although they were careful to caution visitors, the Bells became apprehensive that someone might be badly bitten or clawed, for the cub had grown much bigger and stronger. To distract people from their temptation to touch or feed the wild bear, the Bells pressed Jet into service. They could count on the wonderfully affectionate cocker puppy to lick every outstretched hand, squirm happily as people petted his silky body, and look into their faces with loving soulful eyes. Jealousy would finally prompt Smokey to emerge from under the coffee table to entice Jet to play, and people would delight in watching the two animals dash about the house and brawl.

Smokey and kids

Days passed with no word from Chief Watts at the Forest Service. Although the Advertising Council had dropped their opposition, it was the head of the Forest Service who might still veto the plan. The impasse was almost broken when California officials unexpectedly telegraphed Elliott that they wanted Smokey—because a bear was the state emblem on the California flag. For a short while, Elliott wavered, but Ray was adamant. Smokey was a New Mexico bear. And a bear with a mission—to prevent wildfires and preserve wildlife. If the bear was going to spend his life in a cage, let it be where he could do the most good—for the entire country. Not for California with its big state's pride! Elliott was persuaded and turned down California.

By then, photographs of Smokey had been appearing on front pages of newspapers across the nation. Evidence of peoples' response to the little bear became overwhelming. With such public support, and support from officials in his own department—spearheaded by Clint Davis—the Chief of the Forest Service finally made a decision. The long-awaited phone call arrived in New Mexico. Chief Watts wanted Smokey for the National Zoo.

Elliott Barker shouted across the corridor. Ray and Kay—who happened to be at the office that morning—came running. At last it was settled. The trio beamed and clinked their coffee mugs together at the good news. As he left the others and walked out of the office, though, Ray felt a let-down. It had been exhilarating to work as a team with good men for a good cause. Now they would have to go back to their ordinary business.

As he drove home to tell his family the news, Ray recalled similar excitement working with other men on that very different kind of project—preparing the plane that would drop the atomic bomb on Japan to end the war. It was then that the genie of a tremendously destructive force was let out of the bottle, and the world would never feel as safe again.

As Ray pulled into his driveway, Smokey appeared at the window, and he felt a lightening of heart and soul. It was as if he was now sending out a little bear on a much different kind of mission—this time to preserve the wilderness from fires that careless humans caused. As he sat in the car he couldn't help but feel a stab of sorrow at the personal sacrifice it would entail for the innocent little wild bear. He heaved a sigh, then took a deep breath. He opened the car door, snatched his silver-gray Stetson from the passenger seat, pulled it down securely onto his head and stepped out. Upon opening the door to the house, he called out the news to Ruth and the kids, "We found a good home for Smokey!"

Now that the men at the office knew Smokey was going to the nation's capital, they had to face the next question. How could the bear travel more than halfway across the continent to the East Coast? The three musketeers moved fast. First, Kay Flock asked the United Parcel Service to fly Smokey in one of its planes. And UPS offered to transport him, but only as freight, an arrangement Kay refused. Then Ray called the manager of Trans World Airways (TWA). After Ray spent thirty maddening minutes trying to convince the man to let Smokey ride in a passenger cabin accompanied by one of the team, the TWA manager still wouldn't yield. He'd only send the cub alone in a freight plane — in a crate, as baggage. Angrily, Ray declined.

Desperate for some solution, Ray had a sudden inspiration. It was a long shot. He phoned his good friend Frank Hines, who was the Piper Aircraft dealer in New Mexico. He knew Frank was a generous man. Years before, Frank had rented him Piper Cubs for only three dollars an hour so that Ray could make aerial surveys of wildlife across the state.

Upon hearing Smokey's story, Frank readily volunteered not only to pilot a plane himself and fly the bear to the East Coast, but also to pay expenses for the eighteen hundred mile trip. A few minutes after they hung up, Frank called right back with good news. He had phoned Bill Piper Sr., president of Piper Aircraft Corporation, who offered a spanking new plane for Smokey's trip — a 125-horsepower Pacer — a 'tail dragger' — a new model without a nose wheel.

The next question was: Who would accompany Smokey on the flight to Washington, D. C.? As the director of the Game and Fish Department, Elliott could have claimed one of the seats, but he offered the passenger seats to his men. Ray was the obvious choice, but he declined in favor of two colleagues who had championed Smokey. This act of generosity was part of the cowboy code: You helped other cowhands who needed it. If you won money in a rodeo, you gave some to another cowboy so he could afford the entrance fee to contend.

And Ray had two friends who needed that chance. One was the head ranger Kay Flock, Smokey's new champion. Kay needed some way of getting to a big city where he could buy a car before what threatened to be an outbreak of hostilities — possibly World War III.

The spring of 1950 was an ominous time for the United States. Russia had already moved into Eastern Europe, and by the end of April, Communism had overtaken China and a military storm was brewing over Korea. North Korean tanks were moving south, which Kay feared might precipitate war between the United States and China. The men remembered what had happened on the home front during World War II. All the automobile factories had worked 24 hours a day to churn out jeeps and tanks. For the duration of the war only two hundred new cars had been allowed for the entire population of one hundred thirty-five million Americans.

This time, before it was too late, Kay wanted to nab a new car. The plane could drop him off at the Indianapolis fuel stop, so he could buy a car and drive home.

The other man who needed a ride was Homer Pickens. Ray knew him as a superb animal tracker and fellow Game and Fish Department man. Among other things, as Elliott's assistant director, Homer produced movies. The week before, with Smokey slated to leave soon, the Bells had suddenly realized how much they wanted something to remember him by, and Homer had readily agreed to come over with his 16mm Bell and Howell movie camera to film Smokey, Judy and Jet romping in the living room. So Ray felt grateful to Homer, and knew that this trip would also be the man's only chance to visit his son in Washington. So it was settled.

Chapter 24

Parting with animals is awful: no explanations possible.
–Alec Guinness

Smokey sensed something had changed. The people in his household slumped their shoulders, and Judy sometimes sighed and sniffled when he sat in her lap. He wondered what the matter was. For a short time each day he was being placed in a cage like the one he'd known at the veterinarian's. What did it mean? Was he going to be returned to the vet's?

One afternoon he heard Judy wheedling her older brother Don to put on Smokey's harness and leash. The cub soon gathered what was in store, and got so keyed up that he could hardly stand still for the halter to be buckled. He knew that they were going to traipse across the back yards to little Barbara's house, where he could see the cat Lightning.

Smokey had spent many happy afternoons at the Ragle household. At first Barbara's mother had hovered over the four-year-olds, but now merely kept a watchful eye from nearby as the girls sat on the living room carpet with Smokey and gave him treats.

This time, as soon as Smokey entered the house, he caught Lightning's eye to signal that they should steal a moment to be together. The girls sprawled on the floor with Smokey, but were not playing and giggling. Judy was hugging Smokey and crying. Then Barbara started sobbing and saying, "g'bye." Smokey wrinkled his brow and snuggled with Judy briefly, then escaped to be nose-to-nose with Lightning under the coffee table.

The tiger-striped cat rested her green eyes on Smokey's for a moment, blinked, and then looked away. Lightning said,

"There's no easy way to tell you this, little bear, but the way these girls are acting I think you're in for a change. Have they got out a cage for you at home?"

"Oh, Lightning! Ray put me in a cage for a while yesterday, but maybe it means I'm going home to the forest! And I can see my old friend Strut."

"I don't think so, Smokey. You'll probably never go back to the forest."

Smokey huffed, stood up, bumped his head against the coffee table above, shook his body, and crouched down again. "You're wrong! I have to go back to the forest. It's where I *belong*."

The cat let out a mew of distress. "I don't think so, Smokey. I'm really going to *miss* you." She wailed, "They'll be taking away the first animal friend I've ever had!"

"Oh, Lightning. You're one of *my* best friends! I'm going to miss you, too." Just then Smokey and Lightning heard Don arrive at the back door to fetch the cub.

With a knowing nod to each other, both animals dashed to the bedroom and scooted under the bed. The cat said, "We only have a short time. Don't worry. I'm sure your human family has found a good place for you.

"Remember: If the going gets tough, be *satisfied* that at least you'll have all the *necessities*. That's food, shelter, and safety from predators. It's a miserable life without them; I know, from having been homeless. To be *happy*, though, you'll need a *friend*. You're a smart bear, so make a friend wherever you end up."

Lightning rubbed her chin and whiskered cheeks against Smokey's muzzle. He nuzzled the tiger cat's soft fur in return and said, "I'll never forget you. And I'll remember what you told me. Uh-oh, here come Don's feet. He's going to catch me! Good-bye."

Smokey darted out from under the bed, and, after a short chase, was caught and led home, a very unhappy bear, not knowing what was going to happen to him.

Things moved quickly. It was the day before Smokey's

departure. There was to be a celebration in the evening, with a flight out the next morning. But that afternoon, the Bell household was suddenly thrown into turmoil. Where was Smokey? No one had seen him for an hour or so.

They searched the house and yard. Had someone left the outside gate open? Had he been run over by a car? Judy started crying and Ruth was frantic. The family tried following the spaniel, thinking perhaps he could sniff out Smokey, but Jet was no help in the house or the yard, running hither and yon. Hours went by. If the cub was alive and in trouble, why hadn't he cried out?

Ray's worst thought was that all the publicity had ferreted out some person who took Smokey from the back yard—either kidnapped him for a reward or stole him as a pet. He'd seen people do all sorts of cruel things to wild animals, out of ignorance or selfish thinking—like the gas station owner who had probably shot Ruby's mother to exploit the cub, as if Ruby were a kind of commodity. Some people just didn't think of a wild animal as a real individual with its own life to lead, or, in Smokey's case, a bear destined for whatever future that could best be found for him.

Judy tugged at her father's pant leg and said. "Maybe he's hiding so he doesn't have to go. Maybe he can stay, after all!"

"I'm sorry, sweetie. He's going to get bigger and bigger, and some day he'll hurt someone. And he has a job to do. He has to go to Washington and be an ambassador for all the wild animals so they don't get burned in forest fires like he did."

Judy stared at Ray. "They're going to put him in a *zoo*, and he won't *like* that at all!" She stamped her foot and darted him an angry look.

Ray, Ruth and Don headed into pouring rain to search the neighborhood, calling and asking if anyone had seen the little bear. Left on her own at home, Judy wandered around peering into unlikely places. She was the one to finally discover Smokey—in the empty washing machine in the back room.

Judy called out the back door, "I found him!" and the

others came running, rain-soaked but laughing in relief. She blurted, "I first looked all around the back room, then I looked in the washer—and there he was, fast asleep in his nice nest." The others peered inside the open door to the small front-loading Maytag, and figured out that Smokey must have stretched up, somehow clambered into the washtub and dropped down onto some dirty clothes there. But the little girl insisted that Smokey had been hiding so he could remain home with them forever.

Ruth reached to scoop up Smokey and told Judy, "Sorry, honey, but he has to go. Now, there's not much time for Smokey's bath. Be a good girl. Grab some towels and come help me. This'll be your last chance to play in the bathtub with him."

Smokey's last bath at home

After they had washed Smokey, Ruth let Judy sit at one end of the tub and splash a ball back and forth with Smokey at the other end, until Judy was squealing non-stop. As a rancher's daughter who had grown up with constant danger, accidents and loss, Ruth knew that laughter was the best tonic for hard times. Ruth toweled her daughter, then dried and fluffed Smokey's fur until he was ready for the festivities.

During Smokey's seven-week sojourn with the people of Santa Fe, they had come to love him, so the city had planned a big going-away party for the evening before his departure—June 26, 1950. About two hundred people packed the brightly-decorated community center, with dignitaries on the stage including the town mayor and the head of the Advertising Council—the group that distributed national public service ads and posters for the original Smokey Bear poster campaign.

Smokey seemed satisfied to sit at the head table like a quiet little teddy bear in a high chair, watching the crowd as if he were studying them. Then Ray held up the cub, who twisted his head to fix his eyes on the minister who intoned an invocation.

As the audience clapped, Smokey stood on his chair, alert eyes looking intently at people, sweeping from one side of the hall to the other. When he was seated again, he sat still and was remarkably attentive through the rest of the ceremonies. Speed Simmons stood before the microphone and spoke about the ferocity of the fire and his brave young firefighters who had hunkered down on the rock slide. Then Ray and the vet Ed Smith each told about the rescue of the wounded cub and Smokey's antics in Santa Fe.

Some people thought that the highlight of the evening came at the end when Ray finished answering questions from the audience. He had assumed that the radio broadcasting of the event was over, and was holding the cub in his arms. By then, Smokey had become tired, and was chewing on Ray's gloved hand. Irritated that he couldn't get his teeth through the thick buckskin, he suddenly gave an irritated moan and lunged above the gloves to sink his teeth deep into the man's upper arm. Ray pulled him away, and the microphone blasted to the assembled crowd—and the radio audience—the startled man yelling, "You little son-of-a…"

The crowd exploded in laughter, and Ray laughed with them, and quick-on-the-trigger as usual, he said, "That wasn't fit to go on the air, but that was Smokey's way of making a *speech.*"

Afterward, Ray, Kay Flock, and artist Will Shuster raced to Ragle Airfield nearby and found the Piper PA-20 Pacer. The one favor Bill Piper had asked of the New Mexico team was to paint a bear on each side of the plane. When the men reached the plane, however, they had forgotten to bring a poster of Smokey Bear to copy, so, by a hand-held lantern, Will painted a cartoon image of an injured bear. He slathered lacquer over the watercolors, and the plane was ready to go.

The next morning, June 27th, 1950, the celebration of Smokey's departure was wiped off the front page of the local newspaper by an extra edition of *The New Mexican.*

RCA radio signals from the capital of South Korea had suddenly ceased the previous day. The reason was now known: North Korea's Soviet-built tanks had crossed the 38th parallel into South Korea. The fall of Seoul to the Communists was imminent. The headline read: U.S. ENTERS KOREA WAR.

As it turned out, Kay Flock had been prescient, after all, in sniffing the coming warfare.

President Truman reinstated the draft, and in less than a year the number of active-duty military was 2.9 million Americans.

At dawn the next morning Frank Hines was in the pilot's seat, with Kay Flock and Homer Pickens in two of the passenger seats with thick buckskin gloves in their laps. Outside the plane, Smokey was in his cage on the ground at Ray Bell's feet. His son Don stood nearby, holding Jet's leash. The cocker spaniel strained to reach Smokey and managed to mash his nose into the wire mesh of the cage. The cub sat with his front feet pressed against the mesh, the whites of his small eyes visible as he looked up at Jet. Nearby Judy clutched her mother's leg and sobbed.

The time came to hoist up Smokey, and a heavy-hearted Ray paused a moment holding the cage out from his chest in midair. His eyes misted and he whispered, "Good luck, you little rascal. You'll need it." As arms reached to haul Smokey aboard, Ray found himself touching the brim of his Stetson in a cowboy's salute.

The pilot waved through the window, and everyone waved back. The two-bladed propellers whirred to life, and Smokey's family watched with heavy hearts as the plane revved, taxied away, gained speed down the dirt runway, lifted into the air, and slowly disappeared from sight.

Smokey uneasy in Homer's lap

Chapter 25

O beautiful for spacious skies,
For amber waves of grain
For purple mountain majesties
Above the fruited plain!
–Katharine Lee Bates

As soon as the plane had wobbled through air pockets and leveled off, the three men on board settled back in their seats. In front was Frank Hines, the pilot, and next to him was Kay Flock, keeper of the Santa Fe National Forest. Behind them was seated Homer Pickens, the game warden, and next to him in the cage, Smokey, whom Homer would handle during the trip.

The men squinted above the brilliant early morning sun into the eastern sky ahead. Then they looked down to spot familiar landmarks in the wilderness they knew so well from the ground—dirt roads cutting through the yellow desert around Santa Fe, streams weaving through dark evergreens, and canyons gouging mountainsides.

Tucking his tie into the shirt of his US Forest Service uniform, Kay Flock poured steaming coffee from a big thermos. Kay turned around to the seat behind him to hand a mug to Homer Pickens, the hardy forty-six-year-old looking spiffy in his tan Game and Fish Department uniform—with dark necktie, fancy cowboy boots and Sunday-best western hat.

Homer took the coffee and, putting a finger to his lips, pointed to Smokey on the seat beside him. Both men smiled. They had braced themselves for Smokey throwing screaming fits the whole way, but he looked as cute and calm as could be, asleep on his back, with all four feet straight up in the air. The men raised their eyebrows at each other, hoping the bear cub's quiet composure would last for the three days it would take to fly the eighteen hundred miles to the East Coast.

After a short while, they began the descent to the Texas Panhandle — the first of their seven stops. Breaking through the clouds, they soon spied railroad lines, ranches and grazing cattle dotted across the flat land. When they got low enough to see neat squares of green around miniature houses of a town, Smokey whimpered and pawed his ears. Homer swallowed to clear his own ears, and wished he could tell Smokey how to do the same, but all he could do was make soothing sounds to him.

Smokey and his plane

Frank Hines was an expert pilot, and after they'd bounced twice, they were taxiing smoothly on the paved runway. Since this was only a brief refueling for the plane and a rest stop for Smokey, the cub's three escorts were amazed to find about two hundred people at the little airport waving a welcome to them. Homer wrestled with Smokey to attach a leash to his red halter, and for his trouble got punctured above his heavy gloves with needle-sharp teeth. When they stepped out of the plane, people yelled "Smokey! Smokey Bear!" as flashbulbs exploded.

The game warden quickly led Smokey to a small grassy area, but the cub just looked up at him and moaned. Then Homer remembered what Ray had told him. He called to the nearest people in the crowd, "Anybody got a newspaper they can give me? This is a very neat bear!" Someone handed him an *Amarillo Globe*. Homer hammed it up, elaborately spreading the newspaper on the grass, and the crowd roared approval to see the cub push past Homer and rush onto the papers to do his business.

Catching the high spirits of the crowd, Homer folded the paper carefully and ambled over to them. "Anyone want a genuine souvenir from Smokey?" Holding it up to those close by, he grinned and said, "Take a whiff! I dare you." A few brave souls rose to the bait, howled disgust and the crowd guffawed.

Airborne again, the little plane pierced heavy cloud cover to cruise at four thousand feet directly east over the high plains. As soon as they started their long descent for their second break—at Tulsa, Oklahoma—Smokey grabbed his ears and screamed a shrill protest throughout the long minutes it took to land.

Upon alighting from the plane, the trio of escorts for the cub were again surprised to find so many local families and summer tourists standing at the terminal to greet the cub, clapping and cheering as the bear padded along on his leash. When children stretched their small hands out to pet the cub, Homer, scared they'd be bitten, shouted, "Kay: Quick! Ward off the kids on the left! Frank—take Smokey's right side! I'll watch in front." And they made their way through the crowd safely.

On the way again, this time headed east northeast, the men found themselves leaving the ranches dotted on the flat Great Plains of the Southwest for the grain fields and rounded hills of the Midwest. To pass the time the men exchanged stories about tracking incidents. One of them had been tracking a big mountain lion who'd circled back and suddenly leaped on him from behind. Luckily, he was able to fend it off with the butt of his Colt revolver.

One of them had tracked a male black bear eight miles in a day and told how the bear had the uncanny ability to know exactly when different berries came ripe. He'd seen mothers make their little cubs climb into the upper branches of oaks and shake acorns down to the ground.

This sparked a discussion about how the cub could possibly cope with being locked up. They all knew that bears liked to roam over a wide range.

It seemed a crime to confine an intelligent being like Smokey in a cage with nothing to do, like a life sentence to solitary confinement.

They'd all seen some deplorable conditions in zoos: big animals like bears and tigers pacing back and forth, sometimes with no water to swim in and cool off. No quiet place to get away from the crowds. Animals looking listless. How did that show kids what wild animals were really like?

Kay Flock said, "But when I saw the National Zoo during the war, it didn't seem such a bad place. And recently when I talked with Doc Mann, the one who runs it, he assured me it's one of the best.

"Most people are stuck in cities. Their only chance to see animals up close is still a zoo. Doc Mann told me four million people visit the National Zoo a year. If so many people see animals up close in zoos, they can't help but care what happens to animals in the wild . . . I hope, anyway. Look at this little fellow! You can't help but care what happens to him, sleeping with all four feet in the air like that."

Homer looked over at the cub beside him. "Still, it's going to be a tough life for this furry little guy."

As the afternoon wore on, and clouds cleared enough to see a highway cutting through the fields of wheat, they came upon the thickly wooded rolling green hills of Missouri and began their next descent.

Again, Smokey woke up, clutched his ears and shrieked. The cub rolled his eyes at the game warden as if beseeching him to help. Homer recalled how passenger planes routinely handed out little packets of Chiclets chewing gum to relieve the pressure in passengers' ears. Maybe Smokey would find relief in sucking or eating. He rummaged in his bag for the jar of honey, dipped in his finger and poked it through the wire.

Smokey stopped crying a moment to lick it, and, before the cub could bite him, Homer quickly withdrew his finger. Homer realized that he hadn't fed Smokey all morning. So he slid a small bowl of Pablum into the cage, which Smokey noisily sucked up. Then the cub screamed the rest of the way to their landing at the third stop — the Kratz Airport in St. Louis, Missouri.

Although Homer had just fed Smokey, the cub wasn't any nicer to him when he tried to fasten the leash to the red harness. The little bear fiercely pushed his four feet against the man's arms and stretched up to sink his teeth into the flesh above the gloves. Each bite by itself wasn't so bad, but so many bites had accumulated that Homer's arms seemed like pin cushions. He groaned at the thought that they'd have four more stops to go before Washington, D. C.

The crowd at the St. Louis airport was bigger than ever, and when people pressed forward, the three men were relieved to see Smokey whisked off to the Forest Park Zoo to be fed honey, milk and Pablum, and be housed overnight.

The next morning the Piper Aircraft continued northeast over the flat Indiana cornfields. As planned, the men left Kay Flock at Indianapolis, their fourth stop, to buy his new Oldsmobile and drive it home.

Frank, Homer and Smokey continued their journey northeast over grain fields, which gave way to small towns tucked into the green hills of Kentucky, then factory smokestacks just before they touched down at Cincinnati, Ohio.

Crowds continued to surprise the men at their next stops. Even at the little town of Elkins, nestled among the thick woods and hills of West Virginia, people from the sparsely-populated countryside waited to see Smokey at the brief fuel stop. By this sixth stop, Smokey had the runs from his steady diet of Pablum, and — looking like a very embarrassed bear — did his business the moment his paws touched the paved runway.

On the way once more, the plane pointed east toward the Atlantic Coast. Used to the high, dry desert and western mountains covered with evergreens and aspen, the men gazed with hungry eyes down at the lush, leafy-green deciduous woods of Maryland with glittering streams converging on Chesapeake Bay. At this last stop — the seventh one en route to Washington — a bigger crowd than ever greeted them at the red-bricked city of Baltimore, where a car took Smokey to a veterinary hospital to stay overnight and be given a checkup. Relieved of their charge, the travelers were treated to the hospitality of Marylanders, and attuned their ears to the unfamiliar soft, drawn-out accents.

Unfortunately, on the last morning of the trip, the men awoke to hard rainfall and strong winds. They were due at the reception in Washington, D. C. The city was only forty miles from Baltimore, but it was impossible to take off. Everyone became more frantic as hours ticked by. Finally, by late afternoon, Frank saw the sky clearing a bit and took a chance on making the short hop to their final destination. He arrived at the National Airport just in time for the scheduled reception.

But not without some help. In deference to Smokey, President Truman gave special permission to fly straight over the White House to the airport. And air controllers kept 27 commercial planes in the air until Frank could land, while TWA moved one of its airplanes so Smokey's plane could dock at the assigned gate.

As they stepped out of the plane, the men saw a canopy of umbrellas — five hundred wet people waiting in the sluicing rain. Smokey was led onto the tarmac, and an impressive delegation introduced themselves: Lyle Watts, Chief of the Forest Service; Clint Davis, Smokey's champion at the capital; Bill Piper Sr., the president of Piper Aircraft; and other top-echelon wildlife and Forest Service officials.

Smokey gave his best performance yet to the expectant crowd as many photographers jostled for position. Standing erect holding his paws in front of him, he strutted on his hind legs through puddles, sniffed the air curiously, and gave no heed to the splat of big raindrops—just licked them off his wet muzzle with a long tongue.

Smokey and a Cub Scout

The cub then dropped to all fours, followed by Homer and an entourage of notables, and ambled past a Cub Scout honor guard to the National Airport's Presidential Suite, usually reserved for foreign dignitaries. There, under a *Welcome Smokey* banner flanked by Smokey Bear posters, the cub delighted people by chewing on the green carpet and crunching on the Venetian blinds until Homer pulled him away.

Cued by the photographers, Homer placed Smokey Bear on a table where he sucked warm milk from a baby bottle held by TWA hostesses. Then the cub—his mouth ringed with milky

Smokey and TWA hostesses

foam, sank down and fell asleep. Shortly, awakened by flashbulbs and the high-pitched squeals of little children, Smokey proceeded with determination to mouth an ashtray on the table.

A reporter asked if the bear had been airsick on the trip, and Homer said no, he hadn't. In fact, he'd been a fine flyer. The New Mexican explained that Smokey had grown up at eight thousand feet on a mountain in Lincoln National Forest, and then had lived at seven thousand feet on the high prairie of Santa Fe. Since the plane couldn't fly higher than four thousand feet, the cub had hardly minded the altitude—Homer neglecting to mention the shrieks of pain on descents to airports. In an expansive mood, Homer related how friendly the cub was, but Smokey had become irritable by then and belied his keeper's words by swiping Homer with his pointed claws and biting him, to Homer's chagrin amid a burst of laughter from the crowd.

A motorcade drove Smokey and Homer through Washington, D. C. to the National Zoo. Upon arrival, the zoo director, Doc Mann, registered him as "Smokey, a black bear; Arrival: June 29, 1950; Age: four months old; Weight: eleven pounds." He was now officially checked into his new home, for better or worse.

Smokey with Doc Mann and Homer

Chapter 26

Asusu: To feel unknown and uneasy in a new place.
–Boro language

We remember the bird songs at sunrise.
We remember the grasshoppers jumping at dawn.
We remember the sound of heavy raindrops on leaves.
We remember the song of the male gibbon.
We remember the fruit trees . . . the pineapple, banana, and papaya.
We can still hear the owls cry to each other like we cry.
-Doua Her, Hmong poet

Smokey pattered along the sides of his barren enclosure. After the confinement of his cage aboard the plane, it felt good to stretch his legs and move around. But he didn't like the rough concrete beneath his pads. It was much harder than the cushion of pine needles on the forest floor, or the surfaces back home in Santa Fe—smooth linoleum, a soft carpet, and the grassy lawn. And the cage was bleak, without a trace of wildlife, making him feel disconnected from himself.

His nose enticed him to a pan of moist kibble on the ground. With his lips, he rolled a softened pellet in his mouth. Not bad, he thought, and swallowed it. But his stomach felt queasy and he left the rest for later. He eagerly sucked up water from a nearby bowl, then curled his lips afterward at its strange taste, and snorted out his nose to protest its alien smell.

The cub stopped abruptly a few paces from something odd in his yard—a shiny, silvery surface. It moved like water he had seen, huge compared to the bathtub at home, yet not as wide as the river where he'd seen his father. He stiff-walked over and tentatively pawed the surface. It felt cool and wet, and ripples danced away from his paw to the far corners of the pool.

Smokey wondered what would happen if he went into the water and splashed around, but there was no one like Judy to play with. Would it be hard to get out? Ruth had always lifted him in and out of the steep-walled bathtub at home. He backed away, making a small grunt. He didn't want to try any more new things right now, but he liked the prospect of water nearby.

In the back wall he came upon a dark opening in big rocks that looked like the entrance to a cave. Curious, he was about to poke his head in when he heard a mighty roar somewhere in the vicinity. His body turned rigid. The cub stood, raised his ears, and snapped his head this way and that. Where was the noise coming from? It sounded like a warning call from a giant mountain lion. Fierce snarling erupted as if two enormous cats were fighting over food.

He ran lickety-split toward the tree at the center of his cage and, reaching high with his sharp claws to grip the bare wood, his hind legs boosted him to a large branch. Seated in the safety of the tree, he could tell that the lions were actually at some distance, one growling low and the other grumbling discontent.

From his high vantage point, the cub swept his eyes around the four sides of his enclosure. No big predators in the clearing around his big cage. Smokey was reminded of what Lightning had told him. If you have food, shelter and safety, you have the necessities. He tried to remember what else the cat had said — something you needed to be happy — but he was too tired to think. He certainly wasn't happy. He had not been returned to the forest after all. And his human family had been left far, far, behind.

Smokey raised his nose and deeply inhaled the air. He could detect the faint smell of wet leaves and grasses, mingled with whiffs of pungent and acrid odors from many animals and the stench of their excrement — strange odors he'd never smelled before. And, from the building close by, the faint smell of reptiles, perhaps snakes. There were no animals in sight, except some pigeons walking below on the concrete. He idly watched them, was quickly bored, and looked around.

At least there was this lone tree in the enclosure, but it was oddly smooth and slippery, lacking any bark. And its big branches had no leaves. In fact, the branches ended abruptly only a short distance from the trunk. At least he had a tree to climb and relax in. He sighed, and sprawled prone on a short horizontal branch, letting his four legs dangle below him. After his long journey, he was glad to sleep through the day.

Upon awakening later, Smokey was still curious about the dark opening in the rock wall. Where might it lead? But he preferred to stay at his perch through the long summer evening and night. It was drizzling, and he wouldn't mind some rain penetrating his thick fur to cool him. The air was heavy with the smell of moss, mold and mildew. It was wet air—quite different from the dry air back in the mountains.

The cub listened to the unfamiliar sounds of strange animals settling down for the night. A bird he didn't recognize called out, and another answered from far away. Smokey suddenly felt very small and alone. He craned his neck to look up. The stars were obscured by mist. It would have been comforting to see their twinkling presence. Would the sky be the same here? How could he find out where he was? He could smell a forest nearby, and hoped someone would take him for a walk so he could recognize what animals he'd been smelling and hearing.

The next morning the cub awoke in his tree to a bright sun and a cacophony of noises: trucks coming close, gates clanging, and hungry animals calling. Then, from below him, came a piercing screech, "Heee-yon!" Smokey backed down the tree to the ground. Out from some bushes outside his cage stepped a tall bird that paraded back and forth on the grass, trailing a long folded tail that glittered in the sunlight. Despite being somewhat damp and bedraggled, the bird displayed a majestic bearing. It sashayed over and stood outside Smokey's cage. It slowly lowered its long turquoise neck—sparkling with gold flecks—toward the ground as if it was going to eat something.

Before its head reached the dirt, however, it suddenly thrust its neck upright to emit six more harsh screams. Smokey's attention was riveted on the tall feathered crest jiggling atop its head. Then, noticing some beads of water on its slick back, he was reminded to shake his own damp fur, sending a shower of silver droplets into the air.

Mr. Dazzle   *#146230085*

"*Merde*! Stop that! You're getting me *wet.*" The bird hopped back and fluffed out the emerald green feathers on its shoulders and breast. It tilted its head back to fix Smokey with dark eyes flashing with anger.

Smokey quickly said, "Oh, sorry."

"I *detest* being wet. I'll have you know that I'd almost finished drying my feathers in the sun— enough to preen and oil them—so I could come here and interview you. And look what a reception I get for my trouble!"

Smokey stared at the odd bird. "Stop scolding me! I'm miserable enough."

"Well then, if you don't deign to apologize, I bid you *adieu*!" The bird stalked off a short way on its tall, bony legs.

"Wait a minute, big bird. I apologize. Who are you, anyway?"

"I'm called Dazzle. You'll see the reason for my name sooner or later. *Attendez moi*, so you do not mistake exactly who I am. As you have surmised, I am quite large for a bird, but I am definitely not that oddest of birds — the ostrich. I'm a *peacock*. In fact, a male peacock — not one of those drab little peahens. And, it's *Mister* Dazzle to youngsters like you. I'll have you know that I'm the *only* zoo reporter, so watch your step around me, little bear. Or else I shan't deign to tell you any news. I'm the only animal who's loose in this zoo, so I get around. I investigate anything worth knowing and report it to all you wretched animals confined to cages."

Smokey felt a sudden alarm: How long would he be kept here? He must ask this peacock! But he hesitated to ask. The peacock rattled on about himself non-stop like Lightning did, but didn't seem nearly as friendly as the cat.

"In case you're wondering why I don't have a royal blue neck like those *common* Indian peacocks, it's because I'm a rare 'Green Imperator' from French Indochina. I was born wild in the jungle along the great Mekong River, I'll have you know. After the war, when the French returned, they rescued me as well as my half-starved peahens, and subsequently escorted us to the States as a *special* gift to the zoo here.

"I'm only gracing you with my presence so I can announce your arrival to the others. So would you kindly tell me about yourself? Were you captive-born or wild-born? Of course, wild-caught animals, like myself, are held in higher esteem here at the zoo, since we have known true freedom — to be ourselves."

As soon as the cub told the bird that he had been born wild, lost his mother and was burned by a fire in the mountains, the bird abruptly interrupted. "Well, well, well. You must be Smokey Bear! We've all heard about *you*. This will make the top news of the day for all the animals.

"Let me inform you: You can expect to hear the daily news from now on. That is, as long as you treat me with proper *respect*. Otherwise, famous or not, you're *out of the loop*!" He stretched his long elegant neck over a wing to preen a few feathers, and sashayed away with a slow and stately gait, lurching from side to side on his spindly legs and big feet until he was out of sight.

After the bird had left, Smokey frowned. What highfaluting ways Mr. Dazzle had! So intimidating that the cub had forgotten to ask him about the strange animals he'd been hearing and smelling. He huffed. Outrage filled his chest. How he wished he could shout at that weird-looking bird to come back and answer his questions about the other animals, and how he might escape to the nearby woods.

But he didn't dare antagonize the hoity-toity peacock, for hadn't the bird threatened never to visit again? How Smokey wished to see his good friend Strut. The crow had always been eager to tell him what was happening in the forest.

Suddenly hungry, Smokey ate the rest of his unappetizing pellets, then walked along the front of his enclosure. He passed a series of hard vertical bars unlike anything in nature. So strong that they didn't even move when he banged on them. "Huh," he dismissed them. At the far corner at the front end, he came upon a wrought iron gate. Having seen keepers go in and out, he pushed it with his arms to no avail, then sat and pushed as hard as he could with his hind legs, but it still would hardly budge. That made him so mad he kicked it and bruised the pads of his feet. The other two sides of his cage also had the hard vertical bars like the front.

Huffing to himself, the cub turned tail and cast his eyes toward the back of the enclosure. There was a hill of boulders out of which sprung more upright bars at the far end. He decided not to check it out just now. That way, he might retain slim hope of escape.

A pigeon flew down onto the concrete floor near the food dish. More pigeons came, then the gulls to chase the pigeons away. At least his enclosure cage was wide open to the sky above. How he wished he had the freedom they had. Then he became curious about the big hole in the rock wall toward the back of the yard. Inside the dark cave, he found a large rounded area with rough sides of stonework. It had ample space to sprawl anywhere he wished, but it wasn't at all like his mother's spacious cave that led to endless tunnels. Alas, this den had an entrance but no outlet.

He emerged, blinking in the sunlight, and prowled along the front fence, waiting for something to happen.

Chapter 27

Stardom can be a gilded slavery.
—Helen Hayes

Smokey dons Chief Watts' hat

A whiff of someone familiar reached Smokey's nostrils. Shortly, he recognized the distinctive walk of Homer Pickens, the man who had handled him during the airplane trip. The game warden was accompanied by a stranger in gray overalls who unlocked the gate for the two men to enter. Holding the red halter and murmuring softly, the way he had always done, Homer walked slowly toward Smokey. The cub moaned and mewed to him, glad to smell and see someone he knew. When Homer reached out to touch him, though, Smokey felt an irresistible urge to play, and cavorted away—just out of reach, like he used to do with Ray or Don. The chase was on.

The gray-clad attendant said, "Let me catch him, Mr. Pickens. I know how." The next thing the cub knew, the strange man had lunged, grabbed his shoulders, and pressed him onto the concrete with firm hands. In return, Smokey seized the man's nearest leg with all four feet, bit him hard and raked him with his claws until he pierced the overalls, causing rivulets of blood to run down the leg. The man flinched and cursed, but still held the cub down, swiftly attached the harness, snapped on the chain, and jumped aside. Smokey gathered his paws under him, glaring at the man—a commanding type like Ray whom he'd have to combat with all his strength.

Grumbling, Smokey followed the two men out the gate, but as soon as they were outside the enclosure, he was glad to see his surroundings. To his disappointment, they didn't take him for a long walk, as his family back home would have. They stopped at a large grassy area not far from his enclosure, where a crowd of people waited. Smokey slumped onto the lawn, and let Homer pick up his limp body and set him on a table. It was just another ceremony where people intoned and flashbulbs blasted the air. He sat up and looked around, then, grunting to himself, flopped down to sleep. The photographers shouted to Homer to make the cub do something, so the game warden swung and clanked the chain-leash. Smokey caught the leash with his teeth, yanked it and chewed on it. People cheered—and flashbulbs burst in his face.

The photographers next asked Chief Watts to pose with the bear. When Watts removed his hat to place it on Smokey, the cub quickly rose on his hind legs, reached for the hat and pulled it down on his own head, like he'd seen Ray do with his cowboy hat. The bear's eyes sparkled as they swept over the crowd. Hundreds of people erupted into laughter, and a series of flashbulbs went off again. Smokey turned away. He didn't like bright lights in his face, and, by now, crowds of people soon bored him. The cub sat and wouldn't be prodded to parade among the children. Finally the gray-clad man searched his pockets to pique the bear's interest, and dangled things in front of his muzzle. Soon Smokey was enticed to move forward, trying to clutch with his teeth and chew each thing in succession—a pencil, then a handkerchief, and best of all, a thick leather glove.

Afterward, Smokey found himself relieved to return to his increasingly familiar cage. And he found something new there: a big cardboard poster, propped against his tree trunk. He nosed the Smokey Bear poster at the base, then climbed part way up the tree and bit the top edge of the intruder.

Photographers leaped over the outer railing and held their cameras at the iron bars, aimed at him. More flashbulbs went off. The cub had had enough. With one thrust of his hind feet, he pushed the poster to the ground, swiftly climbed down the tree, went over to the back wall and curled up to sleep — with his rear end facing the crowd.

While the cub was snoozing, he was dimly aware that the same gray-uniformed zookeeper returned to replenish his food and water. Then, later in the afternoon, the man — who now smelled strongly of different strange animals — entered through the front gate once more. Curious, but not wanting to move, Smokey opened one eye to watch. The keeper went over to the far corner, poked the bear scat with a stick, and bent over as if to sniff, then scraped a bit of it into a small box.

What a strange place this was, where a human acted more like other animals. The people he had known so far had never smelled his poop. In fact, his family back home in Santa Fe hadn't seemed at all interested in his or Jet's poop, even when it was still fresh and warm, redolent with scents of food and each animal's unique odors. They made it disappear as soon as they could.

Smokey raised his head to see what this odd man would do next. He fiddled nearby and suddenly appeared lugging a long rubber hose that resembled an enormous snake. Smokey galumphed to his tree and was safe at a high perch when the man held the snake near its head — and let loose a great gush of water to splash onto the concrete floor. After the man disappeared again, the cub climbed down and gingerly touched the floor with his paws to find it wet. Shaking his paws now and then, he minced his way to the far corner.

His poop and pee were gone. That was good; he liked his home clean. Yet it annoyed him too. The water-cleaning had destroyed the entire scent-map on the ground. Now everything beneath his feet was utterly boring: No smells of yesterday's treats on the concrete, no trace of where a bird had alighted, and none of his own body-odor to mark this place as his own territory. After a while he noticed something else that was odd. The floor stayed wet a long time, unlike the forest and the Santa Fe back yard that soaked up rain and dried quite readily, especially on a sunny day. He must remember to glare at that keeper when he appeared with the hose again. He perked up at the thought of swatting the hose from the man's hands.

With the first birdsong of morning, Smokey heard the zoo come awake. There was the same hubbub of truck engines and animal calls he'd heard the day before. The keeper returned, and, oblivious of the irritable looks the cub darted his way, went ahead and filled his bowls with fresh water and food. The strong smell of food compelled the cub's attention and he gobbled it down. By the time he looked up, the man was gone. His hunger satisfied, Smokey sat with his front paws resting on his round belly, relieved to know food would come every morning and perhaps the evening, too, like it had at home. Is this what the cat, Lightning, had meant by 'necessities'?

Familiar screams of "Hee-yon" brought Smokey running to the front fence, where he was careful to properly greet his new acquaintance as 'Mr. Dazzle.' In return, the peacock ducked under the outer railing, pranced a few steps just outside the upright bars, turned to face Smokey to make sure the cub was watching, and said in an imperious voice, "*Attendez*! You will now see why I'm called *Monsieur* Dazzle!" He shook and rattled his tail until it broke open into a wide array of feathers with sparkling blue eyes. Smokey rocked back on his feet in amazement, and said with awe, "Oh, Mr. Dazzle!"

The peacock inclined his brilliant green-and-gold neck in a slight bow toward Smokey and seemed pleased. The big bird folded his tail and came closer. He told the cub that throngs of people outside the zoo were lined up — as far as he could see — to enter the outer gates. It was a longer line than the one for the grizzly cub who'd arrived the day before Smokey. "*Certainement*, you are the biggest star attraction I have yet seen in my four years at the zoo."

Smokey didn't know what a 'star attraction' was. Not

knowing what to say, whether he should act flattered or humbled, he thanked the bird for telling him, and quickly changed the subject to ask if there was any other news. Dazzle told him that the grizzly bear was as young as Smokey, but much bigger—a hundred pounds. Usually people flocked to see grizzlies because they were so big and fierce, he said, but, inexplicably, they all wanted to see little Smokey.

"But—" The cub tried to ask Dazzle why people wanted to see him, and why he was being kept in a zoo, but the peacock brooked no interruption and continued to recount other news of the day. The male giraffe—a spotted animal as tall as a building with very long legs—had started wooing a female giraffe, both moving in a slow dance with their necks swaying together to brush softly against each other.

And the old hippopotamus—a short-legged fat animal like a huge pig—had been groaning all night with a toothache in one of his big yellow teeth—probably from too many sweets. With a disdainful voice, the bird told how this hippo had always wallowed in the water near the fence, his enormous mouth open all day for treats. His rotten tooth was his own fault. Be that as it may, the zoo always tended even such foolish animals. So the white-clad vet was already headed across the zoo to the hippo's wallow.

The cub loved hearing the news, and was about to ask all the questions he had stored up, when they both heard the distant gates clanging open. Mr. Dazzle bid a hasty *adieu*, saying, "Soon they will come! I must depart." Smokey hadn't thought that such a big bird could lift himself off the ground, so he was surprised to see how Mr. Dazzle could spread his wings, whoosh the air, angle up sharply, and disappear.

Before long, the sound of scuffing footsteps and voices came closer, and a stampede of people rushed up to his cage, leaning forward against the horizontal railing outside the upright iron bars. They were talking in high voices and pointing at him. The cub backed up to the rock wall, and sidled toward the dark hole of his cave. Then, curiosity made him amble forth on all fours. He hesitated behind his tree to sneak looks at the people. Most were children. Some were clapping their hands and smiling. Others had long faces, cooing sympathetically, "Don't you think he looks sad?" and "Poor Smokey — burned in a fire!"

Smokey and AAA kids

The cub spied many little girls. Perhaps Judy was among them! He stood erect, walked forward eagerly and pressed his muzzle against the long bars. He searched among the children's faces for his friend. No Judy. He retreated a few steps, sat and sucked his paw.

Then a teenage boy as big as Don threw fluffy things through the bars that landed on the floor of the enclosure. Smokey gamboled over and scooped one up with his lips. Popcorn covered with something like honey! The boy laughed heartily and threw some more before his father admonished him, "The sign says: don't feed the animals." Meanwhile, Smokey smacked his lips and finished the popped kernels. He stood, raised a paw, and stared meaningfully at the boy. The cub knew he had more treats, because he could see the boy eating them out of the Cracker Jack box he was holding. This boy was certainly not like Don, who would have laughed and given him more.

Smokey sighed, and shinnied up the tree to sit on his favorite branch, with his arms and legs dangling. With curious eyes, he watched people come and go until boredom overcame him. His long eyelashes opened and closed, and he yawned widely. This excited his audience who pointed at him—something he didn't like. He glowered at them, backed his way down from the tree, and retreated to sleep out of sight in his rock cave.

Toward the end of the day, a new man entered the enclosure. Dressed in white, he approached quietly, and handled Smokey nicely like the man in the white suit whom he'd first known when he'd been burned. The bear relaxed and let the vet examine him, submitting to the careful touch and muted voice. The routine was familiar: his stomach pressed gently, his ears and mouth examined, a light shined in his eyes, his chest and back thumped. The man also deftly snipped off the tips of each claw. When the vet left, Smokey lay prone on the damp concrete floor and whimpered. He longed to be cradled against Ruth's bosom and fed Pablum. How he wished Judy was there to sing little songs to him.

Smokey was glad to have met one animal at this new place, Mr. Dazzle. The cub wasn't sure he liked the peacock, who was too uppity, but what other choice was there? Then he remembered what Lightning had said. To be *happy*, the cat said, one needed a *friend*. But all his good friends were far away. He wished they could come visit, or that he could escape to the woods nearby and find a wild friend there.

How could he escape? The cub stood and spun around to carefully appraise his entire enclosure for any gap. There were iron bars on the front three sides of his enclosure. Could he possibly squeeze through? Excited at the prospect, he ran over and tried. No, the space between the bars was too narrow.

His last hope was in the back territory of his large cage. He clambered over the hill of boulders to the top only to find upright bars there, too. He looked up at the pale blue sky. There were puffy clouds, so big that he'd never seen anything quite like them. How he wished he could fly out of the cage and see things himself. Or fly away. Better yet, fly home to the forest—back to the world where he belonged.

Chapter 28

To a Louse: O wad some Power the giftie gie us
To see ourselves as others see us!
–Robert Burns

Quales illic homunculi: What weird munchkins.
–Lucius Apuleius

Sprawled on the concrete in early morning sunshine, with his head resting on his paws, Smokey dozed until harsh screeches interrupted his lazy calm. He leaped to his feet and craned his neck toward the front of the cage. There, near the paved path, was Mr. Dazzle with three other peacocks that were smaller and less colorful. They must be his girlfriends.

With his head cocked high, Mr. Dazzle strode up to one peahen—but she continued pecking at the ground here and there. Undaunted, he rushed in front of her and spread his tail in a magnificent display. Without even looking at him, she turned and walked away.

Watching this, Smokey barely suppressed a giggle. Dazzle pranced to the second peahen, but she didn't even look up. The last one whom he courted promptly ducked her head into some bushes and disappeared. Crestfallen, the peacock stood immobile. Smokey chortled.

Dazzle darted an angry look at the bear, hee-yonned loudly and poked his head into the bushes. The peacock then proceeded to enter until his folded tail was almost out of sight, then backed out, catching a tail feather on a twig so it turned askew. He darted his bill at the feather to jab it back in place. Out of the bushes, he shook his head, stomped the ground, and raked the dirt with his big claws.

Seeing Dazzle so mad, Smokey couldn't help but sit down, grab his back feet in front of him and rock back and forth in glee. He hadn't had such a good laugh since he'd been with Strut. It felt so good! Laughter burst forth in loud gasps. "Ha! Ha! Mr. Dazzle. Better luck next time!"

Dazzle stopped scratching the ground, folded his tail tight, and glowered at Smokey. Then, flailing his wings he flew up onto the horizontal railing just outside the iron bars. He arched his head high and fixed beady eyes on the bear. Smokey tilted onto his stubby tail and fell over backwards. Dazzle whooshed his wings so fiercely at Smokey that the cub recoiled from the breeze.

"*Ça suffit. Arrête!* How dare you laugh at me, you little smart-aleck. Enough! *You*: I will not visit again!" He dropped to the ground, wheeled his ungainly body around, stretched his long legs and flew off.

Smokey huffed under his breath. Couldn't Dazzle take any kidding? Strut would have laughed, but not this haughty bird. The cub wondered whether everybody here in this miserable place took themselves too seriously. What was the fun of that?

The cub moped around through the day, anticipating without much enthusiasm the familiar routine: the distant lions roaring for their meal, food and water plunked down by the zookeeper, and the coming and going of people staring at him. He didn't rouse himself more than to eat his food and retrieve popcorn that a boy or girl threw his way.

The next morning he heard "Hee-yon" in the distance several times, but the peacock didn't visit. Time passed slowly, and Smokey slept a lot. By the following morning, he'd been at the zoo almost a week, and life seemed lonelier and more boring than ever. He became so glum that he hardly stirred himself, until he became so hungry that he had to eat his kibble.

Restless in the late afternoon after the people had left, he was grumbling to himself about how hot and humid it was, when the zookeeper entered with his hose. Smokey looked up, and raised his brows in a mischievous way. He ran over and jumped at the water as it splashed onto the floor. The keeper laughed, and sprayed him with a fine mist. Smokey cavorted around the yard trying to capture the spray wherever it hit the floor. It was great fun, but it ended too quickly. The keeper looped the hose over his shoulder and abruptly left.

Running around had heated him up, but only his outer fur had been sprinkled so the bear wasn't cooled off. Until then, he had ignored the pool in his enclosure, except for pawing the water the first day. The cub ventured over and found the broad step below the water line. Smokey summoned his courage and stepped down. Soon he was up to his neck in water. The cool liquid seeped through his long fur and then his thick undercoat to cool his skin.

He hesitated only a moment before he launched himself across the pool. His head went under right away and he gulped water. Frantically clawing, he raised his head and blew it out his snout. Then he stood on the top step in the pool, his breathing rapid, and shook his head vigorously to scatter the drops. Glowering at the pool as if it were an enemy to overcome, he eased his body in again. This time he instinctively raised his muzzle to breathe. With his eyes and nose above the surface, his legs paddled slowly and smoothly. It felt great to swim. How his muscles yearned to move!

He lolled in the pool awhile, dunked his body underwater up to his nose, slapped the surface with his paw, and enjoyed each new sensation. He finally emerged, happy to have found something he liked, and gave his body some good shakes that sent water flying. "Well, Mr. Dazzle," he thought, "I can get along without you!"

One evening soon afterward Smokey was startled by loud staccato sounds. The darkening sky lit up as if by lightning, but not the kind of mountaintop lightning that jangled his head and prickled his fur. A faint smell of fire wafted past his nostrils. Was a forest fire coming? He ran to his den and backed his rear end inside.

Then he heard high-pitched chattering—the happy

rippling sounds that Judy and her little playmate Barbara used to make. He squinted through the dark. Two little figures were climbing up the outside of his enclosure. They paused at the top, nodded to each other, and peered down at him.

Who were these little folk? They looked like tiny adult humans with long arms and legs—but no clothes. In a friendly sing-song voice the smaller one called down. "Hi, we're Trish and Trash. Want a visit?" In response, Smokey mewed eagerly. Using their long curling tails, they swung themselves over the top of the enclosure and down the inside, squeaking with glee. They leaped onto the ground at the far side of the cage and stood upright, clinging to each other.

There, below the tall lamplight, they looked at him with intelligent eyes. They had short gray-brown fur, and furless faces with big eyes and little noses. The base of their pointy ears lay flat against the sides of their heads, like humans' did, and their little paws seemed more like a child's hands than Smokey's own.

Trish and Trash   #75229333

The cub thought they must be some kind of human, so small that, even upright, they'd hardly reach a child's knee. "Don't be afraid," one of them said. "We're just monkeys." Then they crouched on all fours in order to show Smokey that they were indeed wild animals.

They widened their lips to grin at him showing lots of white teeth, and raised their light-colored eyebrows to sparkle their eyes mischievously at him. Smokey mewed longingly and swiftly bowed in an invitation to play. They chirruped, and with feigned charges and fast changes of direction the three raced after each other. The monkeys were quicker than the puppy Jet, and could bound over Smokey and spring up high onto the fence. At last, exhausted, they all flopped on the floor next to each other.

The male monkey, Trash, caught his breath first. "Thought you might like some fun, after your fight with that stuck-up old bird, Razzle-dazzle. Ha! You sure showed him!"

Trish added, "But we came tonight because we've been hearing popping sounds today. So we thought it'd be fun to watch the fireworks together."

The two monkeys lay on their backs on the concrete and motioned the nearby cub to look up at the sky. A loud bang — like a tree exploding in the forest fire — was followed by a bright star that curved higher and higher into the sky until it burst into pink starlets that crackled like bushes on fire. Trish brushed a soothing hand across Smokey's arm, and Trash said, "Don't worry, buddy. Just enjoy the show." Smokey's tense body soon relaxed, and he chimed in with the monkeys' "oh's" and "ah's" at one star-burst after another.

When there was a pause, Smokey asked, "What's this all about?" and Trash sputtered angrily, "It happens about this time every year. Humans are celebrating something, like they're the lucky ones — *free* out there, not in *prison* like us!" A finale of bangs and bursts came, then the sky became black, leaving only traces of a strange burnt smell in the air.

The monkeys leaned against Smokey. He remained still, soaking up the wonderful feeling of lounging beside new friends in the delicious stillness of the night. After a while, he asked them, "How did you get here? Don't they lock you up?"

Trash answered. "You know, monkeys can get out of anything. So before the keeper left our island this morning, we hid his empty banana crate, so we could hold onto it — and swim across the moat. That's why our fur is so wet."

"I'm so glad you came. I've been dying to find out what's going on at the zoo. Especially these last few days, since Mr. Dazzle . . . well, he's mad at me and won't come by any more."

"Just leave it to us. We'll make it worth his while to visit you again. And when he finally does show up, all you gotta do is flatter him—about how handsome and important he is."

The cub remembered the most important question to ask anyone at the zoo. "Were *you* born in the Wild?"

Trish spoke in a soft voice. "Yes, both wild-born in the jungle. I'd ride upside down clinging onto my mother's belly and we'd go everywhere. Until men shot her . . ." Smokey said he'd lost his mother, too. There was silence between them for a long moment. Trash said that he had lost his mother at the same time, so the two babies were put in the same wicker basket. "We liked each other right away, and clung together the entire trip from Sumatra. We've been partners on Monkey Island ever since."

Trash broke in, "Let's tell Smokey about all the other animals." Smokey was glad to hear him describe lions, gazelles and other animals whose fur and food and dung he had been detecting at the zoo. Smokey asked about the mysterious low rumbling vibrations he felt in the pads of his feet from time to time, and Trish told him how enormous elephants are. Smokey was especially happy to have the monkeys confirm the presence of familiar animals he'd known in the mountains whose special fragrance he sometimes sniffed: deer, raccoons, and fat marmots.

All too soon, Trish and Trash reached their arms up the fence to go home. Smokey quickly said, "I can smell the woods nearby. Help me get out of here! I want to run free again. Is there any way I can go there?"

Trish looked at him with sad eyes. "I'm sorry, Smokey. It's so near . . . and so far. Rock Creek Park is just across the road. But you could get hit by a car. And there might not be enough food for a bear there, so you'd end up prowling around houses for garbage—and risk getting *shot*."

Smokey looked at the four walls of his enclosure. Then he heaved a sigh. Although it was a prison, it felt safe, and he could count on being fed. At least he now had two new friends. In good-bye, Trish tickled the cub on the stomach, and the two slipped away, their dancing shadows dissolving into the darkness. They called back to him that they'd visit again. Then the zoo went silent.

Smokey slept late. Upon awakening, he grouched at himself that Mr. Dazzle had probably already come—like the monkeys said he would—so he'd already missed the chance to see him. Then he searched the air for the zoo animals the monkeys had described. He pursued distinctive scents to see if he could recognize certain animals—their moods, the food they were eating, their dung. It made him feel a bit more like his old self in the forest.

Smokey sank to the concrete floor. They were all captive. Moreover, he was in a cage by himself, unlike the orangutans and hoofed animals that were allowed to live with their own kind. Maybe he'd never again get a chance to actually watch other animals. He sighed and tried to cheer himself up. At least, thanks to the monkeys, he now knew the scentscape, and that made life more interesting.

The following morning Dazzle appeared, because, he said, he'd heard from the monkeys that Smokey had been suffering terrible shame for having been so disrespectful to him. The peacock said that Trish and Trash had begged—and remunerated him well—or he wouldn't have *deigned* to hear the bear's apology. Smokey was at first a little taken aback, but lowered his head and mumbled how sorry he was. It wasn't so hard to lie, after all! The peacock looked at him with sly eyes below half-closed lids, and said that he couldn't quite hear him. "Speak up!"

The cub turned away a moment, and, raising his brows to put on a contrite face, declared, "I'm sorry." In fact, in saying it the second time, it almost felt like he meant it.

Then the cub remembered what else the monkeys had told him. He raised his eyes, slowly looked Dazzle up and down, and told him that he was surely the most handsome and dignified bird he'd ever seen. And, in saying it, he realized that it was indeed true. Is that what those wily monkeys had intended? Dazzle jerked up his head, let out a short squawk, and spilled out all the news Smokey had missed. When the bird left, Smokey went over and whopped his tree with both paws, proud that he could handle things so well in this strange place—with some help from his friends.

Chapter 29

To a Mouse: Wee sleeket, cowran, tim'rous beastie!
O, what a panic's in thy breastie
Thou need na start awa sae hasty,
Wi' bickering brattle!
I wad be laith to rin an'chase thee,
Wi' murd'ring pattle [paddle]! . . .
But Mousie, thou are no thing lane [not alone],
In proving foresight may be vain:
The best laid schemes o' Mice an' Men
Gang aft agley [often go awry],
An' lea'e us nought but grief an' pain,
For promis'd joy!
–Robert Burns

Tact is after all a kind of mind-reading.
–Sarah Orne Jewett

Smokey awoke very early and savored the cool morning air. This was his favorite time of day. Amid a chorus of insects, he listened to the ke-ting-ting song of a certain wake-up bird, then the incessant sharp sound of Mr. One-Note, soon joined by a full chorus of twittering birds. The sun soon showed itself orange, then slowly began to thrust its hot breath onto the concrete. The cub gazed at the pale blue sky, and marveled again at the fireworks he'd seen there.

Then, out of the corner of his eye, Smokey saw a man standing outside the enclosure. His presence was puzzling. No one ever came this early. No peacock, keeper or crowd. This man was not large but he had the presence of someone much larger. He just stood, his breathing easy and slow, his eyes in the cub's direction—but not staring. Smokey rose on his hind legs and watched him.

After a long pause, the man clicked his tongue against the roof of his mouth, sounding just like Mother Bear. Smokey leaned toward him and moaned softly. In response, the man strolled closer, opened the gate and slowly sidled in, leaving the door slightly ajar within arm's reach. Smokey eyed him, chomped his teeth together, snorted and charged, then halted several feet away. The man seemed to have anticipated the bluff-charge because he casually raised his arms to appear taller, took one step to the side, lowered his eyebrows and made a low "eh-eh" sound.

Smokey's nose wrinkled and he sniffed hard. This was the man with the fur above his upper lip. On the cub's first day at the zoo, this person had gathered him into his arms like a vet to weigh him. He had also been at the ceremony on the lawn, standing with an air of importance among the other men. Smokey dropped onto all fours. At the same time Doc Mann crouched, resting his eyes lightly on the bear. They both waited.

Behind the glasses slipping down Doc's nose, the eyes were twinkling as the zoo director took a paper bag out of his pants pocket and rustled the paper. He brought out something round and red and bit into it, releasing a sweet aroma into the air. Smokey let out a series of hunger-moans, widened his nose to smell, and stretched his neck closer to see. Doc chuckled, and lowered his head and shoulders in a playful bow. Smokey flashed an open-mouthed smile in return, and quickly made a play bow.

Then the director tossed it, and Smokey ran after the rolling ball and pounced on it. He clutched the sweet-smelling apple between his paws and devoured it with gusto — seeds, stem and all. Then he looked expectantly back at the man still crouched inside the gate.

Smokey sauntered sideways to him, nuzzled his pockets, finding no more apples, sighed and rested his chin on Doc's bent knee. The cub raised his eyes to search the man's face. The zoo director shrugged and showed his empty hands, which the cub understood as "no more." Smokey yelped and spread his claws wide, ready to rake Doc's pants, but the man grunted the 'eh-eh' warning and flicked his hand as if to give a playful swat. The cub skidded a short distance away and looked back in dismay. Doc grinned in satisfaction, and slipped back out the gate. "See you next week, little guy. And I'll bring another surprise." Smokey watched Doc Mann until he was out of sight.

Then the bear scrambled up and down his tree as fast as he could, and dashed around the perimeter of the cage. Maybe he'd found a new friend — someone to look forward to during these boring days.

Smokey launched himself through the air into the pool slapping the water in a loud belly-flop. He swam around, twirling in the water one way and the other. He sloshed through the water to the steps, and made low purring-chortles from deep inside. Finally he emerged from the water, dripping, with his wet fur spiked. The cub's buoyant spirit carried him through the rest of day as Dazzle visited, the keeper came and went, and the crowd grew and then thinned.

That evening, as the sky began to darken, Smokey was lolling inside the coolness of his cave, wonderfully tired from such an upbeat day, when he heard a strange, high-pitched squeak coming from the direction of his food dish. It was a very different sound than the usual cooing of pigeons pecking bits of spilled kibble. Wondering who it might be, he roused himself to amble over. There, standing on its hind legs, was a brown rat, front paws held in front and tightened into two little fists, and a very long coarse tail extended behind him.

The animal looked like it might have poor eyesight because it swayed sideways back and forth as if to see any movements of the cub and catch whiffs of his scent. Smokey sniffed deeply and recognized the trace of rodent fur and dry grass that he'd been noticing lately along the wall outside his cave.

The rat spoke first. "Whadya think yer doin? Ya didn' leave me no kibble!" With ears flattened and whiskers pulled back, he glared at Smokey. "Don'tcha know what happens to wiseguys like you?"

Smokey frowned at the impertinent creature, and replied indignantly, "What are you talking about? That's *my* food."

Squinting his black beady eyes, the rodent stared steadily back. Smokey sputtered at him, "I'm stuck in here. You're out there—where you can get your own food.

Freddie

Go raid some squirrel stash, and leave *my* food alone!"

"Ya big dumb mug. Yer in the city now. And dis is my territory."

Smokey moved closer to tower over the rat. The bear narrowed his small eyes and clacked his teeth angrily. "What's all that mumbo-jumbo? This is not your territory, it's mine."

The rat stood his ground and pricked his ears. "Ya don't get it, do ya? Lookit, I'm yer *protection*. Ya want everybody bargin' in on da action? Pesterin' you? Different gangs scramblin' in here, screamin' bloody murder all night? Just gimme da measly one percent, den everythin's nice and orderly. Think about it."

Smokey was annoyed. The nerve of this tiny pest! "I will not, you toothy little rodent."

The rat smirked. "Ya'd better. Otherwise, as soon as dat keeper fills yer bowl, I'll sneak in here and piss all over it. Make it real tasty, ha, ha." He laughed in a sneery way. "Or ya can stay awake all night wonderin' when I'm gunna creep up and bite yer *toes*!"

Smokey was so astonished that he just stood there as the rat scuttled back through the bars, paused on the other side, and said, "Make up yer mind. By tomorrow night."

All the next day the cub couldn't help worrying what to do about the rat. He debated whether to ask Mr. Dazzle for advice, but couldn't bring himself to admit being intimidated by such a small creature. What would Strut, his cunning crow friend, say to the rat, or better yet, what about the smart monkeys Trish and Trash? Then, as he was going after popcorn thrown on the floor of his cage, an idea came to him. He could hardly wait to see the rat.

In the middle of that long summer evening, the brown rat finally stood before the cub, his brownish-white underbelly showing a fast-beating heart, and his pink rounded ears looking translucent in the fading sunlight behind him. This time, Smokey greeted him cordially, introduced himself and asked the rat his name. "I'm Freddie-da-Rat. But don't try buttering me up wid sweet talk. Dis is *business*."

The cub was momentarily distracted from his plan, but then said, "This kibble is kind of boring, don't you think? How'd you like a really nice treat every night instead? Don't you toothy guys—like chipmunks and squirrels—prefer stuff like seeds and nuts? How'd you like some crunchy popcorn? You won't even have to come inside the fence. In the evening, just hide in the strip of tall weeds outside the fence and I'll sweep kernels of corn out to you."

Freddie rubbed his mouth with his two hands as if he were relishing the taste. "Well, well, well. Ain't you da smart one? Yeah, that'd be okay."

"But there's one more thing I want thrown into the bargain. Mr. Dazzle tells me only news about the zoo. You're wild. You can tell me about the woods and the city out there."

Freddie fixed him with bright eyes. He wiggled the impressive spray of whiskers that burst from both sides of his snout, as if sniffing whether it was a good bargain. Smokey added, "You can even tell me how hard life is out there for you and your gang."

"Really? Agreed, then." And Freddie-the-Rat scurried through the fence and disappeared into his burrow somewhere in the weeds.

The cub gave a sigh of relief. Then he huffed. He could outsmart these city animals any day. You just had to figure out something they'd like—that he didn't need—and give it to them. As easy as that. Strut would have been proud of him. The monkeys too.

Chapter 30

The tragedy of life is not so much what men suffer, but rather what they miss.
–Thomas Carlyle

It has been my experience that folks who have no vices have very few virtues.
–Abraham Lincoln

During the next hot days, whenever Smokey wanted to cool off and take a respite from the crowds, he swam for a while in his pool. It boosted his spirits. He also lounged in the shade, grooming his body and snoozing when he was bored during the day, which allowed him to stay up late and savor the night scents. As early as twilight he sometimes stretched his back on the concrete floor to stare at the sky.

How he liked the long summer evenings. The stirring of animals reminded him of the sounds he'd heard in the mountains back home — the rustling of small creatures on the ground, the last of the calls of the whippoorwills. And he welcomed the familiar conclusion of the day: The soft drone of crickets died down, and the far off hoo-hooing of owls ended. The moon rose late, bats flickered about in the dark, and the nights became still.

In the quiet of one night after another, he discovered that the moon changed until it became a sliver, and by mid-month it was gone, and the night so dark that Smokey found it spooky. In this faraway place where he now found himself, would the moon ever return? He counted on its presence during the long nights. Besides the familiar cricket and bird songs in early evening, the moon was a reassuring presence from his forest home.

On the morning of July 15, after the cub's first scary night in the dark of the moon, the gray-clad zookeeper came early with a spring in his step, whistling as he did his chores. To Smokey, his mood seemed brisk with anticipation as if something good was going to happen. But the man merely cleaned the floor, put kibble and fresh water down without even looking at Smokey, closed the gate, and left.

After lunch time, when crowds had thinned, the zoo keeper returned with Doc Mann. Smokey recognized Doc right away — the man with glasses and fur below his nose — who'd brought him an apple. The two men were in a merry mood as they talked outside the gate. The zoo director handed the keeper a sign to hang up on the outer fence: "SMOKEY GONE — TO MEET HOPALONG CASSIDY."

Doc Mann entered the enclosure laughing, and Smokey ran over to him eager for a treat. While he snuffled the man's pants pockets, his red halter and leash were quickly attached. That signaled something even better than food. It meant they were going outside. A moment later he happily scurried after the zoo director out of the enclosure.

Before the cub could protest, though, he was hastily crammed into a small cage which was hoisted onto the back of a pickup truck. Smokey looked up at the zoo director and moaned. Doc caught his eye and said softly, "It's okay, little fellow. Just give me a chance to secure your cage and I'll lower the tailgate so you can look out back and see the sights."

The cub was left alone. Where was Doc taking him? He pictured the morning that Ray had picked him up in his box from the ranch basement, still terrified and suffering from burns. Ray had gently set Smokey next to him in the front seat of the pickup to be carried away from the forest to another world. Was he now being rescued from the zoo to go back to somewhere familiar — or somewhere new?

The front door of the truck slammed shut, and the engine started. Smokey was distracted from his hopes and worries by the medley of scents from different animals as he traveled through the zoo grounds. Soon the truck left the zoo and sped down city streets, where the breeze past his nose brought a confusing assault of odors—gas fumes, burnt rubber, hot asphalt. Dust in the air mingled with the scent of flowering bushes. It was exciting, but the longer he was whisked through town, the dizzier he became from the succession of sights flashing by—the blur of trees, buildings, and people.

The cub was taken by surprise the first time the truck abruptly braked at a stoplight. He tumbled onto his back and let out a rasping shriek. Smokey hated being thrown off balance! He scrunched up his face in concentration, determined to keep his footing.

The third time the truck stopped he was chortling in anticipation, and when they careened around corners, he leaned expertly to the side with his feet flattened. What a game! People in the convertible following the pickup waved and smiled at Smokey.

The vehicle slowed down as it entered a dirt road leading to a large meadow. Smokey's nostrils caught the heavy scent of buttery popcorn in the air and the sugary smell of pink cotton candy. Shortly after the truck stopped, the cub was released from his cage and set on the hard-packed dirt, strewn with yellow straw. Doc held the leash. Smokey wondered if the immense tent nearby was the next place he was going to live. Thumping music and a loud voice came from inside the Big Top, and the air was filled with trails of strong and unusual scents. The cub's heart beat fast at the musky smell of big animals and their dung. The sweat from some creatures smelled watery with exertion; other sweat was pungent with anxiety. This was a much more exciting scentscape than his home at the zoo.

One woman with flowing red hair and dark blue around her eyes started to saunter by and then stopped. She swept her purple shawl aside to bend down, smile widely and murmur to him. He liked her aroma of herbs. Suddenly the cub flinched.

He had spied something moving. It was a big snake looped around her neck with the rest wrapped around her waist. He was not usually interested in snakes, could hardly smell them, but he stared curiously at this one's thick body and its darting tongue.

He watched the woman leave, walk to her trailer, and open the door. The snake glided through her hands onto the floor and disappeared. It must be a pet—like a dog, he thought. Maybe he himself was going to be a pet here too, and live in one of those trailers with some nice family who'd take him for walks.

Smokey strained against his short leash. He wanted to see the animals gathering at the entrance to the tent, in particular, an odd, long-legged, knobby-kneed animal. Quite tall, with a big hump on its back and flabby lips. Its gait was slow, and as it strolled along, the camel rocked back and forth from side to side.

Then the cub was distracted by workmen who rushed ahead to adjust ropes at the tent entrance. An enormous truck backed up with loud beeps. People were shouting. This place was exciting to see, but awfully noisy.

Smokey's attention was drawn to the strong scents of big wild animals coming from a huge open truck that had just stopped nearby. It was loaded with three cages of tigers. A woman walked with confidence and ease alongside the cages of beautifully-striped tigers, talking and humming to them. Dressed in tight black pants and a shimmering jacket, she carried a long stick that she rested nonchalantly against her shoulder. At certain moments, in rhythm with her humming, she gave a quick twist of her wrist and snapped the leather strips that dangled from the end of the stick to make a cracking sound in the air. Then she hopped into the cab of the truck and headed for the tent.

An elephant lumbered past. A baby elephant hurried to catch up, its trunk raised to hold onto its mother's tail. When the elephant pair arrived to join the others at the tent entrance, the people, hoofed animals, and furry ones moved aside so the elephant pair could move to first place. The animals and people stood casually, as if they didn't mind being so close to each other. But the tigers paced impatiently in their cages until finally, with groans, they relaxed onto the floor, yawned, and waited like all the others.

Smokey was delighted when Doc walked him closer to the entrance so he could watch the waiting animals. From far inside the tent, an elephant trumpeted, and the mother elephant at the entrance arched her trunk and trumpeted back. As if that was a signal, workmen jumped forward to open wide the tent flap and secure it. The little elephant swung its mother's tail playfully and stamped its flat feet in place. Then the animals and people pressed forward and the line bunched up in restless anticipation.

Oompah-oompah music began. And, at the sound of a drawn-out whistle from far inside the tent, the line at last moved forward through the entrance. In the lead was the mother elephant, her trunk coiled high, with the little elephant close behind. She stepped ahead at a measured pace and the procession followed. Next pranced the horses with people astride, then a camel, a person with a red-capped monkey on his shoulder, a group of colorful people with erect postures, and finally little black and white dogs wearing ruffled costumes.

After they had disappeared, Smokey craned his neck to see inside the tent, but the workmen quickly roped the flap shut again. The little bear huffed in frustration. The loud music that had accompanied the procession stopped. From inside came the outbreak of clapping every so often. How Smokey wished he could see what was happening in there!

With the departure of the parade, the commotion outside the tent faded away to silence. Smokey stood alone with Doc. Was he going to be left here after all? The cub felt his throat tighten, and he sighed at the thought that he might never see his new friends, the monkeys, back at the zoo. He searched the zoo director's face and stance for any clue, but could discern nothing.

Then the cub took a deep breath to trace the great array of animal smells still in the air. His heart leaped. It'd be more lively here than in the zoo. These animals seemed to move around much more freely. Most of them were out of their cages, and others mingled easily with people — who seemed more like friends than his own keeper who only brought food and cleaned up.

Smokey wondered, though, whether the animals here were somehow too tame and oddly cautious. He recalled something he'd seen earlier. Did those dark brown spots under the elephant's eyes indicate that she cried in distress? Since she was so big, why couldn't she just break free? Smokey's helpless feelings about his own fate confused him, and so he lay on the ground and escaped into sleep.

A voice boomed from inside the tent and woke him. Rousing oompah-oompah music began again. Smokey stood and shifted from one foot to the other in time with the beat. Soon the same workmen who had closed the tent flap swiftly loosened the ropes so it was partly open, checked their watches, and held the ropes coiled in their hands ready to open the entrance wider. It looked dark inside, but Smokey could smell the sweat of a great crowd of people in the tent.

Doc Mann pulled out the fob from the little pocket at the waist of his pants, glanced at his watch, grunted, and wound the watch absentmindedly while he looked back up the dirt road. Sensing the tension, Smokey sucked his paw. Soon two cars came up the road in a swirl of dust. Men hastily clambered out to greet Doc Mann, glance at Smokey, and linger nearby, fiddling with cameras.

Smokey could tell that the cluster of people gathered around him were in a jovial mood. Some glanced every once in a while at the play of light and shadows that moved just inside the slit of the tent flap. Something was going to happen. At the sound of two short whistles from inside, the workmen leaped to the sides of the slitted opening, pulled the flap wide, secured the ropes, and jumped aside.

Out came a procession—completely different from the one which Smokey had seen enter the same opening. In the lead were two people with red balls on their noses, white around their eyes, and big red-colored smiling lips. They were laughing and looked harmless as they came closer. He liked the funny, sloppy way they walked with their floppy shoes. Smokey stared at them, entranced to see their baggy striped clothes and mops of orange hair. When they came near, they looked right at him, smiled, and both did a flip at the same time, landing in front of him. What strange humans, he thought, like monkeys who were always doing surprising things for the fun of it.

The main procession followed the clowns. First came an enormous elephant, his big ears sweeping back and forward in time with his measured pace. The fringed cloth hanging over his square forehead glittered in the sun, and flashed a purple jewel in the center. Perched just behind the broad head of the elephant was a small man whose hair was wrapped in a cloth. The pink plume above his turban reminded the cub of the bobbles that jiggled atop Mr. Dazzle's head.

Behind the mahout and standing upright on the elephant's back were two long-legged slim women, looking relaxed and smiling. Each was dressed in a small gold top and a short skirt that stood out stiffly. They had almost gone past when one woman spied the bear and pointed him out to the other, who quickly leaned forward and tapped the mahout on his shoulder. Nodding assent, the mahout jabbed a stick into a well-worn spot behind the elephant's ear. The great beast winced momentarily at being prodded by the bull hook, then turned and came slogging up to the cub. His big ears were spread to either side of his head and softly fanned the air back and forth. Up close, his ears looked tattered and sun-bleached, and his gray skin appeared mottled and wrinkled with age.

As the shadow of the elephant loomed across Smokey, he

jumped backward, then leaped up Doc's back and straddled his shoulder, peeking around the zoo director's neck. By then, the great beast had already backed up a short way and was slowly kneeling on his front legs. When the big animal was settled, he looked at Smokey a long moment, appraising the cub. Smokey met his gaze, and was awed at how wise the old eyes looked. Although he felt humbled, the cub dared to look again into the elephant's eyes, and knew, in that moment, that he and the elephant shared a similar sadness.

The mahout prodded the elephant again, so the animal had to turn his head aside. Smokey saw him reach with his curving trunk to encircle the nearest woman on his back around the waist and gently set her upright on the ground. The other woman called out, and he did the same for her. Complaining in muffled sounds, the aged beast rose from his knees and stood.

Both women joined hands and giggled cheerfully like little Judy and her friend Barbara. Smiling broadly at him and cooing, they pattered in their slippers toward Smokey. The cub lowered himself down Doc's back and shinnied down a pants leg, stretched to the end of his short leash and whimpered longingly at the friendly young women. Doc nodded to them, so they slowly reached out their hands, and carefully tousled the fur on the cub's back for a moment. Cameramen flashed pictures. Then Smokey sat on Doc's shoes, and the women stood on either side of Doc, leaning into him. When the two young women slipped their arms around Doc's waist, the man laughed awkwardly, but the cub sensed he was pleased.

The elephant moved on, and the rest of the procession followed. As they went by, some of the performers peeled off the line to get their pictures taken with Smokey, but soon most of them had departed, leaving only the original cluster of cameramen, the two young women near Doc, a few other performers, and Smokey. The group continued to wait, looking expectantly at the opening in the tent.

A man came out and walked briskly toward them. He had an air of importance, like Doc Mann, which made Smokey anticipate that his fate might be in this person's hands. The bear studied him intently as he approached. He was dressed in a white shirt and white bow-tie, black pants, tall boots, a black coat with a red vest showing, and a high black hat. He was quite sturdy and plump. The black coat tails swept down low and his body was rounded, but he nevertheless moved with a stately stride and firm forward footfall.

With one sweeping motion of his arm and a jerk of his head, the man genially but firmly motioned the two women and some other bystanders to move on. Then, beaming, he clasped Dr. Mann's shoulders. "Welcome to the Cole Brothers Circus." He had a mellow voice and a hearty manner that the bear cub liked. Maybe he was going to be his new protector! The man pointed toward the opening in the tent, and Smokey wondered who would emerge next. With a few polite words, the ringmaster departed, and the remaining group waited.

Suddenly from inside the tent a white horse appeared, fancy-prancing in time with the music. Astride him was a silver-haired cowboy dressed in a black outfit with shiny silver buttons and a big-brimmed tall-crowned black cowboy hat. As he rode toward them, the cowboy pushed his hat higher on his forehead with the same slow movement of his hand that Ray did when he greeted someone. The cowboy neck-reined lightly so the horse side-shuffled toward them with soft-falling hoof-beats. As they came alongside, the cub was drawn to the man's calm, easy-going manner.

Could it possibly be Ray, who had come to take him home? He moaned "uh-uh" and strained forward on his leash to see and smell better. Then he stopped pulling. This cowboy didn't smell at all like Ray, and held his shoulders a different way. Nevertheless, Smokey hoped, if his life was to change once again, this man might be his new protector. The cub shook with excitement—part curiosity and part foreboding.

The horse halted to drum his hooves in place as he suddenly caught the scent of the cub. He snorted, his nostrils flared, his ears went back, and he raised his head as if to rear, but the cowboy spoke in soothing tones, and the horse settled down. Doc moved Smokey a few steps back. The horse eyed the bear, and must have recognized how very small he was, for the startled look in the animal's eyes changed, and he soon regarded the cub with a certain nonchalance, if not disdain.

Doc stepped forward with a laugh and called up to the man, "Well, well, well. Bill Boyd, we meet again. You know, I've never seen you up close in that Hopalong outfit—only in movies. What a handsome saddle—must have cost a pretty penny! And that cowboy suit has the softest leather and fanciest fringes I've ever seen." Doc stroked the horse on the side of his neck as well as on the velvety nose. "So this is the famous Topper—a real beauty."

Then Dr. Mann caught William Boyd's eye and stepped aside to bow toward the cub. "And here's Smokey."

"This is the first time I've seen the live Smokey Bear. Isn't he a cute fellow?" The man in black then nodded to the cameramen. "You can get those cameras ready."

Doc Mann took off his heavy leather gloves that extended well above his wrists, and proffered them to the cowboy. "Bill, you better take these. He can be a feisty little fellow—a real terror."

"No need. If I can't handle a little animal like this with bare hands, I'm not Hopalong Cassidy!"

"Well, if you say so, but don't say I didn't warn you."

Bill Boyd quickly took off his own black gloves. He tucked them at his waist so they folded over the low-slung belt that held silver pistols on his hips. He dropped the reins around the saddle horn, leaned over, and reached down. "Just hand that little fellow up here." Doc put his thick gloves back on, held Smokey under the cub's armpits and raised him to the cowboy.

Smokey felt himself grabbed by the loose skin of his neck and plunked down behind the saddle horn facing the horse's neck. He was clasped from behind by strange hands and pressed back against the cowboy's body. Flashes from cameras blinded his eyes. Smokey roared his outrage, bit the wrist holding him, and twisted around to face his tormenter. Then he peed so hard it drenched the front of the cowboy's outfit—from the waist clear down the pants. Boyd yelled and the cub found himself flung through the air to the ground.

The cub caught his breath, sprang from the ground and scurried back to Dr. Mann. Smokey clung to the man's leg with one paw, and sucked his other paw. He knew he'd done something bad and moaned to Doc, who made reassuring sounds. The silence was broken by one of the slim women who had been riding the elephant. She was one who had earlier put her arm around Dr. Mann's waist and had remained at a short distance. She shouted at Boyd. "What'd you do to that little bear? How dare you hurt him!"

Doc Mann sighed, felt the cub all over, and said to Boyd, "Don't worry. It's okay. This little guy isn't hurt; he tumbles easily. This rascal bites so hard that he can make anyone mad before they know it." He winked, but Boyd didn't react. The famous cowboy's jaw was tight as he growled under his breath. Everyone waited to see what would happen.

Finally Boyd shook his head, as if to shake off what had happened, saying, "Well, I'm just an actor, you know, not as perfect as Hopalong, for heaven's sake." He looked straight at them with his good-natured Hopalong Cassidy smile, and let out William Boyd's—and Hoppy's—distinctive and wonderfully hearty laugh. Everyone else laughed too, in relief.

A moment later, though, Boyd shot a commanding stare at the photographers and asked them in a strained voice, "You guys aren't going to use those photos where I goofed, are you? You know, ever since the thirties, Hopalong's been a real hero to children. Not violent. Always captures rustlers instead of shooting them. Never uses his pistol unless an outlaw draws first." Boyd implored the photographers, "We can't disappoint the kids now, after all these years, can we?"

The men joked about how shocking the headlines would be in *The Washington Post* and *The Evening Star*: "Cowboy Idol Slams Heroic Baby Bear to Ground." But seeing how sheepish

Boyd looked, they assured him they wouldn't use any of the incriminating pictures. Before the 'incident,' they'd gotten enough good shots of the cub seated on the horse with Hoppy. Bill futilely flicked his hands over his soggy pants as if to brush them off, pulled at the soft leather that was sticking to his legs and released it to cling once again to his skin. By the time he looked up at everyone he was in good enough spirits to josh with the photographers.

Smokey let go of Doc's pant leg as soon as he sensed the atmosphere among the men had changed for the better. Still, he knew he had angered the cowboy and disappointed Doc. What had happened? Something he'd been wondering about occurred to him again: Men might have such soft skin that a bite or rake of his claws — which wouldn't bother another cub like him with thick fur and tough skin — might actually hurt people and make them mad. How surprising, since men were so big and powerful. Sometimes Jet had yelped when they played rough, but the cocker had always come back for more.

Soon afterward, the pickup drove back on the dirt road, and Smokey realized that he'd be returning to the zoo after all. Tired, he curled up in resignation. At least the zoo was safe and had plenty of food. And now he had stories to tell the monkeys: how he'd almost been given to the dignified man or the cowboy, and what amazing people and animals he'd seen and smelled at the tent. If only he could tell Strut about it!

Chapter 31

I asked him, "How do you keep such a large elephant tied to such a small stake?" He said, "When elephants are small, they try to pull out the stake, and they fail. When they grow large, they never try to pull out the stake again."
–Vivek Paul

Umuofia was like a startled animal with ears erect, sniffing the silent, ominous air and not knowing which way to run.
–Chinua Achebe

As soon as Smokey came back from the circus, he looked over at his food bowl, and was glad to see it full of food. It must have been filled while he was gone. Having missed popcorn and other treats from the afternoon crowds, hunger pangs cramped his stomach. The cub ran over, plunged his muzzle into the kibble and gobbled a mouthful. He immediately spewed it out. It tasted awful. Stepping back, the cub saw drops of yellow liquid on the kibble. He sniffed it. The rat had peed on his food. How dare he!

Smokey stood erect and glowered at the spot where he'd last seen Freddie. From the unkempt weeds on the other side of the fence, a little voice piped up in a rasping singsong: "Nyah-nya, Nyah-nya, Nyah-nyah." Smokey rushed over and whammed the iron bars with his paws. Freddie poked his pointed nose out of the tall grasses, wiggled his whiskers, and sneered, "Ha, ha. Ya can't catch ME!" A roar rumbled out of Smokey's chest and his eyes glared at the impudent face. Freddie stood on his hind legs and stuck his nose up. "Dis is a warning. Ya'd better deliver. Next time ya cut me out of popcorn, I'll bite yer toes while ya sleep."

Smokey's jaw dropped and his lower lip hung slack. The nerve—trying to play tit-for-tat! He thrust his head forward. "You better watch out, you little twerp! Watch out . . . or someday I'll crush you with my foot!"

"Yeah, big guy, but ya have to catch me first."

The little bear turned his back on the rat and huffed. That rodent was due for a comeuppance! With each breath, more anger filled his chest until he thought he would burst. He clattered his teeth, and shook his head as if to rid himself of a buzzing fly. Finally his shoulders slumped and a wavering moan came from deep within. The truth of his utter helplessness in the zoo made him despair. He was a prisoner, at the mercy of everyone—even a rat.

Smokey recalled the sad eyes of the big elephant at the circus. Even that great and gentle creature was captive, too. He remembered how the mother and baby elephant had to wait in line to enter the tent as if they were tame, and how the big elephant had to carry people on his back and kneel when prodded with a bull hook, dug into what looked like a raw wound. The elephants at the circus seemed as helpless as he himself, even though he had seen them walking in the open. Were they caged at other times? Why didn't they try to escape?

He walked over to the chain link fence and pictured how the monkeys had swung up and down wherever they wanted. Smokey reached up, as if to climb the fence, but stopped at a memory of falling backward with a hard thud when he had tried to climb the chain link fence at Ray's house. In frustration, he ran to the upright bars at the front of his enclosure. The cub pressed his face against the hard metal rods until it hurt, as if he could push his way out. Then he yanked at the bars but they were still stronger than the strongest trees and didn't budge. The cub drew back his arm, whacked the barrier and grunted, "Huh-huh!" until the pads of his paws hurt.

Smokey suddenly felt the full exhaustion of his exciting day at the circus as well as his disappointment at coming home to the rat. He pattered to the cave, groaned, curled into a tight ball, and cried himself to sleep. The next day he didn't stir. As if through a fog, he heard Mr. Dazzle's far-off screech followed by the sounds of the keeper coming and going, and a succession of children's voices outside the cave. With his head on the concrete and a dull ache in his chest, he remained very still in the dark cave all day, then welcomed the oblivion of night. In the morning the cub stretched, checked his paws, and when he found that they hadn't been bitten by the rat after all, slumped down again to doze the day away. Another day passed without the cub moving much.

The sun was high in the sky when Smokey sensed someone nearby. He didn't bother to raise his head, just rolled his eyes upward. There was Doc Mann peering into the cave. A woman stood just inside the gate. She caught Smokey's dull eye and held up a bottle for him to see. His throat tightened with longing. "Baa-woo-wooo," he cried out to her in a trembling voice.

The cub toddled over and sniffed her legs. She wasn't Ruth, but she smelled similar to her. He stretched up to her knee, eager for the bottle. In a moment she was seated on the concrete, softly humming the way Ruth had. Smokey crawled into her lap, and was soon cradled in Lucile's arms. She held the bottle for him, and he pressed his paws against her wrist and sucked the Pablum greedily. Doc quietly crouched next to his wife. She nudged him and said, "Ruth Bell was right. He sure loves Pablum." Smokey paused a moment to gasp for breath and chortled low sounds of contentment.

Doc sighed in relief. "What a change! He's been looking so gloomy—hardly ate anything these last two days. Thank goodness there's nothing wrong with him. Just needs cheering up—till he gets used to things. It must be a miserable existence for the little fellow."

Lucile gazed at Smokey's face. "He's awfully young to be left alone. No wonder he got depressed. Maybe he should have stayed in the house with us at first—for at least a little while— like the other orphans do. Babies need some kindness—and some excitement — or they just don't thrive."

"There was too much pressure for the public to see Smokey ... Well, they can do without him this afternoon. Let's take him on an outing. Give him a taste of his old world. How about Rock Creek Park? We can be there in a jiffy. Why don't you wait here while I get his harness and a long leash?"

The two people laughed together, and Smokey sensed that something good was in the offing. By the time Doc returned, Smokey had finished the bottle. He curved his tongue over the white ring of Pablum circling his mouth and licked up drops that he had drooled onto his chin. Then, with his belly round and warm, he clutched Lucile's shoulder to nuzzle her neck, whimpered all his grief to her, glommed onto her ear and sucked it noisily.

Smokey slipped away from the woman's lap onto the concrete floor, ate his kibble and sucked up water from his bowl. Bill had returned, but departed again, saying, "I forgot. I'll have to make a sign for the public." A few minutes later he called to his wife from the front of the enclosure. "Here's what it says: *Smokey Exhibit Closed for the Afternoon by Order of William Mann, Zoo Director.*"

The cub's relaxed face beamed at the sight of his leash and halter in the zoo director's hand. It signaled a walk! He readily complied with being placed in his halter, but when Bill tried to coax him into a small wire carrier, he balked. Treats finally tempted him to enter, and the cub was taken to a car and the carrier placed between the couple in the front seat. During the short ride through the city streets, the Manns opened the car windows to a cooling breeze.

The little bear could tell when they entered the woods — damper and more sweet-smelling than the mountain forest he'd known. The tires made sloshing sounds as the car slowly forded a stream, and then parked on the far side where no cars or people were in sight. Smokey's carrier was lifted out of the car and set on the ground. Donning gloves, adjusting his glasses, and wrapping the end of the long leash securely around his wrist, Doc let the cub out of his carrier.

The moment all four paws touched the grass, Smokey was wonderstruck. He threw himself down and rolled onto his back, feet up in the air, wiggling to rub the grass smell into his fur. Then he bolted ahead and almost immediately was brought up short by the leash. Doc called back over his shoulder to Lucile, "Hurry up, dear. He's stronger than I'd have thought. Off we go!"

On the run, pulling the zoo director behind him, Smokey took big gulps of forest air. It was laden with the sweet scent of honeysuckle and damp leaves. The ground emitted smells of all kinds of small animals. He romped over to some tulip poplar trees—tall and straight like the stately lodgepole pines back home. Sticky aphid goo at the base of a tulip poplar made him snort and sidestep. He reached his front legs up the trunk and dug his claws into the strangely furrowed bark—much more satisfying to grip than that smooth tree trunk at the zoo, stripped of its bark. He boosted himself a short way up the tree and just hung there for a moment, feeling the wonderful stretch of his body as he licked up some aphids.

The cub was itching to climb higher when he heard a squirrel scold him from the adjacent tree. He backed down to the ground and bounced over to climb up the squirrel's tree, hearing the indignant little animal chattering insults down at him. He happily boosted himself up the trunk, but was suddenly stopped by the pull of the leash on his halter. Frustrated at being interrupted, the chubby bear stretched his neck upward, but the insistent jerking continued so he had to shinny down.

If only he was free of the leash and could run and run . . . Yet, he was soon distracted by smells and sights nearby. Everything was tantalizing. He spied a yellow-and-white flower on a honeysuckle vine. Curious, he mouthed it, and loved the sweet new taste so much that he scooted over to a tangle of the abundant vines for more. It felt like home at last.

Soon the bear's nose led him to a spot near the base of a tree where he snuffled a squirrel stash, and his claws dug up the ground. Leaves and dirt flew out behind him. He found a cache of old acorns, their caps partially rotted, but the insides still good to eat. A log lay nearby. It wasn't hard and dry — like the fallen trees in the mountains — but crumbling-soft and damp. This made it easy to claw through the bark and find fat squirming grubs. A black beetle tried to walk away, but Smokey pounced on it, touched his tongue to it, scrunched up his face in distaste and spit it out.

The little bear lifted his nose and inhaled the scent of berries. He crashed into thick underbrush, tugging hard on the leash, and soon found himself in a thicket of blackberries. He passed over all the hard green ones, but here and there spied some berries already ripening: sweet-smelling reddish-purple ones. The little bear stood on his hind legs as tall as he could to enclose the nearest plump blackberry in his loose sensitive lips, easily avoiding the thorns. He savored the taste, and moved on to the next one. By the time Smokey had eaten as many ripe berries as he could find, his long leash had become so tangled that he couldn't move his head.

Smokey shrieked, and was rescued by Doc who led him out of the thicket, and then toward the roar of water at Rock Creek — much larger than the river he'd known back home. The cub surveyed the sharp rocks and the crashing water to find a calm eddy near shore where he could drink. For the first time, he saw a fish and jumped at it, but it slipped away.

Lucile exclaimed, "How he loves to be free! Let's keep having him lead us — wherever he wants to go." Smokey proceeded on the wide path upstream and came upon a strange orange and black rock. He reached out and turned it over with his claws, and was startled to see scaly arms and legs flail the air. Smokey placed his paw on it, and the head quickly disappeared inside the shell. The cub jumped back, then timidly nudged the shell with his nose. Lucile interceded and turned the box turtle right side up. Full of wonder, Smokey sniffed it, tongued it, and stared for a long time until Lucile finally pulled him away from the closed shell. He balked, and didn't budge until he could watch the turtle finally emerge and plod along its way.

Shortly Smokey found a small stream that flowed downhill into the big creek. He wondered why there was no trace of deer at the intersection of the waters, but he did smell the strong musky scent of skunk luring him onto a narrow animal path climbing uphill along the little stream. It led to a well-worn animal tunnel through the bushes. Opening his mouth and flaring his nostrils to inhale a cascade of animal smells, Smokey proceeded to run up the tunnel. But the leash stopped him with annoying frequency. Why couldn't he run free?

The cub looked impatiently behind him where the humans crouched, coming slowly through the low bush-tunnel, stopping to part the higher foliage with their arms. Then they crept on their hands and knees through the dense underbrush. They were such slow animals! Smokey determinedly dragged them forward until he heard Lucile call out in distress. He looked back, and saw that she had fallen on the ground and was untangling her foot from a honeysuckle vine. Doc helped her up. Smokey grunted and pushed on.

When the animal path came to an end, Smokey splashed his way up the middle of the stream and could hear the two people splashing through the water close behind. Every once in a while the cub turned over a rock beside the stream to see what might squiggle in the mud. He found a black-spotted red salamander, which wiggle-walked away on its tiny splayed feet before he could decide whether to taste it.

Eventually the cub emerged from the woods into a shade-flecked area. There, in the middle of a marsh, was the origin of the brook he'd been following. It was a spring-fed pond — wider than Doc's outstretched arms. Smokey peered into the still, dark water and was startled to see a furry animal staring back at him. Alarmed, he jumped back. It jumped backwards too, then could no longer be seen. He cautiously approached the pond and was startled to see the animal again. He sniffed it, making a loud snuffling noise. Since he couldn't smell anything to confirm its presence, he shrugged and warily walked to the other side of the pond.

Smokey in Rock Creek Park

In the shallow water near his feet swam pollywogs, most with just a fat swinging tail behind their bulbous heads, but some already with little legs sticking out. As he lowered his muzzle to suck in the cold liquid, he saw their guardian. Above the surface of the water were two bulging eyes and at each side—two hands with tiny spread fingers. Below the surface, the frog's long back legs slanted down into the water behind it. Once Smokey had seen one frog, he spied more pairs of frog eyes in the pond. When he moved his head closer, they plunged and left only ripples on the surface.

Skunk cabbage lent a musky smell to the marshy area. Smokey ambled around the pond, eating young curled fern-heads in the marsh. He liked the cool feel of his paw pads squishing in the mud. When he came full circle back to the place where the spring spilled out to the tinkling brook, he found small delicate watercress leaves in the running water to feast upon.

Soon flying bugs swarmed around Smokey's head, but he didn't mind. In fact, he liked to snap at flies, bees or wasps and eat them. The cub wondered why the humans frantically swatted the mosquitoes buzzing around them. Why didn't they just eat them? He didn't understand their sounds of distress as they slapped their arms and the back of their legs. They became so agitated that Doc yanked him away from the pond. "Let's get out of here!" Smokey stood his ground and braced his legs, but Doc repeatedly tugged on the leash, then pulled steadily to shorten the space between them.

The cub's irritation grew. He wanted more watercress! Smokey woofed and abruptly stood up on his hind legs, which jerked the line taut and plopped him backward into the pool. Doc, sliding in the mud and holding his glasses, crashed in after him, and they ended up seated side by side in the pond, the man coughing and spitting out water, Smokey with mouth open and his tan eyebrows raised in surprise.

Lucile started laughing. The cub was reminded of Judy giggling in the bathtub with him, so he playfully splashed water at Doc. The man laughed and splashed him back. After a short water fight, Lucile offered her hand to Doc, and he slogged out, his clothes dripping and muddy from the stirred-up silt. Smokey remained up to his neck in water, cooling down from the hot muggy air. But Doc still held the leash and finally sweet-talked him out—a wet, muddy, contented bear.

The cub was still exhilarated, but tired enough to let himself be led up the slope beyond the pond. They entered quiet woods. The bright summer sun filtered down through a high canopy of tulip poplar trees to the delicate dogwoods nearby and kept the woods pleasantly warm in the mid-afternoon. As they walked, the shade trees gave way to dense pines. The strong smell of home assailed Smokey as he crept beneath the pine branches, and felt the thick pine needles cushion his feet.

The bear cub lay down for a moment, and rolled on his back, savoring the familiar smell of pine sap. He hoped he'd be brought to the woods often. Maybe someday they'd let him run free. He longed to stay in these woods and explore other creeks and find new foods, and, best of all, smell the familiar earth and animals like the ones he'd known back at his old home in the mountains.

The three soon reached the top of the slope where there was a small grassy meadow in an old clearing. The Manns lolled on the grass in the sunshine, and let Smokey gambol within a wide circle around them — as far as the long leash allowed. The cub jumped after butterflies and tasted different flowers and grasses. How wonderful to see new things and eat whatever he wanted: tiny red strawberries close to the ground and yellow-centered daisies. He spotted his old favorites — dandelion heads and the blossoms of lavender-pink clover — and ran all around to devour them.

Seeing the little bear look so happy cavorting in the meadow, Doc said, "He sure loves it here! I'm glad we came. Too bad he can't really be free like this! I feel bad putting him back in his enclosure."

The two stood up and heaved out long sighs. They hugged. Smokey looked up at them quizzically, and they returned his look with tender eyes. Doc said to Lucile, "Someday there'll have to be wildlife parks where animals like Smokey can roam around like this. People could drive through and see how smart — and lively — they are in their natural habitat. And why can't orphaned animals be reintroduced to the wild? At least, after their stint at a zoo or wherever, they should be entitled to retire somewhere to a better life."

The little bear was tired enough to pad after the Manns until they reached the car. Doc stood holding his leash while Lucile spread a towel on the driver's seat where Doc, with his wet clothes, would sit, and another towel under Smokey's carrier nearby. The cub strained toward the woods but the man jerked his leash and managed to grab him. However, when he tried to jam Smokey into the small carrier, he resisted with all his might. He screamed and bit Doc. The man yelped, shook his hand, and put on his rawhide gloves. Smokey spread his legs wide, clutched the outside of the cage door and twisted to bite again. Doc pried the claws from the wire and crammed Smokey into his carrier.

"That little tyke can't be much more than the eleven pounds on his arrival, but he's already awfully strong. We won't be able to bring him here much longer, poor fellow. Perhaps one more time before we leave for the expedition in fall. Then, by the time we get back from the trip, he'll be too big. We won't dare take him on a walk then. If he broke loose — then what?"

Lucile said, "I can just see the headline: Famous Smokey Bear lost in Rock Creek Park. Escaped from Dr. William Mann, Director of the National Zoo for the past twenty-five years." They both looked into the cage at Smokey, who raised his innocent tan eyebrows at them, but they couldn't meet his eyes. They turned their heads away and held hands for a quiet moment. "One more time," Doc promised. Lucile said, "Too bad he has to be so confined all his life, to suffer, even if it's for a good cause." Then they started the car and drove back through the park to return Smokey to the zoo.

Back in Smokey's enclosure again, Doc uncurled the hose and sprayed the marsh mud off his own pants and off Smokey. After the man left. Smokey felt tired, and more forlorn than ever at being caged again. He retreated to the shaded side of the rocks outside his cave. Every so often he wistfully lifted his nose to breathe in the windborne smell of the woods.

As he recognized the different smells and tastes he'd discovered earlier in the day, he relived the happiest time he'd had in a long while. Smokey watched the evening fade, and the stars come out. Although he hated the bars on all sides, at least the rare day of freedom had made him feel restored to himself somehow, and he felt light-hearted enough to look at the clear expanse above and welcome the moonlit sky.

In the dead of night, Smokey thought he heard a tiny voice say, "Watch out!" Was it a dream? He didn't want to wake up, but something made him open one sleepy eye. His front paw felt a sharp sting like the prick of a big thorn. By the faint light from the high lamp at the sidewalk, he saw that it was Freddie biting him! He jumped up and swiped at the rat, who sailed through the air and landed with a thud. The rat was scurrying away when the bear pounced on him. His front paw came down on Freddie's long tail, pinning him to the concrete.

Freddie let out a piercing squeal, thrashed his body mightily to try to free himself, and at last managed to turn his head around to bite the cub's paw. Smokey angrily held the rat's body down on the concrete with his other paw so he couldn't move. "How do you like being trapped? Huh, you little rat?"

His chest so squashed, the rat could hardly speak, but he managed to say between gasping breaths, "So ya got me, ya big bully. What're ya going to do? Kill me?" While Smokey paused to think, the rat suddenly squirmed out from under his grasp, and scooted toward the fence. But before Freddie could escape, the cub caught him again. This time, Smokey pressed the soft pads of his big paws together to hold the rat by the tail. Then the bear stood on his hind legs with the rat high in the air. Freddie dangled upside-down, writhing and spitting angrily.

Straining his muscles, Freddie tried to bend his body upward, bared his lips to show sharp front teeth, and snapped at the paws that held him, but he couldn't reach high enough. The rat emitted a distinct odor of fear. Smokey saw yellow liquid dribble down the rat's lower light-brown underbelly and onto his tail. The cocky rat had wet himself in his anxiety. This made Smokey laugh in triumph, and he snorted. "I caught you, you dirty little rodent. Now you can see what it feels like to be a prisoner. And I'm your keeper."

Freddie's body went limp, and suddenly Smokey's gleeful

feelings died. In a chastened tone, he asked, "Are you okay?" He peered into the rat's face, but the eyes were clenched tight. When the eyes opened, they didn't look like the rat's usual flashing eyes, but dull in defeat. The bear grunted, not knowing what to do.

The cub pictured the big elephant's sad eyes. Moments passed. Smokey finally said, "Okay, you little runt. I'll let you go this time. But you have to promise not to bite me, so I can sleep at night without worrying." He paused a moment to think. "And I promise to set aside your fair share of popcorn — but only when I *can*. After all, I was gone all afternoon. No sense your making life hard on me whenever I don't happen to have any popcorn to give you. Okay?"

"Yeah. Dat's a bargain I can live with, seeing how I don't have no choice. Now let me *down*!" Smokey set the rat gently on the ground, and Freddie dashed for the fence and was safely on the other side when he had the last word: "Ya big lug, picking on a little guy!" Smokey smiled at Freddie's spunk, then smiled again at his own triumph. Now he could sleep in peace.

Chapter 32

What is – good? – Good for whom? . . . Is there a common good? . . . Or is yesterday's good today's Vice? . . . Good of this kind is a mere husk from which the sacred kernel has been lost. Who can claim the lost kernel . . . There is everyday human kindness. The kindness of an old woman carrying a piece of bread to a prisoner . . . an unwitnessed kindness . . . This private, senseless, incidental kindness is in fact eternal. It is extended to everything living, even to a mouse, even to a bent branch that a man straightens as he walks by.
–Vasily Grossman

What really has expanded is not so much a circle of empathy as a circle of rights – a commitment that other living things, no matter how distant or dissimilar, be safe from harm and exploitation ... Empathy, like love, is in fact not all you need.
–Steven Pinker

"Hee-yon," screeched Dazzle. At the sound, Smokey jerked his head from sleep, and raced in a bounding canter to the front of the enclosure. In his enthusiasm to tell about his trip to the woods, Smokey shouted, "Dazzle! Here I am!" The bird slowly lowered his gold-flecked green neck, pecked the ground, turned and sauntered away.

"Excuse me, *Mister* Dazzle," the cub called. The bird looked up as if surprised to see the bear. With a grand manner, the peacock fluffed his feathers and slowly settled them. He informed Smokey that of course he'd already heard how Smokey had stood up to the rat. The peacock raised his eyebrows. "I didn't know you had such gumption."

Smokey looked at him with bright eyes. "You should've seen Freddie dangling upside-down. Did he ever squirm!"

As if to hide his amusement the peacock poked a feather in place, then fixed the cub with a stern eye. He rattled his tail and declared in an excited outburst. "What *impolitesse*—bad manners. *Écoute*! Listen, Smokey Bear. *Ce n'est pas comique*. It's not funny—to dangle a small creature upside-down so he's so scared he wets himself."

Smokey looked at the peacock in disbelief. He'd imagined that Mr. Dazzle, being such a snob himself, would be impressed. The big bird continued, "Let me tell you something for your own good." Smokey scrunched up his nose and snuffled out a noisy breath dismissing the lecture he knew was coming.

Undeterred, Dazzle said, "I'll explain. The zoo is a small place. Word gets around, and you're going to be here a long time. So don't humiliate anyone. Especially if you're Somebody, and they're Nobody. When Freddie finds out that everybody's heard that you shamed him, he'll have a *ressentiment*—a grudge against you.

"Furthermore, all the rats know they're considered *excrément*—the scum of the earth. So the whole underground of rats will exact vengeance on you to restore their *dignité*." The bird paused and bore his eyes into the cub. "So, Smokey, do you want advice from this peacock, one who knows something about *pride*?"

Smokey said he supposed so. Dazzle puffed himself up and said with great authority, "A bigger animal, like you or me, has *autorité*—power, so he must be *galant*—chivalrous, toward smaller creatures, *n'est pas*? So you must make *réparation*—reconciliation. And *directement*, before all the rats come and get you!"

The cub slumped to the ground, envisioning a pack of rats pouring through the fence at night to crawl all over him and bite his toes. The cub's eyes beseeched Dazzle, and he asked what he could do now, but the peacock merely gazed at him in an arrogant way, and said it was up to him to make amends. The cub's throat tightened. In bewilderment, he whimpered,

"Uh-ruh."

But as Dazzle turned to walk away, he said over his shoulder that he could mention a secret that might prove helpful. Did the cub want to hear it? Smokey implored him to do so. The peacock raised his eyebrows to look around to see whether anyone was eavesdropping, then confided that there was going to be a big party at the French Embassy in the evening. And, as everybody knew, the French had splendid cuisine, not like that plain food at President Truman's White House.

Then the peacock added with peculiar emphasis, as if it might be a clue, "Too bad all the little wild folk don't know about the feast, because there'll be great leftovers — in the alley behind the embassy." With a foxy glance at Smokey, he paraded away.

The cub looked at the ground and frowned, as if staring at the ground would help him guess what Dazzle meant. At a loss, he shinnied up the tree. It was always easier to think when you were sitting in a high place and could gaze at the sky. For a long while, he was stymied. He felt stupid, and spluttered how mad he was at Dazzle for not telling him more.

After a while, the cub lounged in the crotch of the tree, imagining how luscious French food must be. He could almost smell milk and honey, berries and clover blossoms. As saliva dripped from his chin, he thought he heard a voice say, "What a feast. Too bad the rats don't know about it." There was that odd voice he'd heard before and dismissed, not seeing who it was. He looked all around, but couldn't see anyone. So it must be his own idea!

Suddenly Smokey could hardly wait to tell Freddie about the food. Then the rat would be grateful to him. *His* rat, Freddie, would become a hero among all the rats, and he, Smokey, would be their hero too. And instead of holding grudges, Freddie and the rats would owe Smokey a favor. Maybe that would come in handy someday.

Late that afternoon, after the cub had carefully swept the

popcorn through the fence, he paced nearby, impatient to see Freddie. Before long, he spied the rat standing upright in the grasses, his body tilted forward. The little rodent squinted his eyes and frowned. Smokey knew Freddie was trying to see more clearly, so he helped out by walking half-way to the fence.

Up close, Smokey felt sorry for the short-sighted rat, even protective toward the little guy. A voice from behind the cub urged, "Go ahead. Tell him the secret! However, you must first say you're sorry." Smokey brushed the air irritably with his paw and grumbled that he hated saying those words. Did he have to? There was no reply.

Smokey found it hard to meet Freddie's eyes. He turned aside and muttered that he was sorry to have held Freddie by his tail. The rat heard him. He had shifted one of his ears toward Smokey, an ear so thin that the setting sun shone pink through it. A bit embarrassed, Smokey smiled and quickly added that he would make up for it by telling Freddie a secret.

Freddie looked amazed, and cocked his head quizzically. Smokey walked slowly right up to his side of the iron bars, and urged the rat to come closer. Freddie flinched, hesitated a moment, edged closer, but didn't come through the fence. His whole body was shivering. Smokey said that he wouldn't hurt him, and whispered the secret to Freddie. The rat immediately perked up and beamed at him. "Ya don't say!" He wiggled in delight. "I'll tell my pals." He pivoted around and disappeared into the grasses.

Then Freddie abruptly reappeared. He stood stiffly with his little hands clenched tight in front of his light-colored belly. His eyes narrowed and his voice crackled with suspicion. "Yer just trying to make a fool of me again, aren't cha? Making all us rats go on a wild goose chase. Why should ya be doing me any favors when yer such a stinker?"

Smokey was flabbergasted. It had never occurred to him to make something up. What kind of world was this, where you couldn't believe another animal? He snorted, "Huh-huh" so loudly that Freddie backed into the tall grass until only his shiny eyes could be seen peeking out. In a huffy tone, Smokey informed the rat that he himself never lied, and resented the accusation. The rat said, "Is dat so?" But after turning his head away a moment, he again approached the fence.

The bear sighed as Freddie looked up at him and seemed to study his face. Smokey spoke about his mountain home where animals always let others know where food was. In fact, his mother had told him that when a berry patch ripened, the first bear that found it bent branches to show others the way. And any crow who spied vultures circling in the sky above a carcass let everybody else know about it. He had never chewed on a carcass himself, but sure wished he could have tried one. The cub paused a moment, then confided to Freddie that he had almost become a carcass himself when he was a very small cub. A big bear had attacked him, but a crow named Strut had saved him by flying in the bear's face.

At first the rat looked perplexed while Smokey told him about the Wilds, but gradually his black eyes began to shine. He exclaimed wistfully about what a wonderful place the mountains must be compared to the city. Shyly, he crept closer and clasped an iron bar with his little pink hands as high as he could reach so he was stretched completely upright. Smokey bent down to see up close his soft underbelly, and discovered how clean it was.

For a long moment, Freddie scrutinized the cub's face. "Ya got an innocent face on ya, Smokey, so I guess I can trust ya. Anyhow, what's life widout some risks, huh? We rats are suspicious by nature, but I'll take a chance on ya, ya big lug." He thanked Smokey for the tip about dinner that night and shot off through the bushes to tell other rats about the feast at the French Embassy.

The cub sat for a long time. He missed his mountain home more than ever, but was glad that Freddie might tell him about city ways. It occurred to him that when you're in prison, it's information that is the most important thing—news from inside and outside. He'd need to learn all he could if he was going to live in this prison a long time.

The next day, Smokey found out more about the dark ways of the city. He was idly watching the crowd, always on the lookout for the occasional man with a sun-beaten face and a cowboy hat who might be Ray, little chattering girls who resembled Judy, or boys like Don who'd throw popcorn. Three boys — shorter than Don — came up to the fence, laughing and nudging each other with their elbows. There was something about their tense bodies and strained voices that made the cub uneasy. And their eyes had a hard, menacing look to them. Smokey had learned that staring human eyes don't necessarily indicate an angry threat, but more likely interest, kindness, or even food. But these particular eyes unsettled him.

The boys didn't have any popcorn, but the tallest one grasped something else in his full fist. Smokey was tempted to investigate when a 'threat smell' halted him. At that moment the boy raised his arm to throw, and Smokey felt something sting his forehead. He closed his eyes, made gulping sounds of distress, and hunkered down as another volley of pebbles came through the bars and hit his body. Moaning in fear, he ran behind his tree. The few bystanders — young children — looked bewildered.

Hiding from the pelting behind the protective trunk, Smokey peeked out and locked his eyes on the tormentors. He slowly stiff-walked a short way toward them, his ears flattened, and stopped. With a guttural huff — so low that he even surprised himself — he stomped the ground, and suddenly bluff-charged, snorting, and showing his teeth. He slammed against the iron bars, and all three boys jumped back. The bear bore his eyes into the biggest boy and chomped his teeth at him.

The boys recoiled a moment. Then, the biggest one squealed, whooped, and rushed toward the cub with a mocking face, making growly noises. Smokey stood his ground and stretched his neck forward, ears back, to glower at the sneering face. The boy was taunting him! Smokey was furious. How he'd like to smack them all!

At that moment, an adult came running from the sidewalk and shouted at the boys. Startled, they stopped in their tracks a moment. The cub prowled on his side of the fence, snorting defiance, ready to bluff charge again. Then something happened in a flash. The adult as well as the children turned on the boys in an outraged manner and shouted; the boys shrugged, faces still sneering, but pivoted, turned tail and left.

Smokey remembered what he'd once heard from Dazzle—that people occasionally taunted caged animals at the zoo and pelted them with stones as large as acorns. Sad at heart, the cub retreated to his cave for the rest of the day. At least all the other humans nearby had stood up for him, like crows mobbing an enemy. He pondered people he had known. Ruth and Judy had been nice to him, but Ray and Don had held him down no matter how much he struggled and screamed.

The worst part of the torture had occurred the first week when Ray had torn bandages from his burnt skin. It had hurt terribly. Afterward, Ray had always rubbed something soothing on his wounds. Maybe Ray had bandaged him "for his own good," and wasn't mean after all. At his next thought, though, Smokey whimpered. Ray had placed him in a cage and sent him away to be imprisoned here. Although Doc Mann and his wife had been nice to him, they had returned him to his enclosure and had not taken him back to the park again. Humans could not really be trusted. A cry erupted from deep within his chest.

As dusk descended, Smokey finally ate his food, careful to leave some kibble in the bowl for the rat, who was late. The cub waited impatiently through the long evening. It wasn't until the moon had passed across the sky, and he was dozing near dawn when Freddie finally came. He was humming happily and squeezed his fat belly through the fence. The cub rushed over. This time the rat seemed relaxed enough in Smokey's presence to rub clean his greasy cheeks and lick the pads on his tiny front paws. He pressed each pink ear down flat to scrub behind it. He extended a back leg to scratch an ear thoroughly. Then he licked his fur all over. Smokey was fascinated to see that the little creature groomed himself the same way he himself did.

The rat lifted his head and thanked Smokey for telling him about the feast at the French Embassy. He talked fast with great excitement—how his gang of field rats had gone through sewers to join the Massachusetts Avenue gang, who led them underground, until they came out at the Rock Creek overpass. All the rats had raced to a place nearby where the gigantic mosque was being built, and, in the moon's shadow of the high minaret, they had run behind the mosque to the brick embassy hidden among some great shade trees. It was a rat-feast indeed! Outside the kitchen were garbage cans bursting with leftover food. In a sing-song voice, Freddie happily named all the scrumptious French cuisine he'd tasted.

Freddie confessed to Smokey that he was only a young rat. In fact, he admitted, Smokey had been his first "mark." But, thanks to tipping off the older rats about the French Embassy feast, all the rats now held them both in great esteem. As a reward, Freddie had just been given a longer route for extorting food from more animals in the zoo. Best of all, whenever there was a prolonged scarcity of food, he would no longer be among the "lesser rats" that were always fair game—to be eaten up by the more important rats. And, there was something Smokey should know: The rats wouldn't bother the cub in the future because Smokey had tipped them off and was now their friend, too.

Even though he looked bloated, Freddie nevertheless couldn't resist nibbling kibble. Smokey admitted that he hadn't saved any popcorn because he'd been sleeping in the cave all afternoon, but Freddie said he didn't mind—he'd gorged enough. To prove it, he stood to show Smokey his tight rounded stomach. Then the rat asked how Smokey's day had been. The cub related how a boy had thrown stones at him. Freddie listened not just with sympathy—but also fierce indignation.

The rat was in an expansive mood and asked the cub if he'd

like to hear what the gorilla did sometimes? Did he know what a gorilla was? Smokey remembered seeing one sprawled asleep as he was led through the zoo to the vet's one day. So Freddie told how the great ape got so tired of people staring and kids jeering at him that he'd wait until a crowd gathered. Freddie giggled and said, "Guess what he'd do then?" The rat merrily told how the ape would suddenly throw poop at the people so they'd holler and run. Then the ape would swing on his rubber tire and wait until another crowd gathered, and do it again. Smokey made a joyful snort, and knew that he'd found a new friend in this spunky creature.

Freddie's mood changed quickly. He lamented that people hate rats. But he found it strange—since people are so big—that they scream in fear when they see a rat, or even a mouse. What cowards! They're also piggy. Humans never share their food with wild animals, so rats in the city have to sneak food from dog and cat dishes. And people are so stingy that they even clamp their garbage cans closed, although last night Freddie and the others managed to get into the overflowing French Embassy garbage cans.

Freddie squealed in a high-pitched voice, "Dose humans even put out traps and poison to kill us. We were on dis land *first*! Day are da invaders, building all over our fields. Who gives dem da right?" Smokey enthusiastically agreed with the rat, and grew so expansive in fellow-feeling that he told Freddie about his day at the circus, and all the animals he'd seen and smelled.

Although the rat told Smokey he felt very full, he stood upright, holding in both hands one kibble after another, gnawing away until he'd emptied the bowl. Then he lay outstretched, and burped—quite loudly for such a small animal. Finally, groaning, he tottered to his feet, his belly almost scraping on the concrete, and waddled toward the fence to leave.

At the base of the upright bars, however, the rat came upon low fencing—recently placed there to keep out rodents. He searched for an opening at the bottom of the diamond-shaped chain links, poked his head through, and tried to squeeze his bloated body to the other side. With his belly so fat, he got stuck halfway. He squeaked. Smokey started to laugh, but smothered it as best he could.

"Help me, ya big dope. Do sumpthin'!"

As Smokey stood perplexed, Freddie let out a piercing cry. The cub quickly said he'd help, and lay spread-eagle on his stomach to examine the problem. With his nose close to Freddie's long scaly tail, he saw what to do. Warning the rat about what to expect, he reached out his forearm, placed the pad of his paw on the rat's little rump and pushed. Freddie popped through. The rat laughed happily and said "Thanks, my friend," and scurried off.

The rat had called him a "friend." As if he were under a warm sun, Smokey basked in the thought that he might have an every-day companion at last, like Strut had been. Then, he thought, what if Freddie grew so fat that he couldn't come through the fence any more—to eat kibble and chat—or bite him? He decided that he'd still give his friend some kibble and popcorn. He liked talking to the rat about important things, like how disappointing humans were. And he needed to learn what the rat underground knew about the outside world, so he could be prepared if he ever was free again.

Chapter 33

Pity is feeling sorry for someone; empathy is feeling sorry with someone.
–Martin Luther King

An unexpected sound drifted into Smokey's early morning snooze. He snorted to become fully awake, grouchy at the interruption during one of his favorite times of day. He liked those moments of calm after breakfast before crowds came. Raising his head slightly and tilting it to peer sideways toward the zoo entrance, he could see two little figures whispering excitedly. "So what," he grouched. "Just some little kids — early birds." He flopped his head onto his paws.

In the mornings it felt good to press his belly, tight with breakfast, against the cool concrete. Half-awake, Smokey liked to take in long slow breaths of the moist air, and savor the quiet until the zoo gradually came to life. He had become accustomed to the routine and liked a pattern he could count on. Still to come were successive doors to clank in the distance, tigers to roar for their meat, and finally the talkative people to approach.

He groaned when he realized the two children had already reached his cage. Their whispering continued, very softly, as if the little folk didn't want to disturb him. But their swirly noise irritated him. It was like a fly: once noticed, impossible to ignore as he braced for it to alight on his nose, or worse, settle on the wet spot at the base of an eye. He huhhed grumpily and heaved his head to face away from the intruders. But when their whispering suddenly stopped, his curiosity was piqued.

The children stood close together, one much taller than the other. The girl was almost Don's height, the boy about Judy's size. Their eyes focused intently on him. For a fleeting moment he flinched, remembering the three boys who had thrown stones at him.

Then he realized that these children seemed friendly. A murmur rippled between them and they nudged each other as Smokey gathered his feet under him and stretched his body fully awake. They leaned toward him and smiled. There was something about the two that was different from other people, although he couldn't tell what it was.

As he angled toward them, he saw they were not looking at him with aggressive, staring eyes. Rather, their gaze was gentle and inquiring. An aura of warmth emanated from them—he could smell it—and their eyes brimmed and glistened with moisture. A tear trickled down the small boy's face, and he brushed it aside with his fist. The girl leaned in, and put her arm around her smaller companion's shoulder for a moment. "Why don't you say hello to the cub?" she asked him.

His face brightened. "Hi there, Smokey Bear."

Smokey drew closer. He liked that they hadn't been pointing at him like other small youngsters who chirped at him in high-pitched voices or sounded mournful with pity. These two had furrowed eyebrows and foreheads as if they'd known pain like he had, yet the outsides of their eyes crinkled in greeting. He sensed their warmth radiating toward him like a warm sun. Could they possibly understand what he'd felt, all he'd lost?

The cub mewed and moved toward them. He slowed as he drew near the iron bars, and waited until the boy leaned against the horizontal railing so they were face to face across the small distance. Smokey stood and pressed a front paw against one of the bars. The little boy held his hand up too, as if they could touch each other's palm, and held it there a long moment, and said, "I'm so glad your paws are healed." Smokey took a deep breath, and without quite understanding what was happening, he sensed that they were friends in a special way.

Smokey dropped to all fours, but remained at the fence. Up

close, he noticed something odd about the girl. Under the shade of her hat, half of her face was strangely wrinkled, the tender skin on her neck rough and pink. The boy held out his raw left hand in a tight fist as if clutching something. "See, Smokey? We know what it's like to be burned."

The girl spoke earnestly. "We promised each other — on the Burn Unit — to come see you as soon as we got out, and here we are! I'm Vicky and this is my brother Charlie."

The little boy broke in. "Didn't it hurt terribly at first, Smokey? Then itch a lot? But we always knew that if *you* could make it, *we* could too."

Vicky swept her big hat off the side of her face to show Smokey her twisted lip, scarred cheek, and pinched eyelid with its missing eyebrow. She said, "Look. It's not raw anymore, but it still looks pretty awful. Though *you* don't care, do you, Smokey — that I look so ugly?"

Smokey studied them closely. He didn't know their words, but something about their posture conveyed empathy. He licked his paw. The grave set of the children's lips relaxed and they beamed at him. Perhaps they'd give him some treat, the cub thought. He whirled and wiggle-waggled around in a circle until the children laughed. Then he stopped and looked at them expectantly, but no treat was forthcoming. "See, he understands," the boy said. Smokey kept watching to see whether they'd reach into their pockets.

The spell was suddenly broken when an onslaught of people approached behind the children. The two lingered only a moment to say, "We'll come again, we promise, when the surgery and skin grafts are over. To show you that *we* can heal, too." They waved goodbye and he watched them until they were out of sight.

Ignoring the new horde of visitors reaching his cage, Smokey walked slowly to his cave and lowered his body to the ground. Instead of letting himself become grumpy at people staring at him all day, he wanted to bask in the fellow-feeling he'd sensed with the two early visitors. He let out a sigh and rested his head on his forepaws.

As he lightly dozed, the scene came to him of his mother saying, "You have a special destiny, my son. Don't waste your life. Dedicate yourself to the animals and the forest. That is the good life." Cooped up in the zoo, though, his life seemed wasted. There was no way he could pass on her Medicine Bear knowledge about healing herbs. How he yearned to be back home in the forest.

Yet the burnt children today made him wonder. Smokey sensed that he had somehow helped them.

On a strange impulse, Smokey pulled himself up off the concrete, went over to his pool, and submerged himself up to the neck in the water until his fur was soaked. He then emerged and walked slowly up to the bars to stand, dripping, at the front of the cage.

People grew quiet and watched him with interest. He gave them a roguish look, and suddenly shook his body vigorously. The people in front squealed and ran from the droplets of water, then looked up at the smiling bear—and came back for more.

Chapter 34

Hope is the thing with feathers that perches in the soul.
–Emily Dickinson

The hot Washington sun beat down on Smokey in his exposed yard. By midday the white concrete sizzled the pads of his paws and forced him to retreat to the dark shadows of his cave. Even at night the relentless August heat and humidity made him pant in his heavy fur coat, and he often sniffed the air, hoping to catch a whiff of a salty-fishy breeze coming off Chesapeake Bay. The deep scent of brine was new to him, and so were the kinds of clouds in the sky. Many an afternoon he welcomed puffy clouds, which, after growing steadily bigger and blacker, burst to drench him in a downpour. It meant that he could frolic and splash in the puddles on his rain-scented concrete. And, in the morning, when he awoke in his den, before he opened his eyes, he could tell it had been raining by the sound of cars whooshing by on the nearby road.

Sometimes for days on end, drizzle fogged the air and skies were gray. The light showers brought out the smells of the zoo, but sometimes turned to rain and obliterated the smells and made his world more boring. Then he couldn't even watch people, for they didn't come.

When rain stopped, oppressive heat soon led Smokey to seek relief in his large pool. Slumped on the lower step, he'd loll around with water up to his neck, enjoying the feel of the water slowly seeping through his thick undercoat of fur until it reached his skin. Then he would paddle slowly around, relishing the smooth rhythm of his whole body as the water slipped by. Smokey found swimming satisfying for his restless legs. It was wonderful to pull the water as hard as he could and feel the strength of his arms and legs. Finally he would hoist himself out—panting, tired and refreshed.

Toward the end of one day, as he languidly swam around, he heard Freddie's voice from the edge of the pool where the rat perched. "Rats are good swimmers too!" Freddie boasted.

Smokey raised his head so he was eye-to-eye with the little fellow. "Oh, yeah? Show me then!" With one flick of his arm, he smacked Freddie into the water. After a long moment underwater, the rat's wet snout emerged. He coughed and coughed, his black eyes bulging as he flailed his feet to keep his head high out of the water. Smokey watched him make a beeline for the nearest side of the pool where he scratched at the smooth vertical wall.

Despite his struggle, Freddie still managed to sputter at Smokey, his little teeth gnashing furiously. At first, the bear merely floated nearby, watching the rat flail. But when he saw Freddie gasp for breath and gulp water, the little bear came alongside the rat and nudged him. "Quick, climb onto my head . . . That's right!" Freddie's feet clutched the fur and yanked his way along Smokey's furry head until the bear felt him settle. Smokey was surprised how heavy the rat was. And how loudly he yelled angry accusations right into Smokey's ear.

When Freddie finally stopped for breath, Smokey told him that he'd only meant to be funny. This unleashed such a tirade that the cub winced. The rat informed him with a huff that of course any Norwegian brown rat can swim, but certainly not when thrown underwater in a pool where the sides are so steep and slippery that he is in danger of drowning.

As Smokey swam around with the rat safe on his head, Freddie's mood turned playful. He trilled how much he liked his perch. He urged the cub to go faster so he could feel the breeze go by to cool his sopping wet fur. The cub asked, "Are you game—for a thrill?"

"Yah! Anything's hunky-dory with me."

"Okay then. Hold on tight."

The bear suddenly dunked his head under the water and

resurfaced. Freddie couldn't stop giggling and said, "Wait till the other rats hear about dis!"

Finally the bear lumbered out of the pool, and heeding Freddie's high-pitched warnings to be careful, lowered his head for the little rat to jump onto the pavement. With his nose close to the rat on the ground, Smokey breathed in the swampy aroma of the rat's wet fur. They both shook their dripping bodies. As Smokey watched the scruffy fellow squeeze through the fence and leave him behind, he felt a sense of kinship with the little guy. A whiff of the familiar rat smell lingered around the enclosure and gave his home a familiar family-feeling. He could smell it clearly now — an unmistakable rodent smell, mixed with that of dry, pale yellow grasses turning to dust.

He noticed the trail of small droppings like shiny dark-brown seeds that Freddie always left where he ran along the outside or the inside of the enclosure, interspersed with sharp-smelling tiny yellow puddles. It was amusing that the rat — for all his bluster — edged along walls like that, brushing his whiskers against the sides to find his way, as if afraid to venture forth. Smokey could picture the rat standing up now and then to look around and sniff his way along, trying to decide whether to come in or go out into the open field. Freddie was the constant in the cub's daily life. Every evening, the bear would come upon the rat inside his enclosure or outside, gnawing some kibble and popcorn kernels, always ready to wise-crack.

He liked being with Freddie but what the cub longed for was another taste of real freedom. Day after day, he waited at the gate for the approach of his human friends — zoo director Mann and his wife Lucile. It was disappointing to never know when they might come. By late morning he would bang the concrete at the gate with his paws, mad that he could not go to them. He hated being helpless about something so important. Many times his hopes were dashed by false sightings and mistaken footfalls.

Week after week passed. At last one Sunday the Manns

arrived to take him to the woods again. This time they brought a larger cage and set it down on the concrete floor of his yard. He greeted them with a head bob and a smile. Lucile enticed the cub inside the cage with a treat, and he obliged. Doc carried him to the car and heaved the cage into the space between the front seats. This time, when the car arrived at the meadow in Rock Creek Park, Doc wasn't taking any chances. He snapped the long leash onto Smokey's halter, wrapped the other end of the leash around his gloved hand, and let the cub out. Smokey stood a moment, savoring the air in the meadow, and ran to the base of a nearby tree. He snuffled among fallen leaves and found old acorns to eat.

Nearby the cub came across a small hole in the ground surrounded by a mound of fine dirt. Rows of ants were marching in and out of the hole. When he stuck his muzzle in their midst, curious to see them up close, they swarmed and angrily attacked him. He found that their bites didn't hurt him any more than the stings of the honey bees had, since his muzzle seemed immune to their attacks. So he decided to amuse himself. He clomped his paw down in the midst of their orderly procession, waited for them to climb up his arm, then licked up the whole row, and ate them with a great feeling of satisfaction. Compared to eating his daily kibble, it was much more satisfying to hunt food himself.

Smokey remembered where he wanted to go next. He led Doc and Lucile to the path along the large creek where he turned over rocks and watched for fish, all in vain. Then he found the small stream and pulled the couple up the path to the spring. Most of the short young ferns had uncurled their heads and become a grove of big ferns near the pond. It was a sunny day, and so hot in his long thick fur that he sloshed into the pond, displacing an abundance of frogs, and sank up to his shoulders in the cold water of the fresh-running spring.

Smokey caught a whiff of a familiar smell, more enticing than before. His nose compelled him to scamper toward a meadow. Doc puffed behind him holding the leash. The cub thrashed through brambles, yanking Doc after him. What delirious joy! The blackberries by late summer had become such a deep purple that they looked black. They were wonderfully ripe and sweet, loose enough to drop into his mouth with the slightest nudge of his loose lips. They were so squishy that they dripped sweet purple juice all over his muzzle and down his upraised neck. Swarms of shiny green Japanese beetles buzzed among the overly-ripe blackberries — the ones that smelled rotten. He soon learned to crawl through the shaded brambles to eat the low-hanging berries — the fullest plumpest ones of all.

Then something happened on this trip that made Doc angry at him, angrier than he had ever been before. When, at last, Smokey had eaten his fill, he heaved a satisfied sigh and lay down to rest in the berry patch. Doc and Lucile sat nearby, looking down at him and smiling. After a short time, however, the man looked at his watch, raised his chin to signal Smokey, and tugged at the leash. Smokey understood: They wanted to go back to the car. He turned his head away. He didn't want to leave this wonderful wild place and return to prison.

Doc kept a firm hand on the leash while he untangled it from a thorny blackberry bush, but by then Smokey was determined to escape. He lunged suddenly, jerking the leash out of Doc's hand. The bear dashed along animal-paths through the blackberry patch, dragging the leash behind him, and headed toward the open part of the meadow. The leash occasionally caught but he pulled it free. What joy, to be wild again! He could hear Doc crashing through the brush after him, shouting in a growling and commanding way, but the cub didn't heed him.

Smokey reached the open area. He was free to run! It was a great feeling, and in a fresh burst of energy, he romped toward the beckoning forest on the far side. But the running steps behind Smokey caught up with him at the far side of the meadow just before he reached the woods.

His exuberant escape to freedom ended abruptly when

Smokey found himself tackled. They both crashed to the ground, Doc panting heavily. The cub found himself in such a tight grip that he could hardly move. Smokey clenched his teeth and kept his eyes shut. He hated being held down. He panicked and gasped for breath. He writhed, remembering the torture of being bandaged. With a supreme effort, he twisted his head around and bit the man's arm above his glove as hard as he could.

Still gripped by the furious man, Smokey smelled Doc's strong sweat, as if the man was bristling his hair with fierce warnings. It seemed like the ominous presence of Father Bear long ago when the beast had pursued him, trying to wallop and devour him. The bear cub scrunched his body into a cowering ball for a moment, then slowly turned his head and eyed Doc with a mixture of defiance and compliance.

Resisting with stiff-legged limbs and paws clawing the grass, he forced Doc to drag him by the halter to his feet. And each time the cub diddle-dawdled along the way to the car, the leash was tugged angrily. Smokey grouched the whole time, but couldn't help but register Doc's voice—harsh and distressed. As the man opened the car door and heaved the cub into the cage, his voice turned sad. "Too bad, but no more gallivanting around for you! We can't afford to lose you. You're too important. This'll have to be the last time we take you out." Crammed into his cage next to Lucile, Smokey whimpered, "Uh-ruh."

"It's okay, little bear," Lucile said, but Smokey heard sadness in her voice.

In the days toward the end of August, Smokey wondered whether he'd ever be taken to Rock Creek Park again. He could still count on the couple's visit early Sunday morning before the crowds came, but Doc and Lucile no longer took him out. Still, their visit made the humdrum routine during the week more bearable. Always hungry now, he looked forward to their scrumptious treats. He still climbed into Lucile's lap and almost knocked her off balance because he had grown much heavier.

No longer did she bring him a bottle of Pablum, and after mewing a bit he relinquished her embrace for a chance to play with her husband.

One time, acting dodgy and enticing, Doc held his hands behind him, then whipped forth a beach ball to show Smokey. The little bear backed off, afraid. From a distance, he eyed it suspiciously. After a while, he came forward, stretched to sniff it, and finally touched it with a paw. Doc crouched in play and bounced it toward the far wall. The cub gave chase and tried to grab it, but it was bigger than his arms could encircle. It was strangely slippery and flew from his paws.

When the ball rolled over to Doc, he kicked it into the pool. The cub crashed in after it, and soon learned to slosh it around. The two humans laughed. Lucile said, "Isn't it great — seeing him have fun. If only he could wrestle with another cub!"

At that moment, the ball shot out of the pool to land near Doc's feet. He picked it up and told her, "You said it!" He emptied the pockets of his Bermuda shorts into Lucile's arms, and despite her admonitions, belly-flopped into the pool with the ball. Up to his waist in water, the man called to Smokey. The cub swiveled his body to look, and suddenly flashed on the happy times he had splashed in the bathtub with Judy. He readily batted the ball around with Doc and they both laughed until their stomachs hurt.

At one point Smokey collided with Doc in the water. They jostled each other, then tussled happily, the play-fight halted occasionally by Doc's stern "Uh-uh!" The cub became so happy that he climbed onto Doc's chest. Impulsively, he put his arms around the man's shoulders, looked him in the eyes for a moment . . . and was off again. Smokey could play forever, but Doc got winded first, and stopped for breath.

Lucile called out, "Too bad he can't rough-house with playmates."

"He sure likes it! And he can't hurt me so much at twenty-some pounds. But he'll soon be too big for this. It's good he can have some handling now. It'll make things safer for the vet later." Doc left the ball for Smokey to play with during the week, and whenever he came by and found Smokey sitting forlornly with a deflated ball — punctured by teeth or claws — he shortly returned with a replacement. One day he brought a more durable one of solid rubber that Smokey loved. It was small enough that Smokey could push it under the water with his front paws, and be astonished each time that it popped up to the surface. It was almost as much fun as he'd had back home bending over slender saplings in the mountain forest to see them snap upright again.

The last summer days slid by, the brisk winds of fall whistled past the corners of buildings, and the crowds thinned. Around the zoo grounds, the leaves on the bushes and trees turned bright colors, and flying geese honked overhead. Smokey sensed the change in the air and welcomed it. Dry leaves drifted down into his pen. He crunched them underfoot to hear them crackle, and chased them so they would swirl and scatter. It broke the monotony to make something happen.

It was around this time that Smokey first caught the faint smell of something burning. It was not like the overwhelming smoke of pine trees afire back on the mountain. Nor was it at all like the alluring scent of pinyon, mesquite and sage drifting from Santa Fe chimneys in the evening. The smell came from one direction outside the zoo, then from another. The bear stood to sniff at the threat, his ears held back in alarm. "Huff, huff." He rushed to his cave, curled into a tight ball, and had a troubled night. The next morning he sensed that the fires were gone. During the ensuing weeks of autumn, he noted that the fires always smelled like burning leaves. The cub came to realize that the fire-smell swiftly came and went during the late afternoons or on weekends. So far, it had never approached closer. Yet it always gave him a shiver of foreboding.

That autumn of 1950, Smokey also noticed a change in visitors from the summer. There were more clusters of young men in khaki or blue uniforms, saying the word "Korea" a lot. And, instead of the summer visits by parents with their children, there were groups of children—each group the same size—now dressed in sweaters and jackets. Each group was herded by a woman who stopped them at a distance and talked to them in solemn tones, frowning a lot and using words like "fire," and "careless." Smokey noticed that the children's eyes—fixed on the teacher—became serious, and he was reminded of Mother Bear warning him about various dangers.

These groups always stirred a special feeling inside him, so that he felt mysteriously drawn to them. Something in their manner reminded him of Judy and the rest of the family he'd known in Santa Fe. He'd drift over and make eh-eh sounds and look closely at them. As soon as the children saw him, their eyes brightened. Buzzing among themselves, they broke away from the teacher and ran toward the bars, looking at him with intelligent eyes filled with caring. Bewildered about what he meant to them, he, in turn, searched their faces. Why was he so important to them?

It was confusing and disappointing, though, that these groups of eager children never threw him popcorn or other sweets, which his body craved more than ever in the cool weather. He sensed that they meant well, but he couldn't be sure. He rejoiced when, occasionally, once a teacher moved on, a child lingered to sneak peanuts or another treat through the fence before hurrying to catch up with the others.

During this first fall at the zoo, Smokey was hungrier than he had ever been. He gobbled whatever the zookeeper brought—plentiful kibble as well as apples and carrots—and got more fat and heavy on his feet as the weeks went by.

Soon the clear blue sky turned gray and days got colder. There were occasional snow flurries that muffled sounds and turned the concrete in his yard into a field of white. The snow on the ground was heavy and wet. When it was deeper than usual, his pawprints looked turquoise in the snow. How unsatisfying that the snow hardly ever got very deep but instead soon turned to slush and puddles, then gradually disappeared.

One night, he heard the wind stir and rustle the tree branches, and before long it rattled the nearby roof. The buzz and crackle of electricity in the air made the hair on his back stand on end. A trash receptacle slammed onto the sidewalk and rolled, spilling food-smeared paper that whipped into the air to swirl around and catch on the outside of his cage. He reached his long tongue through the bars to try to nab a piece of paper with crusted food, but the wind whisked it away. Branches snapped and fell. It was late November 1950. The gale-force winds of a great storm had arrived.

Smokey loved the excitement. He shinnied up his tree as fast as he could to watch what else might happen. The bars of his enclosure whistled. A branch split from a tree trunk and thunked onto a nearby building. Then the blizzard thrashed the trees with snow and began to blanket the branches outside Smokey's cage and to whiten his fur as well. Soon everything was frosty-white, and he could no longer see anything but swirling white snow. Happy at having such an unexpected thrill, Smokey watched until dark, then padded through the dusting of snow to his den.

The windstorm rampaged fiercely and more snow fell. Smokey sank into a deep sleep, as snug in his den as he'd been in his birth cave in the mountains. He opened his eyes in the morning to blink in the glare of sun at a snowy world. He pawed the thick snow at the den entrance, then buried his muzzle in the white powder and snorted it out his nose. Cautiously stepping outside he sank so deep—well over his chest—in the soft snow that he floundered at first. But he forged ahead and managed to plow a path. And soon he was tossing his head, bounding across the snow, and romping around the perimeter of the yard as fast as he could.

Suddenly he slid to a stop at the gate. There were his friends Doc Mann and Lucile, bundled in thick clothing and covered with snow flakes. He sniffed a greeting. The zoo director opened the gate, and Lucile held up a plate of strong-scented food. "Smokey, here are Thanksgiving goodies for you." The cub opened his nostrils and closed his eyes to enjoy the enchanting scents of sugary fruit and nuts, and the next instant plunged his snout in the food and wolfed it down.

After Smokey had finished, Doc scooped up snow and whooshed it at Smokey. The cub caught the playful spirit and gamboled about and rolled in the snow. He wiggled on his back with his feet in the air. Doc laughed and clapped his hands. "He's almost as white as a polar bear. He sure loves snow! Maybe he knew it in the mountains. But he'll probably never see anything like this again. Not in Washington, D. C."

The Great Appalachian Storm on Thanksgiving Day, 1950, was echoed by other storms across the world. And the date was also etched into people's minds by world events, for on November 26th China officially entered the Korean War.

By December an extraordinarily harsh winter in Korea — with temperatures thirty-five degrees below zero — assailed American troops in their lightweight uniforms. On New Year's Eve, waves of Chinese soldiers crossed the 38th parallel into South Korea, with heavy casualties on both sides. In the years ahead the capture of the capital city of Seoul seesawed back and forth with great loss of lives. However, World War III was averted, and the war finally ended in July 1953 with the 38th parallel dividing North and South Korea.

As the last month of the year 1950 turned steadily cold and gray, Smokey became increasingly sluggish. Tiredness drew him to his den more often, and he slept more than usual. Only the steady arrival of food each day lured him out. He lazily moved about and cast his eyes on the bleak scene. Not many visitors came during winter.

At last the days grew longer, although the world was often gray and wet. One morning, after a long absence, he spied Mr. Dazzle, looking bedraggled as he sat on a bare branch, his long ragged tail drooping below him. The peacock seemed miserable, and merely nodded at Smokey. The bird didn't look like his usual high-and-mighty self, so Smokey wondered whether this might be a time to ask Dazzle the Big Question that had been on his mind. He had always hesitated to ask the bird something so important, afraid of being rebuffed or given a cynical answer.

"Mr. Dazzle, is there a reason why I'm—I mean—why are we creatures here?"

The peacock raised his head high and answered in a haughty way, "Of course. Every living creature has some reason for being on this earth, although they don't conduct themselves accordingly!"

That wasn't an answer at all, and made Smokey mad. "If that's so, then what's *your* purpose in life?"

"To be beautiful. And to teach animals like you good manners." He tucked his head in his feathers to end the conversation.

The cub persisted. "If everybody has a mission, then what good is that lazy hippo?"

Exasperated, the peacock said, "Here his purpose is to eat and sleep. But there, in the Wild, hippos eat weeds in a river to keep it running, and they poop a lot to fertilize things."

"How about those pigeons and seagulls over there near my dish eating specks of food?

"Oh, those pests! They're not even zoo animals! Just 'trash birds' that have invaded the whole city." The haughty reply brooked no challenge, although Smokey would have liked to point out that Dazzle himself was only a visitor to the zoo, coming and going, and running free.

After a pause, the cub challenged the peacock, "Well, how about the monkeys?"

"Their function in life is to have fun and be popular."

Smokey said, "What good does that do?"

The peacock raised his long leg and scratched his head. "Well, it's good to make everybody laugh. Oh, yes! So people will like them and won't shoot them in the jungle to eat monkey meat. So there!"

"What about the giraffes here? I'll bet you can't answer that one!"

Dazzle shook his feathers and rose to the challenge. "Their

job is to have offspring. And cute ones, so more people will come to the zoo and care about animals. So there!"

Smokey had been waiting to hear what Dazzle said about other animals before he asked why he was there. Now, he found that he couldn't quite bring himself to do so, especially after the bird had so harshly dismissed pigeons and seagulls as worthless. What might he say about captive bears? That bird was such a snob! The cub abruptly said thank you. Before the bird could speak, the bear ended their conversation himself, turned tail, and ran to his den.

Winter finally receded and Smokey's first full spring at the zoo was announced by more rain in just a few days than he'd experienced in his short springtime back West. After a particularly rainy spell of two weeks, the bright sun brought sounds of birds and crickets as well as zoo animals stirring and calling out, as if the world was coming awake again. Smokey wished the monkeys would visit. He hadn't seen them for a long time. Had they been soaked? What were they up to? The bear called out, "Trish and Trash! Where are you?"

As if in answer, he heard a voice behind him. "Watch out. Monkeys can get you in trouble." It was that voice again—the same one he had heard on occasion. He spun around, but there was no one there—only some dumb pigeons to-ing and fro-ing on the ground and a lone seagull pecking at kibble near the bowl. Perhaps the voice came from his own head.

Chapter 35

They also serve who only stand and wait.
–John Milton

This is the true joy of life, the being used for a purpose recognized by yourself as a mighty one; the being thoroughly worn out before you are thrown on the scrap heap; the being a force of nature instead of a feverish little clod of ailments and grievances complaining that the world will not devote itself to making you happy.
–George Bernard Shaw

Smokey was almost a year old that spring. When playful, he still scampered like a cub, but now he walked the length of his enclosure with the smooth rolling grace of a youthful grown bear. He was still lean and had not yet become fat and heavy like older male bears. The rounded ears on top of his head, which had looked quite big on him as a cub, now seemed smaller in proportion to his body. He was handsome. His eyes had turned from the blue of a young cub to a warm brown, and his glistening cinnamon fur was luxuriant—full, thick and long. And his voice was deeper.

Days and nights went by. Whenever Smokey thought he heard monkeys nearby he would lift his head to listen, but it turned out to be baboons screeching or gibbons whooping it up. When the zoo was relatively quiet and the wind just right, sounds of distant squabbling from Monkey Island reached him but he couldn't detect the distinctive voices of Trish and Trash. Were they still there? What if they had been shipped to another zoo? The peacock had said that animals could be suddenly snatched from their best friends and relatives, shipped away and never heard from again. Several times the bear almost brought himself to inquire about the monkeys, but was afraid of what Dazzle might answer.

The night the two monkeys did finally come he was deep in sleep. He had lounged outside his den until late, contemplating a sparkly star low on the horizon, as he waited for the round moon to cast its brightness into his enclosure. The cub reminisced how he had first heard his monkey friends on a moonlit night like this, chattering at the top of the fence before they swung down inside his cage. He wanted to keep awake in hopes they'd come, but his eyelids grew heavier and heavier, his head drooped, and soon he was snoring.

Two spindly figures stood near the gate and peered at Smokey lying in the moonlight. The impish Trash wanted to surprise Smokey — skitter up the outside of the fence and down into the enclosure and poke him. But Trish trembled at the sight of how big the bear was now. She was afraid that if he was startled awake, he might strike out and hurt someone as small as a monkey. Trash boldly scoffed at her worry, certain that he could spring out of the way if Smokey took a swipe at him. "Let's go, scaredy-cat!" He reached an arm up the fence.

Trish rose on her tiptoes and thrust her face in his. "You always think it's fun for someone to be surprised. Well, it's fun for *you* but not for *them*." Trash jerked his head aside and began to climb.

"If you move one more step, I'm leaving!" Trish warned him.

Trash descended with gruff sounds, but quickly brightened with a new idea — to find pebbles and pelt Smokey and wake him. While they looked for small pieces of gravel, Trish came upon a trash container, and boosted up Trash to see what he might find inside. With her mate's feet braced on her shoulders, she saw his head disappear inside the trash can. Suddenly the little female couldn't resist tickling Trash in the ribs — something he often did to her. His muffled giggles and hoots grew hysterical and he pulled his head out. "Stop it! That's funny for *you* but not for *me*!" He bristled and glared at her.

"Now look what you made me do! I dropped a bag of something." Grumbling, he recovered a half-empty bag and handed it to her. It was their new favorite: M&Ms! Smokey should love them, too.

The two monkeys pranced around in the moonbeams on the pavement, and tossed M&Ms through the fence toward the bear. At last one bounced off Smokey's muzzle. He snorted awake. A tantalizing smell trailed across his nose. Still prone, he corralled a little M&M with his tongue. Chocolate. It was raining chocolate! He mewed and ran from one round M&M to the next, savoring each with a smack of his lips. When he had eaten all of them, he noticed chitter-chatter, and looked through the bars to see his two friends on the sidewalk. With a smile from him, they quickly sprang up the outside of his fence and down the inside.

Soon they stood before him, swaying hand in hand. Their bodies were still wet from swimming across the moat at Monkey Island, and Smokey happily inhaled their monkey smell and feasted his eyes on their slender bodies and long skinny arms and legs. But there was something odd about Trish. He stared at her big belly. "Is something wrong?"

"Oh, you mean this," she said, as she clasped her hands on her belly. Smokey leaned closer to loom over her. She said, "Go ahead and touch me." When he hesitated, she took one of his big paws in both her hands and played with it a moment like four-year-old Judy used to do. Up close, he could see that her little hands with their tiny fingernails were like Judy's. Then she gently pressed his paw against the short downy fur on her belly. The cub waited a moment then felt something bump against the pad of his paw. He flung his arm back, startled. To Smokey's astonishment, Trish explained that their baby was inside, and would soon be born.

And the two monkeys said they had come to tell him an even bigger secret. They didn't want their offspring to be captive-born. They were going to escape to the forest nearby and have their baby born free. Wild! And the newborn would be safe from the ornery old female on Monkey Island who had once killed someone else's newborn.

Trish trilled, "We can't wait to taste the fruit we had back home in Sumatra: *papaya, rambutan* and especially *pisang* — those little red bananas. What fun to swing on vines, to be free again!"

Trash fixed Smokey with a stern eye. "One more thing. Don't tell that blabbermouth Razzle-Dazzle. He'll announce it to everyone and they'll make an uproar just when we're trying to sneak out."

They explained their plan. As they had done before, they would hide the wooden crate in which bananas were brought to the island, and when night came, they'd hold onto it to swim across the moat, then help each other over the fence. Trash had already scouted their escape route through the zoo grounds and across the road to Rock Creek Park.

Trish blurted out the question: Would Smokey like to come with them? Trash quickly added that Trish had been practicing with her tiny fingers how to fiddle with a gate like his so that they could release him from his enclosure to join them.

Smokey's chest leaped at the thought. He imagined running where he pleased and inhaling the myriad scents of forests and meadows again. He groaned with longing. His mouth watered for an array of food — sweet, even sour and bitter — any change from his boring diet of pellets. The bear could almost taste the blackberries. He curled his toes, remembering the softness beneath his feet of a forest path, the aroma of earth and mushrooms, and the heavy smell of mud along a river.

Then Smokey's stomach tightened at the thought of actually leaving his cage. He could sense from his outing with the Manns, and what he could smell in the wind, that the Rock Creek Valley was large, but was it vast enough for a bear? What if it was already taken? Would he be intruding on a big male bear's territory? He would have to fend for himself to find food. He already knew how to sniff out acorns. But his mother hadn't taught him how to fish in a creek or where he might find enough insects and berries at different seasons. How could he discover, on his own, what roots to dig and what plants to chew?

Smokey looked from one monkey to the other, bewildered, torn between excitement and anxiety. He lowered himself to the ground and sat, dazed. Trish said, "Please think about it, Smokey. Another thing: Our fur is quite short, so your thick furry coat would be awfully nice to keep us warm if it rains."

Trash gave the bear a puzzled look. "What's the matter with you? Not scared, are you?" Smokey felt dizzy. Maybe he was afraid, but not of the unknown, exactly. He relished adventure. But a heavy feeling in his belly warned him that leaving the zoo might not be a smart thing to do. Hadn't Trish once warned him that the woods here might not have enough for him to eat? Could she really open his gate? Before he could tell the monkeys his worries, each gave him a quick snuggle, told him to think about it, and left. Smokey sat, held his back feet with his front paws, and rocked back and forth for a long time.

Weeks later, the moon had waned to only a pale silhouette as the coming dawn began to lighten the world for a new day. Smokey awoke and shook his head. Had the monkeys really visited one night not too long ago and invited him to the woods? Perhaps it had been only a dream. Suddenly the eerie hoot of an owl nearby made his arms jerk and his whole body shudder.

A voice seemed to come out of nowhere. "That's monkey business! Don't go with those two trouble-makers. Aren't you the Guardian of the Forest? Remember who you are: Smokey — the one who rises from the ashes to bring something sweet to the world. Everyone is counting on you!"

Smokey whipped his head around. He demanded, "Who said that? What do you mean?" Now that he had a chance to escape his worthless life in captivity, he was being told not to go! He galumphed around his cage and grouched, feeling miserable.

At last breakfast came. He ran over and happily scarfed it down. The zoo gates were opening and he heard the sound of people coming. The two burnt children reached him first. They came every week now, tossing him berries and looking at him with eager eyes. Would he disappoint them by leaving? A group of rowdy, happy sailors came and stood nearby smoking. One sailor blew smoke rings in Smokey's direction, and the cub sneeze-snorted and shook his head. He hated the smell of fire and smoke. Vicky glowered and Charlie darted dirty looks at the man, as if the two also disliked the smell. And when the man threw his smoldering cigarette onto the grass, Charlie ran over and stomped on it.

At that instant, Smokey remembered the forest fire and how he had stamped out embers that fell into his hollow tree trunk. Mr. Dazzle had once told him that people visited him *because* he had been burned as a cub and was therefore "the protector of the forest and all its animals." He had never understood what it meant, and didn't quite understand it now. The image flashed through his mind of the terrified animals fleeing from the fire alongside him and his mother. Smokey's throat tightened. The blackness of a heavy burden came over him.

It was at that moment that he had a dawning notion of his mission. And in his gut, he decided: He would stay. It was somehow a relief. His tight stomach relaxed. And he knew that his stomach was always his best guide. Smokey inhaled deeply, and heaved his breath out so strongly that his nostrils flared. He felt very much himself. In fact, he felt *important*, and that felt good. But he didn't know why.

As he was dozing off to sleep that night, he felt a qualm. Whenever the monkeys did come, he dreaded telling them — sweet Trish, who'd be disappointed that he wouldn't be there to keep her warm, and Trash, who'd be contemptuous of him. He turned over with a dismissive groan. He could sleep on it. The final decision — to stay or leave — could wait another day.

Chapter 36

There is a thing . . . most precious to man. Perhaps it is man's essence . . . It is self-respect, but also the basis of self-respect . . . because there is greatness in us. It does not make our bad untrue; one is as poor a thing as one seems; but there is in our being of which no man may speak ill . . . descriptive of our true essence — "self" as it is used in the Upanishads, as the sacred identity within us, and to protect this is our chief aim.
–Florida Scott Maxwell

The next morning Smokey awakened to a breeze that carried the scent of the forest. He raised his head and moved it in an arc, savoring the aromas. Wouldn't it be splendid to run down animal paths in the park and explore all the smells he could find? And do interesting things. Instead of lounging in this boring place, day after day. His seesawing last night seemed far away. The bear decided: He would run away, after all.

When Dazzle came by, Smokey felt smug about his secret, and hardly listened to the peacock's news about the other zoo animals. What did he care about other caged animals—those poor fools? He was leaving!

That afternoon Smokey blurted out his plan to Freddie. Instead of being impressed, the rat cocked his head and eyed him with scorn. "Whaddaya want to do dat for? You got a cushy life here—plenty of food, a nice den, humans to serve you. Anyway, you can't survive out there." Smokey protested: The monkeys had been born wild. So had he. The Wilds was their *home*.

"Those nincompoops! They don't know nothin' about dese kinda woods. Dese ain't no jungle. Dere're no banana trees—

even miles upriver in Rock Creek Valley. And dis park is only a coupla times the big one in New York City—where even *rats* can't hardly make a living dere in Central Park. They hafta go live underground, under the city. So, whaddaya think yer going to do for *food* in dis park?"

Smokey spotted some dandelions on the other side of the fence. "There are oodles of dandelions—and blackberries too! I've seen them in the park."

"Dandelions, yeah. But blackberries—still hard and green in spring. You'll have to eat garbage, like the rats in New York, and ya don't know the first thing about sneaking around." Smokey brightened at the idea of snooping around houses and eluding humans. He loved using his wits. What a game it'd be to outsmart two-legged ones!

The rat returned the cub's delighted look with his own frown. "Listen my friend. They'll kill ya for dat. People don't want no wild animals around their places. They're even afraid of little bitty mice! And humans are too selfish to share their leftovers!" Smokey looked down at his feet. His mother, too, had warned him not to be a garbage bear.

Freddie continued in a shrill voice. The cub and those jungle-monkeys didn't know how to survive loose in the park, less so in the city. And how would they get there? Animal carcasses were found all the time on the busy road to get to the park, as well as on paved roads inside the park. The rat called Smokey stupid to even consider escape. Then, after eating his share of kibble and popcorn, Freddie left, snorting in disgust.

Smokey scratched his shoulders back and forth against his tree trunk. After being confined for so long, his body itched to do something different. He fast-paced along the fence. Should he go or not? He hated making such a big decision.

When people rushed up to Smokey's cage during the next few days, he looked at them wistfully, not knowing whether to feel good or bad about their expectant faces. It was worse when the burnt children came. They talked with him like he was an old friend, showing him their healing faces and arms. He would take a quick look, then turn his head aside, not knowing whether to feel proud that he might stay and remain their friend, or ashamed that he might desert them. Each evening right after dinner, afraid that the monkeys would come before he had made up his mind, he retired to his den to sleep.

Days went by and the monkeys didn't appear. Smokey's qualms mounted. He dreaded telling dear Trish he wouldn't go, and hated the prospect that Trash would scoff at him as a coward, but leaving the zoo had become less and less appealing.

Late one morning Smokey awakened from a vivid dream—like the one he'd experienced back in the hollow tree stump in the smoldering forest. In her 'listen carefully' voice, Mother Bear said, "This tragedy gives you a mission in life. You must go through great hardships. Be a hero, Smokey, and bring something special to the world." Then she'd hugged him, and he'd felt sad and hopeful at the same time.

The cub looked at the sky above his cage and blinked in the blinding sun. Why me? What am I supposed to do? He tightened his eyes shut as hard as he could, blotting out thought, yet the yellow disk shone bright through his closed eyes and he felt bathed in the warmth and the safety of sunlight.

When he opened his eyes, he felt very much himself—important and brave. Although he still thought his life incarcerated in a zoo was worthless, he had somehow reached a decision. He was no longer afraid to tell the monkeys he wouldn't go with them. Without quite meaning to speak aloud, he announced, "I'm staying!"

A voice out of nowhere said, "So you're going to stay, after all, and tough it out here?"

Where was that voice coming from? At first befuddled, then annoyed, because he didn't know who was speaking, Smokey wheeled around to look behind him. Nobody was there—only the usual pigeons and gulls pecking the ground near his bowl, leaving fresh splats on the concrete, already white with bird lime.

The voice asked again, "So you're going to stay?"

Smokey answered to the void, "Yes, I guess so."

"I thought so. Just checking. Good! And, of course, you'll want to be here so that your crow friend can find you."

So surprised was he at the news, that Smokey's mouth dropped open. "What?" He looked all around, but still couldn't see anyone.

The cub's heart raced in excitement and disbelief. Strut! Was it possible that he would once again actually see his spunky feathered friend? He was so exhilarated at the happy prospect that his body trembled. He ran over to his bowl. No food. He huffed at the pigeons and seagulls, and scattered them into a flurry of wings so he could eat the bits of kibble on the ground himself. Then, launching his body over the pool, he belly-flopped with a great splash and vigorously swam about until he was exhausted.

Soon afterward Trish and Trash came, and Smokey related regretfully that he wouldn't go with them. Their little bodies drooped as they mumbled how sorry they were to leave him behind. They admitted, after all, that they hadn't been sure whether Trish could actually pick his gate open so he could join them. Smokey then warned them about what his rat friend had said—that the forest wasn't like the abundant jungle they'd known. The monkeys shouldn't expect to find anything like banana and other fruit trees even if they walked many miles up the creek.

The bear was surprised to find Trash—the bold and impulsive one—turn sober and ask Trish in a worried voice whether they should abandon their plan. Smokey was even more amazed at Trish's reaction. She had been leaning backward to balance her bloated belly, but she straightened her body and stood taller than ever. Looking powerful and determined, she said with authority, "Don't worry, Trash. I'll be safe. We *must* go. For the baby's sake—to know the jungle world." Trash joined in, "Even if we fail, we can tell our baby we *tried* to let him grow up free."

Smokey felt bad. He could tell that they didn't feel as safe in their venture without him. At least he could help them set out. He urged them to wait until very early in the morning when there would be much less traffic on the busy street they'd have to cross to reach the park.

The monkeys agreed to wait, and the three sat together through the night. Trash fidgeted the entire time. Trish looked tired and leaned against the cub. Finally the city quieted, and in early morning the time came to leave. Trish had one request. She wanted to hear Smokey say good-bye in their home language: the farewells to those who are leaving, "*Selamat djalan*," and they'd respond, "*Selamat tinggal*," good wishes to the ones being left behind.

Downcast to see his friends leaving hand-in-hand, Smokey whispered. "*Selamat djalan*," wishing them well on their journey, and heard their sad "*Selamat tinggal*," as they disappeared from view.

The bear felt a lump in his throat, and almost called after them, "Wait for me!" But something held the urge in check, and he merely slumped. The bear felt so forlorn that he had to do something. He sprang up and plunged into the pool. He slapped the water and sloshed it around, feeling angry and strong. As the sun came up Smokey climbed out dripping wet, to face another boring day as a captive in the zoo.

Chapter 37

No standing in the world without stooping.
–Japanese proverb

From the shelter of the den, Smokey grumbled at the unexpected commotion at his gate. He had thought the heavy rain would keep crowds away. Groaning at the interruption, he peered out. Hunched in his raincoat, Doc Mann was coming through the gate, his boots splashing in the puddles. He was followed by Lucile and the veterinarian. "Guess what, Smokey? This is June 29th — the first anniversary of your arrival. Time for your annual checkup."

The new leash that Doc dangled so tantalizingly in Smokey's face was irresistible. It was a chain link one that clinked against his teeth, as if inviting him to play tug-of-war. This led to more ferocious play as he huffed all his frustrations at Doc, who kept laughing. When the zoo director bent to attach the new leash to Smokey's halter, however, the bear got ready to leap and sink his teeth into Doc's arm. Just in time, the man said, "Hey! Don't you want to take a *walk*?" And the cheerful note in the voice halted Smokey. Was something good in store for him?

A new thought occurred to Smokey: If he bit Doc, the man might get mad and not take him for a walk. He stood still for the leash, was led out of the enclosure, and Doc allowed him to pause and sniff wherever he wanted.

As they neared a building, Doc turned to the vet beside him. "Thank goodness he's cooperative today, so you won't have to give him sedation this time either." They entered a white-walled, brightly-lit room. The cub remained in his subdued mood, and, before he knew it, the two men had heaved him onto the shiny table. His feet slipped on the metal surface, so he lay down with his head between his paws, and felt the routine his body was familiar with—smooth human hands holding up his ears, lifting up his lips, and pressing down the sides of his spine.

When it came time for the vet to examine Smokey's underside, Lucile stroked the cub's side, her signal for him to roll over for his belly to be rubbed. Smokey made happy grunting noises, and the vet gently pressed here and there. The examination over, Smokey scrambled upright, and leaped to the floor. Skillfully nudging Smokey to step onto a low platform, the vet announced, "Let's see. Awfully puny at eleven pounds upon arrival at four months old. Now seventy-five pounds, almost on target for a male black bear. Gained a lot here. See that lanky body of a juvenile? He won't be hibernating much in captivity, since he'll probably eat through the winters. So I'd guess Smokey's going to be big—really big—someday."

Smokey listened quizzically to the sound of Lucile's voice as she appraised him from several feet away. "Just look at you! Those cute round Mickey-Mouse ears are much taller now, making you look—what is it?—alert. And you've lost that roly-poly teddy-bear body and have a really chunky snout."

The vet declared, "He's growing up just fine. Let's hope it continues."

Doc interjected. "He's more docile than usual today. I don't know why, since he's been quite dejected lately. But I suppose he's as contented as can be expected . . . Thank goodness he's a survivor. So many of the wild-caught just languish and die in captivity."

Back in his yard, Smokey was gloomier than ever, now that the brief reprieve from confinement was over. Through the morning he idly watched birds chirping and fluttering about as if they expected more rain. He remembered the mysterious voice saying that Strut was coming, then he decided it wasn't true. How could the crow possibly find him? It was too long and perilous a trip across the country.

Dejected, the cub slumped. Then he raised his head. At least, he could smell the air and see birds winging about. By mid-day a breeze picked up, which made him study the sky, and soon he saw puffy clouds with gray-tinged bottoms sweeping closer. He awaited the rain he knew would come, and welcomed the change — any change — in his ho-hum existence.

The wind gusted, and swept in rain that slashed the leaves of the bushes and trees outside his cage. In the early afternoon he lay on the wet concrete as wind-swept drenching soaked his outer fur and trickled through to his undercoat. Suddenly, with a pang, he recalled the monkeys. How could he have forgotten his good friends? Had they found shelter in the woods, or were they soaking wet and cold?

For their sake, he finally welcomed the sounds of the rain's retreat: The steady rhythm of the pitter-patter on the nearby roof slacked off and became a splattering of large drops of water now and then on the concrete, ending in a soft drizzle that finally came to a halt. And by later afternoon the dark low clouds had given way to sunshine. Birds sang, and he heard snorting and whickering and trumpeting from the zoo animals.

Smokey idly watched a pigeon fly down nearby to peck soggy pellets on the wet concrete. As he had learned to expect, many more soon arrived to eat and burble among themselves. Inevitably, seagulls spied the pigeons, dive-bombed with their usual shrill squawking and made the smaller birds fly away. Good riddance, Smokey thought. Pigeons were a nuisance. Anyway, it was rousing to watch the shrieking gulls angrily chase the frightened pigeons who, after dodging and twisting to evade attack, finally flew away, too meek to mob the gulls. Soon the crumbs were gone and the gulls also departed.

The zoo became quiet as the steamy heat bore down. Only a few people wandered by. It was another dreary afternoon. The cub noticed that two pigeons returned, dawdling along the fence, pecking at small bits of food. A momentary impulse to chase them made him lift his head, but he didn't bother to make the effort.

Something prompted him to raise his head skyward to check the weather. The storm clouds had completely receded, leaving a clear sky. He squinted. What was that tiny black speck moving high in the sky straight above him? It hovered there a long time. His heart quickened in his chest. Could it be Strut? He leaped up and stood, swaying from one foot to the other, straining to keep the bird in sight.

The speck in the sky zoomed down toward him. He flinched as a hawk loomed into sight. Its outstretched talons suddenly reached one of the nearby pigeons and clenched it in a death grip. There was a stifled squeak before the hawk flew away with the inert bird in its clutches. The remaining pigeon seemed frozen in place. Then its body shuddered. It looked nervously at the fluffs of down and stray feathers left on the concrete. Then, with an air of composure, the pigeon went back to its business in a matter-of-fact way.

Smokey stood, alarmed that a hawk had come into his cage and killed one of *his* pigeons—right under his nose. He had never thought of them as *his* pigeons until now. In fact, he had always regarded the pigeons as an annoyance. They were always leaving their smelly droppings to be squished underfoot. In fact, he had rather admired the pigeons' main foe—the feisty seagulls, though he now somehow resented their shrieking intrusion into *his* territory. The pigeons were *his* to chase and scatter. It was something to do when he was in a bad mood.

The cub regarded the pigeon remaining after the hawk attack. He'd never looked closely at an individual pigeon before. The pigeons had always seemed dull-gray to him. Peering at this one, though, Smokey noticed that its neck shimmered pink and green in the sun. It was beautiful! And the breast was pleasingly plump with a sparkling reddish sheen to it. The gray back, on closer inspection, was actually a silvery gray-blue. And he liked the two bold black stripes just behind the shoulders. The wings were tucked close to the body, crossed and dovetailed neatly at the ends, making the bird look quite dashing with its black wingtips. The most remarkable thing to him was the color of the pigeon's feet—bright pink. And he noticed the precise way the bird set down each foot as it stepped from place to place.

On closer inspection, this pigeon was pert enough, but had a slight limp. Had its leg been injured— like his own leg had been? When Smokey was tired he still limped, and he felt a sliver of compassion for the bird. He edged nearer. It stepped away. How odd

Sophia © GLORI BERRY

that its head rocked forward and back with each step, as if its head beckoned the legs to move. The bear veered away not to startle it, then very slowly sidled nearby, at an angle, so the bird wouldn't fear being stalked.

Could a pigeon possibly know anything about other birds like Strut? He shrugged. Everyone knew pigeons were too stupid to know anything, much less tell another creature. They only warbled gibberish among themselves. Yet Smokey was suddenly hopeful. He stooped down to look into the pigeon's bright orange eyes with their yellow rims. The bird cocked its head in Smokey's direction and shot him an alert look. Perhaps it was intelligent, after all! The cub eagerly poked his head closer, but the pigeon spooked and flew away.

Smokey was left feeling forlorn. Was he reduced to trying to converse with know-nothing pigeons that only gabbled among themselves? Everyone was gone. Mr. Dazzle wasn't around much these rainy days. No Freddie lately. Hardly any people came by, though in his current mood visitors would have annoyed him. He looked up at the sky where he'd seen the speck—a hawk. What a cruel joke to hope Strut might be coming to make him laugh again.

Chapter 38

He who asks a question may be a fool for five minutes. But he who never asks a question remains a fool forever.
–Tom J. Connelly

After breakfast the next day Smokey stood near his food bowl and searched the open air above the cage. A few pigeons were frolicking in the sky, and one swooped down briefly to inspect his yard, but flew up again. With his paw the cub quickly whisked crumbs from the bottom of his bowl onto the concrete, moved away, and waited. Smokey was delighted with his cleverness when he saw some birds alight on the ground, one of them the lame pigeon. They immediately began briskly pecking specks of kibble before more pigeons could spy them and attract the seagulls.

Smokey knew he must hurry and ask them about Strut, but he felt foolish. How do you address pigeons? Smokey cautiously moved closer. He cleared his throat, wondering how to begin.

The bear blurted out, "Hey, you guys! Do any of you know anything?" Smokey stopped abruptly. None had even glanced at him. Smokey could feel himself getting angry, but before his temper overcame him, he made another try. He crouched low, took a deep breath, let out a sigh, and addressed them in a voice as patient and quiet as he could muster. "Excuse me, pigeons. I'm trying to find out about my friend Strut, a crow. I heard he was coming." One pigeon took a hesitant step toward him and looked up. It was the lame one.

At that very moment, Mr. Dazzle arrived at the gate screeching, "*Mon dieu*! What possesses you, Smokey?" He tilted his head to look first at the cub, then the lame pigeon. The peacock scoffed. "So now you're consorting with pigeons? Those birdbrains don't know anything. Even if they did, those nitwits couldn't tell you." The peacock poked in a loose feather, stretched his green and gold spangled neck and shook the bobbles atop his head. With eyes narrowed, and a tone heavy with condescension, he added, "Poor Smokey. Trying to talk with rock doves! You must indeed be hard up for company."

A wave of embarrassment engulfed the cub, then a tide of anger rose in his chest. Smokey wheeled around and charged the peacock, letting his throat rumble. The rumble was so loud and low that it surprised him. It sounded like Father Bear's roar! Emboldened by his own fierce voice, he grabbed the gate with his paws and shook it hard. The peacock tilted backward, off balance, and flew a few feet away.

It was such fun to scare the bird that Smokey kept glowering. Dazzle took a moment to compose himself, stood tall and announced with a lofty tone, "Everyone knows, *mon petit*, that you can't converse with those dumb clucks!"

The peacock's slit eyes swept over the pigeons, then he arched his head in disdain and declared, "They're good-for-nothings. Taking over the city. Splattering everything. Covering the bridges with their white droppings, hard as rock. Their excrement won't even wash away nicely with rain. Pigeons are a disgrace to all self-respecting birds!"

The cub huffed and said, "I know that! I was just looking for food over there and talking to myself. Those dimwits just happened to be nearby."

"Ha," Mr. Dazzle said, darting the cub a doubtful look. He flapped away.

When Dazzle was out of sight, Smokey slumped, afraid the pigeons might have overheard what he had called them. More pigeons had arrived. He frantically searched among the milling birds to find the lame one to ask her about Strut, but now he couldn't spot her.

By then, Smokey knew he'd missed his chance, for the big seagulls were arriving. They hurtled down from the sky and dived among the pigeons, who scattered higgledy-piggledy this way and that. Smokey yelled at the pigeons, "You cowards. Stand your ground!" A few gave the cub a quizzical look before they all took off.

It was late at night when Smokey awoke. He thought he heard chit-chat nearby. Rousing himself, he peered through the dark and misty air to the other side of the fence. Something was moving against the blackness. Sniffing damp fur, he discerned a familiar smell. A barely-audible sing-song voice whispered, "I don't think we should wake him."

Another hushed voice said, "Oh, come on, Trish. He'll want to know."

Smokey cried out to the darkness. "Trish! Trash! I'm so glad you're back! Come on in!" He saw their shapes slowly move up the outside of his fence, then climb down the inside of the fence to the ground. Soon the monkeys stood before him, but they were no longer their exuberant selves. Wet and bedraggled, they whimpered and looked up at him. His heart went out to them, so he quickly sat and let them nuzzle his long thick fur. They perked up, and both speaking at once, told their story.

The night they had left Smokey, they had braved the road to reach the big park with the creek in it. To their distress, the park was nothing like the jungle. It was just as the rat had told Smokey. No banana trees for food. No fruit, and hardly any nuts to eat, only garbage cans to raid at picnic sites. The monkeys had roamed endlessly in the mist, and had finally gotten soaked to the skin in a downpour because there weren't any trees with big leaves or a high canopy to shelter them from heavy rain.

By the end of the third day Trish and Trash were so miserable and cold that they clung to each other, whimpering and shaking. It reminded them of their grievous time as babies: Their mothers had been shot and fell to earth. Trish and Trash were still clutching their mothers' limp bodies when the shooters found them. They tried to run away, but were caught in nets and crammed into a woven basket.

The two orphans had been chained near a hut and fed rice-water and bananas for a few days. That's when Trish and Trash had become good friends, clinging together for comfort. Then they'd been crammed back into the basket, jostled down a jungle path, and placed in the hot sun at an outdoor market. They had become very weak by the time Dr. Mann found them and brought them on a long journey back to the zoo.

The monkeys told Smokey that by the fourth dawn in the park, they were so hungry and cold they knew they must return to the zoo. But to retrace their steps they had to cross the creek bordering the park. On the way in, it had been easy to jump onto boulders and wade across the shallow parts. After the rainstorm, however, the water had risen to roar over the boulders. As they stood, disheartened, a tree trunk swept past and lodged itself on each bank. They had to move fast in case the tree-bridge was swept away, so they took a chance, ran across, and made it to the other side. They had to wait for traffic to ebb late at night to cross the road back to the zoo.

"You were certainly brave to do that. I'm so glad you made it!" Smokey said, and pressed them against his warm body. The monkeys perked up and smiled with glee, then burrowed into his fur, shivering. The bear commiserated with them, making soft sounds. Smokey told the monkeys that he had worried about how they were faring in the rain. And he had missed them, afraid he'd never see them again.

Trash, who had even quicker changes of mood than Trish, piped up, "Let's show him our big surprise. Now!"

Trish stepped out from Smokey's embrace into the light beam from the tall lamp outside the enclosure. She turned sideways and stood on all fours. The cub gasped. Underneath Trish's body was a little head below hers, and the silhouette of a small upside-down body.

The monkey mother reached to her stomach, gently lifted the baby monkey, and stepped closer into the light. The pale skin on the baby's face was wrinkled and comical-looking with his smooshed nose. He was mouthing his thumb, and his hand—like his parents' hands—looked just like a human's with its joints and tiny fingernails. The wet fur atop his head spiked up to a point in the middle, giving him a quizzical look. And he had pointy ears, shaped like his parents' ears, but very big for his size and sticking straight out to the sides. At the end of the little body drooped a long tail.

Trish beamed and said, "This is *Hopkins!*" Smokey moved closer on all fours and slowly stretched out his muzzle to sniff the monkey's head. His nose homed in on the fresh aroma at the crown of the little guy's noggin, and he softly mewed, "Ummm, ummm." The little monkey squirmed out of his mother's arms despite her protests, and, gripping her fur with his tiny fingers, climbed hand over hand onto the top of her head. Balancing there, with his tail dangling over his mother's face, he leaned toward the bear and looked inquisitively at him with big shiny black eyes. He had a happy-go-lucky air about him that drew Smokey in.

The bear flared the pink insides of his nose as wide as he could and inhaled again the fresh sweet scent of the baby. Smokey wanted to remember this special smell whenever he might catch a breeze from Monkey Island. He sat down, and the monkey family rested, warming up their cold wet bodies as they reclined against their friend's thick fur. They all listened quietly to the familiar night sounds of big zoo animals shuffling about and the distant hoo-hoo of an owl.

As the night progressed, Trish and Trash grew anxious about their pending return to Monkey Island. How would the group of monkeys receive them? Since they had both abandoned their Monkey Island society, would they now be driven off as strangers? Would the sour-faced matriarch attack their baby? If two big males got in a fight, would they toss Hopkins around or even throw him at a tree trunk? Despite these fears—and to Smokey's alarm—before the first light of dawn the monkeys bravely struck out, hoping to find friends, food, and shelter. Over their shoulders they called back, promising, if all went well, to return in a few days to be with

Smokey for the fireworks, as they had the previous year.

Through the next days, Smokey heard explosive noises and whiffed fire and smoke, but recognized them as only signals that the summer fireworks would soon begin.

He waited impatiently. When would the monkeys come for their promised visit? With each passing day, he became more concerned. Had little Hopkins been well-received? Or attacked? Smokey paced along the fence, and sometimes stood still, trying to catch any scent of his friends at Monkey Island.

One day, a boy lingered at the cage, lowering his eyebrows at the cub and compressing his lips. Smokey was instantly wary. From behind his tree, he saw the youngster fiddle with a short red stick until it sputtered white flashes at one end. Smokey hated the acrid smell of fire and backed up. The red stick hit an upright bar and bounced back. The next time a firecracker whipped straight into his yard and exploded. Smokey clacked his teeth, zipped to the top of his tree and cried, "Baa-wooo, Baa-wooo." His eyes on the boy, he uttered gulping sounds of distress to see the boy chortle and fumble in his pocket for another firecracker.

Smokey suddenly found his neck stretched forth, roaring. How he'd like to swat that youngster as hard as he could! At that moment, an older man ran up to the tormentor and shook him roughly by the shoulder and snatched his firecrackers. "You bully! No, you're a *coward* . . . trying to harm a helpless creature."

The cub glowered. The next time he'd trust his instincts and immediately retreat to his den. Or, better yet, roar at the person and charge the fence. The bear came down the tree to firmly place all fours on the ground, practiced some low menacing sounds, and then stretched as high as he could for the great satisfaction of sharpening his claws against the trunk.

One evening, not long afterwards, Smokey heard scattered sounds of firecrackers in the distance, and recoiled at the stench of exhaust from stalled cars headed that way. As the night fell, at last the three monkeys appeared, as they had promised.

Smokey insisted they tell him everything. First, how they had been received at Monkey Island. They told him they had found their banana crate where they'd cleverly hidden it on this side of the moat, so they could swim back to the island. Hopkins had ridden on Trish's back and hardly got wet at all.

Upon arrival, Trash said, all the monkeys had crowded around Hopkins. Then a hush had fallen as they parted for the matriarch to slowly walk up, her shoulders swaying from side to side. She stopped, facing the family.

Trish cringed, and held out her small palm in supplication. The old monkey paused a moment, and then took Trish's hand in her dark calloused one. She peered at their baby boy, and to their great relief, reached out her bony arm and, with her gnarled finger, briefly groomed the sparse fur on the little monkey's shoulder. Their baby would be safe on Monkey Island, after all.

Relieved at the good news, Smokey sat down with the family in the coolness of the evening, looking forward to showing Hopkins his first sight of magical colors popping in the sky. Hopkins was mischievous, crawling all over his parents, wearing his playface and making happy sounds, but the adults appeared subdued. Trish and Trash murmured together about how disheartening their escapade to freedom had been compared to their high hopes. The park was certainly no substitute for the wonderful jungle they had known as youngsters. They and their son must live at the zoo from now on.

Smokey knew that monkeys never stayed in one mood for long, and soon they were chitter-chattering cheerfully about Hopkins, and how he would always have plenty of food, and a whole troop of monkeys to play with—and pester. At that moment, Hopkins held a wad of Smokey's fur in his small fist and pulled hard. The cub winced, and stiffened. Trish quickly pried the small fingers loose. "You see, he's already quite a scamp, but he'll have all the monkeys to keep an eye on him." The little fellow proceeded to mouth the cub's big toe, tickling him, but Smokey merely smiled down at the little imp. The parents assured Smokey that they would often visit so he could watch Hopkins grow up. That gladdened Smokey's heart. It gave him something to look forward to, and would be a welcome break in his routine and loneliness.

At last, a series of rapid loud bangs announced that Smokey's second Fourth of July at the zoo would soon begin. The loud noises didn't startle him much. He had become accustomed to strange noises at the zoo: the clanging of front gates, the sawing and trimming of trees on the grounds, the abrupt and sharp clashing of heavy machinery, and the staccato hammering of new construction. At the first flash of colors in the sky the monkey family leaned against the bear's haunches, and far into the night they marveled at the bursts of beauty in the sky. It was a rare treat in their imprisonment.

Chapter 39

The World is as delicate and complicated as a spider's web. If you touch one thread you send shudders running through all the other threads. We are not just touching the web, we are tearing holes in it. Now think of the web as a safety net. The thin strands of survival. Help us tend it, repair it, hold it together.
–Gerald Durrell

Smokey awoke hungry. It would be quite a while before his keeper appeared with food. His bowl had been replaced with a bucket so he now had more food, yet he still yearned to forage these long summer days of early July. How he'd like to stretch his legs on a path under trees, burst through brambles to find early blackberries, or mosey around in a meadow to feast on clover blossoms to his heart's content. The smell of musty earth came to him on a whiff of breeze and made his claws itch to tear into a rotten log for larvae. Or heave big mossy rocks about and find something wiggly underneath.

The odor from a great body of water nearby, the Atlantic Ocean, heavy with salty marine life tantalized him. How he'd like to hunt in the water for something to eat. He hated being cooped up, helpless with hunger for some different food. Smokey paced the length of the fence, back and forth, back and forth, grumbling low in his throat.

The morning kibble arrived and Smokey wolfed it down. Just in time—as he was about to slurp up the remains at the bottom of the bucket—he remembered the pigeons. He knocked over the bucket so the remaining bits of kibble spilled out. Then he waited, hoping to see the lame pigeon again. He had a strange feeling that she might somehow bring him news of his friend Strut.

Smokey dozed off and on. He heard the pigeons making their soft warbling as they puttered about the tipped bucket and nibbled tidbits. Suddenly their tittering changed into sharp cries drowned out by incoming screeches of seagulls! The young bear snorted and roused himself upright. He strode among the pigeons on the ground, and flailed his arms in the air at the wing traffic of jeering gulls. He roared, "Leave *my* pigeons alone, you—you—hooligans!" To his satisfaction, they stopped their descent and moved their wings slowly in midair above him. Then they flew off. He danced in triumph.

"How gallant! Thank you." He twirled around, and there she was—a short distance away. The pigeon was alone, the others still busy near the bucket. With a composed air, the bird marched a few steps toward him, limping slightly. She cocked her head to look up at him with one yellow eye. "So, you have a question for me?"

Flustered at the pigeon's sudden speech, the cub didn't know what to say. Afraid to frighten her away, he lowered his erect body slowly onto all fours. She remained calm, so he crept in a wide arc just close enough to scrutinize her. Her eyes were remarkably old and wise. "So, why did you save us from the seagulls?" she asked. "Tell the truth. You have to be straight with me."

"Well, uh, yes, of course. I wanted to protect you so you'd stay—and tell me what you might know about Strut."

"That makes sense. Actually, every wild bird knows about your famous friend Strut the Storyteller! It's been heard on-the-wing for quite a while. Here's what I've gleaned so far. In early spring he flunked Nest-Building. And then, of course, the unlucky fellow couldn't build a nest decent enough to woo his sweetheart. So he set out to see you. That was many weeks ago."

Smokey's heart pounded with excitement. Was it true—that Strut was really coming?

"Are you sure? Will he get here soon?"

"Hard to say. He's been moving rather steadily along the

way. It'll be best if he arrives here before the snow flies, so he won't be stranded by winter storms."

Smokey was so excited at the news that he whirled around the enclosure and tripped into the pool so suddenly that he gulped down water and came out coughing. Back on the concrete, he rolled onto his back, and waved the palms of his feet in the air. He flexed his outstretched claws and uttered happy sounds.

At last, with a contented sigh, Smokey lay still. With his head at the same level as the pigeon, his eyes glowed at his informant, who still stood patiently watching him. "Who are you?" he asked. Suddenly he looked at her closely. "Are *you* the one whose voice I've been hearing for quite a while?"

"Yes. I'm called Sophia."

"How do you know things? Even about Strut?"

"There's a saying. 'There are only six degrees of separation between any two birds in the world.'" When the cub frowned, she added, "That means: To find a particular bird, you only have to ask a bird—who knows a bird from another flock, who also knows another, until you reach the sixth bird—the one you're looking for."

Noticing that Smokey looked doubtful, she said, "I know it sounds amazing, but flocks of birds fly all over. Geese are honking news to each other all the time in formation while they're traveling north and south. Crows congregate everywhere and love to talk. Birds are the gossips of the skies. And crows more than any others."

"I see. You seem *very* intelligent," Smokey said, "not just a run-of-the-mill pigeon."

The pigeon cocked her head. "You don't know much about us, do you? Let me explain." Sophia began in a pleasant lilting voice, "I'm a rock dove, the same as the other pigeons here. We're related to homing pigeons, you know. Certainly you've heard about carrier pigeons in the first big war. Those brave birds flew through gunfire to deliver messages. Some even carried tiny cameras for surveillance. And in the second big war, pigeons carried messages for the British and American soldiers."

Smokey looked at her with growing respect. "I didn't know that."

"Well, earthlings like you are confined to only what you smell, see, and hear from the vantage point of four legs on the ground. Winglings fly the skies and that gives us a greater perspective."

She paused, then continued. "Wild birds can sense the larger sun and earth forces so we easily find our direction over great extents of land and sea. And, of course, gifted rock doves — like homing pigeons and racing pigeons — also find our way close to home by following landmarks."

Her eyes swept the other pigeons. "I'll tell you a secret about us *city* pigeons. We can do that, too." She darted Smokey a sharp look. "We're not *dimwits* at all! Smokey, beware birds like that pompous peacock who disparage any mass of newcomers, like us city pigeons. With our illustrious past, pigeons deserve to be held in high esteem. After all, pigeons like the famous 'G. I. Joe' won more medals of honor in the war than any other animal."

Embarrassed that he'd called her a dimwit — and been overheard — Smokey managed to utter, "I'm sorry, Sophia. I'm new here. I didn't know." The pigeon let out a little chirp, and the cub brightened. He announced, "I'll always stick up for you from now on!"

Sophia said, "Thank you, young bear. And certainly I'll do the same for you."

Smokey fixed his eyes on her. "How do you know things about me? Like what I should do?"

"I just do. You can count on me. It's called intuition." Sophia shot him an amused, knowing look. She turned away, and with only the slightest limp, walked in her bobbing-head way to join the other pigeons.

As soon as she left, Smokey realized that all her talk about pigeons had distracted him from the great news: Strut had set out to see him. Cheered, Smokey felt more alive—and impatient—than ever. He eagerly watched the far sky for the crow.

As hot and humid July slid into August, he once again felt compelled to focus on food. He was always hungry. Toward the end of August, the heat and humidity became unbearable to Smokey in his thick fur. Even Mr. Dazzle on his morning rounds looked wilted. The bear retreated from the midday sun to his shady den, now musty-smelling from the green mold thickening on the rock walls. He spent a lot of time in the pool, sometimes with the big new rubber ball Doc Mann had given him to play with.

At last the steamy air that hung heavily over Washington in the summer turned to the brisk clear air of September, and the burnt children came to say farewell to Smokey, using the word 'school' a lot. It reminded him of the tearful leave-taking with Judy. He understood that he was being abandoned again. Before Charlie turned away to leave, the boy tossed something through the fence. It was a small fuzzy teddy bear. "Maybe Teddy can keep you company while we're gone." As the cub placed his paw on the furry thing, he turned and watched the two depart. His stomach hurt like the time when he'd been hoisted onto the airplane back in Capitan and Judy had cried. Smokey understood good-byes.

The cub slowly walked to his cave, and let out a long groan as he lay down. During the following days Smokey felt an irresistible urge to pace in the mornings, but in the evenings he consoled himself by curling up with the furry thing that Charlie had left him.

And as the fall winds became brisk and cool, blowing bright-colored leaves into his prison yard, he chased them in bursts of energy. From time to time he searched the deep blue autumn sky, hoping any moment to see the arrival of his friend Strut. Then, with the coming of the gray skies of early winter, he lost hope. It seemed unlikely that his crow friend had survived such a long flight, what with hawks, strange places, and stormy weather.

Smokey realized one day that his usual grumpy keeper had been replaced. The cub hardly noticed because the man had done his work so hastily. The peacock referred to him derisively as a Sweeper-Keeper. When Smokey asked what that meant, Dazzle said that he was the kind of keeper who just did his job, and hardly looked at his animals.

A succession of other similar gray-clad keepers came — the same ones he'd known on the keeper's days off. He recognized them from a distance by their footfalls and smells. A rapid gait brought Old Sweaty Armpits to the cage; a heavy thud of a walk brought Mr. Soapy-Clothes-and-Minty-Breath. One whistled and sang, another reeked of cigar smoke.

One day, a new person fumbled with the gate lock, like new young zookeepers did, except that this person had the distinctive woody scent of sawdust with a tingly whiff of citrus. He hardly noticed the newcomer, clad in the usual gray keepers' overalls, except to register that she was an older woman with a stout body that moved with a smooth grace.

Day after day she reappeared. He didn't pay her much attention at first. Why bother? Since keepers ignored him, he ignored them. After a few days, though, Smokey wondered if she might be different from the others. The woman hummed softly as she cleaned his enclosure, sauntered about, and sent forth an aura of well-being. Gradually he came to welcome her presence.

One day she stopped, caught his eye, reached into her baggy overalls and threw a carrot in the pool. Then, before he could amble over to the water, she tossed some things that bounced on the concrete. He recognized them as nuts in their shells. He could spend all day wresting meat from them. Smokey stood, torn between which wonderful treat to pursue first.

By the time he looked up, she was leaving through the gate. How he wished she could be his keeper forever. But the next week, she didn't come, nor the next. Would he ever see her again? Was life like that: losing all those you like, one after another?

Smokey forlorn

Smokey hopeless

A swim helps Smokey

Smokey's bored again

Chapter 40

Turn your face to the sun and the shadows fall behind you.
–Maori proverb

The morning after the fire, back in Capitan, New Mexico, more than a year earlier:
Strut watched as the plane carrying Ray and the burnt cub taxied across the field, and rose into the air. The crow flew frantically after it. Not until it was too far ahead of him did he give up and crash-land back on the grassy field. His chest heaving, Strut gathered his legs under him and faced the blank sky. He already missed his friend.

How could he ever find Smokey now that he'd been flown out of sight? Strut had promised Smokey that he'd find him and always be friends, but right now it seemed impossible. When Ray had briefly set Smokey's box on the ground before boarding the plane, Strut had poked his head inside the container to see the little bear. Smokey had looked so frail, lying there, that the crow wondered whether he could survive.

The bird's head drooped in deep sorrow at losing his best friend. And his best audience too. The cub had listened enthusiastically to his stories, and was always curious about his visits to the village. And Smokey always laughed at the crow's jokes.

Strut keenly felt how weary his wings were from his exertions the day before: flying down to Capitan in the morning, wearily flapping back up the charred mountain to find the cub with his head sticking out of a hollow stump, alerting Ray at the fire camp to rescue him, fetching the cub from the ranch house, then watching Ray fly away with Smokey.

He caught a whiff of the singed tips of his own ragged wings. The crow heaved a sigh. There hadn't been any chance to comb his feathers, even though his down was itchy with ashes, and his skin gummy from oily smoke. Too disheartened to do more than peck a few errant feathers into place, Strut shook his body to puff-out some ashes. The crow lowered his body to the ground and his eyes closed.

Strut awoke to the sun high in the sky. The crow stood stiffly, took one last look over the plains to the blank horizon where the plane had departed, and, standing in place, whirred his wings with determination. He bobbed up and down to summon his courage, and launched himself toward the mountain to rejoin his flock.

The crow soared high above the burned-out mountain so he needn't face its devastation up close. He finally reached the other side of the mountain and found the tree that the flock now called home. He settled down on a branch near his family. They were all there, unharmed, and he was touched by how glad they were to see him. Having lost his friend Smokey, it cheered him that his friend Duke flew right over and playfully teased him. Strut's chest expanded at the sight of even those who had earlier taunted him—members of Duke's gang and the bedraggled crow who had pecked him on the head. His hard feelings had somehow dissolved in the greater tragedy of the fire. Strut, once an outcast, felt a sense of belonging like never before.

To his dismay, Strut noticed that some crows were missing. Waiting through the following days, he saw a few stragglers drift in, one by one. Their seared feathers smelled awful and their voices rasped. After that, no more came.

Strut noticed one forlorn female who continued to search the sky for her mate's return. The devoted couple had built a fine nest together early in spring just as they had every year. Strut quietly asked her what had happened. "We couldn't bear to leave our newly-laid eggs, so we waited too long. Then, in all the flames and smoke, we got separated." What could he say?

All Strut could do was stand next to her, and she dipped her head in acknowledgment. Like others who had returned late, the lone crow coughed for days. At last she lowered her head the way grief-stricken crows do, let her body droop, and fell to earth.

Other crows murmured their concern for a moment, then looked away. But Strut was heart-stricken. Why didn't someone do something? Indignant, Strut, who had once fallen to earth himself, flew down to the ground. He hopped about frantically to find a seed for her, but by the time he brought it back, she had crumpled onto her side with her neck askew. He stood over her inert body a long time before he slowly walked away.

During the following days the survivors kept close together in their new tree, legs stiff and claws locked onto branches so they could daydream and sleep without falling. Sometimes one or two grumbled how barren this side of the mountain was compared to their old home. Painful silences followed.

Strange noises startled the flock. Was that movement among the grass a large snake? It was disconcerting to see weary animals come into view and trudge onward, displaced by the fire and searching for somewhere to live. Strut heard the crows' endless complaints: Where were the songbirds they'd always heard early in the morning? Where was the familiar drone of insects in the afternoon? They foraged only beneath their tree. They spent a lot of time grooming — setting straight their errant feathers and combing themselves as if they could make everything right without stirring from their perches.

One day, with an air of disdain, Elder Crow eyed his flock, and stood impatiently on one foot, then the other, from morning to nightfall. The next day, he rustled his feathers with great agitation. By the third day, the old crow sternly urged them to go find food and rebuild their nests. He cajoled. He threatened. He insulted them. When nothing roused them from their torpor, he let out a disgusted caw, slumped his shoulders and tucked his head under his wing.

Days went by. At first the crows were glad to be free of his scolding, for he had been much more grouchy than usual. Before long, though, they missed his large presence in their lives. Strut, especially, was concerned. Although he had feared and resented how Elder Crow criticized him, he was grateful that Elder Crow always championed his storytelling. All in all, he liked the old bird. And the whiny edge to the flocks' mournful caws got on his nerves.

So Strut went to Elder Crow and boldly stood next to him. He stared with alarm at his mentor—a hollow shell of his former self, with his flight feathers ragged and dull-colored, as if he were molting. The wise old eyes were glazed-over. Had the forest fire sapped the elder's powerful spirit? Or was he sick and dying?

Although crows ordinarily went about their business in small groups according to their whim—only summoning the rest when they discovered something special—Strut worried about the flock without their leader. They'd surely miss hearing the old stories from the time before they'd been born.

As Strut gazed at Elder Crow's face, he saw the old fellow surreptitiously raise an eyelid and dart him a meaningful look. That roguish look made his blood pulse. A flush of pride swept through Strut's breast. Elder Crow was counting on him. He must do his noble-best to make Elder Crow proud of him.

Strut stood tall and faced the flock. "CAW, CAW," he declared. "Hey, you fuddy-duddies! Where's your spunk?" He stared at the cockiest young crows until he got their attention. Words tumbled forth to rout the sluggish crows, and he cast his voice into a chanting cadence about new land, wondrous food and adventure. All eyes were on him. "Stretch your wings and follow me!" he cawed loudly.

Without looking back he took flight, hoping that enough crows would follow so he wouldn't feel like a fool. When he dared glance over his shoulder, he saw that a small group trailed behind him. Before they might change their minds, he flew down to a low branch, held on upside-down and beat his wings, dislodging some insects. Two crows rushed to the earth and hungrily gobbled them up. They stayed on the ground to search further afield, and others eagerly followed suit. With their bellies full, the vanguard of crows reported back to those on the nesting tree. Not wanting to be left out, the rest of the crows took off.

Upon the flock's return later in the afternoon, they found to their surprise that Elder Crow had recuperated his strength and become his dignified self again. He called Strut over, gave the youngster a canny, quick smile and said, "Well done." Feeling like a hero, Strut pranced along his branch, tossed a twig through the air and caught it on-the-wing. All evening he basked in the glow of the elder's satisfaction with him, momentary though it might be. He had no illusion that a rebel like himself would remain in favor if he dared overstep the strict rules.

Soon other kinds of birds were busy building their second nests of the spring and laying new eggs to replace those lost in the fire. It was crow custom to do likewise, and following Elder Crow's exhortations, a few couples did so.

By the time summer breezes swept the high mountains, inviting Strut to venture forth, he had forgotten his bear friend. He did not know that Smokey was languishing in the muggy heat of his first summer at the zoo, feeling homesick for the freedom and crisp air of the dry mountains and the company of his good friend, the crow.

Exploring his new area of the mountain, nothing happened to remind Strut of the cub until one day he and Duke happened to cross into their old territory and follow a ribbon of river below. With a jolt of recognition, Strut suddenly swooped down and hovered above a familiar meadow sloping down to the river. The crow excitedly recounted to Duke how terrified he'd been for his friend Smokey, who would have been killed by his own father if Strut hadn't flown in his face and the cub's mother hadn't arrived. A wave of remorse assailed Strut. How could he have forgotten his promise to find the bear someday?

Duke told him there was nothing he could do, and, in his persuasive way, proceeded to distract Strut through the summer.

Autumn came early to the mountains, and the brisk days brought bright colors—deep yellowish-orange to stands of cottonwoods and aspens among the dark evergreens, and red to patches of scrub oak. Soon after, the glistening winter snow of 1950 shrouded the mountain peaks in white, then spread down the mountainside. By late November—at the same time Smokey was being brought Thanksgiving dinner by the zoo director and his wife—the crows were huddled together in the high mountains through the countrywide blizzard. Afterward, the days continued cold and dark. Strut's mood darkened further as his thoughts returned to losing his bear friend. How helpless he felt to ever find him again.

The spring of 1951 finally arrived in the high country. Snowmelt trickled into creeks. By this time, a year after the fire, soil had absorbed the mineral-rich ashes so the burnt meadows and mountain slopes now had a feathering of bright green and chartreuse grasses. Surviving pine trees sported bright green needles; clumps of aspen and cottonwood budded tiny leaves. And here and there, long-dormant seeds that required fire burst into life with green shoots. Insects rustled and flitted about, creating a buzzing hum as background to bird calls and bird song. Not only the crows, but all the other animals scurried about with renewed vigor to start afresh and replenish their numbers.

In the aftermath of the fire, with tall grass and brush burned away, raptors could more easily spot small prey on the ground, but prey were scarce. Many had been incinerated in the fire or starved in the winter. Large hawks and great horned owls had to expand their springtime range to feed their young.

The presence of raptors soaring above their new territory frightened the crows. One evening they noticed that members were suddenly missing from the roosting tree. Elder Crow ominously proclaimed that he suspected airborne predators.

Alarmed, the flock cawed loudly that something had to be done. He cawed back angrily at everyone to desist from their hysteria. Perhaps the crows in question had not died after all, and might yet return. He paced heavily, as if a great responsibility had descended on his shoulders.

Investigating the disappearance on their own the next morning, Duke and Strut spied tell-tail feathers of crows below a tree: evidence of the predator. They quickly dashed away, then did a cautious fly-by past the tree top, and saw the dreaded blue-gray back of a goshawk. For one terrifying split-second the two stared at the fierce, brilliant orange eyes of the hawk—their worst enemy, a big bird whose rounded wings allowed it to pursue crows even through thickets. Beating their own wings fiercely, the two crows swiftly banked away, but not before Duke swooped down and bravely snatched up a crow feather from the ground. Not to be outdone, his heart thumping, Strut did the same.

The two crows carried the crow feathers back and presented them with pride to their elder. Fear flashed in his eyes, and, instead of complimenting the two for finding evidence that confirmed everyone's worst fears, he merely nodded, as a deafening cacophony of alarm calls from the watching flock reached a crescendo. "Caw! Caw! CAWK! CAWK!" The clamor had hardly died down when Elder Crow abruptly left to perch on a branch of a nearby tree. He summoned Strut and Duke to join him. The elder was known to be fair, but at this point he looked more rattled than usual. The youngsters stiffened and braced themselves to be scapegoated as messengers of bad news.

To their relief, Elder Crow began in a reasonable tone. The times required that all crows be diligent and start families so their depleted numbers could increase. Soon owls and hawks would grab crows setting on eggs or steal their baby hatchlings. Furry predators, too, would steal eggs and snatch nestlings. The flock needed parents—and sentinels. Elder Crow's voice shifted to a harsh caw. Strut and Duke stiffened at the inevitable chastisement—for whatever misdeeds of theirs Elder Crow would use to vent his helplessness and wrath.

Elder Crow called them "independent spirits" who had hardly attended Nest-building Class the past spring, and instead had sneaked off to lark around and go to town every chance they had. And the two hadn't "cooperated" in the urgent business of juveniles helping others build nests.

And now came the last straw, the elder said. In recent days he had heard Strut set a bad example for the younger crows, scoffing about memorizing and weaving "those tedious two thousand twigs for nests." What would the two of them do next? Elder Crow demanded. Would they lead impressionable singles to rebel against their time-honored apprenticeship of helping feed the crows sitting on eggs, and, later, feeding the nestlings? The old crow looked sternly at Strut and Duke. "No more shenanigans! I ought to banish you from the flock as good-for-nothings." The two hung their heads in submission, sneaking sidelong glances at each other.

"Caw! From now on, you have to be *useful* members of the community." Elder Crow paused a moment and looked far away. His mood suddenly shifted and the more reasoned cadence of his voice returned. He announced that henceforth they were to work as the official lookouts for winged predators, especially that goshawk who preyed on crows.

Relieved, the two agreed. Guarding the others sounded much more exciting than building nests and feeding youngsters. It turned out that Duke and Strut were a good team. They relished working together. Strut showed how sharp his eyesight was and how smart his strategies, while Duke showed off how powerful he was in rallying his group of raucous crows to mob predators. With their new sense of importance, they preened themselves elaborately in front of the flock and swaggered on the upper roost with heads held high. And soon, busy with a new job he loved, Strut had again forgotten his vow to find Smokey.

Strut neglected his intention to remain in Elder Crow's

good graces. Since being a crow sentinel entailed stretches of time waiting to sight predators, Strut suggested the two take turns being lookout so they'd each have more time for other adventures.

One day, while Duke was standing guard, Strut came upon Kate, a female crow. He was mesmerized by the splendid feathers on her back and wings. While his feathers and other yearlings' were brown, hers had the purplish cast of a more mature female, and her long tail was smoothly rounded at the end, not tattered. What a beauty. With such flight feathers, Kate seemed a strong and feisty enough mate for him. Especially attractive to him was his knowledge that she had always loved his stories.

Strut had noticed an abandoned birds' nest nearby. Why not lure Kate to see it? Ordinary male crows showed off new nests they were building so they could appeal to females, but he would be different. The nest he had found was impressively large, abandoned seasons ago by some birds much bigger than crows, possibly magpies. He enticed her to come with him and look at the roomy nest. On closer inspection, they both noticed that the structure was somewhat askew. Strut tugged impatiently at some twigs, but it only made the nest ominously sag as if the whole thing would collapse. He darted a glance her way, and cringed to see Kate's amused look. Noticing dirt and dust inside the nest, and knowing females were persnickety about a smooth inner lining, he asked her to wait while he flew off to find soft material.

He was carrying a bunch of long grass back to the nest when Duke swooped down and grabbed dangling grasses out of his bill. Strut squawked and chased him. When he couldn't catch up with Duke, Strut snagged a twig with his foot and tried to bait Duke with it. As soon as the big crow gained on him, Strut dropped the twig, then grabbed it again before it hit the ground. Before long, they were playing keep-away and Strut forgot about wooing Kate. Fortunately, no goshawk came that day.

Much later, Strut found his new flame Kate perched on a finely-woven nest. She was standing next to Donny Boy, a stolid older male wearing a self-satisfied smirk. Kate glanced disdainfully across the way at Strut. Her would-be suitor felt deflated. How could Kate prefer a pudgy namby-pamby like Donny to someone sleek and daring like himself?

Strut gazed at her with longing, and she eyed him back. The moment her mate was distracted by some commotion behind him, Kate called over, "Too bad you're all talk and no action, Strut. Donny may be dull but he's a do-er." She sighed. "Did you really expect me to like your cockamamie nest? Anyway, you're much too young for me. After all, I'm already three, and I naturally prefer an older male."

With a sweet voice Kate invited Strut to stay around later to help her and her mate. "You can guard the nest while we're foraging, and fetch food for our young ones. It'll be good practice. In a few seasons you'll be three or four years old, and grown-up enough to mate and build your own nest." He was crestfallen. What a fuddy-duddy she had turned out to be! Kate sure deserved Donny Boy: both boring! A thought flitted through his head — could it be that he'd mainly liked Kate because she'd admired his stories so much? What a dummy he'd been.

He became more incensed. Did Kate really think he would condescend to help her and Donny — in preparation for a humdrum life like theirs? He was Strut the Sentinel and Strut the Storyteller, meant for better things. The crow looked over at the conventional couple. Donny looked so smug that Strut let out a shrill scream and flew at him. Donny and Kate braced themselves, side-by-side, gripped the branch tightly, and pecked him hard on his head and shoulders. As soon as he'd retreated across the way, even angrier than before, he puffed out his feathers to launch another assault.

Duke, eager to join the fight, flew over to his friend's side. "CAW, CAW." He hurled insults at the couple, and thrust out his neck, ready to throw himself at the enemies. Other crows came winging in and swarmed in the air above, cawing with gusto, eager to watch the combat.

The ruckus brought Elder Crow, whose widespread wings suddenly loomed in front of Strut and Duke. "What's all this hullabaloo? Oh, it's you two again!" His severe presence quieted the group, and the two warriors pulled their heads into raised shoulders, waiting to be chastised. Elder Crow pegged Duke as the trouble maker and upbraided the big crow for his blustery ways, as well as the offence of tempting Strut-the-Sentinel to desert his guard duty. "What if the goshawk had come into the territory?"

Strut acted nonchalant and turned aside to hide his satisfaction at not being blamed. As he half-expected, though, he could never conceal anything from Elder Crow. The old crow stared at Strut until he lowered his head. The elder told Strut that he, too, was just lollygagging around and not ready to take responsibility.

Then Elder Crow stood tall. He swept his eyes across all the crows for their attention. He announced that Duke and Strut were to be banished at dawn.

The two birds jerked their wings as if a jolt of lightning had struck a nearby tree. Duke was the first to recover. He narrowed his eyes and glared at the elder, muttering under his breath, "You stodgy old fool. What do I care!"

But Strut was stricken. Here he had been enjoying his new-found status — heroically spotting predators and roosting at the top of the tree. How could he have fallen so far? Did he really have to leave his family, his flock, his audience?

The old crow darted Strut a cunning look and spoke quietly so only Strut could hear. He said that if the young crow really wanted to be a great storyteller, this was an opportunity to see the world. "Cah! It's always good for a storyteller to have a grand and dangerous adventure to tell tales about!"

Chapter 41

To lead a creative life or to create an artistic work, we have to balance all the time with the agility of an acrobat, as if we were on a tightrope stretched across an abyss. On one side the Conformist attempts to restrain us . . . On the other side the Adventurer dares us to embark on a journey of discovery.
–Linda Shierse Leonard

There comes a time in every rightly-constructed boy's life when he has a raging desire to go somewhere and dig for hidden treasure.
–Mark Twain

The two young crows felt subdued all night, so stunned at their swift ejection from the flock that they couldn't sleep. But the next morning they put on a show of bravado for the younger crows and boasted that they were off to see the world. Without any plan, they left their home and willy-nilly found themselves heading for the other side of the mountain. They soon acted as if they were in high spirits, making wide pirouettes in the sky.

However, as Strut passed by the mountainside that had been devastated by the fire, he felt compelled to be alone for a while. He told Duke to go ahead and he'd catch up with him in Capitan.

In the year since the fire Strut had avoided flying back to where the flock used to roost at night. Now, he felt drawn to see it one more time. The big blackened tree was hardly recognizable as their old home. It stood like a bare upright stick. With wistful memories of his lost world, the young crow looked at what was left of the lower branches, poking out like stubby points from the trunk. He remembered roosting there, a junior crow enduring the splats from the older crows above him. The higher branches, to which Elder Crow had finally promoted him, retained some curled brown leaves. And there was some new spring growth, but nothing like the flourishing foliage he had known.

As far as he could see across the mountainside, tree trunks stood like forlorn black poles, some with blackened arms silhouetted against the sky. Beneath them were the upraised skeletal fingers of scrub oak. At least there were scatterings of green shoots underneath the tall lodgepole pines — new life from burst pine cones. He stood on a branch and stretched his neck to the sky. "Caw. Caw! Everything is ruined! I want my home back!"

After a while, he heaved a sigh and noticed emerald green grasses pushing up from the earth. And what was that flash of blue among the stubble? Bluebirds! Strut marveled that they could be finding so many insects in this desolation. Heartened by these signs of life the crow had a sudden compulsion.

Strut took off and flew down to the cave where he had first met his good friend Smokey. The cave was deserted, so he quickly settled on his shelf. Strut poked at lumps under a sprinkling of ashes on his shelf and fanned his feathers to uncover a brass rifle shell, a bottle cap, a clothes pin . . . enough to assure him that everything was still there.

He pictured the little cub standing on his hind legs and stretching his lithe little body to peek at Strut's treasures. Where was Smokey now? Looking down at the spot where Smokey had sat listening to his stories, the crow's chest burst with an impulse to keep his promise to Smokey. He lifted his wings and flapped them vigorously at the thought of a great mission — to find Smokey!

Flying fast, he soon found Duke, drifting slowly on a current toward the village below. In between gasps for air, he told Duke his idea. It might seem like an impossible task for ordinary crows, he said, but he wanted to do it — or die trying! Duke thrust out his big chest and declared that he was certainly game for the venture.

As they approached the village, though, the crows realized that they had no idea how to actually proceed. After all, the wounded cub had left Capitan by airplane in early spring a year before. The two crows stood on top of a lodgepole pine where they could survey the crisscross of streets and all six blocks of houses. Strut's eyes were drawn to an odd landmark, an intersection where four little church steeples pointed toward the sky. Ray's house was only one street over. Strut asked Duke to wait at the tree while he investigated.

Strut flew down his favorite street lined with white oaks and overarching branches of Chinese elms, veered past an empty lot to the spacious yard bordered by a chain link fence and filled with pines. And there it was—the familiar house of yellow-tinted adobe and red-and-white shutters, with a big red chimney all the way up one side.

The crow recognized the concrete stoop outside the back door, where Ray had tossed corn for him. It seemed a long time ago. Then he spied a car in the driveway. Had Ray and his family moved back? He flew to the house and peered in the windows. The shadowy interior revealed different furniture than he remembered from his recuperation there. His human family was gone for good.

Strut pictured the moment when he had frantically pecked the windshield of Ray's big van as the man moved away from Capitan. "Cah," he sighed as the memory came back of his parting gift to Ray—the red ribbon he'd slipped into the band of his cowboy hat, and the wonderful gift Ray had given him— his cowboy necktie made with leather strings capped at the ends with shiny silver.

Looking over at the yard, the crow saw small tan grasshoppers jumping above the tall grass. They were the kind he used to relish, but he was too downhearted to pursue them. Finally, with a sweet, melancholic feeling in his storyteller's heart, Strut turned away from the house. It had yielded memories, but no clues. Yet he left with the conviction that finding Ray would lead him to Smokey. How could he possibly find the man?

Strut returned to Duke. His friend hammered a branch with his beak and rattled, "Cawwk! It's about time." But the crow quickly got over his snit and indicated some crows across the street chattering like a bunch of idle good-for-nothing singles. He readied his wings, and said, "Now that you're here, I'll go check them out."

As the big crow flew toward the youngsters they flinched and uttered harsh caws which Duke answered with louder caws. Strut recalled his buddy to his side and shushed Duke, telling him that he was scaring the young crows. If they both remained still long enough, the town crows would become curious.

After a short wait, a female crow, whose sleek black plumage glimmered with beautiful flecks of fluorescent purple and green, flew over and sidled next to the strong-bodied Duke, who rustled his feathers with pleasure. With low caws, she hastily warned Duke that a strange crow like him, brawny enough to be a bully, might be viciously mobbed. The two strangers should swiftly tell the local crows who they were and what they wanted. Duke met her eye and seemed transfixed by her presence — so bold and beautiful.

While his buddy was still preoccupied with the female, Strut called out to the youngsters that he and Duke were mountain crows. Catching their suspicious looks, he added, "Don't worry. We're only looking for a certain bear cub. Then we'll be on our way." He asked if they knew where his friend Ray was — the guy in a silvery gray cowboy hat who'd lived in the house with the tall red chimney.

The crows looked cagey, nodding to each other in a knowing way. Then they proposed something odd. What favor would the newcomers do for them in exchange for the information? The two were dumbfounded. Mountain crows never bargained to get news. Information was fun and free. In fact, they loved to talk, and, aside from that period right after the fire, yackety-yacked endlessly about the latest goings-on. What else was there to do? But these town crows lived by another code.

Strut was stymied for words, but Duke smirked at the crows and whispered to his friend that he'd take charge. He raised the feathers on his impressive bulk to look even bigger. "CAW-CAW," he began in an authoritative, low-pitched rasp, and announced that he and his friend had the job of mobbing hawks and owls for their flock in the Wilds.

Furthermore, Duke said, even though his friend Strut looked quite small and slender, as a plucky youngster he had actually flown over to a Great Horned Owl and fanned his wings in its face. The group of crows exclaimed with wonder for a moment, then excitedly boasted about all the brave feats of courage on the part of certain town crows through the years. Meanwhile, Strut was seething about Duke's condescending references to him as "small," "slender," and "plucky." Was he grandstanding for that sleek female?

Duke shouted above the din, "Stop all that yakking!" The mountain crows were astonished to find how effective the brassy command was, for the town crows immediately quieted. Duke cast a quick look at the beautiful female who acted nonchalant, but must have been impressed. He declared with an imperious tone, "We—Strut and I—will lead you townies right now and mob anybody you want. Show us where your biggest and fiercest raptor perches in the daytime."

In response, the town crows argued lustily among themselves and reached a consensus. Then, giving a rousing pep talk, Duke and Strut gleefully headed the riotous townies, and with a barrage of loud "kr-aacks," surprised a dozing owl and routed it from its tree.

Upon their return, the two newcomers stood waiting for their reward. The Capitan crows regarded them with newfound respect and rewarded them with the scuttlebutt about Ray. Whenever the man had taken off from the field in his airplane, he had usually flown north, so maybe he'd be found in the cities up there.

"So let's go straight north," Duke cawed to his companion, stretching his neck, ready to take off. But the townies chorused an alarmed "No, you dumb yokels!" Swift winds could lift them into high air currents. They'd be carried off course and get lost in the desert. It'd be better to follow the road out of town to the west—the way Ray's van headed out of town, then turn north when they hit the big highway.

Strut and Duke were perplexed. As country crows, their inclination was to follow an inner compass toward the north. What kind of twerps follow people's roads? How boring! Besides, the few dirt roads they knew in the mountains were long winding ones ending at ranches. The only straight road they'd known was the short one through town here—past the gas station, the restaurants, a few shops and all the bars. How could any road be long enough and straight enough to take them any real distance?

With great pride, the two adventurers explained that they were experts at following the lay of the land—the streams that cut through canyons as well as prominent landmarks like unusual boulders or distinctive trees. And they certainly could navigate any long distance by the sun, wind currents, and by other methods they couldn't really name but just knew.

The townies jeered and called them "country bumpkins." They explained that in the land of people, you follow the big trucks. They went long distances on the highway and led you to truck stops where food scraps lay around for the picking.

A few days' flight away, the newcomers were told, was a sprawling city called Albuquerque. If Ray wasn't there, he'd be farther north in the old adobe city called Santa Fe. Duke interjected, "Okay. Let's split! We've shillyshallied here long enough. We know what to do."

"CAW!" A crow whose feathers were scraggly with age alighted on a nearby branch and imposed immediate quiet. "Don't be so cocksure! You young whippersnappers don't know anything. And what-you-don't-know can kill you."

Duke turned his head aside to Strut and scoffed, "What does that old geezer know? He's just some kind of killjoy. Let's scram!"

The old crow glowered at Duke. "You don't know diddly-squat. There's a mysterious danger along the way. Since you won't heed my authority, I shall have to explain it to you."

The old fellow told them what had happened to him on his way to the highway one day. Along the road he came to a place known for its high winds and dust storms, where he had been spun into the air. Despite pounding his wings as hard as he could, he'd been blown off course. "The hazard lies on the first wing of your journey—on the road out of town. After the rolling hills, you'll come to flat rangeland for a while." He fixed them with his eyes and intoned, "Then beware the desert of white powdery sand."

In a quavering, spooky voice, the town elder told what had happened on the white sand desert five years earlier. Birds had seen humans come south and do odd things out on the dunes at Trinity. Soon after, early one morning, came a horrendous flash of light, brighter than lightning. It lit up the whole desert and a horrendous roar shook the ground. And then something strange appeared: A fire-cloud like a giant mushroom rose from the earth high into the sky and turned gold, purple, gray, and finally white.

All the small furry desert folk at the site were turned to ashes, and the remaining animals for miles around fled in terror. Since then, animals dared not venture anywhere near that eerie place. Certainly no crow ever went there. "Whatever you do, don't let the wind take you over to White Sands and the site of the mushroom cloud."

Chastened, Duke nodded soberly at the elderly crow. And with the frightening admonition ringing in their ears, the two thanked him and the town birds for their advice, and resolved to stick close to the road, until they found the highway north.

Chapter 42

Our doubts are traitors, and make us lose the good we oft might win, by fearing to attempt.
   –William Shakespeare

It is a mistake to look too far ahead. Only one link of the chain of destiny can be handled at a time.
   –Winston Churchill

   Strut and Duke stopped at the edge of the village, their shoulders hunched in foreboding now that they were about to plunge into the unknown. Strut broke the silence. He low-cawed that they could still return home and beg Elder Crow to take them back. Each crow stood on one foot and then the other, afraid to venture forth, reluctant to go back.
   Out of nowhere came the attractive female crow again. She fluttered about them, voicing such respect for their brave mission that the two were embarrassed to confess their qualms. She asked, "What are you waiting for?"
   She readily volunteered to lead her two "mountain cousins" on the manmade road that marked the first short leg of their journey. Duke readily agreed, so the decision was made. First she led them to the garbage cans behind the village restaurant, where she showed how to knock off the lids and slice open the big plastic bags of food with their beaks. Then she led them west out of town.
   The pair were young and strong, so they were dismayed at how fast their guide could fly. Strut—and especially Duke—couldn't admit difficulty keeping up, so by the time they came to the last of the rounded hills and could survey the flatland ahead, the two were exhausted. Their guide indicated a tree

and the three alighted. Strut and Duke gasped their gratitude to her, and she barely stifled her laughter at their heaving chests.

The sturdy young female beckoned with her eyes for Duke to come closer and confided that she'd never seen a male crow as big as he. She called him a "Big Hunk," and said he should "look her up" when he returned.

Duke took a deep breath, nodded his head vigorously and said, "You can bet on it. I'll sure look *you* up when I return." As she leaned her body forward to take off, she gave him one last dazzling look of admiration before whipping her wings into the sky.

Seeing his pal Duke preen a loose feather, the storyteller grumbled to himself. It wasn't fair that his friend—just because of his size—was preferable to someone of intelligence and charm like himself. But, since he liked Duke, he was glad to see his buddy look so happy.

Cheered now that they'd begun their adventure, they followed the manmade road at a leisurely pace, soon forgetting the warning about the white desert. It became tedious to fly straight in one direction above the black strip of road, and it felt downright unimaginative to follow something already laid out. But they stayed the course. The land was very different from their mountain home with its familiar forests of mingled trees, dense undergrowth, and rocky outcrops. Here, the trees on this dry land were sparse—just pinyons and junipers, stunted, with twisted trunks.

The two hadn't seen much cactus in the mountains, but here they saw scraggly-looking yucca plants everywhere. A sharply-pointed spear thrust out of the center of each plant. They marveled at the woody stem that sometimes reached an astonishing height—many times the height of a person. Some stems sported white spring blossoms, others held an old pod. The crows found one bent over to form a perfect perch for them to rest on and watch the ground for anything to eat.

Strut and Duke spied a big anthill, swooped down, and, as

the red-and-black ants ran helter-skelter, quaffed them down. The two birds waited, knowing more ants would emerge and frantically try to carry their juicy larvae to safety. The crows snapped them up too. After the feast, they found a thick sprawling juniper where they could hide from predators for the night.

When they awoke late the next morning, they saw cattle in the distance dotted across the grassland, intermingled with sheep and a few goats. All the animals had their heads down, grazing on dry grass. It looked like a fine sunny day, but as they flew along the road the sky became ominously obscured. They wondered what it meant, but, not knowing what else to do, leisurely followed the road.

By early afternoon the crows noticed patches of white along the road. The white areas looked quite different from leftover snow or cottonwood fluff. They flew down and examined what looked like fine sand, as white as old bones bleached white by the sun. They scratched at the smooth white powder with their feet. It wisped into the air like little clouds and floated away. This must be the White Sands area the elder had warned them about!

While they were examining the gypsum crystals, a breeze came out of nowhere and began to ruffle their wings and gently sway their tail feathers. A short distance away, the first sign of trouble was a curious swirling of the fine white sand arising from the earth like a tiny tornado. A second dust-devil rose across from them, then another close by. Frightened, they beat their wings to loft themselves. An unexpected gust pelted them with wind-whipped sand. Sand filled the air. They could hardly see each other. Suddenly, swift winds lifted them up into a fast current. The ribbon of road far below drifted away.

Strut was being blown off course backwards and to his left. Frantic, he imagined being plunked down who-knows-where, being lost in the vast desert, alone, unable to find Duke. Worse yet, would he be slammed down at the site of the dangerous explosion and mushroom cloud?

A mighty updraft took Strut even higher, as if he were being thrust over a mountain top. Then, he was just as suddenly yanked downward, then sideways. Sand dunes slipped beneath him, the fine white sand whipping him around in great white swirls. Strut beat his wings as hard as he could, fighting to escape the currents. His wings became leaden, and his breathing, short and fast.

Duke, the cool-headed athlete, was suddenly at his side. "You dodo bird! Fold your wings tight. Head down. Drop to earth." But Strut hardly heard him, his eyes glazed in terror. So Duke, with his own bodyweight, pressed Strut downward. As they plummeted, Duke shouted, "BRAKE FOR IMPACT." The earth came up to meet them. Whop!

They lay gasping. When they lifted their heads, they were relieved to see a low-lying building within sight. To avoid the fierce wind, they hunkered down with their heads close to the ground so they could slog ahead slowly and clumsily by foot. The wind coming across the flat land whistled in an eerie way. A round tangled mass of brittle twigs came racing toward them, so the crows quickly ducked their heads under their wings. More tumbleweeds came, and it became a game to avoid a collision and then, after a while, it became exciting to watch the lightweight tumbleweeds bounce past them clear across the desert until the rounded masses snagged on distant barbed wire fences.

The weather grew more ominous. The wind screeched. The fine-grained gypsum changed to grains of sand, blowing so thick that the world became dark. They squinted, their eyes narrowing to slits against the pelting sandstorm. Duke moved upwind to shield his friend. When there was a brief lull, he nudged Strut toward the building. It took all their strength to trudge ahead. As mountain crows, they had often walked on the ground foraging, but found it awkward and tiring to do so for long against the wind.

Finally, they reached the roadside building with its low-slung roof. They hunched on the ground at the leeward side, sheltered from the wind and sand. They heard the crash of a garbage can, and saw a lid rolling away at a fast clip. They scurried to find garbage spilled on the ground and before it could blow away they gobbled down their first Mexican-American leftovers—scattered rice, black beans and yellow cornbread. Comforted by food and fatigued by their escape from the sandstorm, they slumped to the ground and soon nodded off, the wind ruffling their feathers.

They awoke late in the morning: two happy crows. The sun was already bright and hot. They cawed together how they'd braved the tremendous wind and battering sand. They laughed and exclaimed over how dusty each other's feathers were. Tufts of down stuck out of their breasts here and there, but they didn't bother to preen themselves, just swaggered around, proud of their signs of battle. They glowed with newfound camaraderie—closer friends than ever.

Strut felt embarrassed that he'd panicked at being swept away by the wind and had needed Duke to bring him safely to earth, so he was greatly relieved that Duke didn't tease him about it as he would have done in front of his buddies. Strut looked over at his companion with new respect. He could rely on this bold friend's good instincts. In fact, he now knew that Duke would stand by him, more staunchly than his own brothers and sisters. Duke seemed like a true brother.

The small crow looked out across the desert, and discerned the gray-blue jagged outline of the far range—the Sangre de Cristo Mountains. He wondered how far he and Duke had been blown off their road, and if so, how they'd find it again. The winds had completely died down, the only evidence of their churning presence new curving drifts of sand. Elder Crow had been right. They were having quite an adventure here in the wider world.

Strut stretched his wings, then vigorously shook off the dust and sand from his rumpled feathers. He'd just begun diligently combing himself, when Duke suddenly took off. He flew so high that he became a dot in the sky. Was his new pal deserting him? Strut was unsettled a few moments until Duke zoomed down. He had seen their road. Oriented again, they took off and soon saw, from high above, that their dusty road would, indeed, end at the big highway going north to Albuquerque.

Just before the highway, they came upon a big water ditch below them, then flew over the stationary box cars of the Burlington Northern and Santa Fe. Curious about the rusty parallel strips running on the ground as far as their eyes could see, they both alighted at the same time on the railway tracks. "Krawk! Krawk," they rasped as they touched down on hot iron, hastily retracted their feet, and flung themselves back into the air. Nearby they came upon the gathering of small buildings of San Antonio, New Mexico. Duke flew down and gripped the windowsill of The Owl Bar and Café. He ogled the diners through the window, and rattled his feathers with excitement at his first sight of humans up close. He soon found that when he tapped the window pane sharply with his beak, everyone gaped at him, their mouths wide open in surprise.

Soon tired of watching Duke, Strut spied the turquoise adobe across the way with outdoor tables on the porch. Soon both black birds were perched on the hitching post in front of Manny's Buckhorn. Alluring smells of cheeseburgers and French fries reached their nostrils, making them gawk hungrily at the food heaped on plates, so enticingly near.

When they ventured closer and stood on the back of an empty chair, they heard someone yell and a waiter in a white apron rushed toward them flailing his arms. The pair stiffened and gripped the chair, defiantly puffed out their chests and haughtily lifted their beaks. Then, just in time to avoid the man, the crows flitted over to the far end of the porch railing.

Soon the waiter, carrying aloft plates laden with food, approached two seated ranchers. Strut recalled an old trick mountain crows used to play: Two crows would sneak up on a squirrel that was clutching a small nut. One crow would creep up behind it and tweak its tail. As soon as the squirrel turned to look, dropping the nut, the other crow swooped down, seized it, and flew away.

Strut cocked his head, signaling Duke to be ready. The moment the waiter set down the plates for the two ranchers, the small crow squawked and lured the waiter away, so Duke could swoop down to the cheeseburger, place his big feet on the table and plunge his bill into the thick warm meat, tingling his mouth with its dab of green chili. The ranchers made half-hearted attempts to shoo him away, but they were laughing and soon people at the nearby tables were also laughing.

People who had been whooping at Duke then turned their attention to Strut, who had been lured by French fries scattered on the wooden planks of the porch. Once Strut crunched on his first French fry with its soft center and oily goodness, he was hooked. When the fries were gone, he flew up into the air and glided down low to grab crispy potato chips off plates, eluding anyone who tried to swat him.

The waiter pursued both birds, snapping his white dishtowel. The crows gave the man a merry chase as they crisscrossed each other's path and flew every which way. Duke became especially adept at sneaking bites of leftover cheeseburger from abandoned plates.

Outwitting the waiter at the Buckhorn was such fun, and the bonanza of food so luscious, that the two thieves tarried there. Then they became curious that their road from Capitan ended at a highway, so for variety one day they flew up the highway a short way to the little town of Socorro. Corn was still Strut's favorite, and he craved the corn tortillas and the more spicy leftovers wrapped in corn husks found behind the restaurants of the Mexican-Americans and Pueblo Indians. Finally, one evening, feeling groggy at being stuffed with food, the crows decided they must brave the next leg of the trip, north up the highway along the Rio Grande River.

The next morning they set out over the wide, smooth-looking road north. Flying low, they soon found that the highway scared them with its speeding cars. And a truck threatened to suck them into the strong draft in its wake. So the pair rose to cruise high above the blacktop, where they could see across a wide expanse of parched range land. On their left was a big sky with wispy clouds hanging above a long plateau far in the distance. On the other side, close by, were rocky striated cliffs and tree-spotted mountains with great fluffy clouds above their spiky outlines.

Every so often, they came upon a lone house with the weather-cracked paint of hardscrabble living and dry-land farming. And occasionally they came upon a larger homestead with a creaking windmill with a green patch of grass at its base.

Once they flew low, curious to see a big bird running along the side of the highway. It turned out to be a gawky-looking roadrunner that stretched its long legs to run faster than the crows themselves could fly. Farther on, they found their first road kill—the inert, warm body of a rabbit. They yanked at the flesh and managed to fill themselves before the vultures, with their keen sight and smell, circled above them and came down to feast.

Flying low again above the highway as evening fell and traffic eased, they saw specks fluttering in the headlights of an occasional car or truck below. After a vehicle passed, they flew down to sample small white moths squashed on the pavement. When they had eaten enough, they went over to the river that ran beside the highway to roost in the trees for the rest of the night. Strut could hardly fall asleep, thinking of the great stories he could tell about the adventure they were having—just as Elder Crow had predicted.

Traveling by day and resting at night in the trees along the Rio Grande, they eventually came upon their first sight of the Albuquerque skyline. The crows marveled at how tall the buildings looked. As they flew closer, they saw how extensive the city was and how helter-skelter it seemed with noisy cars and people rushing hither and yon.

They flew along the wide lazily-curved river and exclaimed to each other about new things they noticed in different neighborhoods. The outlying ones had sidewalks with lots of ant hills, alongside neat lawns with juicy earthworms and bugs. They were amazed how large and shady the trees were. Strut soon discovered a lawn sprinkler. At first afraid, then fascinated, he ran over and let the droplets strike the top of his dusty body. Duke did likewise, and they soon realized they needed a more thorough cleaning to free themselves of dust, itchy lice and mites. At a nod to each other, they flew to the bottom of the driveway where a shallow puddle had collected. They bowed their necks and shoulders under water, bobbed back up, and churned their wings to splash their undersides. Then they indulged in the best part, slapping their wings loudly on top of the water to really soak themselves everywhere, all the while cawing and splashing themselves silly.

At last, their exuberance spent, they shook their feathers and fanned their wings, sending myriad drops flying into the air around them. Then, they quieted down to indulge in a real grooming fest. How wonderful it felt to thoroughly comb themselves down to the tip of every feather.

In the lull after a job well-done, they flew to a slender tree overlooking the lawn. Duke tucked his bill under a wing and went to sleep. Strut tried to rest too, but after a while some noise snapped him into sentinel-alert. He saw movements in a grand oak nearby. Crows!

At first glance, Strut took them for young bachelors. They tilted their heads to the side and peered down at the newcomers with wary, intelligent eyes. Were these big city crows nudging each other in a superior way because they'd noticed how unkempt the travelers had first appeared?

Strut's legs shook in a sudden attack of stage fright as he tried to figure out how to introduce himself and his mission. Duke, fast asleep, was no help. Afraid that he'd appear too nervous, Strut tried to look nonchalant. He stretched out one wing and then the other. He swallowed hard and cleared his throat a couple of times. In a higher voice than he would have wished, he introduced himself across the gap between the two trees as a traveling storyteller from the rugged and dangerous mountains to the south. Once launched, his words tumbled out and he told *The Story of How I Fell from a Tree — and Stayed with People in Their House*.

By the time he was deep into the drama, he could sense that these plump big-city crows were much more impressed with his storytelling than the scraggly mountain crows back home. From their open-beaked reactions, he figured that the city crows had never actually been inside a house as he had.

The story finished, his audience sighed with satisfaction. The bright-eyed juveniles cawed appreciatively. Strut basked in their goodwill until one smart-aleck with an amused look in his eye interrupted with a loud "Kwaak," and declared that he didn't believe any of it. Strut momentarily quailed before the heckler—a crow that looked disconcertingly like a cross between himself and Duke, that is, smart and brash.

In the uncomfortable silence that ensued, Strut saw the city crows look sideways at each other, then suspiciously—and expectantly—at Strut. How he'd like to clobber that crow! A flash of inspiration came. But did he dare to risk the group's disdain?

Strut held out one leg to show the band that Ray had attached to it and waited for their reactions. They were all agog. They exclaimed to each other that he had indeed hobnobbed with humans in a house. Here was the proof—a shiny bracelet like the ones humans wore on their wrists. Strut could hardly believe that he was being welcomed. Those mountain crows back home had been wrong to snub him. So provincial. He was not an odd bird, after all. He was a hero!

By now, Duke had awakened, and in return for the story, asked for any information the Albuquerque crows might have about Smokey. The city crows surprised them. They had indeed heard, on-the-wing, about a bear. A year ago, he'd been seen in the smaller city to the north called Santa Fe. A cowboy had kept the tiny cub in his back yard. Strut and Duke exchanged a quick look and lifted their wings, eager to set out right away for the mountains to the north.

But the Albuquerque crows, like the ones back in Capitan, warned them about getting lost in the desert. Furthermore, did they know how dangerous flying through a city was? How birds smash into the glass windows of buildings? Collide with cars? Get killed by cats? Therefore, invited to be guests for the night, Strut and Duke graciously accepted.

The next morning, the two crows set off. They soon tired of the monotonous road and preferred the more interesting river that meandered beside it. Flying above the Rio Grande they could spot tasty tidbits on the ground, and disappear into the riverside foliage at the first sign of a raptor in the sky.

As in the Capitan area, there were dry arroyos. Whenever they came upon gullies from the mountain run-off that cut the plains, they marveled at their steepness. Some were deep enough to hide a man astride a horse. Wide washouts crossed the highway to meet the river, but the washes no longer contained any water, their stream beds dried into cracked clay and powdery dirt. There had not yet been the 'green-up' to end the long drought and bring forth native grass. But the pale gray-green sage endured everywhere on the plains and lent its soft color and enticing fragrance to the air.

Something different caught their attention along the highway. They flew over to an adobe wall enclosing a Native American pueblo—a village about as small as Capitan. Inside the walls they found adobe homes with flat roofs, a tiny steepled church, and garden plots. In the sizzling heat of the day, there was scant movement: A man trotted his horse home. A woman drew water from a well and balanced a red-earth jug on her head. A couple of dogs lounged in the shade; another one ran among children at play.

What caught the crows' curiosity was a fat, round-bellied animal that snuffled on the ground. It stopped foraging and looked up at them. Its big long ears stuck out from its head, like a deer on alert. And the snout facing them had a flat round end with two breathing holes. The belly was enormous for how small and trim its fanny was, and it had a curly tail.

At first glance, the pink skin looked smooth and naked. How odd that the animal had no fur, only sparse hair-like bristles. The pig trotted closer on its spindly legs and dainty hooves, and studied them quizzically. It seemed welcoming, so they softly landed on its back, and discovered why it had acted so inviting: There were tiny bugs scurrying around on its skin.

"Let's get them!" the crows exclaimed, and went to work nitpicking behind the ears and at the base of the tail. The pig made low grunts and snorts of contentment as they feasted. When the crows had finished, they stood on the ground in front of the pig. The birds and the pig regarded each other for a moment, with looks of satisfaction and friendliness. It seemed to Strut that the pig must surely be quite smart. After a while, the two crows nodded goodbye, reluctantly left the Indian reservation, and vigorously flew off toward Santa Fe, calling out, "Smokey, here we come!"

Chapter 43

All I can do is wonder and wait. This makes me think about how not knowing is so important. Not knowing makes the world large and uncertain and our survival tenuous. It is a mystery why humans roam, and still more a mystery why we need to feel so connected to the place we've left. The not knowing causes such profound anxiety that it in turn spawns creativity.
–Eric Fischl

If we did all the things we are capable of doing, we would literally astound ourselves.
–Thomas Edison

A few more days brought the crows to Santa Fe. As they flew above the small city in the waning sun, they noticed how different it was from the little village of Capitan. Instead of rectangular wooden houses, there were adobe dwellings with rounded edges. The rows of shops and houses seemed sunbaked in familiar earth colors. There were muted grays, browns, pinks and yellows like the mud and sand along rivers.

To get their bearings, Strut and Duke searched the outlying areas first. Instead of the log ranches back home with their cattle and horses ranging freely over stretches of high mountains and valleys, here they found grand haciendas with soft-shaped arches and sprawling buildings. Livestock were dotted here and there across a vast expanse of land for each hacienda, fenced by barbed-wire.

Cruising beyond the haciendas brought them to desolate terrain and craggy high outcrops of rock. They watched ravens play in updrafts of air currents, glide apart in great circles, and then glide toward each other. How they wished crows could soar as beautifully through the air as those big black cousins of theirs. The crows were tempted to explore the pale yellow canyons that arose toward the distant mountain ridge, and ventured in that direction, but soon learned that it would be too far.

Already, the slanting rays of the sun cast a faint pink light onto the sandy ground, lending trees and shrubs long shadows. It was time to seek a safe roost. The bright globe of the sun had slipped behind the distant gray-purple mountains ringing the city as they wheeled back to the outskirts, bathed in a crimson glow.

They hastily scouted the small hills of the city until they found some crows positioned in a row on a telephone wire. Duke flew across the street and reached out with his feet to grasp the wire. With his usual physical prowess, he quickly found his balance, but Strut teeter-tottered wildly. How could he speak, looking like a klutzy pipsqueak?

His hefty partner filled in the awkward moment with his deep-throated husky voice to introduce "my skinny little friend here who tells stories when he's not doing a balancing act, caw-caw." In response, Strut darted angry looks at Duke.

There was a brief silence in which the local crows looked wide-eyed at them, then all gabbled at once. One shouted above the others, "So, Strut the Storyteller, what took you so long to get here from Albuquerque? We've been expecting you for days!" All eyes beamed at Strut, and Duke shot his friend a dumbfounded look, which Strut returned with a smug blink of his eyes.

Now that he found himself suddenly famous, Strut regained his balance, and nonchalantly honed his bill on the wire, first swiping one side, then the other. He looked skyward a moment, then announced in a sonorous voice that in exchange for important information, he would gladly tell a rousing tale.

The Santa Fe crows said they'd already heard the first story on-the-wing: how Strut had lived in a human house. What happened next? With an air of confidence, Strut gave the assembled crows a grand rendition of *How I Met Smokey Bear and His Mother*. By the time he had finished, Strut could tell the crows were enchanted.

Duke realized that his friend was so full of himself that he had forgotten his mission, so he impatiently prompted Strut to ask where Smokey was. The city crows broke the news: Some had seen the cub in Santa Fe. All talking at once, they squabbled over who would lead their honored guests to Ray's back yard

As the two crows readied to fling themselves into the air to find Smokey, a cascade of crow alert-calls thundered toward them: "KOOO! KOOO!" Then, with big wings outstretched, an elder crow—flanked by two lieutenants—came and announced, "Great horned owls have been sighted. A pair of them hunting food for their young. Go to your roost—the lighted one—as fast as you can!" Strut and Duke hastened to follow the whirr of wings toward the center of the city.

It turned out that the emergency roosting tree was smack up against a grand hotel's entrance that overlooked the city plaza. By sundown the whole area was ablaze with street lights. "Why be so exposed?" Strut wondered aloud to Duke. "How stupid, especially when marauding owls have already been sighted! Don't these ding-a-lings know that crows should hunch together like clusters of leaves in a dark tree?"

"Don't worry." It was the composed voice of a youngish crow who settled next to them. They recognized her as one of the lieutenants who had accompanied the elder crow. "Remember me? I'm Roberta. You can call me Robbie. I'm supposed to, ah, take Strut to the highest branch—the place reserved for Special Guests." Strut flashed Robbie a worried look. He imagined cowering all night, exposed in the bright light, awaiting the swift and silent descent of an owl, its legs outstretched and its lethal talons ready to ratchet closed in a death-grip.

Blustery sounds from Duke cut the air. Robbie scrunched low at the outburst. Duke said, "Strut must be spared. I will stand at the top of the tree!" Strut looked at his brave and loyal friend. He pictured him in a fearless stance, pecking fiercely at a great horned owl's claws as they grappled for him. Robbie looked wide-eyed at Duke and opened her bill but didn't utter a sound.

Strut clutched the branch with his feet, his throat tight with worry. How could he let his friend be killed in his place? But he, himself, didn't want to die so young. He had an important mission: to find Smokey. Moments crept by. Strut took a deep breath and faced Robbie. "I won't let Duke be sacrificed alone. He's my best friend. I'm going with him. We'll cover each other's back." Then, his voice cracked with fear, he appealed to the lieutenant in his most passionate voice. "Listen, Robbie: I have many stories to tell before I die! I'm the only one who really knows about Smokey."

Strut paused. How could he convince her to spare them? Without forethought, out of his bill came a guttural warning in a voice like Elder Crow's. "Beware! If you have us killed, word will get out and our stories about Smokey will be lost forever. And henceforth, you Santa Fe crows will be held accountable by succeeding generations of crows across the entire land!"

Robbie laughed in relief. "So that's what you thought: that we'd put you in a danger-spot? No, no, no. Unless a strange male is trying to steal a female, we city crows aren't like that at all! That's not how you country crows treat newcomers, is it?"

Strut and Duke slumped and Strut explained, "Actually, we never have any newcomers. It's just our little flock of crows and their offspring on the mountain. I guess we don't have a clue about what to expect anywhere else."

"Oh, that makes sense," she said. "Sorry to have given you such a fright." Strut was relieved that she wasn't making fun of them for being so provincial. In fact, he rather liked her merry eyes and the way she then cheerfully explained, "You see, we have to get along here in the city: There are so many newcomers of all sorts coming from everywhere!"

"Then why expose us at the top of the tree where we can be

killed?"

Robbie quickly burbled reassurances. The Santa Fe crows wanted their guests to be above all the crow droppings. The tree would soon be laden with hundreds of crows. She, personally, would spend the night right next to Strut and Duke. Strut liked that prospect. He was starting to find her very attractive.

Robbie explained that her oldest brothers Robert One, Robert Two and Robert Three had been assigned to guard the guests and all the crows through the long evening, vigilant to detect any owl. And after darkness fell, if a night raptor dared come near this well-lit place, the illumination would make it easy for the crow guards to spot it and mob the interloper.

Feeling foolish, Strut and Duke apologized, and Robbie escorted the twosome to the top of the tree among the elders. Below them, crows jabbered loudly, but as soon as Duke perched his bulk on the branch, his head drooped. Strut sighed. How he wished he could be like Duke. That big lug always sank into untroubled sleep, while Strut often couldn't fall asleep for a long time, mulling over what had happened and reliving the exciting moments, the frightening as well as the poignant ones. Despite grumbling about his imagination keeping him awake, he had to admit that he rather liked to weave the dramatic scenes of the day into stories.

Robbie sidled over to Strut and emitted a little chirp to see whether he was still awake. When he took a short step toward her, the young female confided that she, too, had always been a poet of sorts. She shyly admitted that she'd never told anyone before. She didn't want to be laughed at.

Strut inclined his head in an attentive way toward Robbie. How he relished being seen as a wise storyteller. She said he was an inspiration to her. She had always been a dreamer, not really cut out to be a lieutenant, much less a guard like her older brothers. Now, after meeting Strut, she said, she yearned all the more to travel and tell stories like he did.

Hearing such an earnest voice, Strut emitted a long

contented sigh. How he had always longed for such fellow-feeling! It made him realize, with a sudden ache in his throat, how lonely and odd it had felt to be a lone storyteller. He fluffed out his feathers and looked at Robbie with renewed interest. His heart pounded. No one back home admired him so much. Well, perhaps Elder Crow. But that Old Scold hardly ever uttered a word of praise.

Now Robbie was looking up at him with affection, perhaps even attraction. Strut's head feathers rose and his wings spread a little as he made a soft sound, "Caah." He moved closer to gently fence bills with her in a little courtship play. But after a brief moment, to his disappointment, she timidly pulled her bill away and tucked it under her wing to sleep. Despite feeling wing-weary from the journey, Strut was too distracted by Robbie's presence at his side to sleep himself. Why had she so suddenly turned away from him? Was it because he was from the country, and didn't have city savvy?

It wasn't easy to know what to expect — good or bad — out in the wide world in another crow culture. How he missed his home roost. Even with the brightest moon high in the sky, he and the others had always slept in deepest shadow. How could anyone sleep here, among hundreds of crows, in a lit-up tree, amid incessant noise? This city was too full of hustle-and-bustle. How he longed for the quiet of the mountains. There, the evening brought only the comforting sound of frogs and crickets nearby and the mournful howling of coyotes far away. Even the little village of Capitan became dark and quiet at night after people had straggled out of the few restaurants, the bars had closed, and the last cars had driven away.

But from his perch in the trees above the entrance of La Fonda Hotel, he could look down at people in the plaza sitting on benches talking into the night. Latecomers drew up cars to the hotel, and twosomes walked back late at night from restaurants and bars. Tired from his long journey, the crow finally nodded off. Sharp city sounds awakened him off and on, and gave him a chance to find Robbie awake too. She seemed at ease with him again, and he listened to her and encouraged her. Wistfully, he wondered whether she might find him attractive. If so, they'd have to be careful for fear her brothers—the three Roberts—might kill him or at least drive him out of town.

At first morning light, Robert Number One alighted near Strut, cawing while he flicked his big wings, at the same time opening and closing his magnificent purple-black tail. He made sure he caught Strut's eye. Then, with a self-important air, he deliberately held his head up and his shoulders out, looking far more heavy and broad than Duke. The proud crow signaled with low caws to his young sister Robbie that it was sunup. Both were relieved of their duties—he, as a night guard, and she, as an escort for the guests.

Duke opened one eye and grouched at them to be quiet. Then he stirred himself enough to ask if the big city crow would take him sightseeing. Robert One replied that he first needed to sleep off his all-night duty, then he'd meet Duke at the Pink Adobe for lunch. Wonderful meat pickings there, he added.

Strut overheard them, and had misgivings about his friend going off with Robert One. He didn't trust that brawny city crow with those cunning ferret eyes darting this way and that. Be that as it may, he took the opportunity while the two big crows were conversing to quickly speak under-wing to Robbie. Would she lead him to Ray's house? Of course! She'd wait for him on a tree at the far end of the plaza. Strut's heart beat fast. Was his excitement due to the promise of seeing Robbie again, or the prospect of finding Smokey? It must be both.

Chapter 44

If men had wings and black feathers, few of them would be clever enough to be crows.
–Henry Ward Beecher

To attract good fortune, spend a new coin on an old friend, share an old pleasure with a new friend, and lift up the heart of a true friend by writing his name on the wings of a dragon.
–Chinese proverb

Once they reached Ray's house, Strut released Robbie to return home to sleep, saying that they'd meet later. He was reluctant to see her leave, but he wanted to be alone to go about his mission. The crows had told him that the bear was long gone but maybe they were wrong. He flew over the house. It was smaller than the Bells' house back in Capitan. He flew down the driveway to the open garage. There was Ray's pickup! A high adobe wall surrounded a huge back yard filled with tall grass and big trees. That's where Smokey might be! A quick fly-by, though, revealed an empty yard.

Strut flew over to the house and peeked in a small bedroom. Small lumps in each bed looked like youngsters still asleep. In the big bedroom, he spied a dark mass of fur melted into the carpet at the foot of a large bed. He opened his beak wide and held his breath. Could it be Smokey? His heart beat fast as he hit the window pane with his beak: tat-tat-tat. To his disappointment, the clump of fur unfolded lanky legs to become a black dog that jumped to its feet and barked. A head rose from a pillow and a familiar voice yelled, "Jet, be quiet!" It was Ray!

The crow couldn't contain himself and beat his wings

against the window. Jet spied him at the window, leaped and scratched his paws against the pane of glass, barking even more loudly. Ray, clad in pajama bottoms, slid out of bed, and yelled at Jet to no avail. He grabbed the dog by the collar and dragged him out of the room. Flying to the back of the house, Strut was just in time to see Ray open the back door and release the dog.

As Ray turned to re-enter the house, Strut struck his wings against the man's retreating shoulder, calling "Caw-Caw." Ray brushed him away and called out to his wife as he crawled back into bed, "Guess what? I've just been attacked by a danged crow! Can you beat that?"

Frustrated and mad, Strut drummed on the window until Ray and Oh Honey climbed out of bed. He impatiently watched them dress and leave the room. Soon he smelled coffee and hurried to the kitchen window. He fixed them with stern eyes and beat a determined tattoo against the glass.

Ruth was the first to look up. "There're bands on its legs. Do you suppose it's some bird you rescued?"

Ray joined her at the window and raised his eyebrows at Strut. His quizzical expression made Strut's heart plunge. Ray cracked open the window a smidgeon and said, "What are *you* up to?"

To Strut's disappointment, the voice hadn't registered any recognition. Exasperated, Strut thought to himself: What is the matter with humans? Doesn't Ray recognize me? Are humans so dumb that they can't tell one crow from another? I can always pick out Ray from any other person just by his walk, no matter what clothes he's wearing.

Strut had a sudden inspiration. He puffed out his breast and launched into an imitation of the wooden bird on the wall of the Bells' living room back in Capitan. "Cuckoo, cuckoo, cuckoo."

They both looked baffled, then Ruth said, "That isn't *our* crow—is it?"

"That's not likely—all the way from Capitan. Must be one of the crows from around here who just happened to hear our cuckoo clock through the open window."

Strut stared back at them, then pecked the kitchen window until they cranked it open enough so he could fly in. He sped past the two in the kitchen and swiftly searched all the rooms in the small house, ending up in the bedroom where Ray and Ruth had been sleeping. No Smokey.

The two had followed him and were watching him expectantly. How could he get them to help? The crow stood on the dresser and impatiently swiped his bill left and right on the wooden frame of the mirror on top of the dresser. Suddenly something caught his eye. It was the red ribbon, stuck into the wooden frame. It must be *his* ribbon—the one Ray had left to mark the tree Strut had fallen out of. It was faded, but Strut knew it must be the one he'd kept on his shelf in Smokey's den, then given to Ray.

The crow shot the man a disgruntled look. "Caw!" This wasn't where the ribbon belonged. Strut remembered how he had thrust it in the band of Ray's cowboy hat as a parting gift to Ray as he was moving from Capitan and the crow thought he'd never see him again.

Standing on the dresser, the bird pivoted his head around the room, this way and that, until he spotted the cowboy hat hung on the wall. With a quick tug of his bill, he snatched the ribbon. He darted a stern look at Ray, to make sure he was watching, and flew straight to the hat. Flapping to stay suspended in place, he jabbed the ribbon into the hat band.

Well-satisfied with himself, Strut flew down to stand on a chair near the bed. He waggled his tail, and eyed Ray. The man burst out in astonishment to his wife. "Hey-boy-howdy! That really is our crow! He remembered us and came all this way! But how in the world did he find us?" The man grinned so widely that his eyes crinkled at the edges. The crow was delighted at the sight.

Then Strut watched the man stride over to the cowboy hat and pause a moment to smooth the ribbon between his fingers. Ray shoved the hat on his head, and winked at Strut. "What a sentimental bird you are!" He gave the crow his familiar invitation: an open-mouthed smile as he whipped off his hat. Strut's legs trembled with anticipation as he shifted from one foot to the other.

Ray playfully breezed the hat past Strut. "Caaaw-caaaww," the bird sang, dancing in the air around the man, deftly avoiding the swinging hat like he used to. He became so elated that he suddenly rendered an imitation of Ray coming home. "Oh, HON-ey." Then he imitated Ray's laugh—"Yuh-ha-ha."

By now, awakened by the commotion, Judy and Don appeared at the bedroom doorway in their pajamas. It took Strut a few moments to recognize them. They were taller than he remembered from a year ago, but their voices were unmistakable. With his rasping voice, he imitated their exclamations of surprise, and soon the whole family was sitting on the bed, bent over laughing. The crow cawed lustily from his perch on the chair. He hadn't been so happy for a long time.

Ruth beamed at Strut. "Look at his eyes—dark amber. Not that pretty blue anymore, now that he's older." Ray got to his feet and extended his hand toward the crow. Strut crouched with wings half-lifted, and quivered his tail in happiness. Then he bowed in greeting, clacked his bill and hopped aboard. In turn, Ray welcomed him with his familiar hearty voice. "You nutty crow! Danged if I know how you found us. Don't you know you're supposed to stay back in the mountains and have a normal life?"

The Bells returned to the kitchen. Strut, now riding on Ray's shoulder, bit his ear lobe. "Hey! Cut that out!" Undaunted, Strut gave another nip. He spied the watch on Ray wrist, jumped down the man's arm and tried to loosen the band, then climbed out onto the hand to nibble at the gold band on his ring finger.

Strut climbed back up the arm, one sideways step after another, to regain Ray's shoulder. In a quieter mood, he rested his body against Ray's neck. Then he leaned his head down, the same way he would to let another crow preen him, and the man gently scratched on the nape of his neck, as he used to. Strut warbled coos of contentment, and his eyes glazed over.

Then Strut jerked awake. He must find Smokey! He looked expectantly at the people. They just stood there. Hoping that they'd catch on that he was hunting for Smokey, he flew down and searched the small living room—including a look behind the couch. In the children's room, he dropped to the floor, hopped over to the closet and rummaged around. Then he deliberately waddled over to each bed and carefully looked underneath. He did the same in the parents' bedroom, darting meaningful looks at the people, who looked back at him quizzically.

Strut then examined the cluttered back room—even around the small hot water heater, the washing machine and wringer. He tried to yank the strings tying the doggie door so he could poke his head out the flap and peruse the back yard more carefully, but Ray shoved him away. "You don't want to do that. Jet's right out there on the stoop, dying to get in."

At that moment, the dog started barking. Strut stood his ground inside the door and turned to face the humans. If only they could tell him about Smokey! The local crows had said the cub had been at the house! Taking on an air of importance, he turned to each in turn—Ray, Ruth, Don and Judy. His eyes bore into theirs: Is Smokey still alive? The man raised his eyebrows with a baffled look.

"What's gotten into that crow?" Ray said. "There's something he wants, but darned if I know what it is."

Judy piped up, "He's hunting for something! I know he is!"

After an extended pause, Ray exclaimed to Ruth, "Maybe— It's been a whole year now, but I'll bet he's looking for his friend Smokey. Judy, honey, good for you! That's what he's been trying to tell us!"

Ray said, "This crow had a thing for Smokey. You kids know what happened when I went to pick up the cub at that ranch after he'd been burned, don't you? As soon as I got back in the truck—Smokey was in his box—that crow flew right into the front seat with us. And remember how I told you that when I got into the plane to fly to the vet, the crow was determined to get in the cockpit with me and the cub? And made such a rumpus, I had to fight him off to close the door of the plane."

The whole family beamed at Strut and they nodded their heads up and down to him, indicating 'yes,' which made him shiver his feathers with glee. He knew, for sure, that Smokey had been here after all. With a lighter spirit, he looked with renewed hope in closets, under beds and the living room couch.

Judy stopped in front of him, bent over and shook her head. "It's no use hunting. He's long gone. I'm sorry." The crow understood the stance and discouraging tone. Yet he wasn't ready to give up yet. Could the back yard possibly yield some clue?

Chapter 45

At moments of wonder, it is easy to avoid small thinking, to entertain thoughts that span the universe, that capture both thunder and tinkle, thick and thin, the near and the far.
–Yann Martel

Impatiently, the crow sped to the back room. He seized a corner of the leather doggie door with his beak, yanked it up, and squeezed through the opening. Strut landed hard on his back, legs thrashing the air, and quickly righted himself. Jet had arrived just below the concrete stoop, his head stretched up so close that Strut could feel his breath. Before the spaniel could bound up the four stairs, the bird hastily shook his feathers into place, frantically stretched his wings and flew to safety across the yard.

From a safe perch atop the adobe wall, Strut looked down with a self-satisfied air at the cocker who barked non-stop, scraping his claws on the rough wall as high as he could reach. The crow hunkered down, and, giving the dog a disgusted look, squawked right back. To taunt the silly dog, Strut imitated Ray, calling out in a hoarse voice, "Jet, be quiet." This made the dog cock his head in surprise, but the young dog didn't obey Strut any more than he obeyed the man.

Then Strut straightened up. If only he could ask the dog where Smokey was! According to the Santa Fe crows, Smokey had stayed in this back yard during the past spring, so surely Jet must know his whereabouts. But, Strut sputtered to himself, it was useless to ask him. Dogs never talked with birds, just chased them for fun.

Heaving a sigh of frustration, the crow hovered high above the bungalow to find some animal or bird to help him. On a whimsy, he flew up West Coronado as it sloped toward the Old Santa Fe Trail, and turned at the corner to investigate the imposing two-storied houses on Don Gasper Avenue.

On a mansard roof above the entrance to a big house was some kind of furry animal. Cruising closer, Strut saw what appeared to be a young mountain lion kit. She was sprawled on the open window sill upstairs, basking in the strong slanted rays of the morning sun. Feathering his wings softly, the crow flew over the vast front yard and settled on a great fir tree whose branches extended almost to the roof.

He knew the creature hadn't seen him yet because she stretched her gray-and-black striped body luxuriously, splaying her pink paws toward him. She licked the front paws, and scrubbed her face, which somehow endeared her to the crow. Strut gently broke the silence with his most charming, soft voice, "Caah, caah, lovely lion. Can *you* talk—unlike that black dog back there who can only bark?"

She sat up and said sharply, "Of course felines can converse! *We* don't expect much from dogs either. They're not as intelligent as *cats!*"

Strut was delighted. Perhaps she could tell him about Smokey. Before he could ask, she continued. "Those cocker spaniels, in particular, are quite excitable. Jet yaps at the slightest provocation. It's *exasperating*! I'll have you know he's well over a year old now, so he shouldn't be *indulging* in such boisterous behavior anymore . . . Now then, who are you?" She squinted at him. "I can't perceive you well with that bright eastern sun behind you."

Encouraged, Strut hopped to a branch closer to the roof. Crouching, he inquired in his most obliging voice, "I'm Strut, a traveling crow. I'm trying to find a bear cub called Smokey. Did you, such a beautiful and intelligent cat, per chance know him?"

"I most *certainly* did! I'll have you know: I was his *Best*

Friend here. I made his acquaintance the moment he arrived at the vet's. He was suffering from the most dreadful burns. If it weren't for *me*, he would never have survived. And we spent the *entire* spring together in this neighborhood."

She stopped abruptly. "As you may know, I don't usually talk to *birds*. I prefer to watch them, or, better yet, bat them down and eat them." Strut scuttled back and hid behind a thick cluster of long needles.

The cat hastily said, "Wait a minute! Don't be frightened away . . . As you may surmise, I don't have wings. I certainly wouldn't be *foolhardy* enough to venture out on this steep little excuse for a roof, much less proceed onto the main roof and jump."

She tucked her front paws under her body, took a deep breath, and yawned so widely that Strut could see her pink mouth and sharp little teeth. "I'm fond of the one life I have—now that I'm ensconced in a lovely home. It so happens that I'm a *domestic* pet. I'd never leap *down* from the roof to that *flimsy* branch you're on. So would you be so kind as to move closer so we can have a *proper* conversation? I'd love nothing better than to talk about my dear friend *Smokey*."

Strut was so overjoyed, at last, to find someone with news of Smokey that he fluttered to the end of the branch and cawed in delight. "I was his *Best Friend* in the mountains! I am Strut the Storyteller, and I'll tell you all about him if you'll tell me what you know."

The crow continued. "Caah. I've been worried about Smokey. The last I saw him was a year ago. He was whisked away from the mountains in an airplane. I just came from searching Ray's house and couldn't find any trace of him there. Is he okay? Where is he? I must find him!"

The cat answered, "Last time I saw him, he was *fine*. Calm down, Mr. Crow—Strut. We have all day to converse. Let me first introduce myself. My name is Lightning—a tiger-striped cat, I'll have you know. And I want to hear everything you can tell me."

But before Strut could open his bill, the talkative cat launched into her own stories about Smokey, from their meeting at the vet through the times Judy or Don had brought the cub to visit her—and her little mistress Barbara—in this very house. Lightning said that on occasion she herself ventured kitty-corner across the yards to visit Smokey outdoors.

One time, she told Strut, when Ray had brought her and the cub down from a tree in his back yard, Smokey had urinated all over the man's shirt. Recounting how angry it made Ray, her lips smiled and her hooded eyes beamed. Strut gave a lusty caw.

Other times the Bells had trooped with the bear around the block, always stopping here at the Ragles' house. As the cub recovered from his burns, he became the frisky star of the neighborhood. Strut heaved a great sigh of relief at hearing how well the cub had healed.

Whenever Strut could get a word in edgewise, he told his own stories about the cub until it became late afternoon and Lightning suddenly fell silent. She stretched her neck to intently watch the sidewalk below. Soon she announced that her big mistress, Elida Ragle, was coming up the walkway holding the hand of her little mistress, Barbara. Lightning politely excused herself to join them inside the house, and turned to leave through the window.

Strut cried out, "Before you go, tell me where Smokey is *now*! He must be terribly lonesome, and I promised I'd visit him, no matter how far away he might be"

Lightning turned and told the crow that she had no way of knowing his whereabouts. However, the circumstances of his departure might contain certain *clues*, slim though they might be. One day Ray had made a small wire carrier for the cub. She knew what that meant, and had warned Smokey that he'd soon be taking a trip, so they had to say a sad farewell. She had prompted the cub to hide under the bed for a last-minute talk.

Sure enough, the next morning Smokey was put in the

carrier and the whole family drove him away. She had not seen him since. She added that Strut should contemplate an important fact: The family had *shortly* returned home in the car without the bear cub. Wishing the crow good luck, Lightning abruptly entered the open window behind her, and Strut watched the tip of her tail disappear.

The crow flew to the top of the tree and pondered what he'd heard. His breast swelled with elation at sensing Smokey was probably healthy and alive—somewhere. Then he swallowed past the tight ache in his throat, wondering how he could ever find him. By now, his friend could be far away.

From his high stance atop the great tree, the bird surveyed the city spread out before him: half-hidden houses among lush trees along a winding river, the vast prairie beyond, and the circle of mountains far away. Instead of his usual confident refrain, "Smokey, I'm coming!" he hung his head and muttered, "So near, and so far . . . Oh, Smokey, I don't know how I'll ever find you."

The afternoon dragged on. He hardly noticed how the street stirred with life below him: the sound of cars parking, car doors slamming, and people entering houses with cheerful greetings. Then, through dim eyes, he became aware of people again on the sidewalks, walking their dogs and stopping to chat.

The mockingbird across the street, with his interminable array of songs, finally quieted. Soon after that, Strut noticed bunches of crows, here and there, flying overhead toward downtown.

Robbie found him, but Strut was so preoccupied thinking of Smokey that he hardly registered her presence. As they stood side by side, she announced that she'd lead him to the roost for the night. Assembly calls had already sounded, she told him, and crows were gathering early in anticipation of hearing their guest tell a story he had promised them. At first Strut resisted the thought of exerting himself to perform. Then suddenly his heart lightened. Perhaps the crows might have some idea where Smokey had gone.

Strut raised his wings to take off, but when Robbie moved closer, he folded them. In a voice flowing with soft warbles, she asked him whether he'd like to tarry awhile. It would take some time for all the crows to assemble from everywhere around the city.

First, Robbie told him, she wanted to show him how beautiful Santa Fe was. After all, Robbie explained with a whimsical air, she was a poet and this was the lovely landscape of her home. Strut looked at her with longing, fascinated by the lovely trill of her voice. He liked her distinctive accent, different from that of any mountain crow he'd known. When she looked at him expecting his reply, he murmured that he'd never thought much about beauty. He leaned lightly against her and became overcome by languor. Feeling her so close suddenly made his breath quicken and a fresh stir of pleasure warm his body. It felt as if his whole being had turned to liquid.

"Your head's chock full of words," she boldly said. "I'm rather frank, but you must know that you have a 'grasshopper mind.'" Strut was momentarily taken aback at her change of tone and what felt like criticism. Yet Robbie hadn't moved away from his side, so surely she felt the same closeness he did. He was bewildered. She continued in a confident voice, "So I'm going to open your eyes and heart to my land — my homeland. Then you'll be sure to remember this place, and some day return from your journey to me . . ." Her voice had faltered, but then continued quickly, "I mean, so you can return home and describe everything to your mountain folk."

Strut was intrigued anew. He'd never thought of considering the land as part of a story. Nor had he imagined that his journey would someday be completed and he might return to her. Strut looked at Robbie. She seemed so certain of herself! And certain of his return. The image of Kate — his lost love back home — vanished. In its place his heart suddenly ached for this very special female!

Strut and Robbie   #53630956

Strut's voice came out more earnest and melodious than he'd expected. In a tumble of new feelings, he told Robbie that he'd never known a poet before, and . . . He paused in bewilderment, then dared to declare that he'd love to see Santa Fe through her eyes. "Let's wing away, then!" she said and departed.

Leading him to alight on a high rocky lookout, his new friend instructed him to sweep his eyes over the curved line of the hills dotted with pinyon and juniper. "The wonder of it!" she exclaimed. Catching her mood, for the first time in his life Strut felt a great sense of awe as he looked into the distance. The entire city of Santa Fe lay before them bathed in soft twilight. And just below, gently-rounded adobe houses were arrayed in colors that Strut now saw as truly beautiful: some like pink-tinted sand, others like wet mud or the palest of dried gray clay or the light yellowish-brown powder of old wash-outs. With her wing tip, Robbie pointed out her favorite colors—red like old bricks, and bright yellow ochre. She invited him to inhale the sultry pinyon smoke that wafted their way from the adobe chimneys.

Robbie swooped below their high perch to a Rocky Mountain juniper tree and Strut swiftly followed. Before he could burst forth, she shushed him to be quiet so they could listen to the smaller birds twittering. Right below them, the birds made soft evening chatter as they flitted among the feathery blue-green needles seeking last-minute tidbits before settling down for the night. Robbie pointed out the ones she particularly liked — the chickadees in pert caps with black bibs on their white breasts tinted a pale yellow, and the finches with the surprising red-raspberry splashes on their breasts, busy eating and contending over seeds. A flash of beautiful blue led them to lower their heads to peer down through the branches at little bluebirds ground-sallying for insects.

Already standing close to Robbie, Strut inched closer to her until he could just barely feel their wings touch. This time, she didn't stir, and made a contented sound. By the time they looked up again, the big sky had filled with wide shafts of rose and yellow. Side by side they silently looked over the broad plain and rolling hills. Beyond, surrounding most of the city, ridge after ridge turned soft orange, rose, then lavender, until the backdrop of snow-tipped mountains glowed blue-gray.

Strut's chest swelled with joy — and confusion. Was he entranced by her, the beauty of this big-sky country, or both? What did it matter? He breathed deeply. The faint scent of sage and mesquite made him dreamy. All he wanted was to prolong the moment.

But darkness crept closer, the scene turned gray, and the spell was broken. In the distance, the crows' assembly calls became louder and more insistent. They sounded like the calls Strut knew from the mountains, but in a puzzling local dialect. Robbie translated: All must immediately go to the emergency roost. They both knew: Stragglers would be at the mercy of owls, hawks and eagles. "We must high-tail it back, but beware my brothers. Act very cool, or they'll drive you away. Or kill you!"

At a safe distance from the tree, the two parted, and Strut veered over to Duke and Robert Number One as if eager to hear their news. They hardly acknowledged his presence, and their cacophony of jabbering jarred him. More than anything he wanted to resume the special mood of being with Robbie. So, as soon as he'd made his presence known, he nonchalantly left to stand by Robbie on a perch half-hidden in the tree. He inclined his head toward her, and found himself whispering secret sounds of crow courtship he'd never uttered before. His bold companion suddenly dipped her head. He moved closer to her side, and his wing sizzled to feel hers gently press his. So this is how it felt to fall in love! They wended their way farther into the dense leaves.

An elder Santa Fe crow peremptorily cawed everyone to attention to introduce their newcomer—a storyteller. "Strut, present yourself, wherever you are!" Strut awoke from his dreamlike state to momentary panic, but before anyone could spot Robbie next to him, she furtively melted into the thick foliage and flew to another branch. For a moment Strut was confused. His big black feet stumbled to the end of his branch where everyone could see him. He blinked his eyes. Hundreds of crows stared at him expectantly.

Still tingling with the exhilaration of Robbie's presence, he gathered his thoughts. To bide his time, Strut bent down to pick at a tuft of fluffy down at his toes. Then he sharpened his beak vigorously on a twig. "Caw!" he declared.

Strut ruffled his feathers, lifted his shoulders and commanded attention. He wanted more than anything to impress Robbie, but was afraid he'd lose his train of thought if he dared search the assemblage to meet her eyes. Instead, he concentrated on the eager youngsters and launched into eloquent visions of his mountains and the village, hoping Robbie would find them poetic. Then he told the story: *How Mother Bear and I Saved Smokey from Being Killed*. He finished with a loud "CAW" and spread his wings wide in triumph.

Pandemonium broke out: exclamations from the elders, buzzing among the youngsters, questions galore. Strut basked in the attention. But as soon as the hubbub died down, he clutched the tree branch tightly and locked his shaky legs to rest, utterly exhausted from his first full, wondrous day in Santa Fe. True, he had yet to find Smokey but he was hopeful, and today he'd found Robbie and the beauty of nature as seen through her eyes. What more could a crow ask?

In the darkness that followed, he sought a special place among the dense leaves, hoping Robbie would join him. He was eager to hear her reaction to his story. Was she impressed by how heroic he'd been? Did she find his poetic descriptions of his mountain home alluring . . . or too wordy?

Robbie suddenly appeared at his side. Strut could sense her excitement about his heroics and his poetic expression. He tried desperately to stay awake to be with her, but his eyelids drooped. Against his will, his wings crumpled, and he could only murmur good night before he fell into a deep, contented sleep.

Chapter 46

For one human to love another; that is perhaps the most difficult of all our tasks, the last test and proof, the work for which all other work is but preparation.
–Rainer Maria Rilke

The meeting of two personalities is like the contact of two chemical substances: if there is any reaction, both are transformed.
–Carl Jung

The next morning things moved fast. Strut was talking quietly with Robbie when her shoulders hunched in fright. Her brothers approached. She gasped, "Oh, oh! I better scoot. Be careful! Meet me at the cat's house." She left abruptly.

The bulky bodies of Robert One, Two and Three crowded onto a tree limb facing Strut, their heads lowered, their black eyes blazing. "What are you doing with our sister?"

Strut trembled as he clutched his slim branch and leaned back from their menacing beaks. Just then Duke—looking almost as stout as any of them—came screeching into their midst and landed his body close to Strut. The Santa Fe crows shuffled their big strong feet and cast sidelong looks at each other. An ominous pause lengthened as Strut tried to think of something to say.

Meanwhile, Duke silently looked each big crow in the eye. Finally he addressed Robert One. "Hey, pal. Let's not pick on the little guy, okay? He's leaving tomorrow anyway. Aren't you, Strut?" The small crow swallowed, and nodded. Without any noticeable signal among the brothers, they took off. Duke called after them, "I owe you. Let's meet at the Pink Adobe again for lunch, okay?" But there was no reply.

As soon as the brothers were out of sight, Duke started to razz his friend about going so gaga over his new ladylove, but Strut got huffy. He reminded his big friend how he himself had been smitten with that fast-flying female back in the village of Capitan. Wasn't he going to return to *her* after they found Smokey?

Duke blustered awhile, then sheepishly broke the news. He stammered that he was sorry to leave his buddy in the lurch, but he'd decided to go back to Capitan. He was afraid to hang around much longer, with all those crows bigger than he was, skulking about him, *suspicious* that he'd nab one of their females. And he didn't like their strange dialect and odd ways. Anyway, he admitted, he liked being the biggest crow back home in the mountains. It was more fun to be a big crow in a small flock — than a not-so-big-one in a large flock.

Strut was stunned to lose his stalwart buddy. Taking the trip together had been a great lark, whereas the prospect of traveling alone seemed dreary and scary. He could tell that Duke saw how crestfallen he was, for the big guy fidgeted, tearing off bits of loose bark near his feet. A heavy silence fell between them, and they looked away from each other, then down at the ground.

The uneasiness was broken with the return of Robert One, Two and Three. The brothers stared at them and challenged, "What are you two talking about?" Duke huffed out his feathers, snorted a loud caw, and rattled out an excuse that sounded more like bluff than truth.

Robert One stood on one foot and then the other, eyeing Duke warily. After a pause, he announced in a tantalizing tone, "Let's go to the corn fields outside town. We three will escort you. Green shoots of corn are sprouting in the old corn stubble. It's great fun to stand on the scarecrows to squawk and taunt the farmers! Then we can fly out to the distant canyons, and teach you guys how to catch warm thermals up the cliffs and soar like ravens, then dive-bomb down the sides to catch the thermals again." At the prospect Duke cawed with glee and shot Strut a bright-eyed look.

Strut didn't know what to say. He'd caught an aggressive flash in Robert One's eyes. And weren't those *sly* looks on the others' faces? Was this a plot to escort two strangers away from the females, out of town to their deaths?

He turned his head aside and spoke furtively to Duke, "Are you crazy — going off with those thugs? Those big guys give me the heebie-jeebies." But, ignoring the warning looks that Strut darted his way, Duke quickly agreed to go with the brothers. The slim crow feared he might never see Duke again, but heaved a sigh, telling himself that his brawny friend had better take care of himself.

Robert One narrowed his eyes at Strut questioningly, with a hint of threat. The only thing Strut wanted to do was high-tail it to Robbie. He carefully declined the Roberts' invitation, convincing them that he needed all day to search farther afield for Smokey.

Duke winked at Strut, and told the brothers they needn't worry about leaving Strut alone with their females, scoffing that "he's too scrawny compared to all the big guys around here." He beat his wings, and they all flew away.

Ready to set off, Strut realized that he remembered only the general direction of Ray's house and the nearby home of the tiger-striped cat, where he was to meet Robbie. At first he felt at a loss on how to proceed. When he had followed Robbie the morning before, he hadn't paid much attention to any landmarks along the winding roads they'd taken, but he did recall the direction they'd taken from the plaza. So the crow set out on the main road. At first it looked promising, but then it curved like a horseshoe circling the city and he landed right back at the plaza where he'd started. What an idiot! Then he heard a mockingbird off in the distance. It sounded like the one whose incessant song had irritated him the day before at the Ragles' house. Strut cheered up, grateful to what now sounded to him like a marvelous songbird able to imitate so many other birds.

Homing in on the mockingbird, the crow soon retraced his way to the tall evergreen tree. He sounded the contact call: "Ka-kuk, ka-kuk." To his joy, he heard the distinctive trill of Robbie's voice from a well-camouflaged place hidden in the tree. To the music of the irrepressible mockingbird, loudly proclaiming his songs from the top of the tree above, Strut flew to her. The two crows bowed to each other, and Strut found himself ruffling his feathers and shuffling up and down the branch near her, surprised at himself for suddenly knowing how to dance.

But Strut soon stopped himself so he could spill the news to her that he had to leave the next day. Duke was already being lured to some canyon where he might plummet to earth and have his head pecked bloody. And if Duke did survive the day, the big guy planned to desert Strut anyway and return to Capitan. So, Strut said, hanging his head, he must continue the journey alone. And without his bold friend, he would be in danger here, so he'd better leave first thing the next morning.

Strut confessed to Robbie how much he liked her, but added that he couldn't imagine settling in a city like Santa Fe. He turned his head away, heartsick at the prospect of losing her, and sighed.

"Of course," Robbie chimed in. "One must see the world first!"

Strut's heart quickened. Before he knew it, he had cried out to her, "*Come away with me! On my great adventure — to find Smokey!*"

She inclined her head toward him shyly, no longer the forthright female. And, as he looked intently at her for an answer, he saw her slowly move her eyelids over her dark amber eyes in assent. He was so excited he could hardly breathe.

Robbie was the first to break the silence. She didn't quite give Strut the commitment he wished to hear. Instead, she sensibly declared that they had only one day in which to find the trail of the bear cub. They must hurry. Strut felt dizzy as he tried to concentrate. Did she really intend to go with him? Hoping it was true, yet afraid to ask, he plunged ahead and desperately reviewed how they might search for the cub.

Their best lead, he finally announced, would be Lightning. They must ask the cat more questions. She wasn't lounging on the mansard roof, so they quickly descended and looked in each window of the big house. There, on the living room sofa, they found Lightning. Strut tapped sharply on the pane until the cat looked up and bounded to the front screen door. "Caw! Help us, Lightning," Strut pleaded. "We have to leave town tomorrow. How can we find Smokey? Think! Which way did he go?"

Lightning looked aside in contemplation. "Well, let me consider . . . The Bell family departed with Smokey early in the morning. They returned in the car a short while afterward—without him—Judy crying and everyone else teary-eyed. I would surmise that they didn't go too far but not too close either. They must have relinquished the cub to his fate, since no one ever saw him again in Santa Fe.

"However, as you may know, felines have *excellent* intuition." Lightning gave a long languorous stretch of her whole body. "My intuition is that . . ." She paused for a dramatic moment, and her slit green eyes looked through the screen door, past the waiting crows into the distance.

"Pretty cat, wise cat. Please tell us," Robbie pleaded. "Any clue is better than nothing!"

Lightning raised her chin in a knowing way, and said that she envisioned Smokey being dropped off at the *airport*. On occasion, she herself had taken a short car ride to the airport to be with her big mistress at her office there. The crows should proceed to the small runway out of town—Ragle Airfield—and inquire of birds that foraged there. The two thanked her profusely and hastily departed. As they winged their way, Strut was elated. Robbie had committed herself to joining him, and they were on the trail to find Smokey.

Chapter 47

In critical moments even the very powerful have need of the weakest.
–Aesop Fables

The ornithologist David Sibley says . . . he once spotted a bird in flight from two hundred yards away and knew, instantly, that it was a ruff, a rare sandpiper. He had never seen ruff in flight before; nor was the moment long enough for him to make a careful identification. But he was able to capture what bird-watchers call the bird's "giss" – its essence – and that was enough.
–Malcolm Gladwell

Before long, with Robbie leading the way, they arrived at the airport. A small finch, pecking thistle down near a runway, said that Smokey had indeed left in an airplane the past summer. The bird couldn't remember where the plane was headed. Airplanes took off in various directions: north, south, east, and west. With a nod of his head he indicated a wooden sign with arrows pointing different ways.

Strut and Robbie walked over and pondered the wooden sign, but stamped their feet in frustration to understand what it said.

The arrow pointing up to the sky said, "Canada: 1,000 miles." The arrow toward their feet, "Mexico: 300 miles." To the left, "Pacific Ocean: 1,000 miles." To right, "Atlantic Ocean: 2,000 miles."

A fat Canada goose plucking grass nearby lifted her head and lumbered over. Geese, she told them, migrated more than any other birds on the north-south flyways and honked all the time to each other. So she would certainly have heard whether his plane had gone north or south. Therefore, Smokey must have gone east or west. Of course, traveling in either of those directions required a long journey to the edge of the land.

"How far?" asked Robbie.

"If you go west toward the setting sun you'll reach the West Coast after a long trip. Flying east toward the rising sun you'll reach the East Coast, but that's *twice* as far." With a discerning eye, she appraised the crows before her. "It wouldn't be much of a trip for Canada geese, but for crows like you, vulnerable to sky predators—well, all I can say is that you'd better choose the correct one."

Strut and Robbie were distracted by a group of sparrows on the ground squabbling. One sparrow—a real chatterbox—hopped into the air and flew off a bit, then landed and tilted his head as if he was thinking. The sparrow looked over at the two crows in a knowing way. They hastily strode over to him, but he fluttered away. The crows stepped back, and, keeping a safe distance so as not to scare the little sparrow, asked, "Do you know something, little bird?"

"Why should I tell you crows anything? You rob our nests all the time!"

Strut retorted, "Well, that's the nature of crows! We have to eat."

Robbie said in a soothing voice, "I'm sorry. How awful for you—crows eating your eggs! But, you know, we also warn you small folk when hawks or eagles are around. Doesn't that even things up a bit?"

The sparrow lowered its haughty narrow shoulders and mumbled something. The crows kindly asked the sparrow its name, and told it theirs. They earnestly promised, personally, never to rob song sparrow nests again. In fact, they were glad they now had a chance to see how appealing sparrows looked up close with their brown caps—such a rich red-brown—and the dark bibs under their throats. And they liked the energetic way sparrows bustled about foraging on the ground chitter-chattering away. How could they ever again harm their little brethren?

"Well, I do have something important to tell you then!" The crows lowered their heads toward the creature, hopeful for any news. He chirped merrily, "We may be small, but we are smart. We stay around the airport and we *notice* things." He stopped and cocked his head so one eye was cast toward the sky. Was he just teasing them and making something up? "Let's see . . . when did the bear leave?"

Strut replied, "Early in the morning."

The sparrow paused, as if reflecting. "Well, then, those planes almost always head right into the rising sun. That's your best bet!"

Strut and Robbie exchanged a quick look. "Thanks, little guy. So that's the way we'll go!" Satisfied that he could now set his inner sun-compass in the right direction, Strut was eager to set out right away, but Robbie convinced him to stick to their original plan and leave the next morning.

The two whiled away the day together, Robbie showing Strut the things she loved about Santa Fe. First she proudly showed him the tallest tree, a grand Ponderosa pine with its extraordinarily long needles always clasped in neat bundles of three. Robbie dared Strut to stand next to her on its slender tippy-top and sway back and forth. They were exhilarated, and laughed at the squirrel below who angrily chastised them for intruding on *its* tree. After a lengthy tirade, it grumpily moved to branches below.

In the quiet that followed, Robbie pointed out the orange bark on a vanilla tree below, and the flutter of big bluejays among the yellow-green needles of a one-seed juniper. With the warmth of her great love of the land, she told Strut how earlier in the spring the Perky Sue blossoms gave the meadows their first splash of yellow, and the phlox lent its purple colors. She found for him black-chinned hummingbirds that buzzed around the Indian paintbrush to sip nectar from their red flowers. And through her eyes Strut appreciated anew how feathery the mountain juniper was and how bountiful its seeds.

Strut asked if she'd ever seen the mountain bird that was his favorite—the big, speckled woodpecker with its red chin and yellow wing feathers. Oh, yes, the northern flicker, she said, whose melodic song she especially loved. This spring she'd seen one fly into a large round hole in a hollow tree trunk to feed its young. As Strut listened to Robbie's distinctive mellow voice telling him so eloquently what she enjoyed, his heart softened even more toward her.

The more she showed him, however, the more worried he became that she might never be persuaded to leave. Robbie seemed to belong here, among the prickly pear cactus or atop a Douglas fir. How familiar she was with the place: where the garter snake came out on warm days to sun on a red flagstone, where the Least Chipmunks, newly emerged from their winter hideaways, ran along certain rocks and walls. She imitated for him their sharp "chip" call, which he immediately recognized.

At the end of their tour, as the evening sky grew darker, Strut suddenly had second thoughts about embarking on their trip the next morning. Should he take her away from her home? Could they trust the sparrow to have told the truth? Maybe they should go west; it was shorter. Either way, it might be a wild goose chase. They would be risking their lives for nothing. There might be deserts and storms, hawks and eagles.

He looked fondly at Robbie. How could he endanger her? Perhaps she should remain here, find her lifelong mate, lay eggs, and have a safe and normal life. He summoned the courage to ask her whether she might really prefer to stay in Santa Fe where she'd be safe. No, she told him. Of course, she didn't want to stay in Santa Fe—while *he* flew off to see the world. She wanted to have an adventure before settling down to raise a family later, and she wanted to have this adventure with *him*.

Instead of feeling relieved at hearing the good news, Strut gasped and felt his stomach tighten. Did this mean they were committed to being mates—for life? He stammered that he wasn't quite ready to be mates *forever*. She flicked her tail and leaned against him. "Probably we will end up mates for life. But we just met, and we're too young. Let's just see how it goes!"

With bright eyes, she exclaimed, "I can't wait. What a good pair we'll be for this trip! Being a city crow, I know different dialects, and how to find food in cities. You know how to survive in the countryside." She added, "But first, practically speaking, we have to find a way to get out of here tomorrow morning—without my brothers knowing. They'll kill you for taking me away."

"Caaaw! Caaaw!" The assembly calls became more insistent. It was already late, Robbie said. She cautioned that they must beware her brothers: It would be prudent to wing their way separately to the evening roost so why didn't they depart for the tree in slightly different directions?

Away from Robbie's presence, and nearing the roosting tree, Strut suddenly recalled Duke's departure that morning with the three brothers. Had Robert One been hiding a wily look on his face as he invited the two newcomers for a day of fun? It must have been a trap! Strut searched anxiously for Duke among the dozens and dozens of returning crows.

At last, to Strut's great relief and joy, his big buddy flew up and alighted at the roost, exuberant about his great day with the brothers. Strut was taken aback. He wondered whether he had been unduly suspicious of the Robert brothers because he had been concealing his wooing of their sister.

The crow waited until Duke finally ran out of tales about their thrilling escapades. Then, carefully looking around to see that he would not be overheard, Strut told Duke of his plan. He and Robbie would slip away very early in the morning. Would his best friend do him one last favor? If the brothers discovered their departure, would Duke make a disturbance to distract everybody? It probably wouldn't be necessary, but just in case—Duke said of course he would. Then Strut warned Duke that he too had better depart Santa Fe and fly fast to Capitan the very next day before the brothers learned of Robbie's departure and targeted Duke in revenge.

When all the crows had assembled and were waiting for their evening story, Strut told *The Great Tragedy: How a Mountain Lion Ate Smokey's Litter-Mates — but Smokey Escaped.*

Then Strut announced that he'd be leaving sometime the next day. There was a murmur of regret from most, but also hacking sounds of 'good riddance' from some males who evidently didn't trust any stranger around their females.

Later, Duke came to say good-bye. Strut promised him that when he returned from his journey to see Smokey, he'd search for his good friend back in the village of Capitan. Or, if by then Elder Crow had relented enough to permit their return to the flock, they'd meet back on the mountain. A silence ensued as each of them faced the stark reality — that they might never see each other again. They couldn't help but think of all the hazards Strut might face flying into new territory.

In their lives so far, they'd been lucky, for everyone knew the odds. Out of six baby crows hatched in a nest, only three lived past their first year — as they both had. Two of those that were their age now would live to four years, but only one of the six would reach age twenty or so. They banished such dreary thoughts with lusty crowing: Duke was so strong, and Strut so crafty, they'd probably both reach age twenty!

Nevertheless, as the moment of parting drew closer, they bowed their heads in sadness, the way crows do in mourning. Then they raised their heads for one long last look, and wished each other good luck. Duke flew up to his night-time perch near the brothers, and Strut watched until his friend's large body disappeared into the dappled tree with its dark shadows and bright light.

At daybreak, when the first cooing sounds from mourning doves lilted through the early morning air, Strut and Robbie stirred awake. Silently and separately they left the roost, feathering their wings softly away. To elude any followers, each took a circuitous route to the airport.

They met again at a tree there and surveyed the area. Reassured that no crows had followed them, they dropped down to the exposed runway. They stood side-by-side, facing the slip of an orange sun coming up in the east. Both crows took a deep breath and their hearts beat fast. Strut felt exhilarated. He nodded to Robbie, and they flapped their wings to take off. "As the crow flies! Off we go." A moment later he shouted jubilantly to the sky ahead, "Hang on, Smokey, we're coming!"

Chapter 48

Though I do not believe that a plant will spring up where no seed has been, I have great faith in a seed. Convince me that you have a seed there, and I am prepared to expect wonders.
–Henry Thoreau

I'm Nobody! Who are you? Are you nobody too? Then there's a pair of us. Don't tell. They'd banish us, you know! . . . How dreary to be Somebody! How public, like a frog. To tell your name the live long day. To an admiring Bog!
–Emily Dickinson

As Strut reached a high altitude above Santa Fe, he found Robbie missing from his side. He looked right and left, and scanned the sky ahead. Where was she? Then he craned his neck around. There she was, right behind him. He called back for her to come fly next to him.

Fully expecting her to agree and beat her wings to catch up, Strut was dismayed when she remained behind him. After feeling bad for a few moments, he darted a look behind. She told him she preferred being in his slipstream. She asked, didn't Strut know that on a long trip crows fly in single file? Hadn't he heard that in the old days crows migrated in a long line extending from one horizon to the next? No, he admitted, how could he know the *proper* way to travel over the plains, having lived his whole life in the mountains? But, he muttered to himself, "Why should we have to do things according to Hoyle? I hate those rule-bound old-crow ways!"

He decided he'd better be tactful. He didn't want to provoke saucy retorts from this strong-minded mate of his. Strut nicely coaxed her to come up next to him saying he *liked* to be near her. And, he asked, why not make their own rules? Now that they were free of everybody, they could do whatever they liked. He noticed that she brightened at his independent spirit.

As they flew side by side toward the rising sun, they soon saw an inviting river below that veered southeast. The strong tail wind along the river tempted them to follow such an easy route. Nevertheless they stayed the course—straight east over a huge forest covering high mountains.

At the end of the great forest, they faced a similar choice. A road angled northeast this time. Alongside the paved road, beneath layers of dust, they could see the ruts of wagon wheels. But where would this heavily-traveled northeast road take them? Although it looked tempting—more or less alongside the mountains—they decided, again, to continue directly into the sun. Hesitantly they ventured forth, and came upon old ruts and cast-off wagon wheels along a barely-discernible old roadway heading east. Were they making a mistake? It looked like endless desert ahead—tawny grass, sage and only scraggly trees here and there.

Bravely, they winged their way farther over the stark land. They'd been flying only a few hours when Strut found himself hot from the sizzling sun and huffing in fatigue. How he longed for the coolness of the high mountains! He stole a glance at Robbie. She must be accustomed to such heat, for she looked undaunted. The moment he saw her flag, though, he proposed they rest in the shade of a small bush. They landed awkwardly, their legs crumpling on impact, and collapsed on the sand, chests heaving. Still uncomfortably hot, they opened their bills and slowly lifted their wings to cool off. Neither uttered a sound.

After a while, Robbie scratched the earth to find bugs, but her efforts were in vain. She asked, how can you find much to eat in the desert? If they were in the city, she could show him all sorts of tricks, she told him, like how to drop nuts on the road in front of cars so they'd crack open.

Eager to demonstrate his cleverness, Strut picked up a sliver of wood with his beak and probed a hole in the sandy soil. Soon delicious ants were provoked to the surface. Robbie had been watching him carefully, and with a saucy turn of her head, she broke off a twig from the bush, trimmed the end into a tiny hook, and jabbed it into a rotting crevice at the base of the bush. She twisted it back and forth, then pulled out a squirming larva on the hook, and gleefully offered it to her mate.

Strut accepted it, a bit chagrined that she might be more ingenious than he was. Nevertheless, he followed her lead, made a hook, and happily snagged some fat larvae. After their feast, he decided that all-in-all, he was glad she was so smart. He playfully toyed with her foot, and she preened him in return with her bill half open.

As they rested, Robbie asked him out-of-the-blue what kind of sounds Strut's friend the cub made. Strut was delighted to show off his imitations of Smokey: moans of recognition, shrieks of distress, chomping teeth, snorting and woofing in warning. When she asked him to imitate Mother Bear, Father Bear, and Elder Crow he asked her why she wanted to know. She smiled beguilingly and said it was a secret.

Now that they were mates, he said, why should they have any secrets from each other? Shouldn't they share everything? "No," she declared. "It'll be a surprise this way. You'll see soon enough." Strut pondered this mate he had. He liked her spirit, but she sure had a mind of her own. Yet Strut somehow found her all the more intriguing.

"Caw!" she interrupted his thoughts. Was he in the mood to consider a proposal? He wondered what she might come up with next. Curious, he nodded and braced himself. She plunged ahead. If they survived this desert and reached a town, she had the city-smarts to be the one who should *first* approach the flock of crows, wouldn't he agree? He could stay hidden outside town while she prepared the strange crows for his appearance. That way, they would welcome Strut instead of chasing him off as a male rival.

Furthermore, she explained, a speaker needs to be *introduced* well. She declared, "I will be your emcee!" She liked his stories so much that she could whip up any audience to beg him to start. Then, during his storytelling, she had a surprise that would make the audience even more enthusiastic. Strut told her he could hardly wait to see what she would do. That is, if they ever reached a town and didn't perish crossing the desert.

The sparse land finally gave way to richer terrain. Late one afternoon they came upon a sizable river, ranches and railroad lines, and by evening they reached the green grass and shade trees of Amarillo, Texas. As they'd arranged, Robbie left Strut behind, and followed the local crows' loud assembly calls to the evening roost.

Like the Santa Fe crows, the Panhandle crows were all talking at once — in a melodious dialect — but these crows were even more numerous and boisterous. Robbie gathered her courage. Beating her wings rapidly, she suspended herself in the air before them. The Texas crows finally became inquisitive enough to quiet themselves for a moment.

In that lull, Robbie alighted on a branch and quickly asked if anyone had ever heard of Smokey. Yes, one exclaimed, the bear cub had stopped at Amarillo the past spring. "Caw, caw, caw!" They all jabbered at once, telling her how a crowd of people at the airport had laughed when the bear cub in his red halter insisted on having newspaper to poop on. Robbie could hardly wait to tell Strut. They hadn't admitted it to themselves, but they'd been worried about whether they should have gone west instead of east.

Robbie cawed loudly, and said she'd bring them a storyteller from the very mountains where Smokey had been born. The crows shrieked their enthusiasm, and she escaped their loud din to fetch her mate.

Strut arrived to the clamor of all the Amarillo crows vying to tell him about Smokey's touch-down at the airport, and asking him if he'd actually known Smokey. He rose to the occasion as a famous storyteller, fluffed out his feathers, and, with a modest nod, launched into the story he had told in Santa Fe about how Smokey had almost been killed by his father.

Early in his story, he was disconcerted to notice that Robbie had disappeared into a cluster of leaves right behind him. What was she up to? He found out when he began to describe how Father Bear slashed at the cub with his great paw. Strut was startled by fierce rumbling and teeth-clacking, as if a huge bear was right behind his perch. He wheeled around, but heard only smothered snickers from behind the leaves. Robbie! The audience was ominously quiet, their beaks open and eyes wide, and so spellbound that they didn't even jabber. From that point on, astonishing imitations of the cub and Mother Bear punctuated his story, and everyone began to hoot in surprise each time.

At the end, the flock of Texas crows were wildly noisy in their exclamations to each other. When they asked Strut how he had made all the animal sounds without moving his beak, he motioned Robbie to come forth and stand beside him. The two crowed with delight at their first triumphal performance together. What a humdinger!

Afterward, the two performers retreated to a hidden branch near the tree trunk. They basked in the camaraderie of having done so well together. Strut looked over at Robbie with new eyes. He prized her more than ever. They were perfect mates, in fact, mates for life!

He exulted to himself: As a true artist, he had always embraced the art of storytelling as the 'love of his life.' Expressing the artistic spirit was so rewarding, so demanding, that it had to come before anything or anyone else! But now he had found someone like him that way, another artist. And that must have been why he had been so attracted: to the artist in her!

Strut burst forth in a flood of exuberance. The two of them were on a higher plane than other crows: those who remained untouched by dedication to art and the spirit of adventure. He puffed up his body, and strutted up and down the branch. He scoffed at all those silly nincompoops: those *ordinary* city crows, bent on gluttony and cheap thrills, and those *ordinary* mountain crows, bound by silly rules and doomed to domestic life.

In the midst of his outburst, Strut suddenly stopped. He had caught a flash of amusement in Robbie's eyes. Feeling a bit deflated, he asked Robbie what was the matter. With a knowing look, she asked Strut exactly what 'silly rules' he hadn't liked back in his mountain flock.

He flinched and said that he had meant to tell her, sooner or later. Fearful of what she'd think of him, but glad to get it off his chest, he confessed. He had been ousted from the mountain flock by Elder Crow. She pulled the details out of him: how he'd skipped the nest-building classes, caused a rumpus over his girlfriend, and indulged in general tomfoolery with Duke. He hastened to add, though, that Elder Crow had great hopes for him as a storyteller, and thought travel might be very beneficial for that endeavor.

Strut awaited her verdict. She chided him about missing nest-building classes, then asked *what* girlfriend back home? "Oh, no," he told her. "Kate was nothing compared to you. That was in my foolhardy youth. Just a Passing Flutter." He hastily explained that his old flame had already found a proper mate, Donny Boy, and had built a nest with him. The two were a good match, both quite conventional, and would be happy together.

Whereas, Strut said, he wanted someone with gumption, like Robbie. They both had the get-up-and-go to have an exciting life.

"Really?" Robbie asked him, and when he agreed she poured out her hopes—to become a master storyteller herself, one whose stories would be replete with sound effects. Strut looked over at her with alarm. He was the storyteller and she was to be his faithful companion.

Then his eyes softened. Strut moved close, and brushed her wing lightly with his. Fierce artistic ambition beat in her breast too! Didn't that mean that they were two-birds-of-a-feather?

Why couldn't they both be great performers?

Strut felt struck by a strange new energy sizzling his whole being. He found himself reaching out to gently enclose her bill in his, and, after a quiet moment, she withdrew her bill to enclose his. He uttered low kuh-koo calls and she echoed him. Then, reaching over with her bill, Robbie combed the short downy feathers on his head. It felt wonderful and he responded by placing his bill under her chin, and gently tipped her head up to stroke the feathers on her throat. And when she next touched his face with her bill, he closed his eyes so she could delicately nibble around his eyes.

In the next instant, it happened. It was if their bodies knew an ancient dance. The crows stepped apart, bowed their heads, and raised their bills to the sky. Slowly they edged closer and crouched flat on the branch. Next to each other, their wings lifted out to the sides and their tails vibrated up and down. They breathed together and their energy flowed as if they were one being, as if they were lifted together to soar high into the sky.

Suddenly Robbie stepped farther aside, shook herself, and abruptly broke the spell with a jarring tone. "Hey! It's too early for that!"

Discombobulated, Strut stumbled on the branch. His vision of this female as his soul-mate was shattered. Her voice sounded so harsh! His heart plummeted: Maybe she was just like his first flame Kate who chose that goody-goody Donny Boy and then had the nerve to turn around and *mock* him and attack him—Storyteller Strut. He scrutinized Robbie anew, and wasn't sure he even liked her anymore. She probably only wanted some steady-Eddie anyway.

And she had common sense to a fault. Who did she think she was? So confident and sharp . . . Where was the sweet, admiring mate he'd always imagined? Did he really want such a *bossy* female?

After a few miserable moments, he looked at her for a long time with opened eyes. She seemed so real, somehow: awfully intelligent ... and poetic ... and stunningly beautiful. So much herself! She was indeed very special.

And Strut found he was forced to begrudge Robbie some newfound respect. She had actually saved them both! Some canoodling, okay. But real courtship dancing? No! It'd only lead to real trouble — the conventional life of nesting and baby birds to feed! He tilted his head to appraise her anew. All in all, he found that somehow he didn't *like* her quite as much ... but he *loved* her all the more. He had to admit — fool that he was — she was just what he needed, to curb that wayward streak of his that always got him into trouble.

Misinterpreting his scrutiny of her, Robbie said in a soft voice, as if to mollify him, "Someday you can build me a wonderful nest!" Strut swallowed and nodded. It didn't seem like the right moment to open his beak and confess how lousy he was at nest building. Nor the time to broach his clever idea of fixing up other birds' abandoned nests, which would be so much easier than assembling thousands of sticks. Maybe it wasn't such a good idea to confess *everything* all at once, he decided.

Instead, Strut announced with bravado, that he had left the mountains to find Smokey. She and he — both of them — had left behind the humdrum life for a much better one. "Caw-caw!" he crowed, sweeping her into his enthusiasm. There would be plenty of time for nesting later. But they must first be faithful to their splendid destiny: to travel and become great storytellers!

Chapter 49

Hear the whole world as music and you'll find we live inside a plethora of beautiful sounds. . . . Music may be one form of expression that vastly different kinds of life have in common. All over the world – from Babenzele Pygmies to Beethoven – there is human music derived from avian sounds.
–David Rothenberg

Why do birds sing? For the same reasons we sing – because we can. Because we love to inhabit the pure realms of sound. . . .We celebrate this ability in our greatest tasks, defining ourselves, defending our places, calling out to the ones we love. But form remains far more than function. We spend lifetimes immersed in the richness of these creations.
–David Rothenberg

The pair hid in a jumble of bushes outside Amarillo for a day together where they could feather-talk: coo softly, rub bills, and bask in the new heat of their special bond. And they felt free to goof off awhile, knowing from the local crows that they were, indeed, headed in the right direction to find Smokey.

By the next morning, they reluctantly emerged from their hideout to seek food. The local crows, calling it 'sightseeing' and 'Texas hospitality,' proudly showed them the sights of Amarillo. Everything went quite well until the newcomers saw cattle crammed into the stockyards next to the railroad. How could these fenced-in animals enjoy life?

The next morning the two headed out on the highway toward the rising sun. They had been warned that, like the rest of the Great Plains, this was treacherous country. Not much life stirred, so they'd be easy game for marauding birds of prey.

They decided to fly as fast as they could, and, at the first sight of trouble, skedaddle over to any tree they might find. Although much of the prairie land turned out to be treeless, dotted with cactus and pinkish-purple thistle plants, they crossed over it uneventfully.

Upon arriving in Oklahoma City, they learned, to their dismay that the crows there had never heard of Smokey. A young crow had heard rumors of a cub traveling by plane to Tulsa, but that city wasn't straight east. It was to the *northeast*.

Worried the whole mission might hang on making the right choice, Strut and Robbie hesitated about changing their course, and, hoping to be lucky, ended up continuing east on the highway they knew, across the Southern Plains. After all, hadn't the trip so far proven them 'lucky in love'? All along the sides of the easterly road were bountiful wild sunflowers reaching as high as a person's chest. They feasted along the way on the tasty dark brown seeds at the center of the bright yellow petals.

The flat land soon gave way to an array of rounded hills and valleys, streams and lakes, wildland forests and meadows. Now and then they came upon sharp-edged patterns below them of different-colored crops. Fields of tawny wheat flowed in the soft breezes like rippling water on a lake. And the summer corn, which had just emerged from the ground as slim blades of green back in the high altitude of Santa Fe, rose from the rich dark earth here as cornstalks so tall and thick they might hide a standing person.

The crows marveled at trees with great trunks and large branches arched wide, sporting bright green leaves. They were truly grand compared to the gnarled and stunted junipers or even the tall pines they had known back home.

Later on, the smell of fish drew them to the river nearby that ran through the city of Little Rock. The Arkansas crows, like the ones back in Amarillo, hadn't heard of Smokey either. The two crows wondered. Were they on the wrong track? If so, was it possible they'd *never* find Smokey?

By the sixth morning of their journey, Strut and Robbie were discussing whether to change their route when they were distracted by some crispy potato chips on the ground at a gas station. As they crunched the chips they noticed a driver leave his big farm truck to enter the gas station.

Strut and Robbie moseyed over. They heard familiar grunts from the open back of the truck. The two fluttered up to the top slat and discovered eight fat pink pigs. They caught the eye of a pig that looked up benignly at them. Down to the floor they dived to scavenge some spilled grain just behind the truck's cab.

The birds were hungrily pecking up seeds when the cab door slammed, the engine revved up, and the truck lurched out of the station. The two crows were about to take flight, but first looked out the side slats. What they saw made them pause. The truck was turning up the highway. They shot each other an expectant look, and folded their wings again. Why not take a free ride? It was easier than flying, and safer than being exposed to hawks. Whether east or northeast: Let the truck decide.

The nearest pig seemed friendly, and was careful not to trample them with its delicate hooves, so the two scrunched down, wedged themselves near the cab and watched out through the bottom slats, the wind riffling their feathers. As soon as they got their footing amid the bumps and swaying, they enjoyed the thrill of such speed—twice as fast as they could fly. The truck slowed to bypass a large city with its sounds of traffic, and the crows' eyes widened to look down from the Memphis Bridge to the enormous Mississippi River.

The truck rumbled on, then finally pulled over and stopped. Where were they? From the slant of the sun, they guessed they'd ridden east to this city. With an appreciative nod at the pig, the two hopped up to the top slat, launched themselves out the top of the truck, landed on the limb of a nearby tree in Nashville, Tennessee, and promptly fell asleep.

Throughout the day among the pigs, Strut and Robbie had

come to like the country music floating back from the open windows of the truck's cab. It was lively and sometimes sad — echoing how crows themselves felt at times. So they weren't surprised to awaken in the evening to the same kind of music coming from a few blocks away. It was loud and had a lively beat. Drawn to follow the call of the music, they flew to a big red-brick building with arched windows and entrances. Not hesitating a moment, they managed to slip between people streaming into a doorway marked "The Grand Ole Opry."

Quickly surveying the vast auditorium with its overwhelming number of people, the two interlopers sneaked behind the last row and perched in a niche built into the brick wall. Onto the brightly-lit stage walked a man dressed like Ray in a cowboy hat and boots. Unlike Ray's workday leather jacket, this man's buckskin had dangling leather fringes. He touched his hat to the audience and a quick smile flashed across his long face.

The man immediately hoisted his guitar, brushed his hand over the guitar strings and burst into a song that carried loudly over the microphone to the crows. "Hey, hey, good lookin, whatcha got cookin?" The Nashville crowd went wild. They stomped their feet and hooted "Hey, hey!" with him. Strut and Robbie got so excited that when Hank Williams came to the refrain again, their rasping voices broadcast loudly above the crowd, "K-hey, k-hey! Good lookin!"

A woman seated in front of them cast a look behind her, stared right at them with startled eyes, then gave them a quick smile, and turned back. When Hank finished the song, people clapped and whistled, and the crows cawed as loudly as they could. Robbie even imitated some loud whistles.

The crowd finally quieted enough for Hank to sing one song after another, as tunefully as any mockingbird. Strut and Robbie stayed until their eyelids drooped. Before the end of the program, they sneaked out the door and made their way back through the dark night to their tree.

Chapter 50

And at the word 'alone' Will felt a great wave of rage and despair moving outward from a place deep within him, as if his mind were an ocean that some profound convulsion had disturbed. All his life he'd been alone, and this infinitely precious blessing that had come to him must be taken away almost at once.
–Philip Pullman

The next morning the streets of Nashville, Tennessee were quiet. The crows knew their tiredness was from being out late, but why did they feel so restless and ill at ease? Could it be that they hadn't told a story, as usual, to local crows the evening before? In new places, storytelling reminded them of who they were, where they had come from, and where they were going. Storytelling led them to feel like themselves in strange places. The exertion of performing left them fatigued afterward, but energized too.

The couple decided to seek out some crows for storytelling. Strut and Robbie zeroed in on distant cawing and soon spied a flock feeding at some stockyards along the Tennessee River. As the two hovered and looked down, they were shocked again, as they had been in Texas, at the sight of cattle, pigs and sheep confined to crowded feedlots. It gave them the willies. Did humans do this to captive birds too?

Descending to a fence, the two looked longingly at the grain spilled on the ground. Soon the local crows invited them to share the bounty. When everyone was finished, Robbie cawed in an inviting voice to rally the flock. She summarized the earlier stories and introduced Strut for the next in the series. He launched with renewed vigor into the story: *How I Helped Ray Find the Burnt Cub after the Fire*. Behind him, Robbie added sound effects, her imitations and timing perfect, in Strut's opinion.

As soon as the story ended, the two held their breaths, hopeful to hear news of the bear. No, they were told. If Smokey had passed through Nashville, they would surely have known.

The next morning, the Nashville crows wished them well on their journey, but the pair sensed that their gracious hosts doubted that the newcomers were on the right track. The two started east again, but Robbie soon nodded to her mate to alight on a branch. "We're on the wrong track. We've been going east for several days now . . . without hearing *anything* about Smokey."

Strut flared up, "Well, what do you want us to do? Go back?"

"That's no answer! Of course not! Why are you so stubborn? Just because you hate to admit you're wrong. It's about time we tried going *northeast*!"

"Why northeast? Why not southeast?" Strut argued back.

The sharp scold of a robin interrupted them. "What gall you two have — to make such a racket and intrude on *my* tree, near *my* nest!" Annoyed, the pair fluttered to the next tree, but she continued her piercing assault. Strut screeched, "Will you shut up? We're in the middle of something *important*!"

Robbie quickly said, "Don't mind him; he's just upset. Perhaps you could be so kind as to give us some peace? We have to make a decision."

The robin must have been mollified because she declared, "If you two will just shut up and go away, I'll settle the argument myself." She motioned northeast with her beak, saying with authority, "Fly that way. Everything's that way." Then she busied herself turning her eggs and fussily rearranging the inner lining of the nest.

Strut and Robbie exchanged a glance. The word of an angry robin was not much to go on. But 'everything' might include Smokey, so at the next crossroads, the two left the eastbound highway they had been following so far, and, with some misgivings, took the road going northeast out of Nashville.

They proceeded at a slow pace, feasting their eyes on the land. What a change this farmland was from Strut's evergreen forests in the mountains and Robbie's high arid desert, as well as the expanse of sparse, flat plains they had crossed. Here the countryside was laced with streams and valleys unbelievably lush with oaks and willows. Beyond every sloping hill they came upon a prosperous farm. Beside each well-kept wooden house stood a large red barn and a silver silo, with pigs, chickens, and a vegetable garden clustered around the buildings, and the entire homestead surrounded by vast fields of grain.

Trees had great trunks spreading into broad limbs thick with leaves. Here the air was balmy, and the forest beds moist with leaf-mulch. Underneath the layer of leaves they discovered rich black soil, crumbly with bugs and worms. There was an abundance of life along the streams and marshes, where they could see many wings flittering among the trees and catch quick glimpses of furry animals scurrying about on the ground.

Strut and Robbie saw a large flock of crows descend from the sky onto a field of grain. At first, the two foraged at the edge of the field, remaining at a cautious distance from the flock. Soon they edged nearer to the feast. What a bonanza of cutworms!

A loud "Koah!" from the flock's sentinel caused the local crows to disperse with a flash of wings, and the two strangers fled too. Safe in an elm tree, they were told to beware men or boys who might kill crows in one scattershot of their guns, then shout and laugh as crows fell to the ground or flew awkwardly away on wounded wings.

Despite the disheartening news, Strut and Robbie couldn't help enjoying this part of their trip. There was fresh dew in the mornings; the air was damp and warm; the breezes, mild and balmy. When it occasionally became hot, the travelers broke their trip at mid-day to lounge in dense shade near running creeks. At first they found rain showers exhilarating and would babble happily as it ran off their backs. They soon learned from the local birds to hide under thick leaves to escape the more drenching downpours that pelted down for hours. In the wake of a storm, they'd emerge to see the sky wearing the vivid blue of a bluebird or the pale blue of a robin's egg, and huge puffy clouds once again marching across the sky. Then Robbie and Strut loved to listen to their favorite songbird, the meadowlark, pour out its heart in a long, lilting song.

After downpours, the damp earth turned its darkest brown, almost black, and the ground was soft under their feet. The soil smelled good, and it was loose enough for their stout beaks to easily probe for juicy earthworms and fat grubs. It was quite a contrast to what they'd known in the West. There the earth had been pale yellow, dusty or hard-packed much of the time, and, even after snowmelt or rainstorms, the wet heavy clay had soon reverted to cracked parched desert that a crow would have to hammer with his beak to find anything.

They tarried on their way through the prosperous farmland, then rode a high air current across the lush countryside of Kentucky until they dipped down at the sight of factory smokestacks along a wide river. Like tourists in a big city for the first time, they gawked at the red brick buildings of Cincinnati, marveled at the singing sound coming from the suspension bridge, and watched a flat barge moving slowly on the wide Ohio River past scrap yards of twisted metal.

Strut checked the breeze off the river. "Let's go soaring. Have some fun like Duke had with your brothers — the Roberts."

"I knew you couldn't stand it that Duke got to play at the cliffs outside Santa Fe, and you didn't." Catching the disappointment in her partner's eyes, she cawed lustily, "Well, what's keeping you then? Let's go to the skyscrapers!"

They glided over to the tallest tower and examined the brick wall that rose straight up at a greater angle than the steepest canyons they'd known. Strut and Robbie threw themselves into the air, and let a thermal sail them swiftly above the lower floors of the Carew Tower, past the deck where people were gathered, then beyond the tippy-top of the building. Strong air currents whistled and crackled in an eerie way enticing them to the cross-currents above.

What a thrill it was to wheel above the spire, wing tips stretched wide and tails flared. The birds followed their fancy. They'd swoop low until they caught another thermal to swirl them effortlessly toward the clouds, wings spread to float. They barely tilted to zoom past each other in wide crisscrossing loops.

Finally, the two crows veered back down to a tree along the street, their wing tips still tingling in the exhilaration of their sky dance. Happily they billed each other. Their spirits buoyed, they became airborne again, this time to seek birds at an airport who just might know about Smokey.

Raucous sounds near an airfield alerted them to the presence of other crows. Robbie nodded to Strut, and, with trepidation, she asked a question. To their happy surprise, the Ohio crows jabbered that, indeed, they had seen the cub. He'd arrived in a small plane the year before and left the next morning going northeast. Giddy with excitement, Strut was ready to take off immediately, but Robbie cautioned that they should stay at least overnight to feed and rest.

After breakfast the next morning, Strut and Robbie flew to the Cincinnati airport where they could idly watch the early morning planes taxiing and departing. The Douglas DC-3s were bigger than the small planes they'd seen before. They dwarfed the smaller ones as much as a Canada goose might dwarf a duck. Each plane would wait, its two big propellers whirring. Then, trailing black exhaust, it would roar down the runway. The huge silver bird—without flapping its wings and without even flailing its feet on the ground like a heavy goose—would rise in the air and neatly tuck its round feet up into its belly.

Robbie pointed out that most of the morning planes headed toward the sun. That gave Strut an idea: Why not sneak aboard a plane and take a chance that it would head northeast or at least east? He spotted a small tractor on the tarmac with a man on board wearing a yellow vest and earmuffs. The tractor was pulling a line of wheeled carts toward a nearby plane. "Come with me!"

The crows hitched a ride in the cart going toward the front end of the DC-3. The two instinctively cringed as they passed under an enormous shadow. They dared to look up. It was not a giant raptor, merely the huge wing of the stationary plane. The driver in the yellow vest abruptly stopped, jumped off, and began unloading boxes and suitcases onto a conveyer belt. At the open door at the top of the belt another man grabbed each piece of luggage, stacked it inside, and reached for the next.

They nodded to each other: Here's where they could sneak aboard! The two flew up and hovered together above the door. Strut indicated to Robbie that he'd divert the man's attention while she sneaked in, then he'd follow. He flew down close to the man's face, but the man flailed his arms so wildly that there wasn't room for Robbie to fly past him through the small door. Strut shortly rejoined her in the air. The man inside the door, hands on hips, stared up at them, as if daring them to try again.

Just then other carts rushed below them with more luggage, headed toward the tail of the plane, where a line of passengers was entering a door. Could they dart inside back there at the tail?

The two crows flew past a dozen small windows that stretched the length of the huge machine. They perched on the tail of the plane and looked down. Waiting for an opportunity to fly in, the two impatiently watched the last of almost two dozen passengers file into the plane through a small door. Then a blue-uniformed woman reached for boxes exuding aromas of hot food, and swiftly stowed them just inside. To their dismay, the door suddenly closed.

Their remaining choice was the big rear baggage compartment below them where the last bags and boxes from a cart were being heaved from a cart to a man inside. The two watched from the tail for an opportunity to fly in. Finally the cart left. Taking their last chance, they hovered outside the baggage door and saw only one man left, deep inside, his back to them. He was busy securing a heavy box with rope and carefully knotting the rope around rings on the floor. Seizing the moment, Strut flew down to the threshold of the luggage door. "Robbie. Quick. Come on!"

But just then, the man inside the luggage area suddenly loomed over Strut at the threshold. When his hand reached for the door handle, Strut quickly hopped into a shadow inside. As the door was closing, Strut saw Robbie stop in mid-air, flap her wings vigorously and head toward the front of the plane, calling back to him, "Caw! I'll try again—up front."

Inside the compartment, Strut felt stunned. How could they have become separated? Soon the plane rumbled. The powerful propeller on one side whirred, then the other, and the walls of the gigantic machine vibrated. Strut sensed the plane bouncing down a long runway, with its whole body swaying like some heavy lumbering beast as it gathered speed. The floor beneath the bird's feet tipped precipitously at lift-off. He braced his tail on the floor to keep from falling backward, shuffled forward in the dark and found a floor gusset to grip with his feet. It wasn't long before Strut experienced a stretch of turbulence where the floor bounced him up and down, the body of the plane shuddered and the wings wobbled. Later the crow sensed the familiar air pressure he knew at the high altitudes of the mountains back home.

As the plane flew more smoothly and settled into a steady drone, the crow relaxed enough to think. Why hadn't he waited until they were both on the plane together? Would he ever see Robbie again? He emitted a small sad caw, and his head drooped lower and lower until his bill rested on the floor. Exhausted, he escaped into the oblivion of sleep.

Chapter 51

Life's true griefs will eventually make you tougher, more understanding, more tolerant, more compassionate. If you let them, they'll teach the proportions of human happiness.
–Verlyn Klinkenborg

There is no remedy for love but to love more.
–Henry Thoreau

Strut awoke. Through the dark he saw a sliver of light at the bottom of the cargo door. "Caw!" He stiff-walked over and pecked the metal door. Why had it closed so suddenly before Robbie could fly inside? He lifted his tail and angrily splashed his waste on the threshold.

The crow crossed to the narrow open space between the stacks of luggage. Perhaps, after all, he had been mistaken and she had flown inside. He peered through the dark into each corner. "Robbie! Are you hiding somewhere? It's not a joke!" He tilted his head and listened. No reply. It had been a vain hope, for hadn't he heard her—in the moment when the door was closing—call back to him that she'd fly to the front luggage compartment?

Strut let out a great sigh. His mate was smart and fast. Maybe she had made it. He shut his eyes again, but he couldn't shut out his fears: What if Robbie had found the front luggage door closed? She was a valiant crow. Perhaps she would try to find her way back to Santa Fe to await his return there. Could she even make it all the way back West as a lone bird—an easy prey for hawks?

Heartbroken, he could hardly breathe. Is this what growing up was: one loss after another? First losing his family when he fell out of the tree, then losing Ray, then his closest friend Smokey, his flock in the mountains, then Duke. And now, the love of his life—Robbie. Would he never hear her resonant voice again? Do you always lose everyone you *really* care about? It was more sorrow than he could bear.

A hard-sided suitcase tumbled onto the floor forcing Strut to jump aside. Annoyed, he turned to peck it, but found that it had burst open. The crow jumped inside and impatiently tossed the contents onto the floor, until he happened to find a warm jacket. He burrowed inside, and, exhausted, fell asleep to the steady throb of the engines. Hours later he heard a loud announcement through the partition, and the tantalizing smell of hot food wafted his way. He was hungry. How long would he be held in suspense on this trip?

This must be an awful dream. No, this was actually happening to him! Was he still Strut the mountain crow—the storyteller? Panic seized him. "Elder Crow, help me!" he pleaded. An answer came, "Pull yourself together and stand tall like a crow!" His gorge rose in protest, but he could only feebly grumble. Then he dropped into a long and deep sleep.

The next thing he knew, the plane jolted him awake as it hit the runway in the jarring way an awkward goose might land. The plane rolled ahead and came to a stop. After a few moments, the luggage door opened from outside, and a man came in. Strut crept to the side of the compartment and tensed his wings, ready to escape. The plane was quiet. For a moment the crow was sun-dazed from having been in the dark. He squinted his eyes.

"Cah!" He barged past the man who stood at the threshold, and launched himself out the door. His heart pounding, he winged above the men in yellow vests swarming the plane and headed toward the front where the ramp was already in place, ready to unload baggage.

Then the sweetest voice he'd ever heard made his heart burst. It was the distinctive "Caaah!" of his loved one. There was Robbie zooming out the baggage door, pausing in midflight, then coming straight back toward him. His heart ached terribly at the sight, and all the anguish he'd been holding back swept out of him. He hadn't realized, until this moment, how much he loved her. How much she was part of his life now.

Airborne, the crows made loop-de-loops around each other, and then landed atop the airplane's tail, so they could joyfully bill and coo. Then a strong urge seized both of them to poke and comb the errant feathers that had become badly askew during the trip. And they gently preened each other. Feeling quite restored, Strut sighed, and softly held Robbie's closed bill in his for a moment, and she reciprocated and held his a long time.

As storytellers, they were eager to tell each other what had happened. Robbie related how thunderstruck she'd been when the back baggage door suddenly shut—with Strut inside. Desperate, she rushed down the length of the plane, and, finding the front luggage door momentarily unguarded, whipped inside.

She discovered a heavy netting between the cargo and the cockpit compartments, so she could watch the pilots and, past them, through the windshield to the sky outside. The windshield sometimes leaked so badly that the pilots grabbed rubber aprons to shield their laps, and she had to move to the far side of her area to escape splatters of water. At such close quarters with the humans, she kept very quiet, and when it got cold, sidled closer to the small heater in the cockpit. Comforted by the thought that she'd be with Strut again when they landed, she slept through most of the journey.

After Strut related what happened on his plane ride, they congratulated each other on what stories they'd be able to tell the crows back home. They could hardly imagine how fast the plane had gone; it must have gone a considerable distance.

Eventually they sobered up. Was it possible that the plane had taken them back west? Or even south? Strut couldn't tolerate the thought and said that the plane must have carried them in the right direction, northeast or at least east. So, he blustered, they would soon find his friend. He lustily cawed, "Smokey, here we come!" And, to be a good sport, Robbie echoed his call with her full-throated one.

In the ensuing silence, Strut swallowed hard. He had no idea where they were. He scanned the expanse of pavement at the airfield and beyond. The scene yielded few indications of their whereabouts. It didn't seem to him like the West. Nor was it farmland. The air was moist. The trees in the far distance were stately with thick foliage and tangles of green undergrowth beneath.

From their stance on the tail of the airplane, the birds spied a cart stopped below them with metal containers of leftover food trays unloaded from the plane. Welcoming a diversion, they watched a yellow-vested man pull out the top tray, pick up something that crinkled, and tear open the wrapper to munch what was inside. When he dropped the wrapper onto the tarmac, Strut dove down, shook the discarded wrapping briskly with his bill, and hungrily pecked up the spilled cookie crumbs. He looked up, and saw Robbie already grasping the edge of the tray with her feet. Strut quickly joined her to gobble down sloppy mashed potatoes and gravy.

The man looked ready to slide the tray back when Strut saw him halt a moment to laugh at Robbie. She was cocking her head from side to side, eyeing a tiny rectangular packet on the tray. She stabbed it with her beak, but the cardboard packet resisted. So Robbie gripped the box tightly with one foot and tore it open with her beak. Out popped two white squares. She pecked through the hard covering into gummy stuff inside but tossed the Chiclets aside in disgust. Some gum still adhered to her beak, and she had to reach up her foot to claw it away. Standing near the man, who was laughing, Strut laughed too, thinking that crows eat just about anything, but humans eat things no bird would deign to eat. The feast was abruptly cut short the moment a small tractor—pulling a string of carts—pulled up and squealed its brakes. They took flight.

Aloft, they wondered where they could be. Salty air was filled with the mournful, harsh cries of birds they hadn't heard before. Piercing sounds beckoned them to a waterfront of strange-smelling water, where they saw seagulls wheeling in the air. The crows were bursting to find out whether they had indeed come east to the end of the land, and if so, whether Smokey had been here, too, but they couldn't find any way to interrupt the seagulls.

The raucous birds were wheeling above the pier, fighting over bait fish and scraps. As soon as one gull was lucky enough to seize a tidbit, another sped after it, squawking. The first one would be so harassed that it couldn't stop to eat, and was forced to drop the food or else have it snatched from its beak. What aggressive birds these gulls were, compared to crows! Since there was no chance to get any news from the noisy birds, Strut and Robbie returned, frustrated, to the airport.

There, they sought sparrows, and soon spotted the chatty little creatures who had helped them at the beginning of their trip back at the Santa Fe airport. The two greeted the brown-bibbed birds politely, and inquired about Smokey. The sparrows had good news. The cub had arrived at this Baltimore airport a year ago to stay overnight. He'd been brought back to the airport the following morning. And although it was raining very hard the next morning, he was flown out in a heavy rainstorm. His plane was undoubtedly headed to the next big city, Washington, D.C., the destination for many planes from this airport. It wasn't far. A bird could easily fly there and back in a morning. Going southwest, you couldn't miss it. From high in the sky, you could see the city laid out in a grand circle around a round-domed building, with broad streets going out from the center like the petals on a sunflower.

With triumphant breasts thrust out, the two crows embarked upon the last leg of their journey. They made short shrift of flying over Baltimore, just enough to exclaim how big it was with its rows upon rows of old red-brick buildings. Then they winged their way to Smokey.

Chapter 52

I felt it wasn't bears, but the idea of bears that he feared: the unseen, dark forces that lurk in the forest of the mind . . . The bear, as the Ainu say, is the God of the Mountain. His energy, vigor, and alertness are pure expressions of the power of the wild forest. To meet him is not just an occasion of fear, but of delight and awe.
–Paul Shepard and Barry Sanders

Animals were not made for us, any more than blacks were made for whites or women made for men.
–Alice Walker

With heightened anticipation, the crows beat their wings as fast as they could and soon found Washington. In an exhilarated state of crow hysteria, they zoomed hither and yon over the city, hoping to spot Smokey at any moment.

At last, calming themselves, they flew to a high overlook, the statue atop the Capitol dome, and stood on the shoulder of the gigantic bronze woman. People below looked as small as ants, but rather than moving in purposeful lines they briskly crisscrossed each other to eventually mount broad steps into grand marble buildings.

The crows marveled at how endless the roads were, extending like spokes of a wheel into the distance. Although they were impressed by the great city, they felt uneasy on Smokey's behalf. Robbie started trembling and exclaimed, "What a weird place humans have made!" Strut pointed out how leafy the trees were along the streets, and how shady the small parks here and there, but concluded that the sprawling city was certainly no place for wild animals. "I suppose crows and sparrows can manage, but not a *bear*. If Smokey's here, we have to get him out." He launched his body off the bronze statue calling back to Robbie, "Let's go to the river and woods across the way. They are the only places for a bear around here!"

Although the Potomac River was quite large compared to the streams they'd known Out West, it felt somewhat familiar. Brown ducks paddled near the banks, and the fishy, marshy smell reminded them of beaver ponds with their surroundings of lush trees and underbrush. They soon came upon a stream that cut right through the city. On a hunch, they veered right into the heavily forested Rock Creek Park. They spied a starling and asked where they might find a bear cub. Grouching to herself about "all these out-of-towners asking stupid questions," she answered that a bear cub would, of course, be found past Dupont Circle — at the zoo where wild animals were kept. His heart beating fast, Strut asked whether a cub called *Smokey* was there, and held his breath for the answer.

The starling wearily shrugged and said, "Where have you two been all your life? Where *else* would he be?" The two crows lifted their wings and chorused, "We have found him!" The two blurted out how far they'd come and how glad they were at the news, then pleaded with her to tell them where the place called a 'zoo' was. The bird closed her eyes as if annoyed at their naiveté, but then paused and, studying their anxious faces, seemed to have a change of heart. "It's not far from here. I'm going up the park anyway. Just follow me." They poured out their gratitude, and, with great anticipation, flew after the starling.

Their guide left Strut and Robbie at the impressive entrance to the zoo where bronze lions guarded the wrought-iron grillwork of the gates. Streaming in the open gates were children and adults, and quite a few young sailors in uniform with white caps askew on their heads. The crows followed the throng, flying above a woman who pushed a very young child in a wheeled cart, with a slightly bigger child holding onto the side of the cart.

Where could Smokey be? The first animal they came upon was a heavy-set deer. The two crows stood on a branch of a full-leafed tree, gawking at the astonishing horns that curved over its back. It was chewing its cud, the jaws slowly moving sideways. With an air of benign nonchalance, it looked out through lazy, half-lidded eyes at the children on the other side of the fence pointing at it. Two more of the hoofed animals wandered up. Apparently they weren't confined like pets, but allowed to roam, at least within the fenced area extending back out of sight.

The crows looked at each other. So this is what a 'zoo' was — a place where animals were confined so people could look at them. The gazelles seemed relaxed, unafraid of wild predators, nor did they flinch at the humans who extended their arms and stared straight at them.

How had Smokey fared in this strange environment? Strut hung his head, and told Robbie that he suddenly dreaded finding his friend — so full of spunk and joy in the forest — probably utterly forlorn in this alien place. Robbie reminded him that's why they'd come: to find Smokey. Didn't that include cheering him up, if that's what he needed? So, she said, Strut must stop speculating and go find his friend. She would stay behind watching the hoofed ones for a bit so the two old friends could have their reunion together. He should take his time and return to pick her up later.

Taking her advice, Strut left her side and flew away — not without trepidation about what condition Smokey might be in. Glancing down at various enclosures, he ignored all the strange animals, so intent was he on finding Smokey and ending his suspense. More than a year had passed. Would he still recognize the cub? Would Smokey remember him? On his first pass-by of the entire grounds, he found no sign of his friend. With mounting desperation he flew over all the enclosures again.

At last the bird noticed the rounded ears of a large bear

immersed in a pool. He dive-bombed to get a closer look. "Caw-caw!" he called. As if recognizing the crow's voice, the bear moaned, then swiveled his big head around. He jerked his body up out of the water and climbed the stairs. As if in a daze, he stood upright on the concrete, his dark fur dripping.

The animal was almost as tall as a person. Could this be little Smokey? The bear was looking around. Then, with a resigned shrug, he trudged to the bare tree in his yard, shook his wet fur, and shinnied up the trunk to sit on a branch and suck his paw. Yes! It was indeed Smokey. The crow flew over to the tree, perched on the stub of a bare branch just above Smokey and peered down.

Strut spies Smokey

"Caah-caah! I've found you! Hey, you big lug! It's *me*—Strut!" The crow watched the bear crane his neck up and blink at him. The crow squawked, gripped the branch with his feet, and let his body fall upside-down with his wings flopping just above the bear's head.

Smokey heaved out a mighty moan of longing, "Eeeh-eh." Then he huffed and huffed. "Oh, Strut. It *is* you! The same as ever . . . I've missed you so *much*!" The crow spread his wings to drop softly on the thick-furred shoulder, and rubbed his bill against the bear's neck. He'd found his friend.

Chapter 53

Discontinuity and nostalgia are most profound if, in growing up, we leave or lose the place where we were born and spent our childhood, if we become expatriates or exiles, if the place, or the life, we were brought up in is changed beyond recognition or destroyed. All of us, finally, are exiles from the past.
–Oliver Sacks

Annoyed that people were shouting and rushing up to the bars and clicking their cameras at him and the crow, Smokey said to Strut, "Quick, to my den." Once inside, the cub crossed the den to a flat rock that jutted out from the stone wall. "I've always thought of this small ledge as *your* niche—just like the shelf back at the cave where you hid your treasures and told me stories."

Realizing that his lanky body blocked the ledge, which kept Strut hovering in the air, Smokey sat down with his legs in front of him like he used to as a small cub. The crow settled on the ledge and winked back at him. Smokey silently feasted his eyes on his good friend and Strut beamed back. For the first time the bear could remember, his crow friend seemed speechless. Smokey was content to just drink in the sight of his best buddy, returned to him after so long.

The cub finally broke the silence. "Tell me what happened. Did everything burn at home?"

Strut, without his usual inclination for drama, just recited the bad news: the blackening of the forest and the toll the fire had taken on wildlife. Then Smokey heard the good news: many animals had been able to escape the fire. And certain stands of trees on the mountain had survived, and, since the firestorm, no camper had left any campfire to smolder. In the following spring all over the mountain green shoots of grass had sprung out of the ashes. Everyone back home was busy having offspring again.

"I wonder about where I lived . . . What happened to the honey tree? And how's our cave?"

"I flew over to the area before I left the mountain to come here. Guess what? Even though that old honey tree is scorched and more dried-up than ever, it still stands, so sooner or later bees will find it. And I visited our cave. There's quite a layer of dust on my shelf. The den felt awfully empty without you and your mother . . . Perhaps it'll be a home for another mother bear and her cubs someday . . . hopefully a Medicine Bear like your mother, to pass on the lore, or else bears will just have to learn from crows."

Smokey was silent, finally let out a sigh from deep inside, and asked, "What about *you*? Catch me up on everything!" With a brevity unusual for him, Strut told how Elder Crow had chosen him and his big pal Duke to mob hawks. Then he had banished both of them from the flock, so they set out to find Smokey. Then, in Santa Fe, the big crow had deserted him. The bird paused, and Smokey asked, "So you had to come all by yourself?" Strut looked away, made a coughing sound in his throat, and groomed an errant feather. He said that he'd tell the rest eventually, but he first wanted to hear how Smokey had fared at the zoo.

"Ever since I arrived, I've been confined here so people like those," he rolled his eyes out the den entrance to the crowd waiting at the front bars, "can come and look at me. I do get fed, but it's the same old dull food most of the time. It's terribly boring here, the same day after day. I have made a few friends, but I'm afraid you'll laugh at who they are, so maybe I'll tell you a bit later. Certainly no one as special as *you*. But if it weren't for my few friends here, I would've been really lonely. And if I didn't have this pool, I'd go crazy without being able to stretch my legs in this *cage*.

"Hey! Let me show you how I swim!" Smokey galumphed over to the water and threw himself in with a big splash. He soon found Strut flying overhead to dive-bomb him, cawing loudly each time he touched the bear's head with his wingtips. Smokey chortled and swatted water at him.

They played most of the afternoon until Strut stopped a short distance from the pool. Smokey climbed out and joined him. They both shook their wet bodies and Strut flapped his wet wings, then retreated to the den. On his ledge, the crow stood on one foot, then the other, his wings pressed tightly against his body and mumbled, "There's something I have to tell you . . ."

Remembering that phrase from their forest days, Smokey grinned and in a deep sharp voice said, "Speak up. I can't hear you." Instead of laughing, though, Strut looked dismayed. Smokey turned aside, ashamed he'd used such an *imperious* tone, one the peacock might have used. He softened his eyes and said, "You know you can tell me *anything*. We're best friends, aren't we?"

Stumbling over his words, Strut confessed that he had fallen in love with someone who had come across the country with him. By now, she'd been waiting quite some time at the zoo entrance to join them. He quickly asked Smokey not to make fun of them.

Although Smokey paused for a moment, feeling a twinge of jealousy, he rose to the occasion and said he was glad that Strut had found someone special. He knew how lonesome life could be. Strut said he'd better fetch Robbie right away before she became too peeved.

He flew away, and soon the two returned and wedged themselves together on the ledge. Strut introducing her as 'my ladylove' and 'my mate for life.' He pointed out to Smokey the exquisite iridescent sheen of her feathers—blue, green and purple—and told what a talented mimic she was.

Robbie looked down at Smokey, and remarked how surprised she was to find that the 'little cub' she'd been hearing about seemed quite big. Then she boldly caught Smokey's eye, and, with a mischievous look, asked him to make a 'happy' sound. She perfectly echoed his 'Eh-eh,' and he laughed. Next she had him grimace and roar like the father bear, which she lustily imitated. They made sounds until the cub was snorting and sputtering for her to stop. She also imitated those sputterings until he told her she really had to stop because his stomach hurt from laughing so hard. Strut pranced around, fluffing out his wings, looking happy that his loved one was such a hit.

Storytelling was the greatest pleasure for all three, and they caught up on a year of news. The bear told about a few interludes in his boring life, and listened avidly to the crows' dramatic stories about their journey.

In the days ahead, Smokey introduced Strut and Robbie to his friends at the zoo, cautioning the mischievous crows ahead of time not to tease Mr. Dazzle for his high-and-mighty ways, and asking them to honor his friendship with the lowly rat Freddie, whom he held especially dear.

When he told them about Trish and Trash, the crows became so excited that they abruptly flew off to Monkey Island. There, Strut and Robbie easily found the couple and their youngster. The crows learned how grumpy and listless Smokey had become. The monkeys said they often found the bear standing on all fours in the middle of his yard with his head hanging down, then slouching to his den and plopping down for a long time.

Strut was dismayed. The little cub he had known always liked to have fun and was eager for adventure. What a depressing place the zoo must be for him.

Furthermore, Strut informed the monkeys, Smokey had a propensity to be quite serious, like his mother, rather than lighthearted or outgoing by nature. Strut and the monkeys agreed, though, that Smokey had a great sense of humor. He liked to be surprised and laugh — at someone else's antics. He just wasn't a natural-born comic like crows or monkeys.

Trish, Trash, Robbie and Strut concluded that bears were very smart, like they themselves were, and learned new things all the time in the Wild. So it was up to tricksters like them to give the bear some tips. And they had to do it soon, Strut said. He confided to the monkeys that he and Robbie couldn't stay much beyond the upcoming winter. In spring they must return home to the mountains.

The animals plotted together: Smokey's world consisted of people coming to look at him, and he already begrudged their staring at him all day. You just couldn't *tell* a self-contained bear like Smokey to loosen up and engage his audience, like extroverted crows or monkeys could. The strong-minded bear would be stubborn about it. So he'd have to be *shown* how — without his knowing it. By the end of their visit with the monkeys, the crows knew they had to find a way to show Smokey how to fool people and make them laugh.

An opportunity arose the next afternoon when a girl walked by on the sidewalk holding an ice cream cone. Making sure Smokey was watching, Robbie crept up behind her and sang the Nashville song, "Hey, hey, good-lookin! Whatcha got cookin?" The girl wheeled around so fast that the scoop of ice cream plopped at her feet. With a saucy flick of her tail, Robbie looked right up into her eyes, went "Caw-caw," hopped to the ice cream and shoved her bill into it. People laughed, and Smokey thudded his paws against the bars. But that didn't show Smokey how he himself could make people laugh. They'd have to wait for another chance. It soon came.

Early one morning, Smokey heard a heavy truck and the sounds of men shouting at the far end of the zoo. Elephants blasted the air with trumpeting, and emitted low rumbling sounds that shook the ground. Something was up! The bear pleaded with Strut and Robbie to investigate and report back to him. He always yearned to know what was happening elsewhere in the zoo. They sped away and quickly returned with a vivid story. Two baby elephants had just arrived. The old female elephants, with tears streaming down their eyes, were touching the babies all over, blowing air on them, and cradling their trunks around the small bodies. The little elephants leaned against the big legs and snuffled.

The baby elephants were called Shanti (meaning Peace) and Ashok (meaning Without Sorrow). They were gifts to the United States from Jawaharlal Nehru, the first prime minister of the newly independent state of India.

Smokey was grateful to hear about the new arrivals, and explained to the crows that crowds would already be lining up outside the zoo gate clamoring to be admitted, like they had for him upon his arrival. Shortly afterward, the three friends saw exuberant crowds go by, largely bypassing the bear's enclosure. This continued through the next days. Only a few people trickled by to see Smokey, but as soon as they saw other people streaming ahead toward the newcomers, they rushed off.

The bear admitted to the crows that he missed people coming to see him. He had grown accustomed to being popular and being able to watch people, at least now and then. It was a way to pass the time. And it was like a game — to guess who might toss him popcorn.

So as soon as a few people did gather, the two crows seized the opportunity. They entertained the audience with antics, and Smokey was as quick to laugh as people were. And those who did stop remained quite a while, so other people noticed and joined them. This meant even more popcorn.

Strut and Robbie exchanged a quick glance. At last Smokey was motivated. They must take advantage of it.

Chapter 54

Corvids had at least an eight-million-year head start on people in the evolutionary race to intellectual superiority. This very likely meant that early people ... who did not experience a significant surge in brain growth until a mere two and a half million years ago, came face to face with savvy crows and ravens who could easily outwit them. Could this be why our ancestors so admired crows and ravens?
–John Marzluff and Tony Angell

Smokey and the crowd

The next time Smokey plodded back and forth along the bars in front of people, Strut sneaked behind him and lifted his feet high off the ground rolling his body from side to side in time with Smokey, exaggerating the bear's lumbering walk.

When the bear turned his head behind him and saw what the bird was doing, he slumped to the floor with a groan, and Strut echoed this too. People clapped, and the bear couldn't help but notice that Strut's antics held the audience's rapt attention.

What happened next was what the crows and monkeys had hoped for. Smokey gave Strut a sly look, and walked along the bars past the people, exaggerating his own lumbering walk and collapsed with a mighty groan. People showered Smokey with popcorn. The bear shot them a knowing look, and cast a self-satisfied glance at Strut.

Smokey no longer resented — quite so much — the way people watched him and pointed at him. At least he wasn't so helpless about it. Like a clown or mime, he found that all he had to do was be a bear, be himself — but a little more so — exaggerating whatever came naturally and concentrating so hard on what he was doing that people were drawn in.

The crows rejoiced to see Smokey's first original antic: He stopped abruptly at a piece of popcorn on the concrete, fixed his eyes on it as if amazed, crept up and nudged it with his paw, jumped back in alarm, then ever so slowly reached out his tongue and quickly slurped it up. He cast a sly smile at the crowd and got showered with laughter and treats.

Another time, when Smokey was feeling grouchy and had become annoyed at someone who dared to stare aggressively at him, he gave the person 'the eye,' let loose a wild roar like father bear, bluff-charged and banged on the bars, then abruptly sat with his legs in front of him and rocked, sending a happy grin as if to say, 'Fooled ya!' It turned out to be fun and lightened his mood. However, acting like a clown didn't come naturally, and, especially on dank and dark days, he preferred to be alone. Then he was content to stay just outside his den with his tail turned toward people.

Strut and Robbie were glad they'd inspired Smokey to perform some antics, so he wouldn't be quite so helpless during his lifetime at the zoo. Not only had they been good company for him during their stay, but they'd be leaving him with something to do for his future years, if only he had the spirit to keep it up after they were gone.

It seemed as if the summer slipped away quickly and soon ushered in the cool days of fall. Late autumn brought whiffs of smoke in the evenings, especially on weekends. One day, the smoke was stronger. Could there be a fire nearby? Whimpering for reassurance, Smokey asked Strut about it, and said he had smelled fires during the previous fall, too. So far, this kind of smoke had lasted just a short while and disappeared.

Robbie said, "Ah-ha! Like this time of year in Santa Fe: People rake up dry leaves in their yards and burn them in little fires until only ashes are left. It's nothing to worry about, Smokey. Something you can expect every fall." The bear felt a little foolish for a moment, then thanked her.

The deep blue skies of autumn developed into the gray skies of early winter. The bright array of leaf colors faded into browns and then fell to earth, leaving stark silhouettes of empty branches above. At night, without the cover of leaves, Strut and Robbie huddled uneasily in the crotch of a nearby tree trying to look inconspicuous to predators. Smokey sensed their fear and quickly offered them a safe place in his den at night. Up close, the bear noticed that his feathered friends were still thin from their trip and needed to be fattened up, so he told them they could share his kibble.

The shorter days of winter were not as bleak as those of the cub's first winter. The two crows regularly visited other zoo animals and came back in giddy good humor. Strut showed Smokey the funny way each animal moved, while Robbie imitated—and exaggerated—the sounds they made. The bear was delighted to find out more about his surroundings at the zoo.

One day as Strut reminisced about home, Smokey's jaw dropped in astonishment to hear Strut speak warmly of Ray Bell. The bear countered that he'd been bitterly disappointed in the game warden. It was still like a rock in his stomach. Why had Ray sent him to the zoo? And what kind of friend pins you down and rips bandages off you? Strut tried to explain that Ray must have done those things 'for the best,' but Smokey had harbored resentment too long to give it up easily. It grated on his ears to be told how good Ray had been to Strut, and the bear argued with the crow until Strut became so angry he flew off in a huff.

Smokey was left alone to grumble, not convinced that Ray Bell had meant well. His head lowered onto his paws. After a while, though, he found himself heaving a great sigh. As he lay there quietly, the knot in his stomach released. And in its place, the bear was left with a sharp sad feeling. Then hope crept in. Could Strut be right about Ray and his good intentions? How he longed to see Ray once more. If only he could look him in the eyes.

In the days that followed, Strut felt a more urgent need to help Smokey endure his life as a captive bear. The crow reported on the wild animals in Rock Creek Park going about their daily business, so Smokey could better imagine what was happening beyond his cage. What were the raucous sounds Smokey had heard that very morning? Across the road in the park, a blue jay had watched a squirrel hide nuts and, as soon as the squirrel's back was turned, had raided his cache making triumphant, smart-alecky sounds at the squirrel's fierce scolding.

While Smokey was snoozing, Robbie—who liked to surprise Smokey and make him laugh—would quietly sneak up behind him and make the screech of the front gate opening, or the shrill sounds of fire engine sirens or ambulances. She worked magic on him: At times, he found himself remembering and giggling, instead of grouching, when he heard the actual sounds waking him from sleep.

And, just as Robbie had shown her mate how to appreciate the beauty around them in Santa Fe, Strut, in turn, helped Smokey tune into the sounds of nature around the zoo. There were the rise and fall of birdsong in the dawn chorus, the improvised jazz of birds' answering trills, and the haunting echoes of night songs. Whenever the cub lapsed into looking at everything with a dull eye, or sank into a funk, Strut went on alert. He'd tug at Smokey's tail. "Caw! Caw! You lazy bum. Wake up. You'll miss all the action around here! Well, whatever action there *is*, anyway."

Robbie chimed in, "So you're stuck in a cage, Smokey. That's terrible enough. But look: It's open to the sky above. Be a cloud-watcher! The heavens are always putting on a new show. See those big clouds stacking up? And high above, the mackerel sky. Imagine being a bird swept into the swift wind making those streaks."

At the beginning of the crows' campaign to make him happy, their excessive cheerfulness had irritated Smokey. In the zoo, he'd been used to sighing and slouching down to doze, so he didn't have to hope or think or feel. But the two tsk-tsk'd him in the most annoying way when he acted morose, and imitated him outrageously. They were so determined to cheer him up that he was finally persuaded to be a good sport and join them in their fun, at least now and then.

As the last snow turned to slush and the weather warmed, Strut and Robbie at first tried to deny that winter had receded. They tried not to notice the obvious signs of spring. Trees were budding their lacy light-green leaves. Some trees were covered with white blossoms like popcorn. Others were blossoming in delicate yellow or soft pink. Day after day rains drenched the sodden earth until they could hear Rock Creek roar.

When flocks of migrating birds flew across the sky, Strut and Robbie's wings grew restless to begin their journey home. They couldn't explain why they had to go, and they tried to argue themselves out of leaving, but it was a strong instinct: They must fly home.

The crows knew they had accomplished their mission as best they could. They had found Smokey and shown him that he had good loyal friends. It saddened Strut, especially, to abandon the bear to his life in prison. At least, having reported on the surrounding zoo and park, they had widened his world to interesting soundscapes and scentscapes so he wouldn't be quite so bored and could better endure his life. Most important, he'd be left with good memories of their presence and the comfort of knowing that the two would always remember him. And maybe, now and then, he would not be such a helpless object. He knew how to surprise people, make them laugh, and elicit treats.

Days passed as Strut and Robbie procrastinated. More flocks of birds flew by. Others nearby built nests. The crows became homesick. They yearned for their own flocks back West where they belonged. Soon the trees were in full leaf. The two crows averted their eyes from the bear. How could they desert Smokey who had suffered so many losses in his life? Finally, one morning after the zookeeper left, Strut screwed up his courage and announced, "Smokey, we have to tell you something."

The bear, who'd been eating his kibble, raised his head and looked at his friends in alarm, then turned away. Strut plunged ahead and broke the news that he and Robbie must soon leave. At first the bear snorted and huffed as if to shake off the message, then walked into his den and lay down with his tail toward them.

Smokey disappointed

Strut hung his head. Robbie, who had come to love Smokey, lowered hers too. The pair stayed silent a long time. There wasn't anything to say. After a while, Robbie called to the bear, "We're not leaving right away, Smokey! We'll stay until the dandelions bloom, so we can fetch you a big pile of them." The cub grunted, "Eh," so softly they could barely hear him.

Several days later Smokey found a heap of yellow

dandelions outside his den with a sprinkling of pinkish-purple clover blossoms on top. The cub had never before in his life hesitated to gobble up treats right away, but the sight made him moan. Strut and Robbie stood on the concrete beside the pile, their eyes downcast. The bear's heart fell.

The moment had come. Passing by the flowers, Smokey lowered his body to sit and face his friends. "Huh-huh. How I hate to see you go! I'll miss you so much. But I'll never forget what good friends you are."

Smokey then swallowed hard and bravely declared, "If I can't be free and go back home, at least I'm glad *you* can go home." The cub's head drooped and he mumbled a question. "I probably won't ever see you again, will I?"

"Caah . . . No, dear ole Smokey, I don't expect so," Strut said.

"Then this is good-bye . . . Watch out for hawks. And have a safe trip." Smokey's eyes misted, and he said in a little voice, "Say hello to the honey tree back home." Strut nodded solemnly, and the crows flapped their wings and flew into the air. They circled above him and glided down close for a last look. Then they departed. Smokey watched until the two black specks disappeared into the distant sky.

The next day, whenever Smokey happened to look at the empty place on the small ledge in his den or other places where he was used to seeing Strut and Robbie, he felt a sharp pang. He retreated to his cave to shut out the world. Hunkering down in the dark, he tried to recall the good times so he could bask in the afterglow of his friends' presence.

During the rest of the spring and early summer, whenever crows alighted on a tree, his heart leaped until he saw they were only local crows.

One afternoon, in late summer, Smokey was indulging in his new habit of watching the clouds. He imagined pointing out a great stack of puffy clouds to Robbie. Then he pictured Strut lumbering behind him imitating his walk with a cocky look on his face. And his chest melted at the memories.

Eventually, though, upon seeing a flock of birds fly by, he felt only a wistful twinge in his chest at missing his friends. It was a great relief that memories of the crows no longer brought an ache of sadness to his throat. But their visit and departure now left him nothing to hope for. How was he supposed to go on, now that he didn't have the sweet longing that Strut would appear out of the sky someday?

Why couldn't he go home where he belonged? He hated this prison! It was as if a dam had burst with explosive force. Smokey snorted, "HUH-HUH!" He ran over and lunged at the tree trunk, swung his arm back and whopped it as hard as he could. THWACK! THWACK! THWACK! At last his leather-hardened paws became sore. Breathing hard, he ran to his den and slammed himself down.

The next morning Smokey awoke with more energy than he'd had for a long time. It was angry energy. He marched out of his den, sputtering loudly with irritation. The wild whooping of the gibbons made him clench his teeth. He paced back and forth ready to grimace at the coming crowds. The bear looked up the sidewalk for the zookeeper. Late again with breakfast. How he'd like to clack his teeth and charge him when he arrived.

Dazzle pranced up to the gate. Smokey didn't deign to look his way. Why should he kowtow to that pompous peacock to make the bird divulge any news? What an egotist compared to Strut, who happily reported all the scuttlebutt around the zoo, and even added his own humorous asides. How humorless Dazzle was compared to Robbie, who delighted in imitating other animals to make Smokey laugh.

Freddie slipped through the fence, nosed his way along the wall, and stood in a tentative way, facing Smokey expectantly. That selfish, crafty rat—no substitute for his generous crow friends! The bear stared angrily at Freddie who turned around and beat a hasty retreat.

As Smokey lurched around and started to stomp back to his cave, Sophia, his pigeon friend, appeared on the ground ahead. He came to an abrupt halt in order not to squash her with his front paw.

What was wrong with the pigeon that she should suddenly block his way? He paused and looked inquiringly at her. It puzzled him that Sophia was the only creature around who never made him mad. She had an unobtrusive presence that somehow lent him a sense of well-being. He watched as the pigeon proceeded to make contented garbling songs to herself as she searched for tidbits on the concrete.

She seemed so much herself. Something about her calm, self-contained way resonated with a place inside him, like a shaft of sun might penetrate a dark place in the forest. She must be very wise, he thought. Certainly wiser than Mr. Dazzle. And wiser, he thought, than he himself.

That afternoon, the bear lay at the entrance of his den facing his concrete yard. A breeze came up. Past his nose wafted the distinctive smell of dung from the Hoofed Ones. He knew right away exactly whose scent it was, for during Strut's visit, the crow had brought him some straw to sniff from the camel's yard. Then he heard a sharp "tik-tik" from the lawn beyond his enclosure. And he knew who that was! It was the same scolding sound Robbie had imitated so well when the crows related the story of their encounter with an annoyed robin on their trip.

His nose stretched high and searched the rich aromas of flowers from Rock Creek Park that floated his way, like the honeysuckle fragrance he knew from his own excursions there as a small cub, and other scents that were identifiable from the array of flowers the crows had brought him to eat.

A realization burst upon him. Although he might never venture beyond the bars, now he could at least read the smallest clues in the air if he really concentrated. His good friends Strut and Robbie had left him the gift of a wider world. It was as if their presence would always be with him.

In the quiet days that followed, he became more reconciled to his life.

Smokey enjoys a good scratch

As the long summer receded, trees began to turn color again. One day the cooler breezes of early autumn descended and Smokey's legs became terribly restless. He felt hungrier than ever, and felt an overwhelming urge to move around. How he would like to forage deep in the forest of Rock Creek Park! He began walking along the fence for hours, stopping only to gorge on food. Soon the bear kept a steady pace most of the day, along the same path, his footfalls in the same places, as if he were in the grip of a strange trance. Smokey hardly looked up at visitors, stopping only when he smelled a food offering. He'd scarf it down and resume his habit of pacing.

Weeks stretched into late fall, heralding the early days of wintry weather, and he paced endlessly. It turned cold. Few visitors came, and those who did seemed disappointed in him, and, clasping their coats to their necks, soon left.

Chapter 55

Of the sweets of adversity, and let me say that those are not numerous, I have found the sweetest, the most precious of all, is the lesson I learned on the value of kindness.
–Daw Aung San Suu Kyi

The most touching moments of our existence leave us without words. It's very difficult for a mime to lie, because for lying the words are missing.
–Marcel Marceau

It was a cool drizzly day when something unexpected came to change Smokey's world at the zoo. The bear should have registered that something was afoot as soon as the zoo director Doc Mann and his wife Lucile appeared at the side gate very early one morning. At first, the bear continued his grim routine past them: seventeen steps along the front fence swinging his head and turning, then seventeen steps back, in endless repetition. Now and then, though, he did steal a glance at them as he passed.

With the couple was someone dressed in the gray overalls of a zookeeper. However, this one seemed different. She was female, for one thing. Eventually Smokey stopped his pacing, rose upright, arms hanging loose in front of him, and took a few steps in her direction. He turned his head from side to side to catch her scent. She smelled good and wore a small faded scarf holding back thick gray-streaked hair that tumbled almost to her shoulders. A scent-memory stirred. Was this the same woman the director had brought by his cage a long time ago, the one he'd liked, who had tossed a carrot in his pool? Maybe so.

All three stood relaxed, resting their eyes on him in a

respectful and friendly way. Smokey was hungry, and in no mood to be the center of attention unless they were going to give him food. He heaved a sigh and turned to resume plodding back and forth. But something about the way they were standing caught his attention. They were leaning toward him with such interest that he sensed something unusual was about to happen.

Curiosity overcame him, "Eh! Eh!" escaped his throat, and he galumphed closer to them. Doc Mann and Lucile chortled happily. With open palms indicating the third person, they presented the plump woman to him, saying, "We brought you a present: It's *Tilly*!" Somewhat hopeful, but mainly wary, Smokey braced himself for another photographic session with endless popping of flashbulbs. Not seeing any photographers, he turned his attention to the woman. Would she suddenly stare, abruptly thrust her arms toward him, and emit high-pitched squeals?

Continuing to stand easily with her shoulders relaxed, the woman gazed softly in his direction. Her cheeks grew more rounded as she broke into a warm smile. The bear ambled closer, stood on his hind legs and sniffed her body scent. No 'fear sweat' or 'threat sweat' like that of tense substitute keepers. It was just 'contented sweat.' Her clothes gave off the aroma of straw and dusty earth, and the smell on her arms reminded him of Ruth's skin, overlaid with a slightly soapy aroma mingled with a faint tinge of lavender. She smelled especially good up close. She made soft lilting sounds, and he tilted his head toward her.

Doc Mann was saying to Tilly, "He looks healthy, so maybe he's just been depressed. Or bored. And lately, rather disgruntled. We're concerned about him. I know how bears travel great distances in the wild to forage and naturally need lots of exercise. But I'm worried how incessant his pacing is. He's started again. It must be a hard habit to break. It's most of the day, like he's a robot, and can't stop."

He continued. "I'm getting complaints from Smokey's fans.

They're wondering whether he's terribly unhappy to be acting like such a zombie. He's not just 'a bear' to them. They know *him*, in particular, and they care about him like their own dog or cat. They've been seeing newspaper photos of him since he was a little tyke and have been watching him grow up here. And he stands for something too. So let's hope your way with animals is just what he needs."

The man paused a moment. "You know, the traditional way here in the States is for zoo personnel to keep their distance from animals, to remain objective and scientific, rather than *relate* to them as individuals. Of course keepers need to keep a careful distance from the large or aggressive ones. But I've heard *you* have worked close-up in Europe with the big ones like giraffes and elephants, even polar bears. So we hope you might be able to build Smokey's trust and give him a better life."

"I hope so! Look at those dull eyes. As if he has to pace like that to escape into some kind of trance. To escape his boring life. An animal so intelligent and curious . . . to be in a cage, poor fellow. Nothing to do, nothing to look forward to, day after day. Well, something has to be done about that!"

Lucile broke in, "We couldn't agree more. And there are some things you ought to know about *this* bear. He was wild-born. And when he was tiny, only four pounds, he was orphaned by a fire in the West and badly burned. For six weeks or so he recuperated in a household with a family. But in the course of his stay, Smokey had to be manhandled by the men in the family changing his bandages. Apparently he fought back and bit them whenever he could.

"However, it's a plus for you that the cub was quite amenable to being bottle-fed by the woman of the house and even the young daughter. So when he came here, at eleven pounds, both of us made a point of handling him some, though we regret that we didn't keep him in our house for a while, like we usually do with orphans. It's because the public, and also the press, were clamoring to see him. From the beginning here he has behaved surprisingly well with the vet. The main keeper for Smokey has always kept a distance from him, and there haven't been any bad incidents."

Doc suggested, "Take your time to get acquainted and maybe you can work your magic with Smokey. Keep us posted on how it goes. You know, he's quite special to us, and a very special bear to the whole country. Everybody knows about Smokey Bear."

Tilly asked what made him so 'special' here, reminding Doc that she'd been living in Europe all this time. Doc explained that Smokey had already done a remarkable job preventing forest fires in the country. So many visitors had seen and cared about the burned cub—and with Smokey Bear public service ads and posters all over reminding them—that people had dramatically reduced the fires they'd been causing in the wilderness, cutting down on things like throwing lighted cigarettes out car windows and leaving campfires to smolder.

The woman replied, "Well, I'll do my best with him. He certainly deserves it!"

By now, Smokey had stopped his pacing, and stood still, curious about how attentive they were to each other and how earnest their voices were. From time to time the woman rested her eyes on him, deep in thought. The interchange evidently ended when he saw Doc and Lucile smile at her and shake hands. The couple turned and gave the bear a nod. Smokey watched the two walk away until they were out of sight, wondering what was in store for him.

The bear looked intently at the woman who remained outside his front bars. She stood at ease on sturdy legs, her eyes casually looking in his direction, and he dropped to all fours to take her in. A faint trace of lavender reached his nose, reminding him of Ruth and his early days in Santa Fe. His heart leapt. Would this woman be staying? Or was she just another temporary keeper until his regular one returned?

Catching his eye and holding it for a moment, Tilly slowly pulled a carrot out of her baggy pants, squatted on her haunches, and grinned as she showed it to him. Suddenly moaning in hope and fear, Smokey scampered behind his tree and peered out at her. She kept sweet-talking, and when he finally moseyed over, she poked the carrot through the bars. Smokey gently received the end of it with soft lips, and chomped it down. She didn't leave, but remained there.

The next thing he knew, Tilly had sat down on her side of the fence and was humming to him. He sat down too, with his legs in front of him. Could this woman really be a zookeeper? She was very different from his main keeper and the occasional substitutes. None had spoken to him or seemed interested in him. This one appeared more personal, like his human family had been. Like a friendly animal might be.

Out of her pocket came a red apple. She took a bite herself, and held it toward him for a sniff, waved it a moment as she laughed, then tossed it through the bars. It bounced across the concrete into the pool. He capered after it, plunged into the pool and played bob-the-apple with his paw. He could hear her laughing. After eating the apple, Smokey turned around in the middle of the pool to see what she'd do next.

With a matter-of-fact air, as if they were already comfortable old friends, the woman clicked the gate open, entered slowly, paused awhile, then detoured smoothly past his pool, talking calmly to him the entire time. A few strides brought her to his food bucket, where she dumped something.

Smokey had stretched his neck and raised his nose to savor the woman's distinctive clothes-smell as she went by. It was a pleasing medley of sun-dried wood and dank-earth. By the time he climbed out of the water, though, the gate had clicked shut and she was gone.

The bear shook his sopping fur as he ran over to the food bucket, his mouth dripping at the prospect of something special. At first it smelled like the same old kibble again, but what were those red things sprinkled on top? He reached with his loose lips, rolled one inside his mouth with his tongue and enjoyed the sweet-sour tang of dried cranberries. This keeper was different! He liked her and chuffed at her receding back. He hoped she would continue to be his keeper.

Each day after that, he eagerly awaited Tilly's arrival. He recognized her easy-going body language from quite a distance. What a change she brought from the dull routine he'd been used to. She came early with his breakfast of kibble, which always included a few buried treats. And she made unexpected visits during the day. Like the burned children used to do, she enticed him to the fence with a melodic voice and dancing eyes as if he was special.

When she opened the gate, he'd cry, "Uh, uh!" She'd show him her latest surprise: peaches, strawberries and blueberries, or sweet potatoes and other vegetables. He'd smack his lips and receive each prize. There were often challenging things to tussle with, such as coconuts in their tough husks and strong-smelling food tightly embedded in logs. One time she tossed him a large meaty bone to gnaw. He spent days happily crunching it and sucking the fatty marrow.

One afternoon when Tilly passed by empty-handed, Smokey flattened his ears and stared straight at her with indignation, lips pointed in a pout. He spun around and trudged to his cave. The bear loudly sighed and lay down with his tail toward her. A little later, when she returned and cheerfully called out, he huffed with annoyance.

She remained until he deigned to look at her out of the corner of his eyes. This brought something small rolling across the concrete. He flinched, then curiosity won out. At first Smokey sniffed and mouthed the small round treat, squished it with his paw, and smelled it again. With his floppy lips he gobbled it down and dashed to enclose the rest as they rained onto the concrete. He caught her eyes and smiled. He loved grapes! And they were friends again.

The waning days of fall descended, then winter was upon him. Unlike wild bears back home, Smokey continued eating in winter and was not in the habit of hibernating, only napping more than usual. He always eagerly anticipated Tilly's arrival.

Smokey was surprised the first time the zookeeper climbed over the boulders at the back of his yard. He watched her intently. What could she be doing over in that part of his territory? The bear soon found that he had to work most of the day climbing up over large rocks to find raisins and nuts wedged between the boulders or tucked under rocks, and, hardest of all to retrieve, pumpkin seeds sprinkled here and there. She even smeared peanut butter on some boulders, which soon attracted lines of ants for him to eat. And once, when a squirrel hunted among the boulders for nuts, he caught it, tore the animal apart and ate it with great satisfaction.

He could detect Tilly's scent from quite a distance. One day, from afar, he also sniffed something sweet. The zookeeper set down a large bowl. Smokey sunk his snout into cold ice cream and gobbled up the most unusual treat he'd ever tasted.

And, to his further delight, Tilly came to remember his favorite flavor. It was strawberry. She brought it time and again. Whenever she drew into sight, the keeper was always talking with him and he came to relish her voice.

In his ecstasy of eating Tilly's wonderful treats, especially ice cream, Smokey knew for sure that she had a kind heart. Once, while she was still holding the bowl of ice cream before setting it down, he slurped it all up, and then, quite impulsively, gave Tilly's cheek a wet nuzzle. He met her surprised eyes with a big smile.

Furthermore, before she left at the end of her visits, she often left something interesting for him. Once it was a small empty beer keg he could play with in the water. Another time she brought a short log he could roll on the ground, chew, and finally shred with his claws.

With Tilly as his keeper, the unrelenting tedium of his long days at the zoo was alleviated to some extent. He still felt the need to pace, but not as often or at such length. He had other things to do now. The zoo was still a boring place, all in all, but he was more contented than before.

As soon as Smokey's ears pricked at Tilly's approach, he'd

bolt to the bars to greet her. He'd raise his head and sniff her, his eyes sparkling and a goofy smile on his face. Although Smokey still acted entirely like a bear and never tried to actually please her, in fact huffing if she displeased him, in time he learned to trust her and to read her like a familiar friend by her posture, the tone of her sounds and even a few of her words.

Being in her presence daily, as well as being busy foraging for food among the boulders, brought back long-forgotten memories of his freedom as a wild bear. It felt good to picture the old days. How much he missed his lost home in the mountains where he watched the goings-on of other animals, and foraged with his mother. And he cherished the memory of being part of the Bell family, free to explore the house and big yard. Smokey sometimes yearned for Ruth and her daughter Judy. He thought wistfully of the old days when he took walks with the youngster Don, chased around the house with the spaniel Jet and visited his cat pal Lightning.

Smokey reminisced about playing in the yard with the cowboy Ray. He began to wonder whether the crow Strut had been right after all, that Ray had not been trying to hurt him. During the next months, as the sight of Tilly raised his spirits, he longed to once again see his human family from Santa Fe, especially Judy. He sometimes searched the crowds in hopes of spotting the little girl or other members of the Bell family.

Eight years had slowly crept by since the bear's arrival at the zoo, when an event in the outer world unexpectedly made one of Smokey's wishes come true.

On the eighth anniversary of the bear's ordeal-by-fire, May 8, 1958, the first Golden Smokey, a foot-high statue like an Oscar, had been awarded to the village of Capitan, New Mexico. It was Judy Bell who was chosen to receive it on behalf of the children of America, and it was to be presented to her by Dwight Eisenhower, president of the United States, on the White House lawn.

At age twelve now, Judy had become a quiet teenager. Despite being shy, and the fact that her parents couldn't afford the airfare to accompany her, she was persuaded to travel to

Washington on her own. For the ceremony, Judy chose her blue "squaw dress," a typical dress-up outfit for girls in the West. Her mother, who had Cherokee heritage, liked the choice, and her father, Ray, thought it especially appropriate because Smokey was a New Mexican bear.

However, upon arrival at the White House, Judy was abruptly informed that White House protocol dictated that in a ceremony with a president of the United States, any girl honoree must wear a white dress. Alone and embarrassed, Judy nevertheless rose to the occasion, not only as the daughter of two independent-minded westerners but also as a proud

Judy and Ike

representative of New Mexico. She prevailed in her confrontation with the protocol staff, and wore her blue western dress as well as her moccasins.

On the White House lawn, President Eisenhower

graciously beamed at Judy, warmly put his arm around her shoulder, and handed her the Golden Smokey Statuette. It was a special thrill, but not the main event for Judy. She went straight from the White House to see the bear she had known and loved as a four-year-old.

Golden statue in hand, she hurried through the zoo to his enclosure. However, when she reached within six feet of the fence, the keeper signaled for her to wait a moment. Tilly said, "Remember, he's a grown bear now. Not a little cub anymore. He's over three hundred pounds and very powerful. He's going to loom over you when he's standing up. We can't predict what he might do."

Dozing near his cave, Smokey jerked his head awake. He thought he had detected a familiar scent from long ago. Could it possibly be the special presence he'd known back when he'd been so sick and hungry after the fire? His throat tightened so much that it hurt, remembering his many years at the zoo, watching little girls approach, then feeling disappointed that none turned out to be his special little girl.

His nose, though, indicated it might be true this time. Smokey scrambled to his feet, and paused, perplexed for a moment at seeing a teenager. Could it really be Judy, the one he'd longed to see until he had lost hope? Hardly daring to hope again, Smokey padded to the front of his cage. He sniffed deeply and gazed intently through the bars. Could it really be the girl from his early days? He remembered Judy holding his bottle while he was cradled in the mother's lap, at the house where he lived with Ray, Don, and his dog friend Jet.

She smiled at him and hummed the same way she always had when they were together. He snuffled to inhale her airborne scent, and opened his mouth to fully sense it.

For a brief moment he stood confused. It was, indeed, Judy, but she no longer looked like the little four-year-old he had known. The girl was now as tall as he was as he stood upright, and gazed back at her across the short distance. From his chest arose little coos and chirps, summoning her closer to the bars.

Judy gasped a breath, and flashed him a quick smile. Then the calm and gentle girl he remembered looked different. She stiffened her body as she turned her head toward his keeper, and addressed her in an earnest voice, "You must let me go up to the bars! I *know* Smokey. You can see *he* still knows *me*. I know it'll be all right."

She waited in her rigid stance until Tilly nodded to her. But when the photographers burst forward, the keeper halted Judy a moment with her palm, while she quickly instructed them to wait until Judy had a chance to greet the bear. Then they could get their photographs.

Smokey watched the youngster rush to him and duck under the horizontal barrier to reach the bars of his cage. He drank in the welcome scent of the girl's breath. "Uh! Uh!" Her eyes were indeed Judy's, and the face held Judy's familiar warmth.

He sought the teenager's eyes as she said, "Oh, Smokey. I just knew you'd recognize me, even after all these years." Smokey's throat ached with a deep longing as he held his paw against the bars. And through the bars he felt Judy press the pad of his paw with a finger.

They gazed at each other a long time. He didn't understand her words, but he understood her feelings as she spoke. "I've been worrying about you ever since you left, but there wasn't anything I could do. I'm sorry, Smokey. But I'm glad you're looking so good! Do you remember when you played with Barbara and me on her living room floor? We still remember *you*. I can't wait to get back and tell her that I saw you and you're okay."

Judy lingered awhile, reminiscing, as they took each other in. Then, composed like a dignified Westerner, she turned around for the photographers to snap pictures of her and Smokey. One man handed her a poster to hold while they all busily flashed their cameras.

Later, Judy was glad she had posed with the poster. At one point Smokey had reached through the bars and playfully

Judy poses with Smokey

Smokey "signs" Judy's poster

slashed the cardboard, so she was able to bring back to Barbara and the village of Capitan a souvenir of her visit to Washington. It was the bear's claw marks on a Smokey Bear poster.

Weeks passed, and, though Smokey looked hopefully at teenage girls who came up the sidewalk, Judy never reappeared. Once he was resigned to her absence, he looked wistfully for her older brother, Don, who took him on walks. Perhaps the parents Ruth or Ray would appear. He still harbored reservations about whether Ray was a friend. The bear recalled the times his body had been manhandled during bandaging. Resentment still simmered in his chest.

Then, one afternoon, while fooling around on the steep rock wall in the back of his den, Smokey tore his front claw. His foot hurt, and, as soon as Tilly came with food, he walked up to her. He sat down, whimpered like a small cub, and dangled his front paw in front of her. When she didn't respond, he impatiently mouthed his paw and locked his eyes on hers in a meaningful stare.

Murmuring reassurances, the woman lowered her plump body to the concrete and sat across from him. She slowly extended her hand near his front foot, and after a moment's hesitation he rested his footpad on her palm. Tilly clucked to see how his claw was torn a bit askew from its bloody base. The bear felt in good hands, and his wide eyes conveyed his faith in her. Tilly carefully withdrew her hand, and, as she left, her voice promised her return.

Tilly soon came back accompanied by the vet, whom Smokey readily recognized from the periodic check-ups. After a few moments of letting Smokey become accustomed to his presence, the vet had Tilly lift the bear's paw in her hand. He carefully examined the base of the claw as he moved the long crooked claw a smidgeon to each side. "Not torn completely loose. The base is strong. I'll just douse it to clean it up."

The vet opened a bottle in front of Smokey. The bear shook his head at the noxious smell. After a while, unresisting, Smokey let the vet bring the bottle close to his paw, which was still in Tilly's open palm. But at the first sting of antiseptic, he jerked away. He carefully scrutinized their faces as Tilly and the vet coaxed him anew.

Tilly offered her outstretched palm again until he voluntarily extended his forearm. The vet held out a treat and the bear ate it. True to his character, once Smokey made a decision, he kept it. He allowed the vet to drench the wound, wrap gauze around the paw, and apply tape.

The vet remarked to Tilly. "He should heal quickly, much quicker than humans with a torn nail. He'll probably chew off the tape and gauze to lick his paw. So be it. It's unlikely to get infected, but just keep an eye on it."

Smokey sniffed his bandage. Both people gave him benign smiles. "Eh-eh," Smokey exclaimed, and stood back to regard them. Then his eyes shifted beyond them, as if pondering. The familiar smell of antiseptic reminded him of his early days at the home of Ray Bell back in Santa Fe. Was this what Ray had done? Had he meant well too? "Huh!" he grunted. Then he tossed his head and let out a short huff. No! He had suffered too much in Ray's hands, and he'd been holding that grudge too long to give it up easily. But a seed of doubt was planted that day.

Chapter 56

We all know just how difficult it is for most of us to admit that we have been wrong. It is perhaps the most difficult thing in the world — in almost every language the most difficult words are "I am sorry" . . . In forgiving, people are not being asked to forget. On the contrary, it is important to remember . . . Forgiveness does not mean condoning what has been done. It means taking what happened seriously and not minimizing it; drawing out the sting in the memory that threatens to poison our entire existence.
–Desmond Tutu

Four years later, in the fall of 1962, Smokey was a mature twelve-year old bear when he saw an unusually large number of people gather in front of his enclosure. A bunch of photographers milled among the crowd. Everyone's anticipation reached a high pitch as a truck pulled up. Smokey stalked this way and that, one ear pricked forward, the other back.

A cowboy stepped down. It was as if a thunderclap riveted the bear's attention. Smokey's pulse roiled. He felt terribly confused, torn between hope and disappointment. He dashed behind his tree and peered out. The man ambled closer. The bear's nostrils flared and his mouth opened to taste the distinctive scent of sweat-and-leather. He ventured a few steps out from behind the tree to look at the man and was flooded with a torrent of feelings.

Smokey recognized the familiar silver-gray cowboy hat, the jaunty rolling walk, and the boots. And that special broad grin as Ray Bell vaulted over the outer barrier and came up to the bars just outside his cage. Smokey hesitated just a moment, then clamored over to him, emitting the same eager sounds he'd made as a little cub, "Eh, eh!"

With his bowed legs apart, Ray put his hands on his hips and laughed heartily. "Hey-boy-hardy! We sure do remember each other, don't we? What a big rascal you've become!"

Ray and Smokey reconciled

He threw Smokey a wink. "Just wait till you see what I've brought you. It's from your neck of the woods in New Mexico. Around a hundred pounds, not much compared to your weight. What are you, Smokey, three hundred?" He returned to the pickup, reached into the front window and retrieved a heavy leather strap. He shaped it into a wide loop, then strode to the back of the truck.

Smokey noisily breathed in a strong scent that emanated from the cage there. He watched intently. The next moment Ray came back toward him leading a big four-legged animal whose fur sparkled golden in the sunlight.

After a dozen years being bombarded by strange pungent smells and odd screeches from myriad creatures at the zoo, Smokey could hardly contain his excitement. This one was indeed very familiar.

Ray opened the front gate next to his, and led the bear into the adjoining enclosure. He unclasped her leash. "This will give you two a chance to get used to each other." He shot Smokey a stern look. "Now, don't you threaten this nice female like you did that sweet little cub Ruby! You be nice to her."

Goldie

Goldie Bear stood calmly next to Ray inside her gate, blinking in the sunlight, swaying back and forth on her four legs as if to get her bearings on solid ground. Then she abruptly made a bee-line for the far end of the enclosure. En route, not recognizing the water, she tripped into her pool. Goldie panicked, her head went under, and she came up coughing and thrashing.

Instantly, Ray threw his wallet on the ground and cannon-balled into the water with a great splash. With his hands cupped, he immediately cradled Goldie's head above water, careful of her clawing feet. Soothing talk calmed her, and soon they both climbed out.

The golden creature shook herself, and drenched Smokey with airborne smells. Excited, he rose on his hind legs and swung his head from side to side with his mouth open. The supersensitive roof of his mouth caught the distinctive smell of wet fur laced with the sweet intoxicating scent of resinous juniper and sage.

A smile of recognition burst across his face. He was flooded with memories of his mountain and the plants he'd known so well. But a moment later he hung his head and whimpered "uh-uh," his throat tight with longing for his old home.

When he looked up, he saw Ray sit down to work his high-top cowboy boots loose and dump out the water. The man's eyes were sparkling as he laughed, and Smokey recalled how he'd always liked the man's hearty laugh.

Smokey looked at him intently. Seeing Ray up close in person like this, not just the dark shadow in his memory, his heavy resentment somehow dissolved, and his chest felt lighter. Smokey squeaked out a barely audible "eh-eh," and Ray glanced up at him from the other enclosure.

Then, after lingering awhile longer with Goldie Bear, Ray looked over in Smokey's direction again. He remembered how the bear had hesitated to greet him the last time he'd briefly stopped by the zoo years before. Would it be different this time? The bear probably still begrudged being manhandled during the bandaging. He himself winced at the memory of that little cub deliberately lying in wait around the house for a chance to bite him with those sharp teeth.

But he also smiled to himself at the memory of Smokey's wild exuberance and plucky play-fighting with the puppy Jet. And, in his mind's eye, he remembered the forest where Smokey deserved to have lived out his life, instead of being in a cage all these years. Ray looked down and cussed under his breath. Then he said, "I'm sorry, Smokey. It's awfully unfair. But you've been sacrificed for a good cause, know it or not. You've prevented a lot of wildfires that would've ruined forests and hurt a lot of wildlife." He muttered, "Anyway, you were too young to survive on your own. You would've starved or been eaten by a predator."

The cowboy strolled over to Smokey's cage and, arms akimbo, leaned against the front bars. After a moment's hesitation, it was as if Smokey's whole being was drawn forward to stick his nose close to Ray's elbow and drink in the familiar smell of his oily, salty sweat. Smokey's eyes looked intently, then softened, and his mouth dropped open in a smile. The man's eyes twinkled. "So you finally forgive me, huh? Well, pal, I forgive you, too, for all those bites you gave me."

Then the bear blinked his eyes, whirled his hulk away to the back of his cage, paused, and slowly turned to take a long, wistful look at Ray. It had been a short, but wonderful reunion.

From the back of his cage, Smokey heard the man walk away, the truck door close, and the vehicle start up. Like Judy before him, Ray, too, left, and Smokey didn't expect him to return. He snorted and gazed far away.

Meanwhile, the golden-colored bear had scampered right up to the fence between the enclosures. She pushed her snout against the bars to wiggle her nose and snuffle his scent. Suddenly tense, his ears partly flattened in fear, Smokey was ready to roar at the intruder. Yet curiosity won out, and Smokey shuffled a bit closer, his neck swaying to catch a special aroma wafting his way. It was, indeed, the familiar fragrance of balsam firs he'd known in the mountains long ago. He quickened his pace a few steps, stopped short of the fence, and thrust his head forward to better catch the full medley of the animal's smells.

He sensed that she was female. Smokey opened his mouth to drink in her scent, his loose lower lip dripping saliva. She emitted an encouraging "eh-eh," and the familiar yearning sound echoed his earliest memories in the cave of his brother and sister and mother. She was, indeed, a bear like them!

In his excitement, he eagerly flung himself against the iron bars. She flinched and backed off. Smokey stopped, bewildered, and watched her. After a long wait, Goldie Bear cautiously approached the fence again and looked inquiringly at him. She seemed friendly. He stayed where he was. Her scent was enticing. A strong impulse soon prompted him to approach, but this time he did so carefully. Up close, he loomed over her and realized that she wasn't a threat, Goldie, at a year and a half, being only a hundred pounds, not even half his size at age twelve.

He grunted to acknowledge her presence, and she grunted back. Goldie put on a playface and frolicked a few steps to the side. Smokey tossed his head and cavorted on his side of the fence. How amazing to find a creature whose sounds and smells, and whose ways of moving and reacting, were like his. She was the same kind of bear he was!

Smokey could hardly contain himself at this happy discovery. But, close on its heels, came a wave of pent-up sadness at having been deprived of his mother and the other cubs. Bewildered at being sad and happy at the same time, he retreated to his cave in confusion.

With experienced eyes, his keeper Tilly carefully watched the bears for days. They showed some fascination with each other but mostly nonchalance, as if both were used to their independent ways. This boded well for a joint enclosure, so the keeper proceeded to test whether it might work to put the bears together, or would there be problems, especially about food.

When Tilly observed how patiently Goldie always waited for her kibble, the zookeeper thought the time had come to move Smokey's food bucket closer to the single fence that separated the two enclosures. She fed him first, then went through the common gate between the enclosures and fed Goldie Bear nearby on her side of the fence. Gradually, with great patience and close observation, Tilly came to believe it was worth a calculated risk to let the two be together in a joint enclosure.

The next day, after the bears had each eaten especially large breakfasts, Tilly stood outside their side-by-side enclosures until both bears were focused on her. Talking calmly to each one, she entered Smokey's enclosure and opened the gate between the two bears.

At first the bears stayed in their own territories. Showing great restraint and diplomacy, Smokey sidled into Goldie's area at an angle, and, casting an inquiring look in the female bear's direction, wandered past her pool to explore every nook and cranny of her enclosure. As he roamed closer to her, he feigned interest at sniffing the ground while casting sidelong glances at Goldie. He stopped abruptly to intently inhale her fresh scat, his nostrils flaring and his mouth dripping with saliva.

Then Smokey was drawn to her tree. Facing it, he stretched as tall as he could and slashed his claw marks high on the trunk with a great feeling of satisfaction. Finding the rough bark to his liking, he rubbed his back against it to leave a scent-mark, and then scraped his back up and down for a long scratch.

Meanwhile, Goldie, aware of his every move, and seeing him preoccupied, slipped into his territory and conducted her own investigation. After a while, they amicably wended their separate ways back to their respective territories and retreated to their own dens, establishing that both preferred their own territory and privacy.

Tilly made sure there was ample kibble to avoid contentions over food, and in the days that followed, under the zookeeper's anxious gaze and careful steps, at first keeping the bears separate for feeding, then leaving the connecting gate open but using separate places for food — the two bears agreed on an arrangement. Tilly had heard that Smokey had been accustomed back in Santa Fe to eating alongside his generous dog friend Jet. Although he was big and assertive enough to bump Goldie aside and eat all her food, Tilly was not surprised that he only sampled her food, which Goldie amiably allowed.

It wasn't long before the bears roamed the joint space with ease. Like adult black bears that go their separate ways in the wild except for brief mating, they were not particularly chummy. Yet they often noticed what the other was doing, which broke the monotony of their lone existence. If Goldie Bear discovered something of interest, it piqued Smokey Bear's curiosity so he'd mosey over to investigate.

In the coming months, they occasionally rubbed heads in greeting, and got along enough that the zoo staff and public were hopeful that they might mate later in spring and have a cub together.

Goldie and Smokey

Chapter 57

Smokey awaits Tilly

We will be known forever by the tracks we leave.
–Dakota proverb

During the late fall and winter, people flocked to see Smokey Bear and Goldie Bear, intrigued with how the two bears got along — or didn't. They hoped the two would mate and have a Little Smokey. What they saw was Goldie being friendly toward Smokey, but the male bear, after his initial excitement, acting relatively indifferent toward her. By middle age, he was evidently accustomed to a solitary life, and enjoyed the privacy of his cave.

The journalists and radio commentators, eager for a story, were disappointed as the months went by. They became angry and criticized Smokey for his 'inability to perform.' Most people, however, stayed loyal to Smokey and steadfast in their fondness for him.

Tilly hadn't shared the reporters' high expectations. By spring, when the black bears would have normally mated, the two had been together too long as brother and sister to stir their mating instinct. And from her long experience with zoo animals, especially orphans raised by humans, she expected that the captive bears probably wouldn't ever have offspring. She was glad to see the furor eventually die down, and the media forgive Smokey.

It was April 1963. Smokey, alert to the smallest changes in the zoo, sensed something afoot. The first telltale clue, something he'd learned after a dozen years in the zoo, was the gibbons yowling more than usual. Then photographers rushed by. Smokey aimed his nose high into the air and flared his nostrils, consumed with curiosity as to what new animal had arrived at the zoo.

That afternoon, Dazzle pranced by Smokey, tossing supercilious looks his way. But the bear didn't rise to the bait. The peacock was bluffing, too proud to admit he had missed the new animal's arrival before it was quarantined.

So, when the peacock provocatively brushed his long folded tail against the bars, Smokey pretended to look inquiringly at him, raising his eyebrows, then laughed when Dazzle snubbed him. Goldie Bear was surprised at Smokey's reaction, then the savvy bear caught on: It's more fun to be amused than annoyed by such a prissy bird.

Smokey prowled impatiently waiting for news. Early one morning he sensed a new airborne odor of a furred animal. Once the gates clanged open, a crowd dashed by, bypassing the bears' enclosures. This clamor augured a big event, so Smokey felt frustrated not knowing who had arrived. His agitation led Goldie to be upset, too, because she couldn't distinguish whether he was just excited or anxious. She moved closer, as if to keep him company, but he turned his back on her and kept his vigil at the bars. Smokey hated being helpless, waiting to learn anything about his surroundings beyond the cage.

He hoped the monkeys Trish and Trash would soon bring him news as well as their offspring Hopkins. The little fellow still liked to crawl all over Smokey's big furry body. Unless the tyke dared to pull too hard on the bear's fur or tweaked his ears or tail, the bear didn't mind. In fact, Smokey was quite fond of the little fellow. It was a welcome relief from his humdrum life to look forward to something in the future. He liked seeing Hopkins grow up—at first riding on his mother's back, and later romping around Smokey's cage under the moonlight. He had been the object of the whole troop's grooming, and had such a sunny disposition that he liked to groom others, including Smokey. He seemed to have no fear.

But in recent years, as the scamp grew older, Trish and Trash hesitated to take him off Monkey Island for fear he'd run off and explore the zoo on his own. Nor could they leave him behind under the protection of their friends, especially after a disturbing incident. Two rival males had been fighting when one suddenly seized the young monkey and swung his big arm back, as if he might throw Hopkins against a tree. Trish had screeched, leaped up, and snatched her son away just in time.

The bear's reminiscing was interrupted late in the evening by the familiar sounds of giggling outside the enclosure. As if his thoughts had conjured up the monkeys, there were Trish, Trash and a nearly full-grown Hopkins. Smokey welcomed them and asked, "What's the latest scuttlebutt?" They couldn't wait to tell him: A chimpanzee with a weird past had arrived at the zoo. Trish said the chimp seemed friendly, in fact, eager to see 'his cousins the monkeys' after his lonely life in a small, solitary cage.

Hopkins blurted out the story. The new fellow had been born in the jungle, then imprisoned in a lab. Day after day humans made him touch buttons before they'd reward him with his favorite food, banana chips. Hopkins' eyes opened wide to relay that when the chimp made a mistake, they'd punish him with small shocks to the bottoms of his feet.

The chimp had told the monkeys that, after endless lessons, he'd been put in a heavy suit and strapped down. Everyone became tense, but at least someone held his hand and made soothing sounds. Then the door closed on the capsule. He had to clench his teeth to endure strange sounds and air pulling his face, but despite the awful sensations he managed to press all the buttons correctly.

"After all the practice I'd gone through, any nincompoop could've done something that simple," he'd declared. "Though I'll admit the conditions were very tough, so I really had to concentrate."

After he had finished his job, a scary feeling had come into his head as if he were falling out of a tree, then he was bounced around with water pouring into his small capsule. The next thing he knew, his door was opened and people peered at him smiling and clapping. Lights flashed, blinding him. Then came the best part—being fed a whole apple. Trish's eyes twinkled. "That chimp must have accomplished a special mission. Everyone admires him so."

Trash said, "Poppycock! I don't believe all that gobbledygook he told us."

Trish interrupted her mate, "Didn't you see those pictures outside his cage? Ham strapped down with a silver cap on his head, then pictures of something metal shooting into the sky and then bobbing in the ocean . . . and finally Ham smiling at people with all his teeth in a big grin, looking proud and happy, like a real hero!"

Trash said, "Well, if there's any *hero* around here, it's Smokey!" Trish readily agreed.

Smokey looked at the little monkeys in surprise. He protested, "How could I be a hero? All I've done is stay in a cage all my life."

Trash said, "You're a famous star—because you're some kind of hero."

Trish sent Trash a dismissive look and asked Smokey, "All this time you haven't known *why* you're here?"

He huffed. "How could I know? Isn't it so people can stare at me?"

Trish's voice sounded sad. "So you've endured this cage such a long time and haven't even known the purpose?"

Smokey gazed at the ground, and then lifted his eyes to the distant clouds. He shouted, "Mother Bear *did* tell me something! She said that 'I was destined to a life of hardship and had to meet it like a *hero*!' But, being cooped up here, I've missed my chance to be a Medicine Bear and fulfill my destiny."

"Oh, Smokey, we should have told you sooner, but we assumed you already knew. Even Hopkins knew!" Trish explained that she had studied the pictures in front of Smokey's cage. "They showed that you were burned in a forest fire, isn't that right?" Smokey nodded. She said, "You endured that terrible fire and *survived*."

Trash broke in, "That's what made you a hero!" Smokey nodded, but looked perplexed, so he continued, "Oh, Smokey, my dopey friend, not to know for so long that you're an *important* bear!"

Trish explained, "Actually, there're pictures outside your cage of forest fires with words under them, but we don't know what anyone's supposed to *do* after seeing pictures of you and those fires, but—" Her voice petered out.

Her partner concluded, "Yeah, she's right. You're a hero 'cuz you *survived* for some kind of *purpose* or other . . ."

Smokey sat down, stunned. Does everyone have a purpose? He thought of being rescued and sent to the zoo, adults pointing at him, children looking at him in wonder, especially the burnt children, regarding him as so important. Perhaps his life had some kind of meaning, after all!

The bear sat quietly for a long time, still puzzled, and for once the monkeys were quiet too. Then he grabbed his front paws and rocked, and his face beamed. The monkeys danced around him, chortling, and finally slipped away.

The next morning Sophia the pigeon was unobtrusively pecking at something near Smokey's feet, now and then sneaking looks at him. He accosted her.

"Did you know?" he asked her.

"Everyone knows! It took you a long time to figure it out. You have accomplished an important mission on earth. But perhaps it's just as well that you haven't known. So you didn't get a swelled head, like that peacock. Or that chimp. It's for the best: that those who are destined for a prominent role in the public domain remain humble souls who just quietly go about their life."

Sophia continued, "After all, anyone who *survives* something terrible can be called a hero. It's just that some lucky ones have the great opportunity for their lives to actually *change* the world. You are one of those."

Smokey liked hearing that she held him in such esteem, but her compliment left him confused. The monkeys had called him a hero because he had *survived,* but Sophia implied that he'd *accomplished* something important. The chimp Ham had pressed all the right buttons on his trip into the sky, but what had he himself actually done, cooped up in the zoo? He was eager to ask her, but she had already turned away to peck at the ground.

However, Dazzle came to dash Smokey's newfound pride. The peacock strutted past the enclosure with a sense of self-importance as he proclaimed the arrival of the new hero, the chimp Ham. His eyes glinted with triumph as he told the bear that, in comparison, Smokey was now "old news." He should expect to be bypassed by visitors for a long time, maybe from now on. Smokey hardly glanced at the puffed-up peacock, and was relieved when he left.

Through the years, Smokey had noticed an ebb and flow of visitors outside his enclosure, and had relished slack days when he could retreat to his cave. This time, though, he found himself disgruntled at being bypassed.

Two years later the new zoo director, Dr. Theodore H. Reed, came to visit his most famous animal, Smokey. It was 1965, and Smokey had been at the zoo fifteen years. His fame now brought a thousand letters a day to his own zip code – 20252 – in Washington, D. C., and millions of people had visited him. The director came with a group of photographers plus Doc Mann, who had retired from the zoo earlier amid fond farewells from everyone. However, he and Lucile still came occasionally to visit their favorite bear.

One day Smokey scanned the crowd as usual and, to his surprise, found a dog standing at attention on the lawn across from his cage. What a rare treat to see a dog again! Smokey eagerly awaited the upcoming routine: Men would place the two animals together for photographs, so he'd have a brief but wonderful chance to smell and be with another animal up close. He studied the dog across the sidewalk. It had a long pointed nose and flowing golden hair, with a more self-contained and noble bearing than the exuberant puppy Jet, his pal back in Santa Fe.

Smokey soon found himself positioned beside the dog for the photographers to flash their cameras. The bear stood proudly erect, knowing he was a hero, having fulfilled some kind of mission. It was a good feeling, and his chest swelled with a sense of purpose . . . until the collie informed Smokey, in a tactful way, that perhaps the photographers were documenting this occasion because everyone knew Lassie was a true hero who had actually *done* good deeds, such as rescuing others.

Smokey's mail

Chapter 58

I grabbed a pile of dust, and holding it up, foolishly asked for as many birthdays as the grains of dust. I forgot to ask that they be years of youth.
–Ovid

Until one has loved an animal, a part of one's soul remains unawakened.
–Anatole France

Throughout the 1960s Smokey Bear became ever more famous and was often visited by celebrities. He was the recipient of more letters than the president of the country. Children sent a thousand applications a day addressed to Smokey Bear, committing themselves to be Junior Forest Rangers for fire prevention.

As usual, Freddie the rat shared in Smokey's good fortune, for additional visitors to the bear meant more treats for him as well. During the Kennedy years in the early 1960s, the rat had glowed with news about the marvelous leftover cuisine at the White House.

Then, after President Kennedy was assassinated, the rat was dismayed at the abrupt change to the simpler food of the President Johnson White House. Gradually, however, during the Johnson years, Freddie grew to appreciate that the leftovers were quite bountiful. And Lady Bird Johnson and other distinguished persons visited and brought Smokey treats, which meant delicious crumbs for the rat.

In 1972, when the bear was a very mature twenty-two years old, he noticed a new flurry of activity across the zoo grounds. By then, Smokey was reconciled to the fact that his popularity at the national zoo waned for a while when new animals arrived. He soon learned who the latest arrivals were: two giant pandas, Ling-Ling and Hsing-Hsing, gifts to President Nixon after his historic visit to China. Mr. Dazzle reported that the pandas had an elaborate suite of rooms featuring cool air, bamboo, and paw-friendly turf outdoors.

The peacock delivered this news to Smokey with a syrupy sound of admiration for the baby pandas, a supercilious lift of his chin, and a jiggle of the bobs on his head. He was challenging Smokey to be jealous, but the bear didn't give him the satisfaction. How could he begrudge young bears their favorable conditions when, anytime he and Goldie wished, they could swim in a pool to cool off?

Smokey still caged, age 24

More years slipped by, and Smokey turned twenty-five years old in 1975. He had lived a very long life for a black bear. His muzzle was gray-flecked, and his coat was shaggy-looking.

He tired easily, and preferred a quieter life.

Measured in human years, Smokey would have reached seventy years — the retirement age for federal employees. In recognition of the bear's fame and his great sacrifice in serving his nation for twenty-five years, a retirement ceremony was held, and he was honored by becoming the first bear to join the National Association of Retired Federal Employees.

Smokey and Goldie Bear were moved to a small out-of-the way grotto. Since the two had not had any offspring, another black bear cub, called Little Smokey, took over the old bear's job at the zoo.

Smokey Bear spent 1976, the last year of his life, mostly sleeping. The far-away corner on the zoo grounds suited him. Visitors rarely came by the cage. He didn't miss the parade of people, but he sometimes missed the tasty treats they had brought and the titillating aromas that lingered long afterward: buttery popcorn, steaming hot dogs, Fritos corn chips, and, especially, Cracker Jack popcorn coated with sticky caramel. Although he missed sweet junk food, his friend Tilly was an attentive zookeeper, and brought him all sorts of vegetables and fruits. And sweet-scented strawberry ice cream, a long-time favorite of his.

He spent much of his time recalling the mountainside where he had been born. Morning and evening breezes that wafted to his cage from the nearby woods made his nose twitch with the memory of pine trees and musky animals, sunny meadows with dandelions, dew-laden grass, and dry leaves.

Toward the end, Smokey became much less active. His arthritis hurt, and he moved stiffly, especially first thing in the morning. He had a dull ache deep in his abdomen, and an occasional twinge of gut-twisting pain. But his sense of smell was intact and his eyesight was still good. For long hours he dreamily whiled away daytimes observing the drama of the sky's changing scene. Once he imagined he might rise out of his cage and fly freely among the low-lying cloudlets like the birds, or ascend the great clumps of cumulus clouds to reach the wisps of cirrus clouds miles above the earth.

At night, as he lay at rest in a kind of reverie, the bear saw stars scattered across the sky. After his quarter century of predictable routine at the zoo, one week easily melted into another. The bear still liked to snuffle around the edges of nearby rocks searching for dried fruit that Tilly had left him, but it required too much effort to forage among boulders farther away. Most days he was so tired, and his joints so stiff, that he didn't bother to chase noisy gulls from his food. And he was quite content to idly watch the pigeons, whom he'd grown fond of through the years.

Freddie's granddaughter now handled the rat's long extortion route since Freddie had aged and didn't want to work anymore. Like the old fellow, Frederica talked as if she was tough toward those who didn't pay up, but she seemed to Smokey more of a softie than her grandfather had been. After a while, she didn't require any 'protection payoffs' at all from Smokey, and just came by to keep him company. One way that the bear found to prolong her visits was to tell her stories about his early days at the zoo with Freddie.

The old bear soon discovered what fun it was to shock Frederica. Although Smokey had been raised in the Wilds where he'd been taught to tell the truth, he found that he enjoyed making up stories that exaggerated what a hooligan — and hero — Freddie had been in his younger years.

One day as Smokey started to reminisce with Frederica about her grandfather, she interrupted him. She blurted out how worried she had become. The rat didn't venture from home at all anymore. In his late old age, Freddie had gradually lost his strong sense of smell. And, unable to detect what was happening around him made the world a dull — and dangerous — place. His diminished ability to smell had also caused him to lose his sense of taste, so he wasn't interested in the food she brought, even the favorite things he used to crave. And, without smell-memories to prompt him, Freddie found it hard to remember anything, and became disoriented and frightened.

In the burrow she had to approach him slowly so he could gradually sense her presence. Once he recognized her, they'd always nuzzle each other. He seemed very glad to be with her, but otherwise his appetite for life seemed to be draining away.

It was during Freddie's last few weeks, then, that the thin and frail rat ventured forth and his dim short-sighted eyes brought him to the bear cage. Once again Smokey heard the familiar pitter-patter of the small feet, and inhaled the unmistakable scent of his friend's fur with its accents of dry grass and earth. Freddie was no longer his bold self as he timidly asked Smokey whether he could please stay with him.

The proud rat admitted that lately he had become leery of the vigorous young rats in his underground den. They had noticed his strength ebbing away. Freddie knew that they twitched their whiskers whenever they smelled the odor of his anxiety. These last few days their eyes glinted with hunger as they crouched close around him. He knew they were getting ready to pounce and eat him if he sighed or closed his eyes.

Freddie was indignant that, except for a few old-timers, none of them gave him the proper respect he deserved. The younger generations didn't know how he had once gained such great esteem from the pack for leading them to that glorious feast in the garbage cans behind the French Embassy. Now he was considered "just an old nobody," he said.

Smokey told Freddie that he certainly wasn't a 'nobody' to *him*. Well, then, the aged rat asked, since he knew his end was near, could he move in with his big friend? The bear assured the rat that he was welcome to stay and snuggle-up into his thick fur for as long as he wanted. And that is what happened.

The two had a short, but surprisingly good time together. One evening, with Freddie lying close to him, the bear caught the eye of his old friend, smiled, and tentatively nudged him with his paw. The rat promptly play-wrestled with the big paw, a new game for both of them. And when Freddie paused spread-eagle to catch his breath for a moment, Smokey gave him a rascally look and, laughing, dared to turn the rat over and lightly touch Freddie's belly with the pad of his paw. As the bear had somehow guessed, it turned out that the little guy loved being tickled, and emitted high-pitched chirps until he finally collapsed, gasping for Smokey to stop.

The frail old friends had barely recuperated their breath when the bear thought, "Now or never." He tweaked the scaly tail. It was something he'd been tempted to do ever since he'd first met Freddie, and the rat was so giggly that he whooped and play-bit the offending paw. They couldn't stop laughing. Whenever one of them caught the other's eye, it'd start up again. From then on, they found that the silly game had somehow broken down all barriers between them, and they became closer pals than ever before and could laugh at just about anything.

The rat's very last days were a special time for both of them. They reminisced about what had happened through the years: how Freddie had bamboozled Smokey, threatening to dribble on the kibble if the cub refused to give the rat his fair share; how Smokey had dangled the rodent by his tail; and how Freddie had been so bloated from his French Embassy feast that Smokey had to push him through the small opening in the fence. Now these memories had become a bond between them.

The time came when Freddie felt more pain here and there in his old body. He tried to hide it from Smokey, but the bear noticed that whenever the rat shifted position his eyes narrowed, his whiskers drew back, and his ears flattened.

And as the rat became frailer, they both grew sad. What Freddie said at the very end of his life surprised Smokey. The rodent said, "Ya know, I've always told ya that the thing to do in life was to eat and survive — so ya can get ahead." He looked down a moment, as if he was thinking about the hardship in his life, and his long nose almost touched the concrete.

Then he beaded an eye on Smokey. "But, ya know, I've been thinking . . ." Freddie turned his head away shyly, then turned back and announced to Smokey, "Ya know what's important in life? It's to be a good friend. Dat's the thing to be."

Later that day, the bear found Freddie's limp body along the wall, his long scaly tail stretched out behind him. Smokey stood and looked at the dead rat for a long time. It was hard to believe that his best friend, once so blustery and brazen, could not move anymore. Smokey hadn't quite realized how thin the old rat's hair had become. The ever-busy whiskers were still. His spunky little companion was gone.

The bear touched Freddie's body gently with the soft pads of his front paw in farewell, then walked heavily to his den and lay down. That evening, the zookeeper Tilly came and picked up the stiff body and left, but Smokey hardly noticed. By then, he knew that Freddie was truly gone. He was remembering the rat as his lively self: at first, a cunning tormentor, who soon became a cherished friend throughout the bear's life at the zoo.

After that, the bear moped around for a long time. He slept late, roused himself by midmorning to pace the cage a bit, but mostly lay flat on the concrete. His early wounds from the fire flared again, and he licked his front paw constantly.

Smokey Bear could still muster some energy when Goldie discovered something interesting in their joint cage. His nose would quiver, assessing whether it was worth his while to get up, and if so, he would walk to her side and investigate. On occasion, when he was walking slowly around the cage, she'd toss her head and tempt him to trot beside her.

Even fewer zoo visitors came to the bears' out-of-the-way spot, but by now it was a relief for Smokey to be spared their noise and excitement. When someone did come, he made the effort to turn toward the gate in hopes of a treat, and also to smell who it was. If it was Tilly, he'd greet her with an enthusiastic "Eh-eh," walk over and flash her a smile. He liked her warm voice and the treats she'd bring.

At last Smokey became reluctant to even pull himself up onto four feet, much less stand erect on his hind legs. His limbs ached, especially first thing in the morning, when he aroused himself to move to his food bucket and later to relieve himself.

He occasionally panted in pain from something wrong deep inside his body. Goldie Bear noticed, and would come by to nuzzle him. He could smell her concern, and it was a comfort

Goldie and Smokey, old together

to have her lie down by his side. Through the long nights he especially cherished the sound of her soft snoring nearby.

As he grew very old, Smokey stayed in his den, or dawdled nearby and found himself grateful for small things in his circumscribed world. He could count on the familiar rhythm of the zoo. His hearing had dimmed, but he could still relish the calls of songbirds in the quiet period just before dawn. And his sense of smell was still keen enough to catch scents from the woods and other animals in the zoo.

The bear always welcomed the sound of his zookeeper's footfall on the sidewalk. In any case, Tilly clanged the gate so if

Smokey was dozing he'd perk up at her entrance into the bears' domain. With her familiar vibrant voice and cheerful smile, she usually sweet-talked him into eating. Smokey was crafty enough, though, to discover that if he refused his regular meal, she'd return and coax him to eat it by first offering his all-time favorite treat: a sandwich slathered with honey.

By his very old age, Smokey had gradually lost weight, and the time came when he ate hardly any of his kibble. He no longer minded when Goldie slowly walked over to his bucket, tentatively looked over at his face to check if it was okay, and finished his food. In the earlier days, he would have given her a sharp warning—a jaw-popping sound—if she had dared sample his food, and might have slapped her snout. But their occasional spats were increasingly rare.

By now, after fourteen years together, the two bears were good companions, and Smokey found her presence a comfort. In fact, he liked to idly watch Goldie go about her day: pacing along the fence, investigating the floor of the cage for some tidbit, sniffing the breeze, and scratching her back against the bars. Having been at the zoo so long, and watching her familiar reactions, Smokey knew what was happening throughout the day and liked keeping track of the routine—the zoo gates opening in the morning, the lions roaring as they were fed breakfast, the vet stopping by, visitors leaving and the zoo grounds becoming quiet again.

Smokey was glad that Sophia now stayed close by. The pigeon looked elderly, her wing feathers less lustrous and her once-proud tail feathers somewhat ragged. And, in frail old age, her limp had become more pronounced than ever. She often lingered near him, and he wondered whether Sophia now wanted to keep him company. Or was she seeking his protection from the other pigeons that might be tempted to peck the balding spot on her head?

In any case, he found the pigeon's soft warbling a great solace. The sounds reached something deep within the old bear. It was the same spot inside where Smokey had found the golden acorn during the firestorm, the same inner place where he still sensed something special, now and then, as a subtle presence through the quiet of his later years.

Smokey reached twenty-six and a half years, the equivalent of a human advanced to the ninth decade of life or beyond. By this time, his back—as well as all four legs—ached. And he became increasingly weary through the day and slept even more. He was thin, almost gaunt.

One morning the old bear's arthritic joints woke him up. His bones felt cold, as if they could never warm up. When he tried to rise from the ground onto all four feet, it was a great ordeal to gather his back feet under him to stand. Then, taking a few wobbly steps outside his den, he was dismayed to find a hind leg give way. He lost his balance, and found himself suddenly splayed on the cold concrete. Smokey couldn't muster the energy to urge his weak body to rise again. He felt very sick somewhere inside his body.

His pain brought to mind the Ancient Bear's saying: "It's the wounded tree that yields the sweetest honey." He felt a sudden alarm: The time had come to find out what the saying really meant, or it would be too late.

He scrunched up his face in concentration. Leaving home so early he hadn't learned his mother's medicine lore, and confined at the zoo he had failed to pass on what little he had learned. Was there anything else he was supposed to have done?

He called out to Sophia, "Could you please come over here? It's very important." The pigeon looked up, and, seeing his body flat on the ground and his pensive eyes, she ceased nibbling bits of kibble from the concrete. She hastened over with her usual zigzag way of walking and eyed him with concern.

Smokey tried to recall exactly what his mother had once told him. He told Sophia that his mother had looked him meaningfully in the eyes, and said, in her solemn Medicine Bear voice, "Don't waste your life, my son! Dedicate yourself to the animals and the forest. That is a good life."

And he related that, later on, left in a tree stump during the fire, he had dreamed she had come to him and said, "Remember the Ancient Bear's saying: It's the wounded tree that yields the sweetest honey. This tragedy launches you on a path of great hardship. Like that wounded tree, you must meet your special destiny like a hero—so you can bring something sweet to the world."

Smokey related to Sophia that, at the time, he'd been a very young bear cub and hadn't known what Gersa meant. In fact, he wasn't sure he quite understood it even now. The monkeys had told him about the first part—that he had survived the hardship of the fire and imprisonment. He paused, and posed the question: But what "sweet thing" could he have possibly brought to the world in his lifetime?

There was a long silence, in which Sophia stood on one foot, then the other, looking at the sky. Then she settled her body onto the ground. Smokey managed to raise his head from the concrete to face her. As he waited for her to speak, he reflected on the tragedy and hardship in his life: never to return to his home in the forest, never to run free there and explore for food, never again to climb a honey-tree and scoop gobs of honey from a bee hive.

He pleaded, "What good could I have possibly done cooped up in a cage most of my life?" In an earnest voice Smokey asked Sophia whether she knew. If so, she must tell him—now!

The pigeon cocked her eye at him, but didn't open her beak. Was she considering whether he really wanted to know? His voice became an earnest plea. Had he done what he should have in life?

Smokey leaned his head toward her, too close, normally, for her comfort. She didn't respond, so he thrust out his muzzle even farther and demanded, "I must know. Tell me true."

Sophia drew her head back at the intrusion into her space, and backed away. She retorted that she always spoke the truth.

After all, her name meant 'wisdom.'

She pondered a moment to command his full attention. Then, in her usual voice, serious and considerate, Sophia announced to Smokey that he had indeed fulfilled his destiny. He had preserved the sweetness of life for many others — the wild animals, the plants, the trees, even people and their homes. Because of him, others could live in the safety and beauty of the forests.

The pigeon paused to explain. "Listen to me carefully: One can't just tell people the truth. One has to change their hearts. And that's what you've done. You've touched their hearts so they'll be careful about starting wildfires."

With her words so clear about the meaning of his life, Smokey let out a great sigh. The bear felt a rush of warmth, as if a golden glow was warming him deep within his old body. Now he could die in peace. He had, after all, had a worthwhile life.

Smokey struggled mightily onto his four feet once more and held himself with great dignity . . . until his weak frame tilted from side to side. Finally, the old bear succumbed to the weariness in his bones and let his frail body slowly crumple.

The bear lay quietly breathing. With one last effort, he raised his head off the concrete and looked the pigeon in the eye. "Thank you, dear Sophia. Now I'm ready. Mother is waiting for me at Rainbow Bridge, to cross over." His head lowered to rest once again on the ground, and Smokey took one last slow breath.

It was the next morning, November 9, 1976, when Tilly came to unlock the gate, as she had done for so many years. She saw Smokey's mate, Goldie, standing on her hind legs near the entrance, swaying back and forth, mumbling to herself. The golden bear's eyes looked bewildered, and the zookeeper immediately realized something was wrong. Her own eyes glazed over for a moment.

Tilly looked beyond Smokey's mate and the sight stabbed her heart. Smokey was lying very still. The zookeeper slowly walked past Goldie. She stood silent over the inert body for a long time. No longer was there a rise and fall of his chest and stomach. Tilly knelt at Smokey Bear's head. She gently closed his eyelids.

After a moment, she whispered, "I've always wanted to do this, you dear old fellow." She reached out her hand, slowly ran her spread fingers through Smokey's thick fur, and leaned closer to inhale the distinctive scent of his ruff.

Finally, she rested her hand on his forehead and said to him, "We'll all miss you, Smokey. I'm sorry you couldn't spend your life in the forest. But at least you lived to a ripe old age, over twenty-six years — a good long life for a bear."

Tilly lingered quietly with Goldie, then turned and left Smokey for the last time, closing the gate behind her.

The vet came, and Smokey's body was loaded onto a green government truck to be taken to the hospital. The pine casket was ready. No media were present. Only Forest Service and other government officials were allowed to give solemn witness. By afternoon, Smokey's body was packed in a hundred pounds of ice. The shipping crate was loaded with great care into the cargo hold of a Trans World Airways passenger jet for the bear's final trip.

Smokey was going home, at last, to the Lincoln National Forest he had loved and had missed for so long.

Ray Lutz, the pilot of TWA flight 217, happened to be from New Mexico and had always had a soft spot for Smokey. He and the crew were well aware of the significance of the bear: that Smokey had helped save wilderness across the nation. After the usual announcements about the flight, Lutz paused, then said to the passengers:

Sometimes we are honored to have special passengers aboard our flights and today we have a special cargo. We are privileged to be carrying the remains of Smokey Bear to be delivered to Albuquerque. It is my understanding the bear will be interred in New Mexico.

Smokey was flown across the American heartland he had crossed as a tiny bear in a Piper Cub decades before. This time, he was traveling back west from Washington, D.C., touching down in Chicago, Illinois, then Wichita, Kansas, to finally arrive in Albuquerque, New Mexico. A delegation of Forest Service officials and TV cameras heralded Smokey's plane touching down on New Mexican soil.

At 6:30 on that cold November evening in 1976, it was already dark at the Albuquerque airport. Rumors had threatened a possible attempt to hijack the bear's body, so the airport was ready. It took only five minutes for the hydraulic lift to lower the crate — five hundred pounds packed with ice — onto the Forest Service pickup truck and secure it with rope. Flanked by New Mexico State Police cars with red lights flashing, the truck was rushed — sometimes at a hundred miles an hour — through the black night to the village of Capitan.

The barrage of national coverage in the media about the famous bear had flushed out the threat that his remains might be dug up to sell his claws, so the Forest Service had taken the precaution of ensuring that the exact location of the grave would be kept forever secret. On the evening of the casket's arrival in Capitan, three village men had waited until dark to quietly dig the grave with a backhoe. Since the Forest Service had felt an urgent need to bury Smokey before the position of the gravesite could be discovered, the men had almost finished digging the enormous grave just moments before the convoy with the police escorts arrived at nine p.m.

Then, working hastily before the media showed up, the newly-arrived men from the convoy moved their vehicles to shield the grave from sight and turned on headlights so the village men could complete their work. The coffin proved too heavy, so the villagers hastily corralled two Texan deer hunters who happened to walk by, and together the half dozen men lowered the heavy black casket into the ground and covered it with a backhoe. Within thirty minutes Smokey was buried.

Protective of Smokey to the end, the villagers carefully removed all evidence of the real burial site. They finished just moments before the journalists and TV cameramen arrived, very annoyed at being too late to record the historic event.

The newsmen could, however, photograph the gravestone that the Capitan men had earlier prepared nearby. Months before, when the district ranger heard that Smokey would soon die, he and the mayor of Capitan had scouted the high mountainside where the cub had been rescued, in search of a fitting boulder to honor Smokey. They had finally found a granite rock, polished by weather to a natural smoothness.

It weighed a thousand pounds, but that didn't daunt the Westerners. They chained the great rock, and, with the help of a front-load tractor, managed to hoist it into a pickup and drive it down the steep mountain to Capitan. There, a bronze plaque was embedded in the stone.

The gravestone and plaque commemorating Smokey can be seen today in the quiet shady memorial at Smokey Bear Historical Park in the little village of Capitan, New Mexico.

Since Ray Bell was the one who had rescued the cub, and his family had been so close to the bear, the game warden was notified as soon as Smokey died. Knowing that his daughter, Judy, especially, would deeply feel the loss of her childhood buddy during that spring long ago, he called her first, then his son, Don, who had helped tend the cub's wounds. Ray was asked to speak at the memorial service a week later, along with his boss, Elliot Barker, and other officials.

By the time Smokey died, land had already been set aside for a Smokey Bear Historical Park, but it was still a barren lot with one lone tree, so, in preparation for the memorial, local men hastily cut down small live trees from the forest to poke into the ground and give the impression of a forest. But the people of Capitan needn't have worried about sprucing up their town. Flowers flooded their village from people across the country. Floral wreaths lined the sidewalk and filled up the little Smokey Bear Museum and Gift Shop—a log cabin the hometown folks had built with their own hands many years before.

On November 17th, the press and two hundred people gathered to dedicate the memorial to Smokey. In a small ceremony to acknowledge the people across the land who had respected and loved Smokey, TV cameras filmed a little girl placing a single carnation on the stone marking Smokey's grave.

Well-wishers sat outdoors facing a podium sporting a Smokey Bear poster. Judy and Don, in the back row, spotted their father, Ray, on the platform. They listened as distinguished Forest Service officials told how people across America had responded to their beloved bear. Judy and Don already knew how important Smokey had been, but were impressed to hear the full tally of what their little cub had accomplished in his lifetime.

During the quarter of a century, millions of visitors had come each year to see Smokey at the zoo. In the 1950s and 1960s, newspapers across the country had carried stories and photographs of the young bear. By the early 1970s, millions of children had become so fond of him that they had committed themselves as Junior Forest Rangers for fire prevention.

The tangible results were impressive. Although the country's population had increased in those 26 years, the number of acres that were burned had actually decreased. Of course, excellent firefighting accounted for a lot of the decrease. And the Smokey Bear education campaign had a dramatic impact on the reduction as well. But it is also evident that the live Smokey had done his share.

In his lifetime, as a living symbol of fire prevention, Smokey had touched the hearts of people across the country. He had indeed been a true guardian of the land — its forests, its meadows, its grasslands — and its homes for animals and people.

Yet the story of Smokey Bear in this novel would not be complete without the appearance of his special animal friends in the scene that follows in the Epilogue.

Epilogue

Solemn loveliness of the night. Vast star-garden of the Universe.
   –John Muir

The lights begin to twinkle from the rocks;
The long day wanes; the slow moon climbs; the deep
Moans round with many voices. Come, my friends.
'Tis not too late to seek a newer world.
   –Alfred Tennyson

Late that night, after the speakers had left Smokey's memorial ceremony and the last people had departed, the little town of Capitan, New Mexico, seemed deserted. After all the commotion of the long day, there was no longer any movement on the main village road. All was quiet at last.

As the night deepened, two small black figures could be seen under the moonlight walking slowly up the road. They stopped now and then among the bouquets of flowers that lined the roadway.

At the sound of a familiar haunting call, "Hoo — hoo-hoo, hooo-hooo," from the field with Smokey's gravesite, the pair immediately took to the air and winged their way to a tree where they settled on a branch with Great Horned Owl.

The three birds were silent together for a long time. The old owl had a bit of a paunch, but stood as dignified as ever. Strut, the crow, so sleek and sassy in his youth, now sprouted scraggly feathers, and had a bemused air about him. With age, his eyes had grown wiser, similar to the departed Elder Crow's. Unlike his mentor, however, Strut had grown mellow with age, even lackadaisical.

His lifelong mate Robbie had a no-nonsense stance and

looked as sensible as ever, retaining the same bold sparkle in her eyes. Her iridescent feathers glinted purple-blue and vivid green in the moonlight.

The three looked down at the great rock below with its bronze plaque commemorating their old friend. Strut spoke first. "Smokey, when you were a cub, you were my best friend, back when I really needed a friend. I'm so glad you were in my life. You know, buddy bear, you're the one who started me telling stories. What a great listener you were! And you always laughed at the crazy things I did, though I must say your own jokes were atrocious, and —" Strut stopped, forgetting what he was going to say.

Robbie broke in, "But you sure loved to laugh, didn't you, Smokey! Remember, at the zoo, when I made that little girl drop her ice cream?"

Strut continued, "And I'm glad I could bring some fun into your life with my antics. As well as give you some words of advice."

The crow paused. "When you were very young, Smokey, you once asked me whether I'd live as long as you would. And I promised I'd be with you for life. And here I am, your loyal friend to the end." He hung his head and murmured, "Caaah, caaah."

Robbie leaned her wing against Strut and chimed in with a sweet lilting 'caah.' The old fellow choked up, and she tactfully continued. "I loved you too, Smokey . . . Through these years, despite Strut's rather casual nest-building . . . we've raised some fine young crows. And we want you to know that their favorite stories have always been about our journey to the zoo, and about you. And they will pass these stories on: how you've saved lots of animals from being burned in fires, Smokey, and kept our beautiful mountains and forests and meadows safe for all of us."

The two crows burst forth with lusty sounds in unison, "Caw! Caw!"

Great Horned Owl ruffled his feathers, and, with a

commanding presence, rose to his full height. He was silent for a moment before he spoke. "Thank you both for your heartfelt thoughts. I'm sure you crows speak for all of Smokey's friends.

"In closing," the owl said, "I want to pronounce a brief eulogy. I know it is one that my esteemed friend Gersa—Mother Bear—would rightly approve. I deem it sums up Smokey's life, and I address the bear with profound respect: *'Well done, Smokey. You have indeed placed your pawprints upon history!'*

Author's Backstory

Through the thick walls of our log house, I heard the Plymouth Suburban's engine labor up the hill and sputter to a stop, then Dad's footfall on the porch and a click as the kitchen door opened. "Toots! Here's something right up your alley. It's a wild animal. You'll have to see it."

My father knew how much I liked to watch wild animals in our Maryland woods. I'd wade up the creek to see frogs plop into the water, and I'd creep through the pine-cushioned woods to stand so close to rabbits that I could see their noses twitch.

Dad reached inside his jacket for the folded newspaper and smoothed the front page onto the kitchen table. The headline announced, "SMOKEY BEAR ARRIVES AT THE ZOO," and further reported that the tiny black bear had been found among the ashes of a forest fire and named 'Smokey' after the famous poster bear known for fire prevention.

As soon as I could nab a ride into Washington, D. C., I headed to the National Zoo and Smokey's cage. There he was, sprawled in the crotch of a tree, sucking his right front paw. The round Mickey-Mouse ears atop his head gave the cub a perky look, but his small dark eyes seemed sad. What had those eyes seen?

The newspaper reported that after a forest fire in the mountains of New Mexico, the bear cub had been found alone. What had happened to his mother? My imagination ignited. How could this baby bear have survived a terrible fire that must have come roaring like a monstrous train to rain embers onto his fur—a wildfire so hot that it had nearly incinerated the firefighters nearby and left them with scorched throats and shoes that smoldered.

I pictured the cub clinging to a tree after the fire, digging his claws deep into the charred tree trunk and growling as a firefighter shinnied up the tree and grabbed him by the nape of his neck. Smokey must have shrieked as the gloved hand brought him down to the ground, then stopped his protests momentarily to gulp water splashed into his raw throat. Then, I imagined, he calmed down as he was tucked inside a young firefighter's shirt where he could hide. The little burnt creature, not much bigger than a squirrel, must have finally let himself go limp as he was rocked from side to side the long way down the mountain.

A little later, I returned to the zoo to sketch Smokey. As I stood before him, I wondered about his life in the wilderness before the fire, and what it had felt like to be thrust into the alien world of people: first a veterinary hospital, then a game warden's home where his burnt behind and paws healed, and finally stuck behind bars in a zoo, with people crowding close, staring at him and making loud exclamations.

As I stood before Smokey with my sketch pad, the idea came to me that, instead of drawing him, I should write his story. Days later, I returned to Washington and marched into the immense Department of Agriculture building to find out more about the bear cub. However, as I actually faced the door of the Forest Service office I couldn't quite muster the gumption to enter, fearful that officials wouldn't be receptive to a teenage writer.

As I waited, what came to mind was the familiar poster of Smokey Bear—the fatherly bear in his ranger hat and jeans, holding a firefighting shovel and saying, "Only *you* can prevent forest fires." That did it. As if a fist had pushed through my qualms, I found myself rapping on the door. Minutes later, I could hardly believe my good luck: The forest rangers liked my idea of writing a book about the cub, and handed me a stack of dramatic photographs to illustrate his story.

One photograph showed firefighters standing in a hazy scene of the still-smoldering forest. Another pictured a vet tenderly holding the cub's bandaged paws. I puzzled over a photograph of little Smokey in the lap of a very young girl as he stretched his head forward to nose her chin. The officials told me that she was the four-year-old daughter of the game warden, whose home the cub had stayed in until he was healthy enough to be flown to Washington.

My twelve-page manuscript about little Smokey just missed being published at that time, but I was determined to work on it again someday. So I tucked away that early version and the photographs in a trunk that followed me from my home in Maryland, through college in New England, then a lifetime of work in San Francisco.

At last I was perched high in the mountains of Colorado where I unearthed the papers from a musty suitcase. My older eyes saw wonderful photographs and a very short manuscript—about a sweet bear cub living an uneventful life in the forest, saved from a fire, healed, and taken to the zoo.

I knew there was more to Smokey's story and I became determined to ferret out the details of what Smokey had actually encountered in his life after the fire, as reported by eyewitness accounts. That much seemed possible. And I could learn from experts about what bear cubs were likely to encounter in their early life in a mountain forest. But what about this bear cub in particular? Here I found one slim clue. The vet who had saved his life considered him quite small as well as underweight for his age. Why? That's when I imagined a first chapter that would explain what might have happened to the little runt Smokey during the early days in his forest home.

Afterword

Since his 'birth' on August 9, 1944, the famous icon Smokey Bear has been the recognized symbol of conservation and protection of America's forests from unwanted, human-caused fires. His message about wildfire prevention has helped to reduce the number of acres burned yearly by wildfires from about 22 million (1944) to an average of 6.5 million today. However, wildfire prevention remains one of the most critical environmental issues affecting our country.

Many Americans believe that lightning starts most wildfires. In fact, an average of nine out of ten wildfires nationwide are caused by people. The principal causes are campfires left unattended, trash burning on windy days, arson, careless discarding of smoking materials or BBQ coals, and operating equipment without spark arrestors.

The Smokey Bear campaign by the Forest Service, the National Association of State Foresters, and the Ad Council has been spectacularly successful ever since it began in 1944, and continues as the longest-running public service campaign in the nation's history. Posters of the namesake Smokey grace the highways, the parks and the Internet, and his message is still heard on public service announcements, "Only *you* can prevent wildfires."

We celebrate the iconic Smokey Bear's birthday on August 9th every year. On the bear's twentieth anniversary, Ray Bell was also honored as the man who rescued the live cub and had the vision to see his potential service to the country. It seems fitting here to quote from that time what was said about Ray Bell:

"He was a man who came West in a covered wagon, grew up as an ordinary cowhand, served his country in World War II, and then became a game warden. He fought the forest fire where he rescued the

bear cub and sheltered him at his home before sending him to Washington. Let us honor Ray Bell, a man with the great insight and the determination to launch the 'live Smokey' on his heroic journey, by quoting Ray's words here:

'Smokey's early life to me parallels that of a war orphan born at the beginning of a war, parents killed, but somehow surviving, picked up by people passing by and placed in an orphanage to spend a lifetime for people to see and be reminded of the cruel effects of war.

'I hope one hundred years from now that that pitiful little burned ball of fur is remembered and respected as the living symbol of Forest Fire Prevention as he is today. LONG LIVE SMOKEY BEAR!'"

What's Fact and What's Fiction in the Novel

Throughout the Novel

Fact: Historical people (dramatized into fiction): Thoughts, motives, spoken words, and descriptions attributed to historical people (designated by first and last names in the novel) are largely based on William Lawter's extensive and detailed personal interviews as reported in his book. Some conversations in the novel are direct quotes, while others are paraphrases or my conjectures. A few are based on my personal interviews with Ray Bell's son Don, the veterinarian Edwin J. Smith's widow, and Capitan area residents.

Fact: Historical animals and events (dramatized into fiction): Smokey Bear; Schick the horse; Jet the spaniel; Ruby the bear cub; Goldie Bear; Ham the chimpanzee; Ling-Ling and Hsing-Hsing the giant panda cubs; Shanti and Ashok the baby elephants; and Lassie the collie.

Fiction: Other animal characters: Great Horned Owl, Leona the mountain lion, Chittery the chipmunk; Strut, Duke, Robbie and other crows; the cat Lightning; the peacock Dazzle; the rats Freddie and Frederica; the monkeys Trish, Trash and Hopkins; the pigeon Sophia.

By Chapter

Chapter 1 – 8:
Fiction: Smokey's early life in the forest.

Chapters 9 – 22:

Fact: The fire and firefighters; the cub's rescue, his bad night and being flown to Santa Fe; Ray Bell's World War II experience in India and Tinian; the cub's stay at vet Ed Smith's hospital.

Fact: Smokey's recuperation in the Bell family's Santa Fe house with Ray, Judy, Ruth and Don, with the dog Jet, with the cub Ruby whom Ray rescued; with Ray in the tree; and with Ray outdoors playing and disciplining the cub. The cub being photographed. Ray's rodeo achievements are real.

Fiction: The author's conjecture that Ray's experience at Tinian influenced his urge to rescue the cub and save the wilderness from destructive fires; the beaver family; Don telling his father about being thrown by a bull; some details and the timing of when Ray took Don to a rodeo; Ray's encounter with Cy Taillon; Ray's rescue of a particular cow and calf.

Chapters 23 – 25:

Fact: Planning where to send Smokey. The Santa Fe ceremony for Smokey; the cub being lost in the house; the Piper Cub trip to Washington, D.C.

Chapters 26 - 58:

Fact: The cub's stay at the zoo; zoo director Doc Mann and his wife Lucile Mann; the cub's interaction with Hopalong Cassidy at the circus; Judy Bell with President Eisenhower and afterward with Smokey; Ray Bell's arrival with Goldie Bear whom he rescued from the pool, and his positive encounter with Smokey; during Smokey's stay at the zoo, the presence there of Ham, Ling-Ling and Hsing-Hsing; Smokey posing with the famous collie Lassie; Smokey's casket airlifted, his burial in Capitan, and the memorial ceremony there.

Fiction: The cub being taken to Rock Creek Park by the Manns.

The Epilogue:

Fiction.

The Author's Back Story:

Fact: As a teenager the author visited the live cub Smokey at the zoo; went in person at that time to the Forest Service and obtained photos of Smokey; tried to publish a story then; saved the photos and manuscript to re-write later.

Special Notes

Special note about Smokey's life at the zoo: Except for my visits soon after Smokey arrived at the zoo, because of Smithsonian regulations I had no further access (written, verbal or archival) from former or current staff, zookeepers or volunteers at the Smithsonian Institute or the Smithsonian's National Zoological Park.

Therefore, for the bear's long years at the zoo, I relied upon Forest Service photographs, Lawter's few descriptions of zoo life in his biography of Smokey, and, largely, my own imagination about Smokey's life there.

Special note about the zookeepers: In the absence of any information about Smokey's zookeepers, I characterized earlier zookeepers rather unfavorably as brusque, which might very well have been unjustified in real life, for which I apologize. I did this partly for the dramatic effect of introducing a fictitious and positive zookeeper, Tilly, for the later years in the bear's life.

In light of recent advancements in the welfare of captive animals, the conditions and practices in zoos during the years of Smokey's life, 1950-1976, were undoubtedly not as favorable as they might have been, even at the National Zoo. With the introduction of Tilly I could show a somewhat more enriched environment for Smokey's later years, so that readers can imagine how a captive animal might benefit — and thrive to some degree — with a caring and enlightened zookeeper. Today, some zoos have better facilities and enrichment for animals than those depicted here.

Special note about photographs: All photos of Smokey, Goldie and Ruby are authentic, based on archival photographs at the US Forest Service and the Department of Agriculture Library. The photos "Smokey ventures out" (Chapter 2) and "Smokey in Rock Creek Park" (Chapter 31) were not taken in the fictitious settings of those chapters, but of the cub outdoors in Santa Fe.

Special note about activities attributed to Smokey and other animals: In my earliest chapters I imagined Smokey's life at home in the mountains. I admit that he might have been too young to have done certain things such as leaving the den in search of the male bear. Throughout the rest of the book, I relied whenever possible on historical events as well as my own lifetime experience with wild and domestic animals, supplemented substantially by careful observations in books by naturalists, field biologists, and other animal experts who have written about their research and close-up experience with wild black bear cubs and other wild animals (see Selected Readings).

Of course, all of the above became dramatized into actions and dialogue to make a novel. I welcome comments, corrections, and questions from readers and scientists knowledgeable about animals for later editions of the book and inclusion on my website **www.smokeybearanovel.com**.

Smokey Bear's Message

Smokey Bear's message of "Remember - Only you can prevent forest fires" was changed in 2001 to "Only you can prevent wildfires," since unwanted fires occur not only in forests but also in grasslands, rangelands, and city parks. The main message remains the same: Smokey Bear is counting on you to be careful:

Never leave a fire unattended.

Don't burn on a dry, windy day.

Dispose of charcoal briquettes and smoking materials properly.

Don't park on dry grass (the exhaust system can ignite the grass).

Be sure the spark arrestor on your vehicle or equipment works properly.

If you plan to build a fire, be sure you have the proper equipment to put it out.

The best way to put out a fire is to drown the fire with water, stir the ashes, and then drown it again. Feel the ashes for heat with the back of your hand. Remember, if it's too hot to touch, it's too hot to leave.

Websites and Places to Visit

The Smokey Bear public service campaign, begun in 1944, continues today in many forms such as public service announcements in the media and Smokey Bear signs at parks.

The official website *www.smokeybear.com* has such features as a map of current wildfires, the history behind Smokey, information on the prevention of wildfires, materials for teachers, games, and links to Facebook and videos.

The author's website about this novel, and questions raised by it, is *www.smokeybearanovel.com*.

Throughout the year the public can personally celebrate Smokey Bear across the country at the following sites:

Capitan, New Mexico

Thousands of people each year visit this high-altitude village near the Lincoln National Forest where the cub was born.

Smokey's gravesite

Smokey Bear Historical Park. Capitan, NM. Features photographs of the firefighting on Capitan Gap Mountain where the cub was burned, photographs of the live bear and the poster bear. A theater shows videos about fire prevention, and a short video of Ray Bell telling how he rescued the cub. See *www.smokeybearpark.com* (575) 354-2748

Visitors can step outside the building, where they can enter a small natural park and follow a walkway to see Smokey's burial site, marked by a great boulder with a bronze plaque commemorating the bear's life.

Smokey Bear Museum and Gift Shop. Capitan, NM. The original log cabin museum, built by villagers, displays historic memorabilia, such as photographs of the bear and part of the plane which carried the cub to Washington. It also offers for viewing or purchase many Smokey Bear mementoes, such as postcards, coffee mugs, books, pins, and patches. (575) 354-2298

Smokey Bear Days. Smokey Bear Historical Park, Capitan, NM. The first Friday and Saturday in May each year. A parade, a chainsaw carving contest and auction, and live entertainment. See *www.smokeybeardays.com*. (575) 354-2748

The Smokey Bear Stampede and Rodeo. Capitan, NM. The Fourth of July weekend each year: a parade, a 4-day rodeo (age 7 on up), footraces, live music, fireworks, and extensive displays of Smokey Bear mementos for viewing or purchase. See *www.smokeybearstampede.com*.

Local, Regional and National Sources

Smokey Bear Association. The SBA's comprehensive website lists many of the iconic Smokey Bear's local, regional and nationwide events. Also on the website, Smokey fans and collectors can view or purchase a vast array of memorabilia (from little statues to posters) depicting the iconic Smokey Bear. See *www.smokeybearassociation.com*

<u>Smokey Bear Balloons.</u> Albuquerque, NM. The most famous regular launching of the giant Smokey Bear Hot Air Balloon is in the fall at the annual Albuquerque International Balloon Fiesta, Albuquerque, NM. The contest draws giant balloons of many kinds from all over the world. For the Albuquerque fiesta as well as other Smokey Bear balloon events across the country, see *www.smokeybearballoon.com.* Inquire at *info@smokeybearballoon.org*.

<u>The US Forest Service.</u> At the Department of Agriculture, Washington, D. C., the USFS has a small exhibit about the iconic Smokey Bear and firefighting. Please check with your nearest National Forest for Smokey Bear programs and exhibits; a list of Forests may be found at *www.fs.fed.us*. In addition, other wildfire prevention information may be found at Smokey's website *www.smokeybear.com*.

<u>National Association of State Foresters</u>. This is a non-profit organization comprised of the directors of forestry agencies in the states, territories, and the District of Columbia of the United States. Contact your state forestry agency to schedule a Smokey Bear wildfire prevention education appearance. Contact is available through websites at *www.stateforesters.org/contact-your-state-agency*. To purchase NASF educational materials, go to *www.stateforesters.org/store*.

Wildland Firefighting Training

There are wildland firefighting training academies across the country. For information, see the National Interagency Fire Center website at *www.nifc.gov* or contact your nearest land management or emergency management agency.

Wild Animals in Confinement

Although the novel depicts wild animals in the Bells' household—two bear cubs, a crow, and a family of beavers—this is not intended as a precedent for current times. Back in 1950, in the absence of rescue organizations or rehabilitation facilities, game warden Ray Bell rescued wild animals in apparent distress. He had no choice but to take them to the local vet Ed Smith for treatment, then care for them in his own home until he could release them in the wild.

Note to readers: If you feel inclined to rescue a wild animal—a very natural and compassionate impulse—be aware that it might be unsafe, harmful to the animal or oneself, unduly burdensome, and, in most jurisdictions, illegal for you to capture wild animals or confine them as pets, whether in the house or yard, caged or uncaged.

The prevailing view, now-a-days, is that wild animals that appear to be very young, injured, or orphaned, can best be helped by leaving them alone in the wild or reporting them to appropriate government authorities, rescue organizations or animal rehabilitation centers for knowledgeable assessment, treatment, and eventual return to the wild or other disposition appropriate for the welfare of the animals and the public. See *www.humanesociety.org/injuredwildlife*.

Questions for Discussion

Should Smokey have been rescued or left alone after the fire?

Why do you suppose Ray was so determined to rescue Smokey?

Do you agree with the cat Lightning's advice about what you need to be happy?

Is it ever justified to confine wild animals in a zoo? A private house or back yard? A pet store? A laboratory? A training facility for entertainment? A roadside attraction?

If you were caged at a zoo, what would be your greatest hardship?

Strut found one way to handle the bully Duke. What else might have worked?

Why did Strut undertake his heroic journey? Was it a selfless deed?

Does it count if a heroic deed is imposed, rather than chosen?

What makes a hero? Was Ray a hero? Ham? Lassie? Smokey?

What made Smokey finally forgive Ray?

What made the rat Freddie change his mind about what's most important in life?

What did Smokey finally discover was his mission in life?

What's most important to you? What might be your purpose in life?

Acknowledgments

My profound gratitude to William Clifford Lawter, Jr. for his prodigious research in the book *Smokey Bear 20252: A Biography*, with its myriad historical facts upon which much of my novel is based. I am grateful for his scholarship, his vivid descriptions of pivotal events and his quotations from the people he interviewed—an invaluable boon for dramatization in my novel.

I am also grateful to Benjamin Kilham and other authors whose research and personal experience with wild animals contributed substantially to this novel. (See Selected Readings in this novel, and any updates at my website *www.smokeybearanovel.com*.)

Throughout all the drafts I have treasured the wise editing as well as the extraordinary support from fellow author Ann MacLeod. I'm grateful for the encouragement and advice from fellow author Allan Chinen. Dear to my heart and a source of joy—during the long hours throughout the decade spent writing the book—have been my dog companions: the Australian shepherd, Koko, and the miniature poodle, Bingo.

In my New Mexico research: special thanks to Don R. Bell at Las Cruces, who gave me extensive personal interviews about the cub's presence in his home, verified certain USFS photographs, and gave me his photos of the cub and Bell family for the book. He also let me see a home video of Smokey with the cocker spaniel Jet.

I found Capitan people rightfully proud of their Smokey and very helpful, notably Eddie Tudor and David Cunningham at the Smokey Bear Historical Park; Fred "Peg" Pfingsten in our telephone interview about his role in the fire; Tim and Cyndy Livingston at the former Firefighting Museum; Joy Slane;

Angelina Provine; Cherie Holmes and Jean Cunningham at the log cabin Smokey Bear Museum and Gift Shop; Pat Garrett and volunteer assistants at the Capitan Public Library; and Robert Olguin, owner of The Buckhorn Café, in nearby San Antonio, N.M.

In Colorado, for early drafts of the manuscript, I appreciate the suggestions from Carol Bell, Karen Chamberlain, and fellow writers in the Glenwood Springs Writers' Group. Thanks are also due Aspen Summer Words Literary Festivals and the Colorado Mountain Writers' Workshop for inspiration. Thanks to Karen Bergethon for her enduring support, and to Anita Witt in Basalt for her personal knowledge about western ranch life in the early days. Sherri Tippie in Denver shared her extensive and close-up experience in rescuing beavers at Wildlife 2000 and gave me a photo of a beaver kit for the book.

At the nation's capital, special thanks for crucial support from Helene Cleveland and Lew Southard at the US Forest Service Headquarters; and thanks to Emilie Rubin and Susan Fugate for their assistance at the National Agricultural Library.

At Avian Haven in Maine, Glori Berry gave me three of her special photos of birds for the book.

In India, thanks to Manish Sharma and his team at photozworld.com for authentic coloring of black and white photos for e-editions and the cover.

I appreciated encouragement at important times from Jan Fite of the Hot Foot Teddy Collectors' Association (now smokeybearassociation.com), and from Sue Houser, the author of a book for youngsters, *Hot Foot Teddy: The True Story of Smokey Bear*.

Selected Readings

Animal Intelligence and Emotion

Bekoff, Mark. 2002. *Minding Animals: Awareness, Emotions, and Heart.* New York: Oxford University Press.

Balcombe, Jonathan. 2010. *Second Nature: The Inner Lives of Animals.* Hampshire: Palgrave Macmillan.

de Waal, Frans. 2009. *The Age of Empathy: Nature's Lessons for a Kinder Society.* New York: Harmony Books.

Engel, Cindy. 2002. *Wild Health: How Animals Keep Themselves Well and What We Can Learn from Them.* Boston: Houghton Mifflin.

Shepard, Paul. 1996. *Traces of an Omnivore.* Washington, D.C.: Shearwater Books.

Von Kreisler, Kristin. 2001. *Beauty in the Beasts: True Stories of Animals Who Choose to Do Good.* New York: Tarcher.

Bears & Smokey Bear

Lawter, William Clifford, Jr. 1994. *Smokey Bear 20252: A Biography.* Alexandria, VA: Lindsay Smith.

Kilham, Benjamin. 2013. *Out on a Limb: What Black Bears Taught Me about Intelligence and Intuition.* White River Junction, VT: Chelsea Green Publishing.

Kilham, Benjamin, and Ed Gray. 2002. *Among the Bears: Raising Orphan Cubs in the Wild.* New York: Henry Holt.

Houser, Sue. 2006. *Hot Foot Teddy: The True Story of Smokey Bear.* Evansville, IN: M.T. Publishing.

McClellan, Harry "Punky." 2010. *Remember . . . Only You: A*

History of Forest Fire Prevention in Outdoor Advertising. Evansville, IN: M. T. Publishing.

DeBruyn, Terry D. 1999. *Walking with Bears.* New York: Lyons Press.

Petite, Irving. 1963. *Mister B.* Seattle: Seattle Book Co.

Anderson, Tom. 1992. *Black Bear: Seasons in the Wild.* Stillwater, MN: Voyageur Press.

Shepard, Paul, and Barry Sanders. 1985. *The Sacred Paw: The Bear in Nature, Myth, and Literature.* New York: Viking Penguin.

Masterson, Linda. 2006. *Living with Bears: A Practical Guide to Bear Country.* Masonville, CO: PixyJack Press.

Zoo Conditions

Grandin, Temple, and Catherine Johnson. 2009. "Chapter 9: Zoos." *Animals Make Us Human: Creating the Best Life for Animals.* Boston: Houghton Mifflin Harcourt.

Poulsen, Else. 2009. *Smiling Bears: A Zookeeper Explores the Behavior and Emotional Life of Bears.* Vancouver: Greystone Books.

Shepherdson, David J., Jill D. Mellen, & Michael Hutchins. eds. 1998. *Second Nature: Environmental Enrichment for Captive Animals.* Washington, DC: Smithsonian Institute Press.

Perry, John. 1969. *The World's A Zoo.* New York: Dodd, Mead & Company.

The Humane Society of the United States. *www.humanesociety.org*

Crows and Pigeons

Marzluff, John M., and Tony Angell. 2005. *In the Company*

of Crows and Ravens. New Haven: Yale University Press.

Woolfson, Esther. 2009. *Corvus: A Life with Birds*. Berkeley: Counterpoint.

Kilham, Lawrence. 1989. *The American Crow and the Common Raven*. College Station, TX: Texas A & M University Press.

Haupt, Lyanda Lynn. 2009. *Crow Planet: Essential Wisdom from the Urban Wilderness*. New York: Little, Brown.

Kirpluk, Barb. *Caw of the Wild: Observations from the Secret World of Crows*, 2005. New York: iUniverse.

Heinrich, Bernd. 1999. *Mind of the Raven: Investigations and Adventures with Wolf-Birds*. New York: HarperCollins.

Savage, Candace. 2005. *Crows: Encounters with the Wise Guys of the Avian World*. Vancouver: Greystone Books.

Savage, Candace. 1995. *Bird Brains: The Intelligence of Crows, Ravens, Magpies, and Jays*. San Francisco: Sierra Club Books.

Blechman, Andrew D. 2006. *Pigeons: The Fascinating Saga of the World's Most Revered and Reviled Bird*. New York: Grove.

Schwerin, Doris. 1976. *Diary of a Pigeon Watcher*. New York: Morrow.

Montgomery, Sy. 2010. *Birdology: Adventures With a Pack of Hens, A Peck of Pigeons, Cantankerous Crows, Fierce Falcons, Hip Hop Parrots, Baby Hummingbirds, and One Murderously Big Living Dinosaur*. New York: Free Press.

Barber, Theodore Xenophon. 1993. *The Human Nature of Birds: A Scientific Discovery with Startling Implications*. New York: Penguin.

Rothenberg, David. 2006. *Why Birds Sing: A Journey Into the Mystery of Bird Song*. New York: Basic Books.

Elphick, Chris, John B. Dunning, Jr., and David Allen Sibley, eds. 2001. *National Audubon Society: The Sibley Guide to Bird Life and Behavior*. New York: Knopf.

Rats and Beavers

Hendrickson, Robert. 1983. *More Cunning Than Man: A Social History of Rats and Men*. New York: Dorset Press.

Panksepp, Jaak. 2007. *Rats Laugh When You Tickle Them* [video]. Free Science Lectures.com/videos/animals, YouTube.

Long, Kim. 2000. *Beavers: A Wildlife Handbook*. Boulder, CO: Johnson Books.

Tippie, Sherri. 2010. *Working with Beaver: For Better Habitat Naturally*. Denver, CO: Wildlife 2000 and The Grand Canyon Trust.

Fire

Ravage, Barbara. 2004. *Burn Unit: Saving Lives After the Flames*. Cambridge, MA: Da Capo Press.

Maclean, Norman. 1993. *Young Men and Fire*. Chicago: University of Chicago Press.

Taylor, Murry A. 2000. *Jumping Fire: A Smokejumper's Memoir of Fighting Wildfire*. San Diego: Harcourt.

Egan, Timothy. 2009. *The Big Burn: Teddy Roosevelt and the Fire That Saved America*. Boston: Houghton Mifflin Harcourt.

Rodeo

McFadden, Cyra. 1998. *Rain or Shine: A Family Memoir*. Lincoln, NE: University of Nebraska Press.

Westermeier, Clifford P. 1987. *Man, Beast, Dust: The Story of Rodeo*. Lincoln, NE: University of Nebraska Press.

Eugene J. "Gene" Lamb. 1956. *Rodeo: Back of the Chutes*.

Denver: Bell Press.

The Enola Gay/Hiroshima

Thomas, Gordon and Max Morgan Witts. 1977. *Enola Gay*. New York: Stein and Day.

To my readers:

I hope you enjoyed your journey with Smokey! I'd appreciate your writing a review on Amazon, even if only a line or two. You are invited to see extra photographs and scenes about the bear on my website *www.smokeybearanovel.com.* Your comments and questions are also welcome.
Karen Signell

Our family

Made in the USA
Monee, IL
11 December 2022

20813258R00282